EVERYTHING I NEVER WROTE MOM

ABOUT THE U.S. ARMY AND VIETNAM

OR

The U.S. Army: An Amusement Park for Adults

BY

BOB LENNOX

i

Acknowledgements:

This work would not have been possible without the invaluable help of many people. And I would like to take some space to thank them here.

First of all these stories would have remained buried in my memory if it was not for the question asked by two friends after a long absence. The Jensen sisters, Linda and Julie, asked me what the heck I had been doing these past years, and all these stories started as a letter to the Jensen sisters.

The love and encouragement from my wife Nancy and our two daughters, Jennie and Sara, helped me to bring this work forward to publication. They helped in many ways; proofing and encouraging me when needed. Thank you for all of your efforts.

Cecelia Cronkright, son-in-law Mike and my brother Alan helped with proofing, grammer and spelling issues.

I would like to thank the inventor(s) of spelling check for his/her invaluable help, whomever you may be.

Big Jon, Orosz, Lou, Perkins and Billy "Badass" all helped with continuity and forgotten stories and personalities, and all of them contributed photographs which added so much.

I would like to thank Dan Burchett for the photographs he provided as they filled in some very empty spaces.

Table of Contents

Dedication:

To my Mom, a wonderful woman, mother, and through her love was a great supporter of me – I miss you. And to all Moms everywhere who sent their kids off to do their duty.

This appeared on one of the never ending streams of mimeographed jokes that made their way around the Army. I saved a copy as I was pretty sure that it summed up a lot of guys, including my own, experiences in the U.S. Army.

A Soldiers Lament

Here I am drunk, tired, pissed off, lonesome, flat broke, homesick, got a terrible hangover, no pussy for over a month now, no mail for days, no friends, damn few relatives, out of cigarettes, and missed bed check last night.

I am in debt, poor character rating, promotions frozen, pay all screwed up, food lousy, no clean clothes, laundry rejected, leave cancelled, pass pulled, restricted for a month, lost my shot record, got guard duty tonight, CQ tomorrow, KP next weekend, got a mule drivers MOS, three days AWOL and the First Sergeant wants to see me after this formation.

Got a Dear John letter, the old lady ran off with the milk man, the kids got malaria, the rods blew outa my car, I'm thirsty, sleepy, my shoe string broke in three places, my watch quit running, I've got an in-grown toe nail, a hard-on, just getting over the clap, about to shit in my pants and the latrine is OFF LIMITS until after the inspection, and some son-of-a-bitch just asked me to RE-UP.

Author: Unknown

Chapter 1

Greetings Brain Surgeon

I guess my military life really began on my 18th birthday. The day was like any other January day in Southern California, gray and overcast in the morning, which turned in to the usual washed out sunshine in the afternoon. The kind of day that tempted you to sleep in, because it seemed like there was no great urgency to get things done.

There was one thing that had to be done on this day, a chore that fell to all young men of my age. We had to go to a designated place to be counted. It was the law that all young men must register for the draft on or about their 18th birthday, and I being a good citizen I did my duty. Besides, there was a strong threat of jail time for those failing to comply with the law, and I have always responded well to duress and threats.

California in the 60's was considered by me to be the land of fast cars and slow women. As I was in school I had already become aware of fast cars, slow women and the war in Viet Nam, but I paid scant attention to it on the news or to the emerging protestors at school. Give me the fast cars and some of them slow women, every time. I was a kid looking for a good time, whether it was surfing, cruising, loving, or going to school I didn't care, but the trip to the draft board woke me up to the reality of the situation.

I arrived at the draft board fashionably late; at 10 in the morning, and immediately became one of a crowd of seemingly identical young men all clad alike in blue jeans, plaid shirts, sneakers and a wind breakers. I was apprehensive, I didn't know if I wanted to be part of this draft process or not, but here I was. There was a mixed bag of 17 and 18 year olds hanging around the counter, a river of blue jeaned, plaid shirted and wind breakered kids. As I looked closer and watched some of the registrars in operation I was amazed, this was my first contact in what was to be the "The System," or "The Green Machine", and I was enthralled by some of the actions that surrounded me. Here were four or five dear, sweet, blue haired old ladies, each of them was somebodies Mom or Grandmother, all in their 50's or 60's handling the draft board needs of two or three dozen plus teenage young men. The sweet old dears were listening to sob stories with sympathetic ears, helping those faking to be the village idiot to find their name and address in the local telephone directory, and informing the surly ones, gently but firmly, that what "Mom" said was the law. The gray haired ladies did all of this and more with a sweet motherly disposition and a cheerful word for all.

As I watched I learned, by the time I arrived at the board I had heard all the stories, (I had even thought of performing one or two of the less peculiar ones), about swishing into the room and kissing the doctor, plus innumerable others, and here before my eyes were these tails being acted out.

Registrars asked all of the right questions to some of the more serious draft avoiders or seeming resistors.

"And how do you spell your name, I'll write it out for you? Does that look right or we could write it this way?"

"If you don't know the street number of your address, do you know where it is on the map?"

"There are 17 Keatons in the phone book, what is your mother or fathers first name?"   I was handed forms that required that I answer all the questions correctly, (under pain of death or staying after school), I gave all the required answers and left thinking no more about it, after all I was a college student.

In high school the draft was a faraway thing, we had what seemed years till the draft. In discussions with other high school classmates regarding future employment or carriers the Army rarely came up. In face amongst us high schoolers the words "Brain Surgeon" rarely came up as well. Came up, hell most of us couldn't even spell "Brain Surgery," or couldn't even imagine what it entailed. (The term Brain surgeon was a known quantity at this period in the U.S., it was what your classmates used to indicate smartness. The term Rocket Scientist was not in vogue yet and was not used as a measure of brain power. Brain Surgeon was a measure of brain, oh never mind). There were also other words that where left out of our discussions, the words "Accountant, Lawyer, Dentist, Ornithologist, or any other kind of unpronounceable Ologists" these were never even thought of words. There was the occasional reference to becoming "President of the United States," but we discounted that as some idiot who believed anything his parents told him. The California town that we lived in was an oil town, an oil town with a harbor. So for those reasons your dad either worked in the oil fields and refineries or the docks. There were the rare ones whose dad was a cop or a fireman, but in my group of associates there were no exceptions to these rules. The guy who talked about college or a higher purpose career was not of the majority and was usually found at meetings of the chess club.

What was ahead for all of us was "The Big Day," the day you finally got laid for the first time. Before or after that there was going to be some form of high school graduation. Beyond that there was this big blank space. As a group we had talked about the "What Next," and what was next wasn't much. The docks, the oil fields, or for a few of us the affordable state college, that is if you had the grades. If you didn't have high enough grades then there was junior college. That is all that was ahead for most of us. At the school lunch table or school bench we talked in twos, threes, or more the subject of the Army, Navy, Air Force or Marines was discussed briefly. What did we know about the Army and Air Force; they had beaten the snot out of the Nazis in Germany. So the war movies told us. The Marines and the Navy beat the Japanese in the Pacific in World War II. There was no hurry to decide, and no conclusions were ever come to about getting drafted or enlisting. We had nothing but time.

What was the Army anyway? To us it was World War II and Korea. War movies, and America wins every time with Audie Murphy leading the charge. We were so ignorant and so American.

College

As a college student I was having a wonderful time, college was nothing like high school (a monastery with women), had been. Where high school demanded long hours of homework, hard work and attention to the rules so that I could be acceptable to a college. College was to me like a country club, (with lots of women), I set my own pace, if I didn't show up on time or at all no one made a fuss, and all I had to do was to pass the finals.

To show how seriously I took my new college life, I had selected Anthropology as my major course of study. The reason I had a major of Anthropology was not because I liked Anthropology, or ever intended in becoming an Anthropologist. The real reason was that my councilor demanded that I have a major and Anthropology was the first one on the list.

It didn't take long for me to discover that my heart wasn't really in Anthropology or for that matter in my college studies. I, like a number of people my own age, had not taken college seriously, and figured I could party all I wanted and study just before a final and still make the grade. It was not to be. I lasted a semester on the skin of my teeth, and I was out on my ear after the first year. In that time I had discovered some inevitable truths about myself:

1. Man does not exist on three to four hours sleep per night for long.

2. To party you need money.

3. If you have a job to get money to party, and you do party, you don't study, and you don't sleep. You don't pass.

Notice to Report

The notice to report for a pre-induction physical did not disturb me in the least, what could they possibly want me for. I was skinny, underweight, and pale as a ghost, and not the all American specimen they would be looking for. What did disturb me about having to take a draft board physical was I had to get myself to and from downtown Los Angeles, and I had to be there at 7 a.m. in the morning. This was no mean feat for a boy from the suburbs, downtown L. A. was almost at the end of the earth. I being a party guy and having a job I also had the most essential item for both, my own car, but transportation was not the problem. The induction center where the physical was to be held was in a part of downtown Los Angeles where people of a certain pale skinned ethnic majority did not hang around, especially after dark. But, to tell the truth I was scared, scared that they might find something wrong with me that would keep me out of the Army. I was doubly scared that they would find nothing wrong, and then take me into the Army.

On arrival at the appointed place and time I was pushed by a very loud voice through the unusual battery of military paper work. The loud instructions stated, "state your name in a military manner, (lastnamecommafirstnamemiddleinital)," all said in one enormous breath. Write your name in a military manner, (lastnamecommafirstnamemiddleinital), I even had to write the date in a military manner, (daydashmonthdashyear). If some military type had not been there to show us how it was done, I'd probably still be processing in with most of the others.

With the paper work out of the way the fun began, we were all complete strangers to each other, and a mixed bag of shapes, sizes, and colors. Together we were collectively stripped of our clothes, (de-jeaned, de-plaid shirted, de-sneakered and de-wind breakered), and stripped of our dignity at the same time. Not knowing what to say to any of the staff or each other we tried to help each other by pointing and nodding to where to go and what to do next. It is tough to look or be helpful when the only thing you are wearing is a pair of under shorts, in various stages of cleanliness and disrepair. The white uniformed staff gave us more loud verbal instructions on what colored line to follow on the floor, but I was as confused about what was said as the next guy. We were paraded around in our underwear; we were led self-consciously before an all-male staff of white coated medics. On arrival at the first station, (this first area sported heavily padded walls and ceiling supports. I suppose they were there for the very squeamish, or to prevent the very determined from bashing their brains out and ending the military process). We were greeted by the loud cheerful words, "First man over here," we were roughly handled and shoved from man to man, eyes, then ears were checked, then the pause until the announcement, "Yes two of each." I was poked and prodded in every opening in my body, all body fluids sampled, (I even helped the nervous pimply faced bean pole next to me pass his urine test, when he couldn't muster a dribble. I filled his paper cup and my own. That third cup of coffee had sure come in handy.), all bodily functions checked. At each station on our route we were greeted by cold tile floors, frigid walls and radiators, (everything painted a two tone green which reminded you of any old high school classroom), and the cold stares of a non-caring and inhospitable staff. What a wonderful uplifting experience this was for young men considering whether to enter into the service of their country. I remember saying to myself,

"If this is anything like the Army, I want no part of it." Surprisingly enough the treatment I received at my pre-induction physical was indeed very much like the hospital treatment I later received while in the Army.

Now that we were exposed to the military we were also exposed to the "F" word as a regular part of speech. Most of the military people relied on it heavily as the third Fucking word out of their Fucking mouths during any Fucking communication. While in high school, it was while in the gym or the locker room you may have heard the occasional "Asshole," "Damn," or "Shit" usually followed by snickers and giggles. Very, very rarely did the "F" word come up. In the Fucking military you couldn't complete a Fucking sentence without two Fucks and at least one Goddamn. The first set of instructions given to us by our military captors containing more than one "F" word brought snickers and giggles from this troop of near naked men. From that time on we were cured of our verbal virginity. Most of us novices however, took to this military language right away without difficulty, and before our physicals were over we were "Fucking" this and "Goddamning" that with the best of them.

After abusing us to their own amusement the medics then administered our final test of our physical, it was in fact an oral examination. It was delivered to us by a very large, burly man in a white medical coat; I believe he was the largest and burliest of all these medics. He came up to our group while we were practicing our new profanity, and demanded and got our attention and our immediate silence. I remember him distinctly by the way he told us to pay attention to him, the shear eloquence and veracity of the man was amazing. In an overly loud voice he commanded our attention by saying, "O.K. you fucking shitbirds you better Goddamn listen up, for the next one of you yaa-hoos I catch fucking talking or dicking around will have to carry his balls around in his Goddamn neck, after I get through kicking them up there." Immediate and utter silence followed.

7

Our burly loud leader next administered his white coated military exam, we were each awe struck by the sheer simplicity and at the same time the magnitude of what we were hearing "Can anyone here not hear thunder or see lightning?" I personally was left dumb struck. Every time since then that I have witnessed a thunder storm I have tested myself to make sure I was still up to the military criteria. Again silence followed this utterance from our inquisitor, everyone looked around quizzically at each other, (unable to speak because of the large lumps formed in our throats), until all eyes were turned as one to the one lone hand that was raised in the rear of our group. The medic's demeanor was unchanged except for the slight smile forming on the corners of his mouth.

"Alright Goddamn it, you come with me, the rest of you fucking shitbirds stay here." said the medic grabbing the offender and dragging him forcefully down the corridor. The perpetrator was marched off to the psychiatrists office to answer for his crimes, the rest of us were left to shiver in place until we mustered enough courage to begin "fucking this," and "Goddamning that" once more.

After the revelation about weather phenomenon our ordeal was at last over, the rest of us were once again paraded down the two-tone green corridors to the place where our civilian identity was waiting for us. We were each given a chit for lunch at a local beanery around the corner, and we were told not to throw the chit on the floor if we didn't want it. We were also reminded that any destruction of military property, (such as our lunch chits), was punishable by the government. The worst punishment any of us could think of at that moment was being subjected to another physical. After donning our civilian attire and once more feeling at ease, we left calling to each other "Fuck this" and "Goddamn that," and throwing the lunch chits on the ground. Once back outside and after looking around the neighborhood of the induction center most of us agreed that we definitely did not feel safe eating at a local beanery free or not. Most of the chits ended up on the sidewalk and the gutter in

8

front of the induction center. This sidewalk had seen guys like us and chits like those scattered there for more years than I could think of. Our chits mingled along with the other chits there from previous physicals. With all those chits all over the place I assumed that the local winos didn't care to eat in the beanery either.

I went home and forgot all about it, I felt immune to the draft system, and how could they possibly want a skinny specimen like me. I felt that way until my new draft classification notice arrived in the mail 2 weeks later, changing my draft classification from student "1-S," (the best possible classification to have was 1-Y `undesirable' otherwise known as "women and children first") to "1-A." A draft category of 1-A meant that I was a prime candidate for the "Green Machine," numero uno, and top of the list for the DRAFT. How could they do this to me? And at the same time, how can I get out of this? I went and talked to old friends both in and out of college, some of the suggestions that came up were:

"Join the Navy," was one suggestion.

God no! I get sea sick in the shower. As a kid I had had the experience of crossing the Atlantic Ocean in a steam ship. I had done this in late winter, complete with monstrous 30 foot waves. I had puked from Ireland to Nova Scotia, every foot of the way. So with that memory reasonable fresh in my mind the Navy was out.

"Join the National Guard," was another.

You've got to be kidding me they have got a waiting list 3 years long, and I'm no senators son.

"Get back in to college," who ever said that hadn't heard what the college had said to me when I was told to leave.

"Get a government deferred job," this was about the best suggestion. Unfortunately the government wasn't granting any job deferments to short order cooks or dishwashers.

One old family friend did say, "Why don't you enlist, then you can choose what you want to do. Believe me you'll have a ball for a couple of years, and at the same time learn a new trade?" I thought about this seriously for about 30 seconds, and then second nature set in. A little voice inside my head instantly went off and screamed, "are you kidding, you go to be out of your Fucking mind! Drafted you only had to spend two years in the Army, enlisting you had to spend three or four."

My Dad was a WWII hero with a chest full of medals for doing whatever he had done. He had been a British Naval Commando, and had served in every theater of that war. Like most WWII veterans he never talked about his experiences. But he was one tough son of a gun. I was not thinking of letting him down in any little way. I was proud of him and wanted to be like him. It was too bad that he was gone. He had died when I was 17; he died of his third heart attack. I was going to do my duty no matter what that duty entailed. There was going to be no avoiding, no running away, and no shirking responsibility. I was expected to do my bit. It wasn't any plainer than that. I waited for the Army to make the next move.

Life went smoothly along until the next notice from the military, which was a complete and total surprise to me. After my physical they had given me enough time to get lulled into a sense of complacent security about them ever getting around to doing anything with me at all. After all there were all those other guys getting physicals, and they would probably take all those healthy people before they got around to me. The next notice read, "You are ordered to report for pre-induction testing," what in the hell is pre-induction testing? I just had a physical, now that was a test, what else could they do to me. I was left with a sense of foreboding.

Once again I mustered my courage and drove myself to the downtown Los Angeles induction center for another 7 a.m. start. Man these military types start early. Again no mean feat considering the Los Angeles freeway traffic in the morning and some of the locals that hung out at the induction center, I had viewed them on my last visit. I parked my car within up-chucking distance of a couple of winos, the car wasn't much but I was rather attached to it. It was paid for.

10

I was allowed to keep my clothes on this time, and once again I was ushered in to a room full of strangers my own age. I did not recognize anyone from the group I had my physical with; they must have already been drafted. I didn't want to start up a conversation with anyone, so I took a seat and waited. A few minutes after the room filled up with young men, and after the coughing, sneezing and other bodily sounds settled down a Sergeant from the Army walked in. He was tall with dark closely cropped hair, dark rimmed glasses, he wore a total of two medal ribbons on his chest which I didn't know from nothing, but I could tell he was a Sergeant because I had watched Vic Morrow in "Combat" on T.V. and this guy had the same number of stripes as Vic did, six, three on each sleeve.

He called us "Men," that was news to me, and he also explained that the tests we were about to take were very important, that they could determine what our job would be in the military. I was now worried, what if I failed, would this mean they wouldn't take me in the Army, Hummm!

We were each handed test forms and booklets, and were then issued instructions on what to do. It seems that all paper work is handled in the same way by the military, we were told to write your names in a military manner, (lastnamecommafirstnamemiddleinital), and to write the date in a military manner. I was catching on about this military stuff, if I put the last word first on everything and put a comma after it I would be doing everything right. This was just like a grown up version of Pig Latin, Last name first, day before month, I before e, pearls before swine, I should do well. Or in military parlance, "well, I should do."

I took their test. I began when I was told to begin, I didn't look on my neighbor's paper for the answers, and try as I would there was no way I could have failed this test. 100 questions that a ten year old could answer were going to determine my military occupation, after this test I was going to be a general or a Brain Surgeon. I breezed through in no time, and handed in my paper.

11

I had forgotten completely that my original thought was to fail deliberately, as soon as I saw how simple the first question was, and I was sure after word that I had gotten them all right. I had been sure to make all my marks neatly between the lines as instructed and of course I had made erasures cleanly.

I left feeling great, I was sure that I had passed. Passed! You idiot, you were supposed to fail so the Army wouldn't take you. The Army had played on my baser instincts, never pass up a good deal.

So I went home again to once more enjoy the good life, but always there was that threat of something yet to come. I passed my time in idol prattle, not caring what happened until the next notice arrived. It was early in January when I got the official letter from the draft board, I was somewhat apprehensive, I was hoping for a reclassification from 1-A to something like 1-Z (Your mother will be picking up a gun and putting on a uniform with you, and you both will be heading to the beach to repel the invasion). It was not to be, this next piece of correspondence contained those four little words that all males my age just hated to hear, "Greetings from the President." I had been drafted, and I had to report for induction on January 23rd.

It is January for God's sake, how could they draft anyone in January, don't they know it is winter wherever they are sending me. I thought better of appealing their decision; after all if they are going to take a skinny, smoking, physical wreck like me they must be desperate.

Induction

I resigned myself to my fate, and showed up at 5:00 a.m., (Oh Five Hundred Military Time, or Oh my God that's early for civilians), at the local bus station. I had said my good-byes to family and friends, but I did tell my Mom that I'll probably be home in a day or two once they took a good look at what the draft had drug in. It was cold and dark at 5 a.m., a fitting morning for my resignation from my youth. I stood in bored acceptance to my fate, with the others of my own age and sex, called together in the appointed place. So there I was standing on the sidewalk, my toes on the curb, shivering and wondering "What next?" I had a strange feeling in the pit of my stomach a feeling I had had before. It was a very empty hollow feeling, but very different from hunger. I had felt it before, usually before a fist fight, and I would have it again and again over the next few years. It was fear! I was facing the unknown; I was going to a place I had no familiarity with. I knew no one going with me and I knew nothing about the place I was going. I was completely alone even amongst the group of strangers around me. We stood shivering, standing with our backs and our wind breakers and jeans against the cold ocean breeze, shivering until the chartered bus picked us up and took us away to the Army. The bus was not driven by a soldier, nor did it take us directly to some Army post, it took us straight to the Los Angeles induction center, the scene of all my introductions to the military system. It was interesting to listen to the conversations going on around me, both waiting at the bus station and on the bus. There were several who had received the same advice I had about the Army, the war, and how to get out or in to one or both. There were others in this group of strangers all from my town, who decided that they had an edge to getting out of the Army.

"They won't take me, I've got seven traffic tickets." said one member of our group.

"They won't take me, there's a paper warrant out for my arrest in Orange county." said another.

"Not bad," I thought

"I've got a case of the clap."

"I'm telling them I'm queer."

No matter what was said, in the end those that rode with me to the induction center in Los Angeles, rode with me the rest of the way into the service. They took them all.

In the Los Angeles induction center we were all given another physical, this one was more an inventory process of

13

body parts than a physical. We were met by another group of white clad medics, identical in every way to the first group I had met weeks before, (I suppose the U.S. Army mastered the cloning process years ahead of anyone else). We were ushered down the same puke green, ice cold, halls to a large puke green room. A large white square was painted on the ice cold tile floor, and we were told to each stand on a smaller square which were painted around the large white square. We were then ordered to take off all our clothes and stand back on the square, my first exposure to mass goose flesh. A doctor, (I suppose he was a doctor, in his white coat he could have been an auto mechanic, a butcher, or something else, and in that case he may not have objected to being kissed), walked around the inside of the square, and then around the outside. We were told to put our clothes back on. We were accepted.

There was just one thing left to worry about, at this time in the Vietnam War people were being drafting into the U.S. Marine Corps. We were all lined up and an announcement was made asking for anyone who wanted to volunteer to serve in the Marine Corps rather than the Army to please raise their hand. I kept my hand down, the fear rising in my stomach, I may have been crazy but I wasn't insane. I looked around me and noticed that there weren't any insane people with me. After the Marine request volunteer announcement, there was another announcement made, this time a list of names were read off. These were the names of those from our group who were "volunteering" to serve in the Marines, whether they wanted to or not, since mine was not one of them my stomach and I breathed a huge sigh of relief.

By noon we were marched around the corner from the induction center, to the local beanery I had successfully avoided before, and we were force fed lunch. At this time we as fellow travelers had started to get to know each other, and a pleasant give and take conversation about the benefits of the draft over a sumptuous repast would have been very nice. However, there was no sumptuous repast; if memory serves me right the meal consisted of shredded cardboard and library paste. There was no trouble with chits and litter this time as we were all under the charge of a Sergeant with more stripes than Vic Morrow, and he made sure that the Army got what it paid for. We were all still numbed by the induction process, and this numbness covered all of us as we awaited our fate. The now usual Army way of talking, the "Fucking this" and "Goddaming that" had not quite got under way yet. Those sitting at my table for lunch settled for airing their misgivings and rumors about what to expect or find in the way of treatment once we got to our next destination.

"We're going straight to Vietnam from basic, as infantry."

"We're going straight to Korea from basic, as infantry."

"They put salt peter in all your food, keeps you from going queer. Just smell this piece of meat, and compare it to the salt shaker. Don't it smell funny to you?" "Don't drink the hot chocolate; they put most of the Salt Peter in the hot chocolate."

After lunch all of us going into the Army were sworn in, those not wishing to take the induction oath were invited to step into the next room for transportation to the nearest federal penitentiary, there were no takers. After which we were each handed a box lunch with the name of the local beanery on the outside and escorted onto another chartered bus. Fort Ord here we come would have been the cheerful refrain had anyone been cheerful, I was sitting next to a very sad Mr. "I've got an Orange County Paper Warrant." Like I said they took ALL of us.

Chapter 2

Welcome Private Lennox

The bus trip to Fort Ord was boring and uneventful, uneventful that is except for the bus being pulled over by the California Highway Patrol for littering. Apparently some members of our party decided to express their opinions of our box lunches, and had heaved some of them out of the buss's windows. We arrived at Fort Ord at 10 p.m. in a freezing rain, and were at once welcomed as brothers in arms by those in charge. A man in an O.D. Green uniform, with yellow stripes on the sleeve, entered the bus and began to berate us, calling us all kinds of filthy names and screaming instructions at us in a language other than English. This was all done to the accompaniment of his wildly waving arms. I immediately thought that news of our run in with the Highway Patrol had preceded us, but I was wrong, this is the way that all new arrivals were treated. The people in the front of the bus began to jump up and run off of the bus, while this man kicked and screamed at them. By the time I ran past him he was somewhat sedated from his initial efforts, glassy eyed and with bits of froth at the corners of his mouth, but generally looking like he was having a good time.

We were left standing out in the rain and harassed by different green clad individuals until our tormentors got tired of it, and after that we were just left to stand in the rain. Eventually we were brought in from the rain to a large wooden building and forced to fill out paperwork. The inside of the building we were taken into was painted exactly the same two shades of green as the induction center in Los Angeles, "someone must have found one hell of a sale on paint," I thought as I glanced around my surroundings. Once inside it was: write your name in a military manner, (lastnamecommafirstnamemiddleinital), write the date in a military manner, and for good measure write your religious preference in a military manner.

This didn't take long, and once finished I was on my way back outside to rejoin the rain festivities.

"What's this shit?" I was asked upon submitting my completed paperwork to the Sergeant sitting at a table.

"My religious preference, number 33 from the list on the wall, `OTHER'."

"You trying to be fucking funny? Asshole!" He exclaimed rising from his seat.

"No sir."

"Sir!... Who the hell you calling SIR, shitbird. I work for a living." He said menacingly at the same time leaning over the table toward me.

"I call anyone sir who's as big as you."

"Listen asswipe, there ain't no fucking atheists in fox holes. Now go put down a fucking religious preference." He explained shoving my paperwork back at me.

"OK."

"OK what?" He demanded.

"OK.......dokay."

"Getthefuckoutahere."

I had only been the Army a few hours and I had already added a new word to my
personal vulgar vocabulary "Asswipe" and I had been branded as a trouble maker. Boy, the Army was certainly living up to its

reputation; so far it was just fun, travel and adventure. And I was certainly being all that you can be.

I was not an Athiest by any means, I had been going to church of some kind for as long as I could remember. In my religious education I had attended services at: Church of England, Church of Scotland, Presbyterian, Baptist, Quaker, and Catholic services. It all came down to what was available where my family had settled. In reality I didn't know to which one of the above devotions I belonged so I selected "Other" to be on the safe side.

Once our paperwork was properly in order we were sent back outside to enjoy the weather, and we had only been there a few minutes when a rather large Sergeant, (all Sergeants in the Army are rather large), came outside and called my name. At last, they have discovered their mistake and are putting me on the next bus home, I ran over to the Sergeant full of anticipation. On the other hand perhaps they were going to straighten out a new trouble maker, me, apprehension promptly turned to fear. I was wrong, it had been discovered that I was an alien, (from a foreign country not a different planet). Well I always knew I was a little different but..... I along with my family had emigrated from Great Britain (that's another way of saying England); to the U.S. of A. when I was a lad of 10 years, and though my parents had become citizens, for some reason I had not. Hence forward I was to be treated as a pariah to my fellow conscripts from my home town and I was separated from them, but what did I care I was now warm and dry out of the rain, Fuck 'em!

The U.N. Platoon

It was from this point I was treated like a human being, (for the present only), I was escorted to a nearby wooden building which turned out to be a warm, dry but empty barracks, and I was given a bed, tucked in and bid goodnight. In the morning I was awakened by the gentle strains of a whistle being blown in my ear. It was then that I discovered that I was truly, once and for all in the Army, and that I was not alone. Others must have arrived during the night. There were now five of us, and a Sergeant came in and had us line up outside in the continuing rain for breakfast. Getting acquainted with my fellow travelers I discovered that we were all aliens, maybe the Army had ideas of starting a club, or were they putting all their rotten eggs in one basket.

When I woke up for the first time IN the Army I received my first real shock realization about the Army. There were of course several things that shook me up in the next few days, but the top of the list was the lack of privacy. That fact hit me right in the face as soon as I woke up on my first morning with strangers sharing my bedroom. However, it really came home when I went to the bathroom, it wasn't that the Army didn't have bathrooms but latrines; it was the fact that the bathroom for 40 plus people was one room. A row of sinks, a shower with row of five nozzles, a trough for a row of six or more guys to piss in at one time, and a row of toilets without anything dividing them was all there was. In the Army you could do everything in the latrine holding hands with your neighbor, and if you wanted to follow local news or sports all you had to do was read along over your neighbors shoulder while going to the toilet. I had been in sports and group showers and locker rooms were no surprise, but this communal crapper was the hardest thing to get used to.

The second great shock I received was being woken up in the morning by a whistle blast or a trash can crashing into a wall. Later.... as my new diminutive Japanese buddy complained, "What ever happened to the bugle, I thought we would be woken up by a bugle in the Army?" My new buddy was obviously someone who had seen too many old movies.

"The guy who played the bugle has already been shipped to Vietnam," said Jesus my also new Latino American buddy, a fellow alien from Guatemala.

19

The building we had been assigned to was one of dozens of identical barracks buildings crowded together at the highway 1 entrance to Fort Ord. The barracks were close together, so close together that they were separated only by an asphalt strip of road two car widths wide. The road was used as a mini parade ground for each barracks group, and drilling and marching went on around us every hour of the day and night. (The amount of midnight marching depended on how much the new recruits pissed off their new overlords). Also, this was the waiting area for each group until it was time to be fed, given haircuts, or Army clothes. The Army didn't want us wasting our time just hanging around in the barracks. Row after row of barracks were used for recruit reception and processing, each row was capped at the top by a headquarters building and at the bottom by a mess hall. Everything outside the barracks was painted a uniform tan color, the buildings the rocks, the weather. At night, since there were no drapes (a Peeping Toms paradise), the buildings blended with the night sky leaving a scene out of Halloween, rows of jack-o lanterns lit up with rectangular eyes and mouths glowing yellow against the night.

This was now my world, a sea of green roofs supported by tan canyons. I was to see little else for the next week. Each morning in my new surroundings as it dawned a dull slate gray, I was there ahead of the sun to make sure that the sun did rise, (at least it became light), and to make sure that the rain was thrown in for good measure. I spent the next two days meeting new people as more aliens arrived, and filling in the same forms over and over again. For some reason the Army had us fill out the same government forms at least four times, this was interrupted by breaks to stand out in the rain while waiting to be fed. We had been joined by two groups of National Guardsmen from Oregon and Hawaii, volunteers from Guam, more aliens, and several people with criminal records pending action, one or two individuals with social diseases, an albino, a congenital dwarf and some other undesirable elements. By the end of the second day the first and second floor of the barracks were full of these people.

This group I was now attached to was not your "A" typical Hollywood World War II Army platoon. My new acquaintances were indeed a varied lot, but they were mostly from one group of the American social structure. Not the above the boulevard or below the boulevard type. Nor were they the above the tracks, or below the tracks variety. It was the group that was either dumb enough not to have gotten their citizenship papers, dumb enough to get drafted, or dumb enough to volunteer.

The group as a whole was eager to get along, after all we were all in this mess together, and a strong feeling of camaraderie began to emerge. However, with so many strangers, nationalities, and tempers crammed into a small space something was bound to give. There were one or two short fist fights, brought on by one strangers "big mouth" and the inability of others to be tolerant. But I was surprised when my new buddy Jesus decided to exert his dominance over the group and tried bullying us.

Jesus was of medium height but of excellent build, I had him by at least three inches in height. He looked like a California beach life guard, as he paraded around the barracks in his underwear. He was about 19 and seemed intelligent, cocky but intelligent, but who was to know. He gave me the rough edge of his tongue one morning, telling me to "get my ass in gear," or he was going to kick it for me. I replied reminding him that he did not employ me, and that he had better come down off his high horse. He did not respond so I thought no more about it. Jesus did however, and he caught me alone that evening as I was taking care of business in the latrine. I guess he decided to do a little enforcement of his self-appointed authority with his fists. I was young, skinny, but I was not a fool and I was not undefended. My father had been a professional boxer for some years, and he had spent many of the happy years of my childhood teaching me and my brothers how

21

to take a punch. The lesson on how to throw one had not been forgotten either. Jesus caught me from behind with a Sucker Punch, a fist to the side of the head, as I stood relieving myself at the urinal. His stinging blow sent me reeling, whizzing all over myself and the latrine floor. Shock abated as fear immediately welled up in my stomach, I regained my balance and with my ear throbbing and pulsing I turned to see what the hell had happened. I was surprised that it had been Jesus, but Jesus was completely surprised when I hadn't collapsed on the floor from his blow to the head. My head hurt like hell, but I had been hit before. And right at that moment I just couldn't remember when. So concentrating at my problem at hand I faced this squared off man crouching in a boxers stance, and with the fear turning to anger I stepped into him and nailed him in the nose with a straight left, right between his wide open fists. His head shot back as the blood exploded forth from his broken nose, a look of shock on his face. He staggered backwards throwing his hands up to cover his damaged face. If he was shocked I was utterly surprised, I had expected to see some blood on the floor, my own. I stepped back, shaking my left hand vigorously, because it now hurt like hell. Jesus staggered back further on his feet, and then sunk to his knees on the concrete floor, clasping his open hands to protect his broken and bleeding nose.

"My naaz, my naaz," he moaned, from behind his hands.

I stepped up in front of him, "Jesus...Jesus did I hurt you?" I asked.

"Yaah maaan, I think you broke it," he said opening his hands to show me. I popped him again on the nose with a right this time, and he screamed and collapsed in a sobbing heap. My Dad had taught me that you always finish a fight, but like I said he had been a pro fighter.

I stepped around his curled up body, and went to the sink and washed the blood off of my hands before leaving. Jesus was still moaning on the floor.

Jesus left that night, in and O.D. Green Army ambulance, for the hospital and never returned. I thought to myself, "I was better off doing it now, instead of having to put up with 10 weeks his crap as my own personal Sergeant." There were no admiring congratulations, no pats on the back, and luckily no court-martial. I guess Jesus decided not to press it.

Shortly after Jesus had left that night one of the biggest Mexican men in our group came and stood by my bed. I was sitting on the side of the bunk taking off my blood splattered t-shirt. Ramon gazed down at me and asked, "Did you do that to Jesus man?" I thought for a minute before answering, Ramon was one big dude, and one mean dude if I read things right. "Yeah man, he hit me from behind." "You know something," said Ramon smiling, "I never did like that cocky little shit." I was left alone from that time on; the other emerging bullies decided it just wasn't worth pushing me around.

The next day, after we were fed breakfast, the real processing in began. We were all given a new identity, an Army identity, and it was given to us in the form of two metal disks. This was our "Dog Tags," to be worn around our necks on a chain from now till eternity. On each disk was stamped our new names, Last Name, coma, First Name, and middle initial, period. Next on each disk was our new Serial Number, the real name we would be known by and called by from then on. All of our numbers were sequential in our platoon, and that gave us a feeling of belonging, but not for long. The disks also contained our blood type and our religious preference. This was so that when we gave our soul to God and our ass to our Drill Sergeant, as we were to find oput later, they knew which God to send our soul to.

If the number wasn't demeaning enough we next had all the hair on our heads removed, all of our hair. It took a lot less than sixty seconds, no conversation, and no formality, just ZIPP....ZZZIPP......, NEXT. For this service we paid, that's right WE paid, the standard Army haircut price of 35 cents, I considered it way overpriced. Then we had our last vestige in individualism removed, our civilian clothes were stripped from us and sent home, after which we were clothed in proper baggy Army attire. Our old selves, wind breakers, jeans, sneakers and plaid shirts were packaged and sent back to loved ones, in a forlorn looking cardboard box, all that was missing was a note from the Army saying, "Dear Mr. or Mrs. So-n-So, here is what you can have back of your son, we kept the rest. With the removal of all civilian attire we were marched into a large room and soldiers in O.D. uniforms started handing is Similar O.D. clothing. Our arms bulged with new things all colored this O.D. color, and we were introduced to a new term, G,I, which stood for Government Issue. We were issued other look alike gear, steel helmets, (interestingly enough called brain buckets by the people issuing them to us, and I didn't find out if this was an apt name until later). Mine had been personalized by the previous owner; it had "SPEED KILLS" printed on its front in 3" high white letters. We were also issued other essential field gear that we would need for training. One of the items issued was First Aid kits, I was immediately curious, why they gave us First Aid kits, is Basic Training dangerous? Yes, the answer was Basic Training was dangerous! We were next given free medical treatment in the form of five shots in rapid succession, and by rapid succession I mean just that. We walked through a room with padding on the walls and ceiling supports, and within three steps we had two shots in each arm and the fifth one added to either arm. The medical stuff over we were paraded to the P.X., (P.X. stood for Post Exchange, an Army combination corner drug store and Army surplus store). We went there for a shopping spree of shoe polish, brass polish and other militarily essential items all at less than bargain prices. Those with money could pay; those without money had to borrow money from someone at exorbitant interest. Loans like these were called "Payday Stakes," you were staked till payday. That is when the lender would be waiting, (usually at the end of the pay line), for return of the money at rates such as three for five, two for one or whatever was agreed to. After these events we were now left to ourselves to apply the polishes to our equipment in a military manner, that is except at meal times, at which times different people would come by the barracks, and it seemed with great delight, interrupt our boot polishing bee. We would be mustered into a formation outside on the street (in the still continuing rain), where we would stand motionless until completely soaked and then we were either fed or returned to the barracks.

I must say that my first encounter with Army food was surprising, it seemed quite good and there was plenty of it provided you weren't at the end of the line. One must realize, however, that by the time we were fed we had been standing outside for what seemed hours. We were usually weak from hunger, and being young men we could and would eat ANYTHING.

We were governed in our daily activities by two soldiers that directed everything, almost to the point of stating when and where to make our bodily functions. These two's rank was referred to as Specialists, reflected by the eagle patch they wore on the arm of their starched fatigues. They were both Vietnam Vets and knowledgeable soldiers, but at the same time they both seemed to be marking time in life. This was certainly true as they were only minding us and waiting for our permanent Drill Instructors to arrive.

Meanwhile we were learning a lot, each night we stood guard inside our own barracks. A fire guard had to remain awake all night since the barracks had been built during World War II and were constructed entirely of wood. Because of its construction a "T" was printed in front of its building identification number. The "T" stood for Temporary, I guess that temporary to the Army was relative, and I guess 20 years plus IS relative. There was a great danger of fire with wooden buildings of that age, and so we all took fire guard seriously.

So we learned how to stand guard freezing in our underwear, how to carry a flash light, how to turn it on in a military manner. How to stay awake for two hours in the middle of the night when your body screamed for sleep, and how to find your replacement so you could get that sleep.

We were finally introduced to our new Basic Training leaders, Drill Instructor Sergeant Jessie from Guam and Drill Instructor Sergeant Arturo, also from Guam. We had in our platoon eight or nine other guys from Guam, but our Drill Instructors were giants compared to my fellow conscripts. Those of our platoon were no taller than 5' 5", and a scrawny lot, except, that is except for one rather rotund cherubic individual who weighed in at what seemed around 300 pounds. Both of our Drill Instructors on the other hand were over six foot tall and were very well built, both sported combat badges and unit patches from units serving in Vietnam. I was not looking forward to having these two go to work on us.

Sergeants Jessie and Arturo presented a very glamorous picture of the U.S. Army. Both stood ramrod straight at over 6' tall, each topped by a regulation "Smokey the Bear" campaign hat. They were the epitome of the D.I., the recruiting poster variety. Both of them had bulging muscles, were tanned, and were very athletic looking. They didn't need to pose defiantly or shout to get our attention they just entered the barracks quietly through the door. Here stood two giants in faded but immaculate, starched, crisp fatigues, gleaming spit shinned jump boots, and instantly every head and eye were turned toward them and every mouth shut.

Our introduction to our D.I.s was accompanied by a speech. This speech was in fact their giving us the rules to live by while in their care, and they referred to the NO word in a big way. The NO rules were delivered in true Abbott & Costello style, Sergeants Arturo & Jessie playing both parts of that duo alternately.

NO TV.......said Jessie
NO Candy......said Arturo
NO Cokes or other soda pop......Said one of them
NO Smoking in formation........said the other

"You people will not smoke in formation, and any two men I see walking together IS a formation."

NO Walking

"You people will double-time everywhere. The only time you may walk is in your sleep."

NO Social contact with the opposite sex

"No Jones queers are not the opposite sex. If any of you assholes want to claim to be queer in an attempt to avoid military service step forward now, you can demonstrate your talents here in front of the platoon."

NO Beer

NO Fun

NO Laughing

 "Unless you are ordered to."

NO Phone calls, in or out

NO Crying, moaning, or whining

"If you are homesick and want your mommy, let me or Sergeant Arturo know so the rest of us can laugh at you."

There was a NO for everything.

There were to be a great many periods of instruction like this to follow. Whether the instructions were from our D.I.s or other NCOs the instructions, they generally centered around two phrases, "You will," or "You will not," or this was otherwise stated as "You will at no time."

Taking their first look at us our D.I.s decided what to do with us almost immediately. We were divided into squads of 12 men, squads were the standard maneuver elements for an Army platoon, and there were higher military uses besides. The method that was used in the selection of leadership seemed somewhat archaic. The standard that our D.I.s used seemed to be might over right. Some of us to this point in our military careers had displayed some sort of leadership potential, but this did not count for anything. As far as our D.I.s where concerned, brawn not brains was the watch words of the Army. Basically they didn't care how smart you were, and brilliant didn't count for nothing. That is unless you were a great hulking brute afflicted with brilliance. No muscles, you got nowhere, and it seemed that the bigger the guy the higher the rank. So, with no reluctance on my part, I settled for a leadership role somewhere down the totem-pole of life. I was to be in charge of me, which was very OK by me?

The next day it finally stopped raining and our Drill Instructors, now firmly in charge, took us outside to play. As our first lesson, we were introduced to our left foot and then our right and we were instructed in their correct positioning on the surface of the earth as the U.S. Army intended. "No you assholes your military Left," was the popular form of correction for we novices.

My platoon was considered by the senior NCOs and drill Sergeants as the UN-platoon, and this metaphor followed us all the way through Basic Training. We were the UN-platoon for two reasons: first because of our composite make up of people from all over the world, (United Nations), and secondly because we could not stay in step, march properly, or it seemed do anything in a military manner. So the name the UN-platoon stuck, and being true to our name through all of Basic Training we would not stay in step, march correctly, or do much of anything in a military manner.

Testing Testing 1, 2, 3

As our next phase of indoctrination into the U.S. Army we were each given aptitude tests to see how we would best fit into the Army. (Apparently the Army's pre-induction testing was just to see how we would pre-fit into the Army). Those amongst us who had enlisted instead of being drafted started whining immediately, something about having signed a contract with the Army for a specific school or training. Our Drill Instructors looked at each other knowingly, smiled and said, "So what!" The Sergeants then showed these volunteers the fine print on their contracts. "Subject to the needs of the U.S.

Army" was printed on each, microscopically printed of course, but never the less there it was.

The tests were on Electronics, (to see if you would prefer to be electrocuted by the enemy rather than shot), Morse code, math and general knowledge. After all the tests had been administered and all the papers collected, several names were called out, mine was one of them. Everyone else was ushered out leaving me to wonder, "What have I done now?" I had passed with a score sufficiently high enough to qualify to be an officer, ridiculous, me an officer. So we were then given the special Officer Candidate Test, and again the papers were collected. After some time some more names were called out and again my name was one of those called. The group remaining kept getting smaller and smaller, and we were now given the Very Special Officer Candidate Test. This test had all the special questions, "would you rather go to the opera or to a football game?" I passed this test, and this entitled me to a free interview, and I was taken by an NCO to a small room and told to knock on the door and then report to the officer inside. Inside meant an eight foot by ten foot office containing one O.D. Green Army desk, Army chair, Army file cabinet, a waste basket and one Army officer. The officer was an aging Captain, (I knew he was a Captain immediately because he told me he was one), gray haired and very over weight, and he gave me the good old Officer Candidate School sales pitch. I had the grades, I had the physical requirements, (I breathed), and I looked like officer material. If he or I looked like officer material we as an Army were in deep shit, I asked if I could smoke and got a dirty look. (No O.D. Army ashtray was visible). I as a good potential customer sat up properly and paid attention, and after listening to his spiel I asked the one proper question. "What does it cost?"

The price was, "Six years." SIX YEARS! A little fuse went off in my head, and with it a red light started flashing a warning "WHOA THERE, WHOA BOY!" After I caught my breath and thought about it for a while I said, "I'm sorry sir but I cannot become an officer," and stood up to leave.

"Why not, Lennox?" The captain inquired.

"Sir. My parents were married."

"Lennox take this slip and go next door," as I left a rather red faced captain was scribbling furiously in my file. He as probably writing the words "Smart Ass."

The real kicker about signing up to go to officer training was that you made the commitment for six years of service just to sign up for the course. Whether you managed to graduate as an officer or not you still did the six years.

I took the slip handed me by the Captain and went next door, as instructed, there I found an identical office, including the O.D. Green furnishings, but a much younger sleeker Captain behind the desk. I presented myself as told and was promptly given the sign up for Officer Flight School sales pitch. Become a highly paid, highly esteemed helicopter pilot. I had the grades, I had the physical requirements, and I looked like officer material. This was beginning to sound remotely familiar. As a good potential customer I sat up properly and paid attention, and after listening to his spiel I asked the one proper question. "What does it cost?"

The price was, another "Six years." And still a little fuse went off in my head, and a red light started flashing a warning. I turned him down stating, "If God had wanted man to fly, why did he put all that traction down here on the ground for us to fool around with." That drew a dirty look and I was quickly sent on my way back to my barracks.

I was disappointed, I was expecting other small offices and further interviews, and I figured that there had to be someone to find me an officer job in a branch of the Army just right for me. It was not to be, I had blown it.

After our test scores had been processed the Army gave no indication as to what job or training you were going to be given after Basic Training, and that is if you survived. The Army gave no guarantees, those qualified to be Brain Surgeons could end up being firemen, but the Army did allow you to shorten the odds somewhat. You could enlist for a school, and they would do their very best to see that you got what you had coming to you. Of course enlisting required some small sacrifice on the part of the enlistee, it cost you one to four more years, depending of course, on how much they could talk you into.

To differentiate between those who had enlisted into the Army, that is those who voluntarily went to an Army recruiter and said "take me!" and those that had been drafted. Drafted meant being dragged kicking and screaming into the Army, the Army used two little letters. Those who had been drafted were given the letters "US" standing for "U-is Screwed" in front of their Army serial number, and a serial number starting with a five. Those that had enlisted in hopes of avoiding the draft had the letters "RA," standing for Regular Army, in front of their serial number, and a serial number starting with a one or a two.

If you were a draftee and took the Army up on its kind offer allowing you to enlist, your "US" was replaced with an "RA". There after anyone spotting an "RA" in front of a serial number starting with a five, knew what you had done and you were treated as the scum of the earth from then on. If you are drafted, by god take your medicine, let the Army dispose of you as it will.

Along with three or four other draftees from my platoon I succumbed to the Army's siren song and enlisted. I really didn't have to be talked in to it; the specter of me ending up a Brain Surgeon did it. I now had three years to serve in the active Army and three in the inactive reserves. Under the draft the deal was for two years active and two years active reserves, (playing weekend warrior with the Army reserves), and two years inactive. I along with my fellow conscripts had all opted for electronics courses, three of us for the same course, and so after our dastardly deed we all slunk back to the barracks feeling, and hoping our peers would not notice the brand on our foreheads or ask any embarrassing questions.

Why electronics? Well why me in the first place? It was the one subject I knew absolutely nothing about, this is corroborated by my scores to the tests given by the Army, electronics was the lowest score I had. Electronics isn't very glamorous, in the 60's you generally associated it with nerds and weirdos. It wasn't out of patriotism; no one gave a stirring speech about the need for electronic technicians. So why did I choose to enlist for an electronics school? Because I was there and the opportunities offered outside of electronics appeared to be even less inviting than electronics.

These are some of the other military careers I could have selected, and their actual meanings that I discovered later.

Fireman - Stoking a furnace somewhere.

Ordinance engineer - Move heavy explosive objects from place to place.

Law enforcement - Breaking up fights between people who would rather hit you than each other.

Administrative - A clerk, male typist.

Ordinance removal engineer - Mine detection.

It was take electronics or let the Army do with me whatever they wanted, that thought did not instill any confidence in me.

Getting acquainted with my fellow cell mates was made much easier after the Army had us issued Army clothes. The name tag, neatly printed and sewn over the right shirt pocket made introductions simple indeed, and life was now a piece of cake for those prone not to remember names right off. But no matter how big your name was printed on your clothes it seemed that no NCO cared to look at it. The only thing an NCO called you by was one of a variety of generic Army names; such as "Hey you," "Boy," "Private," "Soldier," "Trooper," or "Troop." For those of us with un-pronounceable names, those that were extremely long, (these where the guys who had to hold their right arm out so that you could read ALL of their name tag), or names that did not contain any consonants, the NCOs had another method of address. All of the above were simply called "Alphabet." The NCOs could also be very cruel about names. If you had something strange or humorous about personal appearance, this would immediately invoke a nick-name. "Wing-nut" was the name for someone with big ears. "Goofy" if you had buck teeth, but the name "Shitbird" was used to describe the majority of us.

Going Up the Hill

It dawned bright and sunny, the big day we were to transfer out of the receiving barracks, fluffy white clouds drifted in from the Pacific Ocean. I was to be a big day, finally, when we were to be transferred to a Basic Training company, this was known as going "Up the Hill." Army semi-trucks pulling open topped cattle cars arrived at the top of our street. All the barracks on the street were emptied out. We assembled on the street outside our barracks with brand new duffel bags crammed with our new O.D. Green wardrobes. We were counted, sorted, checked off and counted again before we were herded onto the trucks for our trip "Up the Hill." I hugged my duffle bag with my equipment bag balanced on top to my chest as we jolted along the road. We all watched the panorama of Monterey Bay unfold behind us. The view was spectacular; Fort Ord is situated on the California coast, north of the city of Monterey. This was the first really sunny day since we had arrived, and this added to the beauty of the view, several miles of California coastline north and south with the Monterey peninsula to the south and the sea sparkling in the sun shine. It all was so breathtakingly beautiful it seemed almost unmilitary.

Chapter 3

They Could Cook Us/They Couldn't Eat Us

Our new home was a three story concrete barracks that housed a complete Basic Training company, and this new home was just one of a row of three story concrete barracks that marched up the hill from the beaches to the water tower on top of the hill. Our company was divided in to five platoons, each platoon had its own living area of the building, and our Un-platoon was on an end of the second floor and consisted of one bedroom for 40 of us and one bathroom. The acting NCO's appointed over us, (Squad leaders, platoon leader, armorer etc.), shared two or four man rooms, but they shared our one bathroom.

We were unloaded and formed into platoons and hauling all our belongings we were taken and shown our new home. Compared to our old tan wooden barracks down the hill in the tenement district, this was a palace, things were looking up. We took our belongings and picked out our bunks and got settled in. We were then marched down to the basement of the barracks and each of us was issued a genuine Army rifle, a genuine rifle serial number, and a genuine Army gas mask. At last we had what real soldiers were supposed to have, a rifle, but they wouldn't trust us with any Army ammunition. Five minutes later, back in the barracks, I found out why. People started taking aim on each other with their rifles and pulling triggers. This was unnerving, walking in the front door of the barracks and being greeted by a volley of clicks, firing pins falling on empty chambers. The ones who got the most pleasure out of shooting each other were the guys from Guam. I hoped that most of them would get all the firing at live target mania out of their systems before we were given live ammunition.

Now that we had rifles we were a proud lot we each sat with our new weapon and stroked and caressed its parts. We marveled at the moving parts and how heavy it was. School about the rifle began immediately when we were all assembled with our rifles. We were to memorize our genuine rifle serial number, and had to be able to recite the number without error at any moment, day or night. We were to be regularly tested on our knowledge of the number, standing trembling before an officer or an NCO, with them making sure that the number recited was indeed the number stamped on the weapon. For those with poor genuine serial number retention there was the punishment of running around with your rifle held over your head until your memory improved. I can still recite mine to this day, and get a queezy feeling in my stomach if I take more than five seconds to bring it back from memory. I didn't know that such a number could have such an effect on me. Outside of memorizing the multiplication tables as a kid, no numbers had ever intimidated me. To my dismay, no one in the Army, outside of Basic Training ever asked me for my genuine rifle serial number ever again, but hey, ours was to do or die.

Along with a rifle we were each issued a bayonet, but no serial number was required. What I expected to be a formative weapon turned out to be a rather dull knife that we would use to stab old rubber tires tied to stakes. (It all seemed quite kinky but the Army had its reasons). Then bayonets were even more tightly secured than rifles; they were locked in a footlocker and only handed out on special occasions. The Army had a special love for the bayonet, as I found out later in my Basic Training.

The Army considered the rifle a stick on which to attach a bayonet, and that is what you did most of the fighting with.

Memory Tests

Along with your own individual serial number and your genuine rifle serial number there were any number of things that we were expected to know by heart. There was also an individual punishment for each one that you failed to memorize and then recite correctly.

There were various parts of a rifle to be remembered, how to assemble those parts and make your rifle function the right way. Nobody wanted bullets coming out backwards. We had a platoon name and number and you had to know your place to stand when the platoon was assembled. We had various cadences for marching, and you had to memorize your left foot from your right. All of these we were tested on repeatedly, but the grand daddy of them all. The hardest thing to memorize and recite correctly on demand were your General Orders.

General Orders, and for us trainees there were only three of them, were our bible for standing guard. The three General Orders were simple rules on how to behave or make others behave while you were posted to a plot of Army ground and told to protect it with your empty rifle and your life. You had to be able to recite these rules, word for word, at any time anyone in the Army demaded that you do so. Failure to perform this fete of brain power brought instant disgrace and punishment. No mumbling was allowed, if you had an accent in your speech, get rid of it. The Army brooked no deviation in the recitation of the General Orders. After all, Orders were Orders.

Events

Basic Training was hard grueling work, and only a few events really stand out in memory. For the most part it was long hours, miserable treatment, starvation, and a great deal of physical exhaustion.

The one thing I remember most is the constant hunger; we did so much physical activity that we burned up a lot of energy. So whenever we were offered food we devoured it quickly and with great gusto. (The Sergeant or D.I. screaming at you to get moving had nothing to do with how fast you consumed your food. Digestion was a waste of Army time to our superiors). The weather added to our discomfort. There was a constant cold and gray countenance to everyday. We awoke to freezing windy mornings, windy rainy days, and freezing windy nights. This lasted from January until the end of March when spring finally arrived. Spring came bringing us not so freezing, windy mornings but sunshine and butterflies.

Why the weather is so vivid in my memory is because we had to sleep with all of the barracks windows open, you didn't have to wonder what the weather was like outside, you just had to open your eyes. This was part of the Army's Spinal Meningitis control policy that was in effect at Fort Ord. All basic trainees wore white tags above their names, with their company number stenciled on them. You were not to mingle with members of other companies, anytime you went anywhere you went as a company or as a platoon, even to the P.X., your unit was the only one allowed there. This was true except for sick call, when you went there everyone was intermingled, I guess it was OK if you got Meningitis when a doctor was present.

Driving

On my second morning in Basic Training there was a call for all of those with valid California driver's licenses to come forward. I immediately grasped the possibilities of this situation, drivers licenses meant driving, and that meant riding instead of walking or the more frequent; RUNNING. I came forward license in hand and offered my services without regard for the admonishments of friends from civilian life who had told me, "Never Volunteer." My services were accepted and I was assigned to a drivers pool.

My first driving assignment was handed to me the very next day; I was to drive the Training Brigades Sergeant Major anywhere his little heart desired. Being a brand new enlisted man a Sergeant Major was the closest thing to God I was ever to encounter, as far as the Army was concerned, and I was told to act accordingly when driving the Sergeant Major around. They sent me to the motor pool to pick up the Sergeant Major's Jeep. It was brand new, just like they had just taken it out of the box, a nice shade of O.D. (Olive Drab) green, and it had Sergeant Major's chevrons painted on little red signs attached to the front and rear bumpers. The Jeep was really a stripped down vehicle. A steering wheel, a couple of peddles, and a stick shift. No radio, not even an ash tray. I signed out the Jeep and following my map I found the Sergeant Major's office, and presented myself as his driver.

To me, almost all Sergeant Majors in the Army were giants, not just in rank but in physical stature. I would say that 90% of all of the Sergeant Majors that I met were huge men; all well over six feet tall, and with a general fatherly disposition that could turn into that of a mad dog at the blink of an eye. This one was no exception.

It was a beautiful sunny day with a slight breeze, and the Jeep had no canvas covers on it so the Sergeant Major had no trouble heaving his huge bulk into the front passenger's seat. Under the Sergeant Major's instructions I was to drive him to rifle range number 32, and I had a general idea where that was. All the rifle ranges at Fort Ord run along the beach, and you had to drive under highway 1 to get there. I proceeded at the proper speed limit trying my best not to do anything that would piss this guy off. I smiled to myself as I drove, and congratulated myself of my insight. I was now driving instead of running. I drove through the tunnel under highway 1, admiring the white cloud formations that were drifting in from the ocean, and came to my first problem. The rifle ranges ran to the left and right from the tunnel, separated by the crotch of a "Y" in the road. Being right handed I naturally leaned toward going right and headed down the right hand road.

The Sergeant Major immediately came to life and growled, "No shitbird, go left." Being the perfect underling I responded instantly. My left foot jammed on the breaks, and my right foot crammed the gas pedal to the floor, clutched and I dropped the gear shift from third to second gear, and I spun the wheel hard left. (A text book example, just like your teenage Californian street hot rod drivers manual tells you to do in situations like this. Under the fear and evasion heading). The Jeep leaned wildly over as we veered left, and fish-tailed crazily on the loose gravel in the center of the "Y" as I accelerated from second back to third gear. After the Jeep straightened out and was now heading in the right direction I breathed out and glanced over to the Sergeant Major to see if he approved of my California driving ability. Well, the Sergeant Major wasn't there!

I blinked, my brain at first refused to believe what my eyes had seen, I looked again at the empty space next to me, yep, he was gone alright. There was a voice screaming somewhere in my head. "You've lost the Sergeant Major; they are going to kill you!" I took a large gulp of air and looked once again at the empty space to my right, yep, no doubt about it, he was gone. In a matter of seconds my brief life passed before my eyes, and the full meaning of SHEER TERROR entered my brain.

With my adrenaline pumping madly through my body I reacted, I slammed on the brakes and looked around,... nothing. I was 400 to 500 feet past the "Y" in the road, and no one was in sight. Only the sound of the surf and the Jeep's engine ticking over accompanied me, plus a couple of stupid birds merrily chirped their brains out nearby, serenading me in my moment of turmoil. Other than that I was all alone with my conscience. The voice inside my head said, "Drive on, act like it never happened," but reason prevailed and I slowly turned the Jeep around and headed back the direction I had come. I creeped along dreading what I might find, saying to myself, "buy, I bet that when I find him he's gonna be pissed!"

As I reached the "Y" in the road, the Sergeant Major came staggering out of the ice plant and tumble weed that lined the side of the road. He was carrying the passenger seat from the Jeep, and was he ever a mess. He looked like he had a run in with a rabid porcupine, scratched all over, pieces of tumble weed in his hair and to his uniform. I was scared shitless.

As it turned out it wasn't my fault at all, whom ever had assembled the Sergeant Major's Jeep had never put in the pins that secured the passenger seat to the Jeep, and when I swerved left the Sergeant Major was holding onto the seat's frame and he and the seat had flipped out of the Jeep. (I won't mention the fact that the Sergeant Major had neglected to fasten the safety strap across the Jeep entry way, as prescribed by Army regulations).

When I managed to creep the Jeep back to the Sergeant Major's location, (I found it very difficult driving with my fingers in my ears and my eyes closed), I dreaded the next few seconds, I hoped my next breath would not be my last. The seat suddenly flew past my head and crashed into the back of the Jeep and the Sergeant Major swung in after it. "Let's go back to the motor pool son," he said to my extreme relief, and I took off at a sedate pace trying not to rock the boat.

I won't comment on the scene that followed when we got back to the motor pool, or what the Sergeant Major did with the Jeep seat, suffice it to say that it was not a pretty sight. I made sure to stay outside so that I wouldn't get any on me. Buttons being melted off of someone's shirt is not my idea of a good time. This one little incident did end my driving career, and I was sent back to trudging along with the rest of the troops. There was an occasional snicker behind my back once the story got around, and my Drill Instructors would often say from then on," I need a volunteer, anyone but Lennox" much to the delight of themselves and other members of the platoon.

I was not the only member of my platoon to have an ordeal while driving for the Army. Private Anthony had the misfortune to drive over a pot hole while chauffeuring the senior Drill Instructor around the base. The Drill Instructor screamed at him, "Stop this Motherfucking truck right now!" Pvt. Anthony stopped the truck where he was, in panic, in the middle of an intersection, and then the Drill Instructor screamed, "Drop boy, and give me 50." Pvt. Anthony did his 50 push-ups in the middle of the road, traffic and all.

Running

In Basic Training you ran everywhere, and I do mean everywhere, marching was a rest period. Being grossly out of shape, and having smoked for the last two or three years did not endear me to my Drill Instructors. I would go wheezing along as far as I could go, and when the air finally ran out so would I, I would drop out to catch my breath. I would then do my best to catch up, the Drill Instructors running as comfortably backwards as forwards, would call out to the rest of the platoon on my progress. "Here comes 'Speed Kills'" (referring to what was printed on the front of my helmet), or "Speedy's" coming on strong." It took a couple of weeks to get my wind back, but it was a long hard climb up hill.

I won't say that I was slow, but the first time that the Drill Instructor took us out to run the mile, a sort of steeple chase course that went up hill at one end and downhill through a mud hole at the other. By the time I made it around the course for the fourth time to the finish line, the Drill Instructor was half way through his second Benson & Hedges cigarette (the then very popularly advertised "seven minute cigarette").

I was finding out that becoming a soldier was no easy thing to do. It took hard dedicated work, physical work. A little thinking was required, but the thinking part of soldiering you could pick up on the job. The Army did not want thinkers in Basic Training, they wanted doers. The actual part of becoming

41

a soldier was a dedication to your platoon and company and that dedication was a determination to make it without quitting. You had to run, jump, squat, exercise, and endure. It was one tough thing to do. There was no I'm too tired, no I'll do it tomorrow, there was just go, go go from very early morning till very late at night. Gee! Those Hollywood movies made all look so easy. They lied.

In my first note home to my mother I wrote, "Dear Mom, It's a Bugger. Hopping you are the same.

Short Timer

Almost with my entry into Basic Training, I was introduced to the two words that meant the most to any enlisted men in the Army, "SHORT TIMER." In the Army you were constantly comparing how many days you had left, left in basic, left before leave, but especially left in the Army. It seemed to me that most enlisted men took a great deal of pleasure in yelling "SHORT" to one another. I could hardly wait till I had something to yell "SHORT" about. After one of the drafted math majors had done the math, we who had enlisted for a school had well over 1000 days to go in the Army. There was nothing to yell short about that.

Basic training platoons or companies would yell what week their respective unit was in in the Basic Training cycle. All of us could not wait for it to end, so that we could get on with our new Army lives.

K.P.

I remember that Basic Training life was hard, but it became harder when I encountered the Army's own form of slave labor, K.P. (K.P. stood for Kitchen Police. There was never any policing about it). Toiling from 4 a.m. till midnight, often soaked to the skin, always hungry, needing a cigarette, and being constantly harassed by petty tyrants were everyday occurrences, but K.P. took this misery to new heights.

When it was your turn to go on K.P. you would arise early and hustle down to the kitchen hoping against hope that you were not the last one to arrive. Those who arrived first got the relatively speaking "better jobs," and those who arrived last got Pots and Pans. Under K.P. rules you could become the D.R.O. (Dining Room Orderly), and spend most of the day with a mop in your hands and a cook nagging in your ear. There was Dish Washing, where you spent half the day washing dishes and the other half with a mop in your hands, with the same cook attached in the same way. But then there was Pots and Pans, where you never stopped, never sat down, never got time off for a smoke, and it seemed never got done. It was a continuous chain of greasy or burnt, heavy metal objects and you scrubbed each one until the cooks thought it was clean enough.

After the first week in Basic Training word filtered down through the ranks, "Don't get pots and pans, it's a fate worse than death." Try as I would I never got there early enough; I always ended up on pots and pans. In fact I was so popular on K.P.; my picture appears in my Basic Training souvenir book, while I was on K.P.

The Army cooks in the barracks took great pride and pleasure in handing out the same tyrannical treatment and abuse to both K.P.s and anyone else close at hand. I can remember standing in the chow line for breakfast one day and heard the head cook admonishing the men in front of me. "When yo men pass by MY mess hall, yo will omit nothing from yo bodies. One of yo assholes walks by MY mess hall and coughs up a green lunger and expectorates it onto the sidewalk in front of MY mess hall, and fo yo knows it a fly comes along and wipes his feet in that green lunger. Then that fly comes into MY mess Hall. That is why yo people will omit NOTHING from yo bodies when yo walk by MY mess hall." After such statements it was guaranteed that he would also add, "Hey yo, Asshole, I got yo name. I'll have yo ass on KP."

Having your self pointed to by a cook and the "I'll have your ass on K P " tag was as good as a black spot to a pirate. It was a death sentence. Cooks had long memories and they loved to dish out harsh punishments for any infraction. The worst punishment of cleaning out the grease trap was usually reserved for those requiring special punishment.

Working all day soaked from chest to knees in greasy water was definitely not my idea of fun. But what was even more demoralizing was witnessing what Army cooks did to Army food. It was amazing, they could lay bacon in a cake pan, shove it in an oven and have it come out burnt on one half of a rasher and raw on the other half, and that could be accomplished on the same side. There were some pretty amazing mistakes coming back to the pot and pan area.

Sick Call

By the second week in Basic Training most of us in the barracks were hacking and coughing with colds, and drowning in our own phlegm from a malady called the Fort Ord Crud. I had it along with a lot of my platoon mates, and none of us shook it off until two weeks after we left Fort Ord.

For those who went to sick call there wasn't much in the way of relief. A soldier would sniffle and cough his way down the hill to the first aid station, and then sniffle and cough his way back. To show for his efforts he would return with four throat lozenges and two bottles of cough medicine, referred to as G.I. gin. Soldiers were quick to discover the use of pain killers. The lozenges were stuffed into a pocket, and one bottle of medicine labeled "take 2 tbl spns every 2 hours for cough or cold" was downed in one draft. The other bottle was saved for later. For the rest of the day that soldier didn't care that he had a cold, or anything else. He was so loaded on codeine he had no way of knowing.

Darvon capsules were another popularly abused pain killer dished out by the handful by Army medics. These were prescribed for everything from a sprained ankle to a gunshot wound. "Take 2 every 2 hours for pain or discomfort. "For the sprained ankle you got an added bonus of a bottle of Winter Green liniment. G.I.s would take the capsules apart; discarding the white powder and gel capsules and pop the little pills inside four or five at a time. Like Codeine this had the desired effect.

There was a down side to going on "Sick Call," and that down side was what did you do with your rifle and gear? You could not take it to the medics; they would not let you in with it. The answer was that your platoon mates carried it for you. That's right, collective punishment of the platoon for any platoon member being sick. I at times carried two rifles all day, or two packs and harnesses. Also, some guys had to carry mine when I could hack the "Fort Ord Crud" no longer.

Payday

A soldier in Basic Training has few pleasures, but the one pleasure we all agreed upon was the day that they handed you money, payday. Personally I never met a payday I didn't like. My first payday was very memorable. The Army made a ceremony out of everything, and payday is one that they loved most as everyone had to attend. To heighten this experience the Army usually held payday in a dimly lit windowless room, with the money, (all in cash), spread out on a green surface, a pool table was most frequently used for some reason. My first month's payday was, as it was meant to be, an awe inspiring experience. I was marched alone in to the darkened room, I performed the secret handshake and other hand Army signals, stood reverently for the required time, recited the sacred words, and was presented with about 50 brand new dollars for my efforts. With all this exercise, free food, a warm bed, and free clothes (the preverbal "Three Hots and a Cot"), we were paid too, Golly Gee. One of those drafted math majors in the company worked it out to about 11 cents per hour based on a 24 hour day. After the government took out taxes, an allotment for a savings bond (everyone HAD to have a savings bond allotment), laundry, and other incidentals there wasn't much left, but one rude awakening was the price for the $10,000.00 G.I. life insurance was also taken out. It wasn't free! They did not forget to ask for donations for the Old Soldiers Home and the Army Relief Fund, (I suppose the Sergeants were making sure that their retirement was being taken care of). After I got through paying for cigarettes and shoe polish there wasn't much left for frivolity, I had about as much left over for one six-pack of beer, if I had been allowed to have one. The Army also showed me that I had something that I didn't know I had I now had a payroll signature. Instead of the newly drummed in "Lastnamecommafirst," it was "Firstnamemiddleinitiallastname." I was delirious with joy being able to sign my name in the old civilian manner.

Free Time

We worked hard seven days a week; we were given a half day off for free time on Sunday, if you went to church. But, if you went to church there was a good chance that you would miss breakfast. This was a big bone to swallow; starving soldiers do not want to miss a meal. Missing a meal was serious stuff as we were not allowed to buy candy and care packages from home were rare, and life was a constant state of hunger. Those caught with candy had to eat it all by themselves, in front of one's peers, who took a dim view of not getting any. Any care packages received had to be divided amongst all the members of the platoon, after the Drill Instructors had taken out what they didn't think the troops should have. In either case all contraband had to be consumed before the sun went down.

But if I learned anything in basic it was how to be resourceful, and a starving G.I. is one of the most resourceful people you'll ever meet. Getting a temperature of over 101 got you a trip to the hospital to see a doctor, who sent you right back. But if you were resourceful you also got a trip to the hospital P.X. to fill up on the forbidden candy and Coke. Illicit candy stuffed into pockets was hauled back to the barracks and usually sold for exorbitant prices to those starving enough to pay.

In the mess hall during meals any number of tricks, threats, or even out right bribery was used to get past the guard on the mess hall milk machine for that second cup of milk. But the milk usually ran out before a meal was over.

But the most creative troops were the ones who had friends on the outside send them marijuana. The Army was constantly on the lookout for drugs, especially in packages sent to the troops. So the contents of "CARE" packages from home were often rifled and objects removed before they were delivered. But a lot of civilians were just as crafty as the Army in disguising drugs as the Army was in finding them. One of the most common methods of disguising "Grass" was by baking it into brownies. These were popularly known as "Alice B. Toklas Brownies."

There were however several strange and humorous arrivals of these illegal goodies. The normal way that they were prepared was to run the Grass through a blender before mixing into the brownie mix. For those who omitted this step it produced some humorous results at the receiving end. The brownies would resemble mini bales of hay when turned over, and anyone getting a look at the straw like bottom knew right away what they were. If the marijuana laced brownies got through G.I.s would chew on them like farm animals with stalks, twigs or leaves sticking out of their mouths.

Sundays were visitors days, just like the penitentiary, families could come and visit their son, and they could bring all the food that sonny could consume. The visitors, sonny and the food had to stay in the company area, and families would picnic on the grass surrounding the barracks. Those of us who did not have visitors were supposed to shine shoes, rifles, windows, and perform other soldierly functions as those in charge could dream up. Most of us found time to hang out of the barracks windows longing lustily after what had been brought to eat, and lustfully longing after the sisters, wives and mothers who brought it. All of us hanging out of the windows definitely appreciated a glimpse of lace, a shapely leg or two and a little cleavage when it was offered.

Humor

There was no lighter side to Basic Training; however, there were a few lighter moments. The most common of these came when you caught someone who had inadvertent put his skivvy underwear on backwards. The Army issued only boxer shorts underwear to all its inductees at this time, and for the guys unused to this form of dress it was easy to make a social mistake. The only attire we had was Army; anytime we wanted to relax we stripped out of our fatigues and went around in our underwear. Troops caught parading around with their fly opening to the rear was addressed accordingly. "Say honey, I see you got your skivvies on backwards for me. I'll see you later tonight," or "hey baby, I see you is expecting me later. Most of us dreaded making this same simple mistake, and becoming the butt of your buddy's jokes.

There were lots of other strange episodes in Basic Training, but one of the funniest was from the smaller guys in the platoon. Going in or out of our new barracks was an event in its self. Three platoons of troops entering one doorway was traumatic enough, but for the small guys it was even more so. Some of them swore that going up or down stairs at peak rush hour was so jam packed that because of the human press sometimes they never put a foot on the floor, from landing to landing.

Ever since I had come to Fort Ord I had noticed a bit of local graffiti showing up again and again. Three letters were scratched, written, and sometimes panted on vertical surfaces all over the Fort. The three letters were FTA, but you did not see

48

FTA on helmets, G.I. equipment, Army vehicles. It just appeared randomly around the Fort. What did it mean, was it a secret sign, a show of G.I. happiness, or a good luck symbol? It was neither as I found out. FTA stood for Fuck The Army, and was probably a sign of soldier exasperation with the Green Machine. So there was discontent in the ranks. The NCOs would make lite of the graffiti by calling it Fun Travel Adventure, just what the Army was all about. We got the message about not saying it in front of our NCOs or scratching it on your gear. The NCO's would deal harshly with anyone threatening their livelihood. So FTA remained a soldier's symbol of defiance.

Gas

They gave us gas training, how to handle a gas mask in a gas attack. We were marching to the gas training area, were we were attacked by unfriendly gas, and even unfriendlier Sergeants, who were the tear gas instructors. Everyone stood courageously still and put on their gas mask, just like we had practiced. I held my breath while I put on mine; once it was on my head and properly adjusted I exhaled and took my first deep breath, of real strong tear gas. It was here on this first day of gas training that I discovered that my Army gas mask did not work, and the first time I realized true fear. Fear that I might not escape the Army alive. It was a profound shock, a white cloud surrounded and engulfed us, but I had my own private white cloud inside my gas mask. Two very red and blood shot eyes peered out of my gas masks eye pieces, but I stood my ground, I choked and gasped and hung onto my nearest platoon mates instead of running for clear air.

As soon as the gas cleared I reported that my mask had not worked, the instructors had already known it by my choking and gasping, and a group of instructors descended on me with advice. Every NCO and officer associated with our company or gas training took it on himself to fix my mask by pulling on the rubber adjustment straps on the back of my head. This didn't fix anything; it only forced my head further into the stretched rubber mask. After a few adjustments like this, they would throw me back in and put me in more gas, and I would report again that my mask hadn't worked. This would then produce another series of adjustments by another officer or NCO and back into the gas I would go.

I never did escape the gas, I would hold my breath as long as I could, and then just gasp for air and cry from that point on. Even wearing the gas mask during training where gas wasn't used I thought something was wrong with it. Normal breathing was hard; I was barely able to suck in enough air. In the opinion of my companions the mask didn't suck, the Army did. But anytime gas was used it got right through in large doses. Several weeks later the Army finally acknowledged that my gas mask was defective when I was turning it back in after Basic Training was completed. The company supply Sergeant inspected it, he took one look at it and said, "This ones no good, you are one lucky troop, this one wouldn't stop any gas for you." I walked away in disgust, but I was according to him, "Lucky."

Rifle Range

The rifle range was two nerve wracking weeks. Concentrating on how to do it the Army way was hard. You had the rifle's front sight, the back sight and the target. You had to line up all three, but sometimes you got the order mixed up. Our senior Drill Instructor did not make it easy for us. He liked to stand behind people when they fired. If your marksmanship didn't measure up to his expectations he beat you about the helmet and shoulders with his red and white safety paddle. This produced some astonishing results, as bullets would be careening and ricocheting all over the place, as troops would be trying to fire live ammunition with a maniac beating on them. When he came down the firing line in my direction I

50

would cringe. When he stood behind me I found something within myself and shot expert, I just couldn't miss, all he did was offer me slight adjustments to my firing. Incentives and positive reinforcement do pay off.

Hazards

One hazard was running afoul of your D.I. You never wanted to hear one of them say, "Lennox, I want to see you in my office." D.I.s didn't have an office. What usually happened is they would march you out the back of the barracks and into a secluded area near the supply office, and there beat the shit out of you. I always managed to avoid this treatment, and I have always said that one object lesson is worth 20,000 words.

Also there were other dangers. Unfortunately in Basic Training my bunk was first one inside the barracks door, therefore it was my job to announce anyone and everyone of importance who entered. Since we were recruits, and the lowest of the low everyone and anyone who entered and was not a recruit was of importance. Our senior Drill Instructor had explained the pecking order to us on our first day on the hill.

"You people are `croots, re-croots,' the lowest things on god's green earth, you are scum. If my dog walks down the company street you will salute it and call it sir. That's how far down the Fucking ladder you assholes are." Our mentor informed us forcefully. Being referred to as `Scum' did not bother me, but I did take exception when a fellow recruit would refer to me in that way. "That's PRIVATE Scum to you," I would retort.

I had made the horrible mistake when shown our new sleeping quarters of picking the first bunk inside the door. Big mistake on my part! I should have been more choosey and gone further and selected a bunk further down the line. After my bed selection was made, our D.I. informed me of my new job. I was to be the announcer. So my lot in life was to announce people properly, I had to jump to my feet as soon as anyone entered.

Stand at attention, and in a loud voice I was to call everyone else in the barracks bay to attention. When they left I had to call "At ease," in the same loud manner. This is how things were supposed to work, and it is not, unfortunately for me, how they did actually work. I never saw anyone of importance come through the door, NEVER. I was always off somewhere else in my own little world. I was shining my shoes, cleaning my rifle, or dreaming of someone's sister. I was never where I was supposed to be or doing what I was supposed to be doing. The company cook walked in one day and I was looking the wrong way, it made no matter of rank I made no distinction, I missed him too, I missed them all. For this neglect of duty I was always given a punishment of push-ups to perform for my inattentiveness. Our Drill Instructor Sergeant Jessie got so used to my lack of attention that he would announce himself to the barracks with the following statement, "Attennn-Shunn, Lennox drop and knock 'em out till I get tired." This would happen whether I was there or not.

You would think that I should have caught on at some time, everyone learns through repetition. After doing thousands of push-ups I did learn something. I noticed that whoever issued my punishment went on about their business without paying any more attention to me. So the next time someone entered who gave me push-ups to do for not announcing him, I waited till he walked further into the barracks and got out of sight. The only way he knew I was performing my punishment was by the sound my Dog Tags made striking the floor with each push up. So I took my Dog Tags off from around my neck, sat down on the floor and jingled the Dog Tags up and down on the floor making the same sound as a push up. My dereliction was not noticed, and when my tormentor started to leave, I replaced the Dog Tags around my neck and continued to do push-ups. Having to step over me to leave, I was usually told to stop with the admonishment of, "And let that be a lesson to you, be more alert in the future." It definitely had been a lesson, this ruse worked for the rest of my time in Basic Training.

As I said I never saw anyone of importance coming through the front door. I lived on the top bunk, and one of the guys from Guam lived on the lower. My bunk mate was never singled out for not being alert. He was very quiet and soft spoken. He was quiet and soft spoken because he hardly spoke English, and besides that he had a mouthful of rotting teeth. To add to that Mr. Guam was a short little runt, and quite a bit slow on the up take. I had been given the top bunk above this guy by the D.I. so that the Drill Instructor could have someone looking after him. I did that, I looked after him by doing his push-ups and mine, I even looked after him on the rifle range when it was discovered that Mr. Guam couldn't hit the side of a barn from the inside. I shot his targets for him, as well as my own at rifle qualification; under duress, of course.

One evening I was sitting on my foot locker just inside the barracks door, I was in the middle of the delicate task of reassembling my M-14 rifle, (yes the M-16 had been invented and been in use for some time, but they had to use up all that M-14 ammunition somewhere). When a 2nd Lieutenant from another platoon came through the front door, and as usual I was in my own little world and never saw him. I was in the middle of compressing my rifles operating spring, (this was a three foot long coil spring steel that you compressed down to six inches with a metal bar). I had the spring compressed by sliding the operating rod down the center of the spring, (that six inch long bar of metal), I was holding the spring in place with my thumb, and was about to insert the pin to hold the guide and spring into place. The Lieutenant seeing my inattentiveness and not wanting to wait for me to become conscious, announced himself. He screamed, "Atten-shun!" I dropped what I was doing and sprang to the position of attention. In doing so I dropped my rifle, letting go of the operating guide, which was immediately propelled in the direction of the 2nd Lieutenant by the decompressing operating spring. The guide struck the door post millimeters from the Lieutenants head and I don't know who was more surprised, the Lieutenant or me. His eyes became big and round and his face turned beet red, I suppose I did the exact same thing. The barracks room became deathly quiet as all the air in the room was removed with a loud sucking sound, it was being removed by everyone present inhaling simultaneously. The operating rod continued on its journey across the silent barracks until it clattered to the floor in what seemed to be 5 minutes later.

The Lieutenant was taken aback, and for a moment he didn't know what to do. "Do I have him arrested, do I turn and run, do I what?" A little light bulb finally went on over his head and he regained his composure with the statement "Drop Lennox and knock 'em out till I get tired."

That particular 2nd Lieutenant never did visit our barracks again, and I am sure he raised the question with the C.O. and my Drill Instructor of the legal ramifications of being fired on by his own troops. The next day I was balled out by my Drill Instructor, in front of the entire platoon, for failure to properly salute an officer. It wasn't supposed to be done by a flying operating spring guide. My Drill Instructor did his best to keep a straight face as he scolded me about how dumb I was with a rifle, and how all along he thought I was a better shot, and he concluded with, "Second Lieutenants are definitely out of season, no matter what your motives Lennox." My bunk remained however, by the front door of the barracks, but no other strangers ventured in to see what kind of greeting they would receive.

With time we grew used to each other and our Army surroundings, the longer our length of service became, the more salty our language became. The "F" word began to show up in our language again, and though we were considered "Recruits" (trainees, rookies) by most, our language was anything but.

A Hard Price to Pay

Basic Training had a price, but it was not paid by all of us. There were a number of broken arms, legs and heads, and a smaller number of people who left us from things like raging fevers, going to jail, or they just went AWOL.

The physical demands of Basic Training were at times severe, but they never seemed excessive. We double-timed everywhere, and after many trips we were all used to our steel pots wobbling on our heads and the feel of a rifle held at port arms as we jogged along. One soldier in our platoon continually had a hard time with the running. This kid would go along with the rest of us for so long and then he would collapse to the side of the road, a gasping heap of exhaustion. Before he learned to fall out to the side of the road he would just collapse onto the ground wherever he was at the time. He did this little trick one morning on a run to the rifle ranges, he managed to hold on till he was in the middle of the tunnel under highway one, and that is where he collapsed. Unfortunately for the rest of us he was in the first few ranks, and he piled up the rest of the company. Just like putting five pounds of potatoes into a two pound sack. Helmets, rifles, and bodies were massed into one squirming pile inside the tunnel, which took several minutes of cussing and screaming to sort out.

No matter what the threats or punishments piled on this kid still kept falling out on the runs. Sometimes the NCOs would order some of us from his platoon to drag him along, and one on each arm the kid was dragged gasping along while others of us hauled his gear. This brought resentment and derision from the other platoons, and the term "Pussy" was heard more than once. At other times our entire platoon was pulled out of line and told to double-time in a circle around this troop until he could manage to continue on. We began to hate this special treatment and this special kid. The word "Pussy" was heard within our own ranks. Much later in training, on an evening return to barracks, the kid performed his usual trick, but this time he refused to get up and rejoin us, while we circled his prostrate form. We were all tired and near collapse ourselves by the time it was decided to leave the kid in the care of two Lieutenants while we went on to the barracks. Running in sand, wearing heavy boots and gear, and while carrying a nine pound rifle ain't easy. But the rest of us had made the grade. As we ran on in the night the kids name was called out and terms of abuse and derision were heaped on him. He was now a candidate for the proverbial Army blanket party, pull a blanket over his head and pound the lumps out of it with fists, boots, entrenching tools. We arrived back at the company area in pitch darkness, late for dinner, and ready to kill the kid. But to our surprise our CO, the captain was waiting for us on the company street, and after giving us a minute to catch our collective breath he made an announcement in a quiet fatherly manner. The kid had died were we had left him, a heart attack. He had been a RA volunteer, 19 years old with a wife. The platoon went to bed that night in a state of shock, and rather chastened from our thoughts of this kid.

In the last two weeks of Basic Training the sun began to shine daily, and the rain puddles dried up. I even noticed that I had developed a sun tan, I took off my Army shirt one evening and I could see that my hands were brown, I went to the latrine and tried washing the brown off before I realized what it was, a sun tan. Normally I never got a tan, (I still am the THE pale male), I burned beautifully every time I exposed any part of my body to the sun, my body usually had an ashen white pallor, and people would tell me they thought that I had spent most of my life in a pool hall. This Army stuff must be healthy?

At last came graduation from Basic Training and with that our orders sending us to where the Army wanted us. A few of us would meet again in faraway places, but this was more the exception than the rule. Some of us had become friends, and we vowed to keep in touch, especially if someone had a good looking sister, but this too was very rare. (Rare that we would keep in touch). We had been strangers when we met, and mostly we separated the strangers we had always been.

Chapter 4

The Signal Corps

After Basic Training I was shipped off to Augusta Georgia, culture shock for someone from California. I was going to Fort Gordon for school, but it snowed in Georgia and when it snowed in Georgia the whole world came to a stop. At the airport I had to spend some time waiting for transportation to make it back on the roads. Not only the weather, but the Army surprised me. I had been granted the training I had re-enlisted in the Army for. So I was now in the Signal Corps, and I was destined to become a signalman. To me the Signal Corps was a little known part of the U.S. Army. Everyone had heard of the infantry, armor, artillery, engineers, and even the quartermaster corps, but the Signal Corps was a blank, I had heard nothing to recommend it. There were no movies about it from World War I or II, or even the Korean War, Hollywood had seldom if ever mentioned it. There were hardly any news reel footage of heroic signalmen signaling, and this led me to wonder just what I had gotten myself into.

There were three of us, from the same Basic Training platoon, taking this airplane trip to Augusta together, and all of us were destined for the same signal school. The trip was eventful enough, we arrived in Atlanta on a jet from the west coast, but we then transferred to a small propeller driven plane.

That plane had seen better days as the plane looked tired, the seats looked tired, and the stewardess definitely looked tired. The whole trip between Atlanta and Augusta was a lot like those old 30's movies, flying in an old prop plane in the middle of a great storm. The flight was in black and white, with the plane bouncing up and down as it droned on through a thunder storm, lightning cracking all around, while a thin stream of oil streaked out from the port engine. The plane was of such an age that I think it was started by the pilot leaning out a window and pulling the starting rope on each motor.

I had only flown once before, and that was on the flight from the west coast I had just gotten off of. I really began to wonder if aviation had really advanced as far as the airline commercials led us to believe. On this prop flight, the skies weren't that friendly as the stewardess never bothered to come by, but the plane was really moving its tail for us; all over the sky.

Odd Jobs

Arriving at Fort Gordon I really considered myself an official soldier, having just survived a brutal Basic Training, and I figured I was man enough for anything. Well the Army likes to have you believe these little fantasies, just so they can dash them. I ended up doing dirty details in a receiving barracks identical to the one I had started out in at Fort Ord. The only difference between the two was everything at Fort Gordon was painted an orange tan, rocks, buildings, sun sets, as an opposite to the California's Fort Ord where everything was painted a tanner tan.

The big difference between Basic Training at Fort Ord and training at Fort Gordon was freedom. We now got to walk where we wanted to go instead of run. In basic it was "double-time" everywhere, with a steel pot wiggling on your head, a pack slamming into the small of your back and a rifle weighing down on one shoulder. This was now the Signal Corps, no rifles, no steel pots, and no packs. There were no supervising Drill Instructors appearing night or day, no going places only in a platoon, and no Meningitis control. Here in our off hours our time was our own. Now at our new training base, we strolled around the barracks leisurely, taking our time going from place to place. We still performed the normal G.I. rituals, police call, the ever popular K.P. and guard duty, but mostly we were now treated as soldiers. Not as "Shitbirds, Fucking idiots, or Re-croots."

Spring was definitely in the air by the time we got to the receiving barracks, the snow was gone and the south had survived another winter. With spring arriving the days grew longer and they also grew warmer. Fort Gordon was set in the middle of a sea of pine trees, everywhere you looked you could see a horizon of dark green made up of the tops of thousands of pine trees. The post itself was carved out of this dense pine forest; the trees grew in great abundance anywhere they had not been greatly displaced by a building or other construction.

Fort Gordon was enormous; it was a major Basic Training base for the south east, the center of both, the Signal Corps training, and the Military Police for the U.S. Army. Several square miles of Georgia were consumed for these purposes, and all activities on the post involved approximately 46,000 soldiers at all times.

I spent Easter in the receiving and replacement depot because the Army has a sense of humor, I was sent to Georgia at a time when no schools were scheduled to begin. It was the same week as the Masters Golf Tournament, and there was no place to go and nothing to see, outside of the post, that did not require a lot of MONEY. I had a whole two weeks of dirty details waiting for me. I and my fellow travelers spent Easter week scrubbing and cleaning everything the Army could find. It made us think that maybe this re-enlisting thing was not all it was cracked up to be. However, I was very used to hard physical work, and did not shirk. And the work filled up the day nicely. We did get time off to attend Easter Sunday services, if

I was going to be in the military for long I was going to end up very religious. I went to church regularly, not for the sake of any religious conviction, but for the sake of reducing my Sunday work load.

By stroke of luck I was chosen to be a payroll guard. I was given the honor of providing armed escort for the officer handing out travel pay to those being transferred out of Fort Gordon. I was given a loaded M-14 rifle and a Second Lieutenant with over $120,000 in brand new bills to guard. After picking up the money at the post finance office, the Lieutenant and I went away to count the lovely stuff. There I was in a locked room, in a secluded barracks, me, my loaded rifle, the Lieutenant and all that money. I had never seen or been so close to so much cash in my life, for a moment temptation did raise its ugly head but naw! I would never have gotten away with it; they already knew where I lived. The toughest thing about payroll guarding was to staying awake while the Lieutenant handed out the money to troops standing in line, who were trying to stay awake to receive it.

School

I finally got out of the reception barracks and the dirty details and got assigned to my school, and within the first five minutes in class the Army found out what I already knew about electronics. I didn't know beans about electricity.

"Where does electricity come from?" We were asked by a Sergeant.

"It comes from out of the wall," was my answer.

"OK which of you has any electronic experience?" We were all asked. I raised my hand, and the Sergeant in charge asked me to stand up, which I did.

"My names Lennox," Sergeant.

"OK Lennox what sort of electronic experience have you had?"

"I can see lightning and hear thunder Sergeant," I replied. That was my only real electronic experience I had.

"Sit down smartass!"

New Freedoms

I was going to be trained to repair communications gear. As the Army saw it, anyone could be made into a technician; anyone, no experience was necessary. In civilian life I had trouble replacing a house fuse by myself, and ever since the day as a small child that I had experimented with electricity by putting my finger into a light socket I had been less than thrilled to be around electronics. Let's just say that I was slightly skeptical of what was ahead of me. Well the Army realized this, and through their training system they spoon fed me the training, they tried to point out where all the light sockets were, and where not to put my finger, so everything was going fine. They stayed away from electronic theory, why confuse people with details, if they are going to get electrocuted let them wonder why.

Unlike Fort Ord we now had complete freedom of the post on weekends. Not yet ready to venture out on the town of Augusta, I settled for exploring the main post on my first weekend off. I jumped into a set of civilian clothes and with three new acquaintances walked the mile or two from our barracks to the main P.X. This P.X. was a marvelous place, a shopper's paradise, clothes, cameras, stereos, along with the standard brass and shoe polishes, and other bits and pieces for your uniform. All you needed was money. So after exploring this emporium of unearthly delights, and having and ice cold Coke at the P.X. snack bar. What to do next? Why my monthly pay allowed for me to go and see a movie, but not much more than ONE movie, and there certainly would not be any popcorn.

We were soon to discover that there was one movie house on main post, and it showed one movie, continuously. We walked up to a ticket booth at the theater, and when we asked for tickets the person behind the glass pointed to a line of troops behind us. Oh! We had to wait in line. So we trudged on looking for the end of the line, and we trudged and we trudged it was a block and a half away. "So now what are we gonna do guys," well, let's wait in line for the next show. We were used to waiting in line, so we waited.

After two hours and our conversation of acquaintanceship had finally petered out, I noticed that the line behind us while edging forward about one block was just as long as when we started. And the people in line ahead of us and behind looked remarkably familiar to me. They all wore civilian clothes, sports shirts and slacks or Levis, and they all had very little hair on their heads. Why they looked just like us!

We stayed the course and waited for what was the next, next movie before we finally spent the 35 cents required to see some first run, epic, "B" grade, pot boiler of a movie, but we enjoyed it immensely. There was not a dissenting vote or action when before the movie we were all required to stand and salute the flag. We were all enjoying the freedom of a Saturday off, and doing it on what was left of $84.00 a month, Army style.

It was at this point in my army life that I learned about a strange enlisted man ceremony that went on in the week or two before payday. It was called the "Vampire Weekend Pass," and I learned about it from a Specialist 4 standing in line with me at the movies. This guy gave me the name of the place to go and how to find it from the bus stop downtown. This ritual involved finding your way to downtown Augusta Georgia and there you would go to a certain store to sell a pint of your blood. That's right folks, sell a pint of blood, for which you were paid the tidy sum of five U.S. dollars. Five dollars may not seem like much, but to a guy making less than $100 a month it was the difference between having enough to get a 35 cent haircut before inspection, or to have some smokes to get you through till payday.

I did this myself on more than one occasion; as $5 was a lot of "Jack" when you didn't have any. I was not alone in my selling of my blood there was a line of soldiers to get in, and a line at the pay window. None of us were ashamed of doing this five dollars meant a lot.

Freakencys

Electronics was and is wonderful stuff, but I had no idea about what I was doing. Surprisingly enough I was having some success learning how to repair equipment by associating symptom and the function of the equipment. One of the draw backs about learning electronics without all that confusing theory getting involved was I had no basic electronics to rely on to answer a lot of the WHYs that were coming up each day. Secondly, learning electronics from people with pronounced southern accents added new meaning to the word confusion.

"Y'all gotta find the rat freakency, boy," this statement threw me for a loss for two days before I understood what was being said. I wasn't dealing with "A large southern accented chicken," (of Warner Bros. cartoons fame); I was supposed to find the "right frequency," not look for demented rodents. Electronics was totally baffling until I got passed the language difficulties with some of my instructors, after that electronics seemed only confusing.

The instructors were benevolent to a point, spending time individually with the slow people like myself, and offering words of encouragement where needed.

"Lennox, y'all betta get yo' head outta yo' ass an' learn some of this hea' e-lectronics stuff if y'all is fixin' to graduate.

"Sarge, (we were a lot more familiar with our superiors after basic), I'm doing the best I can."

"Yo' problem is that there capacitor boy!" He said leaning his enormous belly on my work bench and pointing at something with a pudgy finger.

"What's a capacitor?"

"That there is a capacitor, boy." The same finger indicated a red plastic square,

"Oh!"

"Lennox, y'all betta get yo' head outta yo' ass an' learn some of this hea' stuff if yo' is fixin to graduate."

"Graduate!"

I was being trained on the repair of Radio/Telephone communications equipment, and this was an exciting new field for me. Not only was I learning a new trade, that the Army swore was worth its weight in gold in civilian life, but a whole new language in terminology

"Freakencys, I mean frequencies."

"Hertz" not the car rental company, but the discoverer of "Freakencys"

Besides all the new stuff about electronics and communication there was a new idea for me to swallow. The new information was a new type of electricity in all the equipment we worked on, now I had to deal with a new way of thinking. This new thing was DC electricity, probably named for our seat of government, because this idea was very taxing. It was confusing enough with learning about the stuff that came out of the wall, the stuff you had to change fuses at home for. The AC stuff, but now I had to figure out what am I dealing with AC or DC. I was not pleased with this new electronic information, because I now knew there were two types of electricity that could kill ya.

If DC wasn't hard enough to figure out there was all kinds of new things and terminology to learn. I was told about AM and FM, but hey, who didn't know about those, but then they threw in HF, (High freakency), UHF, (Ultra High Freakency), and VHF, (Very High Freakency, and they [robably threw in a FUHF Friggin' Ultra High Freakency). Then there were also capacitors, diodes, resistors, triodes, pentodes and all kinds of 'odes' to follow up with. I was lost.

The new gear I was learning I found out was not new gear, in fact it was rather old gear. Not "state of the Art" which is the correct term then in high tech. circles, then as now for the latest high technology equipment. This stuff I found out was older than I was, massive pieces of equipment, all run by electron tubes, and with limited range and capability. It also had enough electrical power to fry you quickly and deadly. But I didn't care I was learning something new and to me as to most of us in the Signal Corps, it was exciting.

Being in the Signal Corps was not like being in the rest of the Army, and not like Basic Training at all. The one big difference was that they didn't give you a rifle or weapon of any kind, you got school books. Everywhere you went you marched along carrying your books, no manual of arms, no bayonet training, and no target practice. At parades the Armor drove by in their tanks and other weapons, the infantry marched by carrying their rifles, artillery drug their guns by, but the Signal Corps marched along empty handed.

Like in civilian life, electronics in the Army was associated with nerds and weirdos, the Signal Corps people were the egg heads of the Army. (The Brain Surgeons of the Army were not in the Signal Corps, they were the whiz kids of the Medical Corpse). We had our share of whiz kids who had had electronics training on the outside. I hated them with a passion. I would slave over a repair problem for hours, and one of those brains would pass by my bench, lean over my equipment and point to the problem.

"There's your problem Lennox."

"Hey thanks a lot, man," and under my breath, "why don't you go and play with a live wire."

These big brains were great at theory and electronics but a major portion of all the repairs of equipment were mechanical. This is where I got to catch up to the smart guys and in most cases I passed them by. The brains certainly knew about diodes and capacitors but all that electronics stuff was attached to something mechanical and that was their Waterloo. When the instructor said, "Take out a spline Allen wrench." All he got were blank looks from the brains. What's a spline Allen wrench? As a young man I had been fixing cars for a long time, you had to be able to fix a car so you could use it to go somewhere, and usually fix it again to come home. I had a ball at the mechanical alignment; I even showed some of the smart guys which way to turn a screw.

The Army's method of training was to provide you with nothing but broken pieces of equipment, they must have had good ones somewhere, but they never trotted them out for us. This was done so you were given as wide variety of symptoms as possible to train with, in the hopes that we would remember one or two of them if they ever came up in real life, I have to say that I did learn a great deal about trouble shooting this way, however, I also created a few new symptoms of my own. In my eagerness to discover the cause of one or two symptoms I inadvertently broke something or burned a component or two up. Anyway, I changed the original symptom or adding a new one of my own. Well instead of reporting it to my instructors and perhaps incur their wrath I just put the piece of equipment back on the shelf. After all this was training, mine and the guys to come after me, so I left my own technical legacy at Fort Gordon.

The First Sergeant

Our unit was governed by a new force in our lives, in basic it had been our Drill Instructor, now that we were with the regular Army it was the First Sergeant. Our First Sergeant was a Puerto Rican of diminutive stature, all of five feet tall. First Sergeant Jesus treated us each as a son and gave freely of his fatherly advice, but he broke our balls when he had too. He had been in the Army system long enough to know how to work the system to his advantage or our advantage, and he really opened my eyes to a lot of possibilities.

I remember him telling me, "Lennox, 'choo better get 'choor head outta 'choor ass an' learn some of this stuff if 'choo is gonna graduate."

Spring turned into summer and I was not prepared for how hot it got in Georgia during summer. Marching to school on a nice sunny summer's morning, in a freshly starched uniform was something I will never forget. The half hour walk would leave all the starch in our uniforms around our ankles, we had sweated so much that we had soaked our fatigues through and the starch was completely gone. Marching back to the barracks at noon for lunch left you wilted without much of an appetite, and no energy at all for the march back to school for the afternoon session. Luckily the class rooms were air conditioned, otherwise I would have had definite trouble staying awake for the entire afternoon.

On the other hand our barracks had no air conditioning, and you became creative on how you kept cool. All the windows were left open night and day, and big electric fans blew air into each end of the barracks. After a long hot march back from school one evening a group of a dozen or more of us were lined up at the water cooler trying to suck the pipes dry. While we were doing so we were overcome by a great stench, each of us looking to the other to see who was the offending one. It was none of us, the stench was coming from the fattest member of our unit standing in the front of one of the fans and the breeze was bringing us the full flavor of his steamy, over heated condition right through the barracks.

At night I would take a wool Army blanket into the latrine and wet it down on one side in the cold shower. I would lay the blanket wet side up, and I would sleep on top of that. In the morning the blanket was usually dry.

The heat and sunshine in Georgia could be murderous in other ways other than sweating the starch out of your uniform. Many is the Saturday I spent standing on the concrete parade ground waiting to be inspected by our C.O., and as I stood at attention I watched perspiration stain the uniforms of the troops in front of me. I'd feel my own moist rivers of sweat coursing down my body, while I stood and waited in complete steaming boredom.

My in attention to my immediate surroundings was occasionally disturbed by a loud "TTHWA-APP" sound. The sort of sound you hear when someone's drops a watermelon in the supermarket. This particular noise was made by a soldier collapsing on the concrete. Men would keel over forward, backward or just crumple in a heap, but mostly they fell over like so much lumber. (It was remarkable that no serious injuries occurred from their abrupt contact with the cement. From those I talked to about fainting on the concrete received nothing more than a bruise or a lump on the head). As the inspection droned on, there were more and more bodies sprawled at our feet. No move was made to pick up these poor souls, and haul them to the shade or see to their wounds. They were allowed to slumber until normal consciousness returned, or the inspection ended.

Fire

We lived in some more of the left over wooden World War II "T" for temporary barracks that were even more run down than those I had experienced at Fort Ord. These barracks had coal furnaces for heat in the winter time, and large coal bunkers sat beside each barracks. The barracks were as much a fire hazard as the others I had been in, and to prove that fact one evening ours burned down.

I never found out how it started, and there wasn't much left but a pile of charred match sticks after the fire was over. The fire had started on the second floor around mid-night. My bed was on the bottom floor and I bailed out one of the windows as soon as I heard the alarm given. No one was hurt as most of the troops got out the same way I had, but then again no one was foolish enough to try and fight the fire. The Army fire department showed up within 15 minutes, but by that time the building was fully consumed in fire. They were in time to hang around with the rest of us to feel the toasty warmth of the flames from our personal possessions going up in great volumes of smoke. The more perverse amongst us cheered at the blaze, but most of felt the sad loss of our prized civilian clothes greatly.

I don't think that this had been part of the Army's policy of urban renewal; some of us suspected that it was probably suicide on the part of the barracks. The old wooden structure just got tired of supporting all those G.I.s, or it's 20 plus year old wiring and many layers of paint had a nervous breakdown.

We each lost everything, we only had one or two minutes to get out once the alarm was sounded, and we had come tumbling out of every exit in the building. I ended up standing in the middle of the street wearing nothing but my underwear and my boots. It was June and I didn't have to worry about getting cold, the fire department never turned a hose on our barracks they just kept the fire from spreading to its neighbors. For the next few days we were housed in another "T" for temporary fire trap near the sight of our current disaster, so we would feel right at home. After which we were moved into the remaining barracks in our training unit's area, crowding in on top of the present occupants, and making already hot and steamy living conditions closer and less personal.

It was unfortunate, I lost all my personal possession, clothes civilian and military, pictures, addresses, and most important of all my money. The Army replaced my Army clothes but that was all, and I was allowed to put in a claim for loss of my personal items. I never saw a dime, any day now it should finish being processed through the pentagon, and it will probably be kicked out because I didn't fill in something in a military manner, skiviescommawhitemens, as in (firstnamecommalastnamemiddleinital).

Pots and Pans

In just the few months I had been in the Army I had performed K.P. many times. In all I did not try to avoid the work, as I was no stranger to the long and dirty hours of labor involved. I did object to working under petty tyrants and

69

bullies that seemed to be in every Army mess hall. At Fort Gordon K.P. took on a new dimension. The training unit was larger than a Basic Training company, thus requiring more K.P.s. Each mess hall served more than one unit, and made meal time an elongated affair. The experience of K.P. was less terrifying than it had been at Fort Ord, but it was just as long and exhausting. The cooks and cooks helpers played a little game with the K.P.s, and after my first encounter with it I decided to play right along with them. The game I called "Hey You!" no matter how busy you were or what you were doing if someone yelled "Hey, You!" and you looked up, or responded in any way, YOU were the one they wanted. I took special pride in tuning everything around me out, and was able with deep concentration to ignore even a loud "Hey, You!" from people in my immediate proximity.

As you may gather, this is where I started to rebel somewhat against the system. I had suffered the degradation and intimidation on several occasions in Basic Training, and now in a new environment I decided to test the waters and see how far the authority of the cooks actually went. As I had discovered in basic that they could cook me but they could not eat me. Sometimes it got to be a real test of wills, to see who would give in first, those who were yelling "Hey You!" in my ear or me ignoring them.

After working long and hard on K.P. without a break, I took it on myself to get myself and my fellow slave laborers a coffee break. I marched into the Mess Sergeant's office and asked for his permission for my friends and me to sit down and have a smoke. The Mess Sergeant was somewhat taken aback, because he really didn't have anything to do with the K.P.s in the kitchen. He usually said O.K. without thinking anything of my reasonable request. I would then take myself and a cup of coffee and sit down at table in the middle of the mess hall. Those of my companions with enough fortitude joined me. This set off a great hullabaloo of "Hey, You!"ing and the noise grew proportionately to the length of time we sat ignoring it.

Some of my companions could not stand the pressure and got up and slunk back to their duties, I remained stalwart in my quest for nicotine and caffeine, and so remained at my post, coffee cup in one hand cigarette firmly in the other. Finally one of the cooks came over to see what was going on since he was not getting the correct servile response to his previous inquiries.

"What the Fuck do you think you're doing?" He inquired.

"We're having a coffee break," I replied.

"The Fuck you are, get back to work," he said grabbing me by the front of my shirt and pulling on it. I stood slowly, controlling my rising anger with difficulty, and faced him, I could smell his hot breath on my face, and by the smell this guy must have been rooting in the garbage. I made sure that he could smell my breath in return. His hand still twisted tightly into my shirt, as he glared at me menacingly pulling me slightly toward him. Looking him straight in the forehead, I was taller, my left hand reached out and I back handedly picked up a mess hall chair by its back rest, ready to swing it over my head should the scene get any uglier.

I was not normally prone to violence, but I was past caring after several hours of slavery. Besides, I was tired of having this guy bully me and others, and I was just generally pissed off enough to do something stupid.

What was left of my group of comrades now sensing what was about to happen got up from their chairs and backed away from the table and from this menacing cook. They tried to do a good imitation of not being part of what was going on. I figured I was on my own from here on, except for one companion; it was me and my chair.

"We are having a coffee break, because the Mess Sergeant said we could have one," I informed my attacker, giving him a firm push in the chest with my other free hand.

I had brought up the subject of rank, and this seemed to confuse him momentarily. Mentioning someone who was superior to him meant that he could not very well countermand his superior's words. I had noticed that my assailant had as many stripes on his sleeve as I had, none, and therefore was in no real position of authority. I went in for the kill.

"Why don't you go and ask him?" I asked.

His eyes darted around my group, his eyes also darted from my face to my hand on the chair, and back again. He released his grip on my shirt and stepped back a pace.

"Who said you could take a Fucking break?" Obviously memory retention was not his strong point.

"The Mess Sergeant," I reiterated, smiling knowing I was winning, and my antagonist deflated somewhat. He walked off leaving us with the admonition, "You come and see me as soon as you get finished," and I assured him that I would. I sat down and finished my coffee, and I never did "come and see him." I spent the rest of the day being inconspicuous.

I disliked K.P. at Fort Gordon even more than I had disliked it in Basic Training, and for the very same reason, I was always assigned to pots & pans. The reason was I was always the last one to arrive for K.P., and so I got stuck with the job that everybody else hated too.

I would spend the interminable hours sweating over a stinking, steaming steel sink full of hot soapy water, scrubbing a never ending stream of oversized steel objects. My belt buckle hooked over the lip of the sink, and my body soaked from chest to knees by hot greasy water. Here after enumerable hours on pots & pans I would again stretch my wings and push the authority of those in charge. When thoroughly bored with my existence, and devoid of any hope of the day ending any too soon I would begin to play games with the cooks. I would take the heavy steel cooking implements hold them high over my head and drop them into the steel sink.

KAA-RRASHH!

"Hey, You! Back there, (KAA-BLAAMM!), quit making so much, (KAA-RRASHH!), noise back there."

One dismal day toward my last days at Fort Gordon, a rather rotund cook came back to my position at the back sink and interrupted my scrubbing and rubbing reverie. He got me to notice him by shoving an enormous steel mixing bowl up against the steel leg of my sink. I looked at him and smiled stupidly.

"I want this back in five minutes, clean," he ordered. I continued to look at him and to smile like the village idiot. I made no move toward the pot or even acknowledged that I understood him.

"What the Fuck you looking at? Asshole," he inquired.

"I'm trying to see the needle marks in your arms," I replied still smiling but holding my temper in check.

He didn't say anything, knowing better than to argue with us fools.

He left me to my task, as he walked away I looked into the monstrosity that he had left in my care, it was half full of instant sweet potatoes, old, dried sweet potatoes. From the vessels weight and the consistency of the contents it might as well have contained a mass of dark brown cement. The top of this mess had a powdery dull brown crust on it, and underneath enough viscus mud to cement a few dozen bricks together.

I took my new burden outside to clean it out with water from a hose, and on the way outside I thought, "This guy is not going to leave me alone, he's going to check on me." Sure enough, as I was hosing out the contents of the bowl, out came my fat friend to have a smoke. I busied myself whistling tunelessly as I sluiced the goop away. Satisfied that I was doing what I was told to do, he turned to go back inside, grabbing the double handles of the double mess hall doors. His hands flew off of the handles like he had received an electric shock, he examined them in disbelief. They were covered in brown instant sweet potatoes. I whistled away watching him out of the corner of my eye; he started to come towards me, a look of anger on his face. I rose up from my task and turned, with the hose still in my hand and with water pouring forth, in his direction, he stopped. Thinking better of it he turned about and went back inside mumbling revenge, what could he do to me, put me on K.P., big deal.

Sunday Breakfast

I was not the only one airing some discontent against the tyrannical cooks. I was standing in the chow line one Sunday morning waiting for breakfast and watching the cook fry eggs on a huge hot plate. The cook had a baby face and was very over weight for such a young guy. He sweated heavily as he worked and beads of his perspiration would drop from his forehead and spatter sizzling on the grill.

Being it was Sunday and an official day off, the men waiting in line to be fed wore a wide variety of military and civilian attire. The third guy in front of me waited patiently for breakfast was one huge dude, and he was wearing a white T-shirt and blue jeans. When it became his turn he stepped up to the counter in front of the hot plate and told the cook how he wanted his eggs cooked. The cook looked at him and said, "Go put a shirt on, I ain't feedin' you till you put a shirt on.

"I got a shirt on," came the reply.

"You heard me, that ain't a shirt. Now get your ass out of here and go put a shirt on."

"Man, you are wearing a T-shirt just like mine," said the soldier. He was right the cook wore a T-shirt under his apron. The argument continued back and forth with both sides getting heated, until finally the cook yelled, "I SAID, GO PUT A FUCKING SHIRT ON."

Frustrated and mad the soldier reached his arms over the counter and the hot plate and grabbed the cook by his apron straps and his T-shirt, and with bulging muscles pulled the cook towards him. The soldier brought the cooks face a foot from his own and screamed back, "I WANT MY EGGS OVER EASY." The expression on the cooks face turned instantly to agony, and he looked seriously like he was going to cry. Not because an argument had gotten out of hand, or over a couple of eggs. But because the soldier had put the cook's big belly just a few inches over the hot plate when he pulled him forward. The cook started hopping up and down and screaming unintelligibly, until some of us who were watching got the G.I. to release his grip. Breakfast was delayed slightly that morning until some burn ointment was liberally applied to a very red stomach. Nothing further was ever said about attire in the Sunday morning chow line.

The White Bus

Arriving at this new duty post was exciting in that it gave you a reason to go exploring, see the sights, and find out new things. At Fort Ord we had not been allowed passes to town at any time, this again was part of Meningitis control. Besides, if I had got to town I would have been sorely tempted to stay there. We were cloistered in the Basic Training area from our arrival to our departure, with only a glimpse of the local area from our bus windows. It wasn't till after I arrived at Fort Gordon that I discovered what dens of inequity surrounded military establishments.

One trip to down town Augusta told me everything I needed to know, this was a real Army town. The part of Main Street surrounding the bus terminal was full of pawn shops, liquor stores, and bars. Away from the bus terminal and off of Main Street the rest of town was beautiful, a little bit of Americana. There was a well-kept side of town with its fine houses and trimmed lawns, but there were the surrounding environs of Main Street with older, dusty, red brick and clap board hotels, shops and other buildings. Outside of the built up town were rural areas of spaced farms and acreage, carved out of the red Georgia clay and the deep dark pine forests.

The only way to get to down town from Fort Gordon that a private could afford is by the Fort Gordon shuttle bus, (unless you were a rich G.I. and had a car), it cost 25 cents each way. On $84.00 a month you went beyond cheap in governing your activities. The Army contracted with a company which used an old white school bus, (with ancient springs and ancient seats), to transport the troops in to town and back. They provided basic transportation, three or more to a seat, plus standing room in the aisle on the way into town. Saturdays there was always a long line at the bus stops, and no seat was ever went vacant day or night.

On the way back from town, especially on a Saturday night, the transportation was even more basic. 25 cents got you a seat next to any drunk you chose, and there was usually one hanging out of every other window. One or two drunken soldiers were passed out on the floor, and they would be sluiced forward and backward on the floor along with a large pool of vomit. The vomit and the drunks would roll forward when the bus braked and back to the rear when it accelerated.

On Saturday nights a little gray haired old lady dressed up for church would ride the bus with the soldiers handing out religious literature. She was a sweet old lady who never preached or admonished anyone for their drunken state, but she would smile and offer her literature and was pleasant to everyone. It was my misfortune to sit behind her one night, yes I too was drunk out of my mind, and with every mile of the jolting bone jarring trip my stomach revolted. The "urge to regurge" finally became too strong and whatever was in my stomach started to come up. Seeing the old lady in front of me, I almost panicked, but I got control of myself at the last second and kept it down, twice. I left the bus at the first stop and took care of my most pressing need, and then walked the three or four miles back to the barracks letting the long walk and the cool night air help to sober me up.

I'm no saint, and this was not the only time I went and got shitfaced drunk downtown, but after this episode I avoided the old lady like the plague. If I wanted to toss my cookies I didn't need anyone cramping my style.

Women

I found out early on these trips to town that it was not wise to go alone, there were a lot of people down there ready to separate you from your money, and alone you were easy prey. But in going down town it was wise to pick your friends very carefully. You didn't want to go with someone who just wanted to get drunk and pass out. The short little guys were no good to go to town with either. If they got too drunk you had to bring them back to the barracks over your shoulder, and they were a burden all the way. Some guys your own size were an even bigger pain. If they got too drunk it took two of you to drag them back to barracks with their arms draped across your shoulders and their toes dragging in the dirt. Some G.I.s going to town wore their military dress shoes, and scrapping the toes along an asphalt or concrete road just made them real hard to shine up nice and bright. Besides that you had to listen to the owner bitch about how we ruined his spit shine while he tried, usually in vain, to put it back on.

The main reason that anyone went to Augusta was not to see the sights, the reason was horniness. Anyone horny enough or desperate enough would go and chase women in Augusta, and anyone that horny had to be crazy to try it in Augusta. The local population knew what soldiers wanted with their daughters, sisters, or mothers, and because everyone knew from years of experience what a soldier wanted a soldier couldn't get to first base with any female there. I being slightly more creative than the average pussy hunting G.I., I tried picking up women in church. I would attend Sunday services in my class "A" uniform decorated with every piece of tinsel I could buy at the P.X. I would sit in the back row and look forlorn as all the families paraded their daughters past me, but even going to these lengths I had no luck. I also tried the local dances, but I got tired of being asked to dance by some ones grandmother. The U.S.O. was a stag party of G.I. men, and so were all the bars in town. Any available women in Augusta hid or were hidden, this was to be the same sad story for every military town I was ever in.

The military and civilian families alike with eligible daughters kept a close eye on them, and they definitely wanted nothing to do with G.I.s. Some guys were desperate enough to chase the local bar girls; I never was that desperate or had the kind of money it took to get them interested.

So if you were horny in Augusta, you were usually horny when you left Augusta. There was that other well-known mode of satisfaction available, and some did take advantage of it. I myself was of a mind not to pay for gratification so I went without. Besides paying good money to a total stranger to visit a sleazy flop house with the outside chance of meeting some mean, ugly and generally pissed off individual with a baseball bat hiding in a closet. That wasn't my idea of a fun night out on the town.

Transgressions

One of the biggest deterrents to raising hell in and around Fort Gordon was the fact that Fort Gordon was the training area for the Army's Military Police. M.P.s and local police crawled over every inch of the area looking and hoping to find some reason to exercise their authority. I unfortunately, gave them the excuse they were looking for one evening.

I was enjoying myself in one of the down town Augusta bars. Enjoying yourself in Augusta, (now that was a relative term), meant sitting at a table of total strangers, the only thing we had in common was that we were all soldiers even though we were all disguised in civilian clothes. All of us were half drunk, so we didn't mind the fetid stench of stale beer that surrounded us and mingled with the stench of tobacco smoke, as we continued to guzzle beer without conversation. The music from the juke box was belting out of the speakers at two decibels below brain damage level, and if and when the puny and disinterested bar maid decided to parade around and serve drinks, this was considered the floor show. Conversation at this point was a dead art.

I was having my "good time" wondering at what time I would catch the white bus back to camp. My fellow drunk across from me gave up his pretense at having an interest in what was going on around him, and he collapsed noisily on to the table sending beer bottles flying. I certainly hadn't gotten to that state yet, and I felt a certain injustice had been done to me. One of the beers spilled was mine and as it ended up in my lap, an experience that I didn't care for. My assailant wasn't unconscious just clumsy in his drunkenness. When he came around after a few minutes I pointed out the price of his clumsiness.

"Hay man, that was my beer you just spilled!" I stated.

"Go Fuck yourself." He slurred

"I think you had better buy me another beer." I warned feeling the anger turn the beer in my stomach to bitter acid.

"Go Fuck yourself."

"Pal, I think you owe me a beer." I reasoned, holding my angry feelings in check.

"Up your ass."

At this point in our conversation I gathered that the wet spot covering my lap was all I was going to get for my trouble. So I decided to take the price of a beer out of this guy's hide. I picked up my empty beer bottle, stood up and laid it across my drunken comrade's head with a beautiful round house right. The beer bottle exploded with a crack and a thousand angry brown diamonds flew about his head like angry bees. "Go fuck yourself," I said under my breath as I starting to come back on him with my left. My target crashed noisily down onto the table and then slid out of his chair and onto the floor, spilling more beer and his blood in the process. This is all that I remember of this little field trip, as my own lights went out. I awoke with my head throbbing fiercely as I was being drug from the bar and thrown into the back seat of an M.P. car, and shortly thereafter I was taken and introduced to the Fort Gordon stockade.

What I didn't realize at the time was when I hit the guy across the table; every M.P. in the world was standing behind me. As it was described to me later, they all had seen what I did and were standing there with their night sticks ready. Not only did they decide to administer justice in their own way, but with their own hands. Let us say that they got right into the swing of things, and the hits just kept on coming.

The stockade was not a happy place and I was definitely not happy there. I was certainly not a happy person when I learned that the guy I had hit was an off duty M.P.

I greeted the bars of my cell several times that night, with my forehead, the old water soaked mop handle in the back of the head trick. I had had better nights out on the town, but right at that moment I couldn't remember when, and certainly none recently had had more excitement. When they were through having there fun I was left alone with my conscience and my pain, to ponder both my past transgressions against the Corps of M.P.s and my fate.

In the morning I was drug before the provost martial, who had received a full report of my deed from the arrest sheet. My commanding officer was summoned from home, and this pleased him no end. It was a Sunday, his day off. The C.O. had to come down to the stockade and sign for my remains, after which I was then returned to my company and the wrath of First Sergeant Jesus. The First Sergeant had also been summoned from home, and he now became the instrument of the C.O.'s will. I wondered how many times I was going to pay for this escapade, and the answer was many, many, many times. I was later given Non-Judicial punishment of extra dirty duties to perform and a large fine. I didn't mind the work but I missed the money terribly.

A Souvenir

Other members of my training platoon also knew how to have a good time down town. One member of our platoon Private Bob went out by himself on a weekend binge and according to his after action report didn't remember not having a better time. I and the rest of the platoon found out how much of a good time Bob had had that Monday after he came back. Monday night I went to take my evening shower, and there was a group of semi naked G.I.s crowding around something. I went and checked out what was going on and it was Private Bob's own nakedness they were congregating around. Bob had a new tattoo, and that was the main interest. I joined in the group's disbelief of what Pvt. Bob was displaying. Sometime over the weekend he had acquired a tattoo in the shape of a dwarf, and this is what we all stood staring at, it was quite a bit of multi-colored art work. The dwarf's legs ran up the inside of Pvt. Bob's legs the dwarf's feet started inside Bob's feet. The dwarf's arms ran down the front of Bob's thighs and each hand grasped a knee cap. The dwarf had no body, just feet legs and a head. The dwarf's head was in Bob's groin, nose and chin were created out of the privates, and the dwarf wore a really surprised expression as his eyes looked out over the top of a bushy beard. I might add the dwarf's expression was no more surprised than those of us admiring Bob's new needle work. He didn't remember getting it, but it was a work of art, and I'm sure that where ever Bob ended up he was a definite hit at parties, christenings, family reunions, etc.

Odd Jobs

On Saturdays there was no school, and the Army used us as training aids for other schools. Several times busses or trucks would pull into the company area on a Saturday morning and haul us all away to perform some task or another as Guinea Pigs for the Army.

The tasks we were to perform for the Army turned out to be both perverse and different. On two of these Saturday outings we were all taken for riot training. This may seem that we were to be shown how to suppress riots, but that is just part of the illusion. After breakfast we were told to get dressed in civilian clothes and get aboard the busses that stood on the road in front of our barracks.

Rumor run rampant as we progressed toward our destination, no two troopers agreed where we were being taken or why. We were driven down to a concrete parade ground where the Army had a Hollywood town set up, and it was quite realistic. The town was several blocks of canvas and wood with painted store fronts. It was here that the Army M.P.s practiced riot control, and they were itching to practice on us. We were going to be the rioters and the M.P. troops were going to do the riot controlling. Getting off of the bus I began to worry as a non-committal NCO handed me a Styrofoam brick, and others getting off the bus were given an assortment of foam rubber rocks with the same delivered indifference given me. These prop items didn't look like much, but their presence in our hands didn't bode well for the future.

Having never been part of a riot before all of us just milled around smoking, joking, and comparing rocks and bricks until the riot got underway. The Troops dressed in steel helmets, flak vests and other combat gear, like rifles with real bayonets attached, descended on our milling band from one end of the Hollywood town. You cannot imagine the feeling projected by a troop of soldiers, three rows deep, all identically dressed and filling a street wall to wall. Each soldier in each rank is pointing a rifle with bayonet at you at a forty five degree angle. The M.P.s advance steadily toward us, they stamped their right foot as they stepped toward you one relentless step at a time. All of the advancing troops chanting loudly the same guttural grunt, HURRA! I got real worried with this development, but I got positively paranoid when they started throwing tear-gas at us. The troops descending on our disorganized mass chanted blood thirsty oaths as they came on, pointing their rifles and bayonets at us in a very menacing way. And so as if in unison we rioters all took the queue, we all saw the better part of valor, and all tossed our phony bricks and rocks in the general direction of the troops coming our way, we then retired at a dead run down the Hollywood street. The troops with the real weapons threw back more tear gas and our retirement then became a race to get away from the gas. Down to the other end of the three block long town we all sprinted, only to be met by another wall of troops and more gas. Back we came, to the opposite end of the town toward the first set of riot controllers we had met. This kept up for two hours while the riot troops herded us up one street and down another, we had already exhausted our supply of rubber items, so we were just herded until our clothes stunk of gas, tears streamed down our faces, and we were all too tired to be chased anymore. I had never been part of a riot before, and if that is how rioters get treated I wanted no part of it.

Sergeants in Frilly Pants

Like riot control there were all kinds of these jobs showered on us, one of the more exciting Saturday details I performed was admiring the women in the Army. The lovely and very female Army WACs. The WACs had a Basic Training area set up near the main post P.X., and a group of us were sent down to their parade ground to pull weeds. The Army's idea of a fun day was 30 men picking out crab grass by hand, and on their hands and knees. The WACs were not really interested in us, but we were interested in anything to do with women. The WACs were out in force this Saturday. So were their female Drill Instructors, and they were in fine voice. It was one of the most disgusting, and at the same time one of the most delightful, displays of filth and vulgar language that I had ever heard before or since. To our own NCOs in charge of our detail it was a lesson in brutal eloquence, and it was awe inspiring as well as mystifying.

There was something less alluring about a woman in uniform, it must have been those huge, black, men type shoes they had to ware. But those shoes never stopped us from ogling them, or trying to imagine what was beneath that O.D. green uniform. But when stripes appeared on those women things sort of went out the window. All of us on the grass detail stood or kneeled in reverent respect of those Sergeants with frilly pants. We were amazed by their veracity:

"When I call you bitches to attention, I want to hear 72 pussies slam shut." This almost brought a cheer from some of us.

"Point them titties to the sky." This brought snickers of delight.

"Don't be eye balling those pussy hungry troops over there girls. Anyone of them don't have enough to satisfy me anymore than you." Our NCO began to turn a shade of red I had not seen before, and the rest of us just giggled and nudged each other

But when the dissertation continued with "You won't be getting none of that hard Army cock for some time. So you bitches better start thinking with your heads and not with your cunts." Our crab grass exercise came to a complete halt.

God they were filthy, and we reveled in it. After a few minutes of listening to the sort of abuse the WAC NCOs dished out we were reluctantly moved to the far end of the parade ground. There to continue our crab grass extraction, but without the social education.

Other Odd Jobs

The Army had many varied tasks for we young troops. One Saturday I spent the day and the night guarding a herd of goats, they were residents of the ammunition dump. Guarding them was easy, tedious, and embarrassing. Motorists driving by would Baaa out their car windows at us while we walked our guard posts.

To add a new dimetion to the chore of guard duty the three General Orders we had memorized in Basic Training were no longer good enough. We were now required to have complete knowledge of 11 General Orders. Oh agany! Before I was assigned guard duty I was handed a neatly printed card, a little larger than a standard business card, and on one side of this card in microscopic print were written all 11 of our new General

84

Orders. Those who wore glasses had an edge on the memorization process, but those like me without glasses could only squint at the small text. Those of us assigned guard spent hours testing each other on the knowledge required. None of us wanted an NCO or, heaven forbid, and Officer to ask us our seventh General Order and then find any of us lacking in that bit of knowledge.

All 11 General Orders were then memorized and tucked away for use later on. The card went into my wallet, as I was sure I was going to need it again later. Sure enough these 11 bits of memory were called on again and again, as NCOs everywhere wanted me to remind them of the contents of one General Order or more.

But on my last Saturday night before leaving Fort Gordon the Army finally out did themselves. I was resigned to any fate the Army was dishing out by this time, so I didn't bat an eye when my name was called out during the morning formation. I was assigned to a very special and prestigious detail for the day, I along with several others were marched down to the M.P. area of the post. There we were given instructions that we were to be the final exams of the people finishing the armies C.I.D school, (C.I.D. Criminal Investigation Detachment, the people who investigated crimes within the Army or as we called them the Army's Gestapo). For final exam purposes we were supposed to have been involved in a crime and were to be arrested, booked and interrogated by the C.I.D.

My bruises had not yet healed from my last encounter with the M.P.s, and here I was back in their arms once again. My faith in justice was shaken once again when my assigned graduate was one of my inquisitors from my last incarceration. He had not been one of those smacking me with a broom handle, but I had seen him there watching what went on. If he recognized me he never let on, and I had no desire to raise the question of our acquaintanceship. So I did one of the smartest things I have ever done in my life, I kept my mouth shut.

As my role in this criminal masquerade, I was supposed to have been involved in a P.X. robbery. I was arrested, searched, finger printed, interrogated, confronted with the evidence against me, and then encouraged to confess. I was already aware of some of the M.P.s means of encouragement, and I quickly decided on my best course of action.

"OK Lennox, we have your finger prints off this beer bottle, (I knew they were my finger prints for he had me put them on it), and these items were in your possession, and they came from the P.X.". The items in question were my own and they consisted of a 10 cent plastic comb and half a pack of gum. So after these revelations about my wrong doings came the admonishment of "Why didn't I make a clean breast of it and save us all a lot of time." I had one or two revelations of my own for my inquisitor "I don't think you understand," I said, "I'm not confessing to anything, and you haven't got anything you can use on me." A look of astonishment crossed my interrogators face, "Just what the hell do you mean?" He said rising menacingly above me. "It's simple, you haven't got a case or the right to put me before a courts martial," I explained. I could see the anger rise up in my graduates face, "listen you little son-of-a-bitch!" he menaced, "You confess to this crime or else." I was not impressed and stood my ground, so the instructor came over to see what was going on. I was admonished for my lack of cooperation, and the two of them tried to bully me some more. "I've had enough of this," I announced, "Your boy here hasn't advised me of my rights, so he hasn't got a case." This was greeted by a blank look from the instructor, and eye balls rolling skyward from the student. We started over.

Graduation

As far as my electronics training, I had found the technical ability along with the talent to pull my head out of the nether world. I was going to graduate along with my fellow classmates from my electronics course; apparently it took quite a bit more inaptitude that I had shown to actually fail an Army course. Graduation day came and we had our last formation in the street outside our barracks. The C.O. came out and wished us well and bon voyage, and then the First Sergeant Jesus handed out the diplomas. With the diplomas came the announcement of every ones new duty assignments. As had been the case with the graduates who had preceded us in our course, all of my graduating class was to be shipped to Vietnam as replacements. This bit of knowledge was greeted by groans that got louder as each name was read off, and the announced destination, Republic Vietnam. The actual Way the destination was read by First Sergeant Jesus was "Republi Veetnaaa" which added to the remembrance of the event. Everyone was going to "Republi Veetnaaa", all that is except me, I was to be sent to Fort Riley Kansas.

Chapter 5

Sergeant Bigbelly and the real Army

Here I was on my way to my first real duty assignment, and I didn't know what to expect. I was nervous about my ability as a brand new electronics technician, and I was nervous about fitting in with a brand new bunch of guys I didn't know. I was going to be a rookie once again; first it had been new to the Army, then new to electronics, and now new to Fort Riley. It seemed that no matter how much time I had in the Army or whatever I was still going to be a rookie. Not complaining about it, just acceptance of the circumstances.

First Impressions of Kansas

By the time I reported for duty at Fort Riley it was late October, and I was flat broke. I had taken two weeks leave at home, the first in almost a year, before reporting in. I had spent my time at home finding out what I had been missing since my induction into the Army. I had been missing plenty. Things were not the same around the old home town; for one thing the attitude toward the war had changed. None of my old friends wanted to be seen with someone with short hair, a dead giveaway for someone in the service. It was very disheartening to find out that being part of the Army was unpopular. I had a lot of pride in myself as a soldier, and I was proud of what I had accomplished to become a soldier. So I spent my leave staying home, and seeing my girlfriend only once or twice as G.I. money just didn't go far in a civilian world. Without much money there was nothing else to do I waiting to go back to the Army.

The bus ride from Kansas City across the center of Kansas to Fort Riley was dull and uneventful; leaving me to wonder what life would be like here in the corn belt of the USA. Kansas scenery seemed all subdued, mostly grays and browns, wrapped in its autumn colors, the road was gray the fields light or dark brown the rolling hills tan and the trees black and leafless. There didn't seem to be a whole lot to Kansas that was animated, the land undulated westward, brown hills interspersed by flat plain. A popular saying in Kansas, I was to find out, was, "You can go for miles and miles and see miles and miles." The miles unfolded one after the other and the only contrast was the sky which stayed a vivid shade of blue for most of the day. This clear sky brought with it a cold greeting in the morning, reminding me that I wasn't in California anymore, Toto.

In California I had been accustomed to only two seasonal changes a year, summer and spring. Fort Riley exposed me to the pleasantries of the other two, temperatures in October dipping into the 30s and below, producing that invigorating crisp slap in the face when I stepped outside each morning, and felt those icy fingers stabbing through my chest. This did not bode well for the future.

Fort Riley was a relic from the long past, left over from those horse cavalry days of the 1800s and 1900s, and that era had definitely left its mark on the post. Massive stone buildings were everywhere on the main post, only in the outlying camps did the old familiar wooden World War II structures reappear.

I spent several days in the fort's replacement barracks eagerly awaiting for a duty assignment, and even more eagerly waiting for payday to arrive. I made the usual use of the time in a replacement barracks by honing my manual labor skills on the menial tasks assigned me. Also, after normal working hours I spent time trying not to be found for late night guard duty or other all night duty. Finally I was assigned to a unit on the post and I was surreptitiously transferred out of the replacement company to my new assignment in the middle of the night. I was taken to the compound of the 724 maintenance battalion, part of the 24th Mechanized Infantry Division; there I was greeted by the ubiquitous World War II, tan painted, wooden barracks and the friendly words of "Christ! Not another radio telephone repairman, we've got five already!" To say the least I was dismayed.

The Seven Twenty Fourth

The 724th took up one row of barracks, eight in all, from a giant grid of barracks called Camp Funston, situated by the back gate of Fort Riley. The whole area did its best to impersonate a prison, up to and including the use of cyclone fences and concertina barbed wire. The wire and fencing circled the important buildings such as finance and intelligence, and it also marked the boundary of Fort Riley. My new world was the company area an asphalt strip ran down the row of company buildings. A one story mess hall building topped each end of the row of two story barracks buildings and there was a one story office building in the center. Other asphalt streets crisscrossed the barracks grid, thus separating the 724th from the other units in camp.

I was deposited into the barracks for the Electronic repair platoon of the maintenance battalion, it appeared no different from other Army barracks from the outside but this barracks was busting at the seams with soldiers. It was definitely over crowded, double bunks two feet apart, wall lockers crowding the center aisle, and bodies everywhere. In my previous barracks at other posts no more than 48 men used one barracks, this one held over 70, and more were scheduled to arrive daily. As it was put by one of my more articulate roommates, "It's so crowded in here you can't turn around and swing your dick without hitting someone."

As luck would have it I had been shipped to a division scheduled to go to Germany on NATO maneuvers early in January, and the strength of the unit was being built up for that purpose. Germany! Now that showed promise, a Rhine cruise, beer festivals, quaint alpine villages, beautiful blonde women all these came to mind, yes I was definitely dreaming.

As one of the first formalities I was introduced to my new Platoon Sergeant, someone I was going to grow to hate in the next few days. Sergeant Bigbelly made an immediate impression on me, but the thing that impressed me most about him was his girth. Looking at Bigbelly for the first time I thought, "Hmmm, this guy hasn't missed many meals." Sergeant First Class Bigbelly weighed what seemed to me to be well over 300 pounds and consequently everything about him was large. He had a large bulbous nose stuck in the middle of a round fat face, which also held two dark little eyes that darted around lazily under a huge brow and two wild bushes of dark hair for eye brows. For all his bulk Bigbelly stood only 5' 6", which made him seem all the larger, as his round beer gut hung close to the ground on stubby, tree trunks of legs. He was not an old man, he was neither gray haired or wrinkled, his fat and florid countenance did allow for double chins, but not wrinkles. He welcomed me to my new outfit with a wave of a pudgy hand and by telling me "Christ! Not another radio telephone repairman, we've got five already!" My technical skills duly noted, as was my name in his fat little notebook with a stubby pencil. I was now just another warm body, and he immediately assigned me to raking leaves, I just knew we were going to get along.

Lifers

Normally NCOs were referred to in the lower enlisted ranks as "Lifers," but Bigbelly was referred to as a "Fucking Lifer," by ALL of us of the lower echelon, he was a special case. What Bigbelly was able to do for me within my first two or three days in the 724th, was to show me how the Army really worked, and to graphically explain the pecking order within the Army. There was THEM, the Lifers which were any NCO, (Sergeants with three or more stripes on their sleeve), grade E-5 or above, and then there were US, grade E-4 and below. Up until my arrival at the 724th the impression I had about Sergeants was that they held command over us by their presence, their leadership, their command ability, and the instilling of fear and intimidation. What the real Army was like was that Lifers held command by the rank on their sleeve, and if you didn't do what they told you they went and told the C.O. and he punished you. Punishment consisted of extra work, or a fine and extra work. For really bad behavior they put you in the Army jail, The Stockade. If a Sergeant was decent you called him "Sarge" as a show of respect and gratitude for that decency. If he was mean and not fare with his treatment of you, you called him "Sergeant. "Hey Lennox, what's the difference between the Army and the boy scouts?" "I don't know what?" "The boy scouts have adult leadership."

Another often heard joke going around the lower ranks was, "Why are Lifers like flies? Because they eat shit and bother people." This summed up our feelings about Lifers. The 724th was loaded with NCOs of all kinds, and if one of them couldn't find you something to do another one would.

On my first day in my new company I received a handful of my new division's shoulder patches, (to sew on everything I owned but my under wear), and the C.O.'s canned speech of welcome. This was in addition to Sergeant Bigbelly warm speech of welcome. I had never received this sort of admonishment in the past and this speech included encouragement to work hard, get along with others, don't make waves, looking before I leap, watching my step, not to call the kettle black, don't sit under the apple tree with anyone else but me, and to keep my wick dry. Summing it up I was told "Today

92

is the first day of the rest of your life. Don't Fuck up." I must have impressed the C.O. with my soldierly bearing as I found myself on K.P. within the week.

I was issued am M-14 rifle, complete with a paper tag tied on the muzzle break, stating "DANGER!!! DO NOT FIRE." The Supply Sergeant noticed the tag and ripped it off for me; I thanked him, and made a mental note never to fire this one. I was also issued field gear which included cold weather clothing, and almost at the same time I was issued an Army drivers license. Obviously the report of my driving record at Fort Ord had not preceded me. There was no question of could I drive, no test, no introduction to the care and feeding of large O.D. green Army vehicles, they just handed out a drivers license like they handed out pairs of shoes.

Work

The Radio Telephone Repair section I was assigned to consisted of four Specialist 5th class, equal to a three stripe Sergeant, and two privates first class (PFC), me and a guy named Roger. I had received a promotion from private, also known as "slick sleeve," shortly before finishing repair school at Fort Gordon.

This was the real Army, the Army that Hollywood had depicted for years, a melting pot of American society. The Army of Farm kids, Texans, American Indians, City kids, and small town kids. The American people's Army from every point in the American compass, every walk of life, and from all races and backgrounds. This Army also contained Veterans from Vietnam, professional soldiers, semi-lifers with more than one hitch under their belts, but only two stripes on their arm.

We had several things in common from the very start. One thing besides being total complete strangers to one another, and within a day or two I realized what that was. All of us were counting the days until we got out of the Army, and all of us had a distrust and loathing of Bigbelly.

Specialist 5 Wash, a lifer with over 10 years in, was my new boss, and he turned out to be quite a decent sort. In Army theory, Specialists even though equal in rank to Sergeants and such, were technicians rather than NCOs. They could issue commands or orders only when these orders were to do with their particular specialty. I was somewhat confused by all of this Army mumbo-jumbo about rank, stripes and no stripes, but as Bigbelly had explained it to me, "mine was to do or die."

The other members of the Radio repair section were:

SP5 Cliff a Cherokee Indian from Oklahoma who was a Vietnam veteran, who worked on the interesting philosophy that you had to be able to sleep in any position on any type of equipment or you were not a true electronic repairman. Cliff was definitely waiting to get out of the Army. I naively asked Cliff what his Indian name was, he replied, "Specialist Cliff."

SP5 Barry another Vietnam veteran, also waiting to get out. Though not as laid back as Cliff he knew the score and knew what he had to do to get by, that is as far as it went with Bigbelly, he wasn't anxious to find himself doing extra work like training a new rookie. Barry was married, with a kid on the way, and he and his wife lived off of post.

SP5 Bud who had seen service in Germany but not Vietnam. He was also waiting to get out. He was an eternal optimist always smiling and cheerful, it made you sick to watch him for too long; he had the bad habit of making sound effects with his mouth while working on equipment. His favorite being the Road Runner of cartoon fame, after 30 or 40 minutes of Beep Beeps his life was usually in danger.

In addition to me there was also PFC Roger, an artillery computer repairman on temporary assignment. Roger was learning a new trade. Not only did the electronic repair platoon have a surplus of Radio Telephone repairmen but also a surplus of 11 artillery computer repairmen. They were surplus because of the simple fact that there were no artillery computers to repair. Plus the unit had several helicopter electronics technicians and no helicopters to repair. This may seem odd, but keep in mind that the Army was only interested in counting noses to fill slots in a unit scheduled to go overseas, and the Army didn't care what the noses were attached to.

So on the first day of work on my new job, there I was face to face with my new work mates, and after all the greeting formalities were over Barry and Cliff sat grinning at me. After a few minutes of this sort of treatment I felt somewhat self-conscious, to say the least, uncomfortable. To break up this grin fest I tried to start up a conversation. I began, "By the way you guys act you must be glad to see me?"

"Did you hear that Brother Cliff," said Barry, "the new kid has something to say."

"I didn't hear anything Barry ol' buddy."

"Why's that Cliff?" Smiled Barry.

"Why because I'm so short." responded Cliff still grinning.

With that comment both of them turned back to me and Barry asked "tell me, new fish, just how much time have you put in in this man's Army?"

"Huh, Humm I've been in ahh! Nine, huh nine months," I responded, nervously. I checked my math quickly by counting each month out on my fingers. I smiled back at them more confident now.

"Did you hear that Cliff ol' buddy, the new kids been in for nine months. Positively amazing."

"I didn't hear him," said Cliff, "I'm too short."

"Why Cliff, just how much time do you have left in this here Army?"

"Why Barry ol' buddy, I have 107 days left. How about you?"

"I have all of 91 days Cliff, only 91 more days to go."

Both men grinned broadly at each other once more. I got the message real quick when they turned to me and Barry asked, "Say, a-huh Le-Nox," he said pronouncing my name with exaggerated care, "How much time do you have left in the Army?"

I shuffled my feet and mumbled my answer "900 and some days."

"Did you hear that Cliff, the kid has 900 plus days left?"

"I didn't hear him," replied Cliff, "I don't converse with anyone with over 200 days left, I'm too short."

Our repair shop was not a large spacious, well-lit depot with work benches and lots of test equipment, as we had had in school. Oh no, our work space was dark, dank and cramped. It was in the back of a truck (a 2 1/2 ton truck with a shop van body) backed against a decrepit wooden structure; the structure supplied us with electrical power thanks to an extension cord We had enough electrical power to run a heater inside the van to keep warm. There was a problem with running a heater as we only had enough electrical power to run the heater, but not enough to run the equipment for repair and the heater. So every morning a vote was taken or a decision was made by our leader, either warm up the equipment or to warm us up.

On this first day of the new job the four Specialist 5th grade tested me on my technical knowhow. I had to show them that I was proficient enough technically to remain in the shop van working with them or to be sent back with Bigbelly's labor battalion. My memory did not fail me I could turn on and operate the equipment we were to maintain. The others had made the great sacrifice of turning off the heater long enough for me to prove it.

It was crowded with six people in the van, there were two work benches one down each side and a small aisle down the middle. You stood or sat where you could, with the equipment placed on a bench to be worked on or on the floor as a seat. It was even more crowded with SP5 Cliff sacked out on a stool and laying across a piece of equipment, or sprawled out on a work bench. Working around Cliff was challenging, as he had a mean disposition if awoken. Why didn't the Army provide a decent shop to work in, you may ask? The Army did provided a shop for us, it was in the decrepit structure we parked next to. The shop had some serious draw backs to it, it didn't have any

96

heat, there was no running water, no bathroom, and worst of all Platoon Sergeant Bigbelly hung around in it.

Odd Jobs

Each morning, after formation in the company street, Bigbelly would hand out a list of Dirty or menial jobs, and assign people to them. The more time I spent standing in formation the more I realized two things. 1. That the same poor souls were given ALL the dirty details, and 2. I was one of those poor souls.

So I promptly picked the brains of one or two of my new acquaintances, and discovered the real rules of the elaborate game of "Them" against "Us." As a good soldier it was considered your duty to avoid any detail if possible, to "Ghost" out. Or "Don't be found to be fired." And any elaborate ruse was OK as long as you didn't get caught. You could not avoid work assignments when you were standing in front of Bigbelly after morning formation. You took your lumps and went to work. However, if that job was completed early you didn't go back and seek another task. You didn't go back to the shop where Bigbelly could spot you. You disappeared! The Specialist 5s that were supervising us knew this also.

The E-5s (Specialist 5s) which included most of the Vietnam veterans had sort of a club thing going, where one would cover for the other. They were always unavailable or otherwise engaged when Bigbelly wanted them to "help out." We new troops had to figure things out for ourselves.

So if I couldn't get help from above I decided to start my own club. I would give myself points every time I got off of or avoided a detail and I would give "Them" points every time I got put on detail, or when "They" paid extra attention to me. This made the daily drudge a little more palatable, as it now became a game. I explained what I was doing to one or two others and they too took an interest in playing. Within a day or two several more got into the act, especially my new buddy

Robert. Whenever Bigbelly handed out the daily chores Robert would whisper from the back of the formation, "Ding, Ding, Ding!" After our assembly had been dismissed I asked him what he was doing, "Why that's the sound of the chicken shit counter adding up the points Bigbelly just got." The dinging was picked up by others and was part of our morning rituals. "What the hell is all this Ding Dong crap I hear?" Asked a belligerent Sergeant Bigbelly. He was answered by silence or a muffled cough. The dinging in formation continued, and became a trade mark of our platoon for many months.

To avoid Bigbelly's claws there were certain places where you didn't go. The local Camp Funston snack-bar, the lifers were there before you. The barber shop was only good for a short time once a week and you had to be on the look-out for prowling M.P.s. The barracks was no good until after lunch, too many inspections. The best places to go were in an area of the Main Post were you weren't known. Hop a bus and ride to another part of the post, and hide out in their snack-bar or EM club.

How to Get Away from Sergeant Bigbelly

It didn't take me long to get fed up with raking leaves or painting rocks white, and it was for this reason that I decided within two weeks of my arrival, that Fort Riley was not the happy place I thought it was going to be. I decided I had better find another home. Where to go seemed to be the most pressing question so taking advantage of the advertised "Open Door Policy," I went and asked the company First Sergeant.

"Boy!" he said, "there's only one damn place you can go to from here and that's Veetnaam."

"Where?" I asked.

"Veetnaam boy, the Republic of Sauth Veetnaam."

I got the message, so I filed my papers with the company clerk volunteering my services in the Republic of Sauth Veetnaam, to any side willing to take me, just so I could get myself out of my present predicament and the clutches of Bigbelly.

M.P.s

The most depressing thing about Fort Riley was not that it was in Kansas that is a moot point. Besides the reality that it was the home of Sergeant Bigbelly. It was the fact that Fort Riley was home to three battalions of M.P.s, more M.P.s than there had been Fort Gordon, which is their training ground. I had already met all the M.P.s I could stand, personally, while I had been at Fort Gordon, and now I was faced with a possible repeat of my encounter with the M.P.s and a water soaked mop handle.

The Army was taking its convalescing soldiers from Vietnam and making M.P.s out of them. M.P.s were everywhere, directing traffic, cruising the boulevards in their M.P. police cars, waiting to check passes at the fort's gates. The M.P.s had a ticket system called DRs that were issued for infractions of dress or military code, DRs were handed out like goose bumps at a nudist convention. They were given out for speeding, having a button undone, walking in an un-soldierly like manner, breathing incorrectly. Each M.P. had a quota of DRs to hand out. God help you if the M.P.s singled you out for attention. You could get a DR standing in line at the barber shop for needing a haircut.

Further Training

Duty in the 724th was the normal Army work week, we worked five and a half days a week, and the half day was on Saturdays. Each Saturday morning was devoted to training. We would be harassed by lectures, movies, or demonstrations, each one trying to fill our heads with something the Army considered useful. Most of us found some way to spend part of these education sessions sleeping. I being the hopeless insomniac spent my time watching, listening, and day dreaming. For obvious reasons there wasn't a great deal of interest generated in "The Care and Feeding of the Army PRC-25 Radio." However, everyone sat up and took notice during a full color showing of that ever popular classic film "The Care and Feeding of Venereal Disease."

On one Saturday the Army got around to something really useful, we were given instructions on international road signs and driving rules. We were going to take the driving test for an International Drivers License. The Saturday following our instruction for the license the company were marched off to a classroom and given the International Drivers License Test. I along with two others were the only ones who passed the test, three of us out of more than 300. The C.O. was pissed!

That following Saturday the test results were announced at a formation of the entire company. All members were assembled in platoons lining the company street, and all of us were balled out by the C.O. No one was going to be allowed to leave for the weekend until they passed the test. My name and the two others who had passed were called out and we were told to stand by as the entire company was marched back to the classroom to retake the test. Me? I was put on K.P. so that one of the K.P.s could retake his test. I couldn't win.

Maneuvers

In mid-November the 724th Maintenance battalion was sent out into the field for maneuvers, and to practice its ability to freeze to death collectively. We were to camp out in the boonies for three nights, playing soldier while we were to be attacked by another Army unit. I hadn't gone on a field exercise (FTX) like this since Basic Training, and with the daytime temperature hovering around 15 degrees above zero, I was not looking forward to it.

We dug fox holes in the frozen ground and pitched our pup-tents out in the grass hills of Fort Riley, guarding our bivouac in frozen disgusted boredom. I had buddied up with Robert, a 6' 2" kid of 19 from Washington State. He was a college dropout like me, and through our conversations it seemed that we both shared the same brand of off-the-wall humor. Though not as skinny as I was, Robert was just another bean pole kid with glasses, but whose infectious smile and ready whit had easily made us friends from the first day he had arrived. Now he smiled at me from deep inside a parka hood, as we stayed huddled day and night in our mummy sleeping bags and blankets trying to keep warm and out of the intermittent snow flurries. To fight the boredom Robert took to reading the sound effects from Sergeant Rock comic books out loud." "BLAMM, BLAMM,.... RAT-ATAT-TAT-TAT,... KERPOW KERR-POW,.... MA-R-RINE YOU DIE!!!" and such would be loudly yelled to the frozen world outside.   This brought strange looks and comments from the other campers nearby, and the occasional admonishment to "Keep it the Fuck down will ya!" from a passing NCO.

"God it's cold Lennox," said Robert, arriving back at our tent from somewhere.

"A mere understatement," said I, "It's Fucking cold."

"Roger that! Boy you're telling me! I just went to take a piss. And I reached in through all the underwear to pull my cock out and I couldn't find it. I thought I was a girl. It took me two minutes of persuasion with a wool mitten to find out what sex I am."

"Maybe you'd better tell me what you found out."

"You'll be disappointed to hear, that I'm still a guy."

"Sure I'm disappointed but nothing is going to get me out of the pair of Long Johns I am wearing." I retorted.
My god it was cold.

"I heard that Fred went out in the field to pee but he couldn't. He says everything in his groin is frozen and his balls are blue," said Frank from the next hole.

"Roger that!" Came the response to this statement from another hole.

"I'm not lending him my fur lined Jock Strap," I replied through chattering teeth

"I've got it on, and three pairs of underpants over it."
Dear God it was Fucking cold.

We stood a 24 hour guard to prevent the "enemy" from attacking us. They never attacked; they were too busy keeping warm. But on or off guard the main occupation was keeping warm in that deep freeze of the Kansas grasslands. The first night there a stove in one of the larger tents, where the company clerks slept, got too hot and set the tent on fire. I and 20 plus other G.I.s wearing gas masks kept the fire from spreading by beating the flames out with entrenching tools, boots or anything else that was handy.

The second night another tent went up in flames for the same reason as the first, but this time a vicious wind pushed the flames through the grass faster than the troops with shovels could move to cut it off. The fire began to spread to other parts of the bivouac, and a general alarm went out. I and the other troops on the fox-hole perimeter began hurriedly packing up. Whole tents were drug down in seconds, without regard to their contents, and the tent and some of the contents were man-handled onto the back of trucks, Jeeps or anything not yet moving. Men ran around yelling and screaming at each other trying to get everyone and everything out of the path of the fire. Things got out of hand rapidly, as the fire began consuming pup-tents and other equipment, blank ammunition began to explode in the grass where it had been left as a mass evacuation was conducted in pitch dark.

The fire raced at the heels of us left on foot who were trying to keep from being run over by the mass of vehicles leaving the area. I headed out without my rifle, pack, tent or anything else. I ran through the freezing night air, gasping and falling with everyone else. We ran until we had left the heat of the flames far behind. Finally stopping when we had exhausted ourselves, and reaching a dirt road. It was the network of dirt roads crisscrossing the Kansas plains that finally stopped the fire from consuming a major part of Fort Riley. But several square miles of grass and brush were now just a black chard nothing. The 724th's field exercise was over. No one was killed or badly hurt, but the evacuation had been only partially successful. Rifles, tents, two trucks, and a lot of other gear had been left behind and destroyed, along with the C.O.'s credibility.

The Holidays

The holidays came around and since I was not going anywhere I resigned myself to dining at the mess hall. For each of Thanksgiving and Christmas holidays a formal dinner was announced. Along with this notice was a demand for ties to be worn if wearing civilian clothes, or class "A" uniforms to be worn. Either way, no tie, no eat. On the day of each dinner the barracks would be in turmoil as 70 people were trying to remember how to tie a tie in something other than an overhand granny knot. And 70 people trying to use the six mirrors in the latrine to try and tie their tie.

The cooks and the Mess Sergeant out did themselves, little nut cups for everyone, the officers eating with the enlisted men, separate tables of course, and the turkey loaf was done to a tee. These were the first meals in the Army where I could remember getting enough to eat, and actually enjoying the meal at a leisurely pace.

The Chow Line

It seemed to me at the time that I spent a lot of time in a chow line, basically I thought I was doing my best to dispel the old soldier's statement of "I've got more time in a chow line than you've got in the Army." But I did spend this chow line time wisely, getting acquainted with more and more members of the 724th Maintenance. I had become acquainted with a lot of 724th members while we had shared chores during K.P., and a day of shared penal servitude was a good way to get acquainted. Another way of getting to know your fellow soldiers was while shivering together in the cold, outside the mess hall, waiting to be allowed in for a meal. On one particularly cold evening waiting outside I met a group of mechanics from the motor pool. We all knew each other, as the motor pool and the signal section were very popular on the K.P. roster. While he was standing talking and shivering one of the mechanics said, "Hey Joe, why don't you show Lennox your clip board?" Joe was someone I recognized, and I got curious about what Joe had to show me. Joe's buddies encouraged him again to show me his clip board. It turns out that Joe was a "Short Timer," a real short timer with only 10 days to go. Joe's clip board was his "Short Timers" clip board complete with some of his processing out paperwork attached. He wasn't loudly bragging the fact that he was getting out he was just standing in line with the rest of us. His buddies were pointing him out to all around. "Show him your clip board Joe, show it to him," said his buddy turning to me excitedly. "Man you have got to see this it is so cool." "Come on Joe show him," he cajoled his friend. Joe slowly relented; he was sort of embarrassed by the whole thing. He held up the clip board for me to see, "I sort of personalized it," he admitted, pointing to one or two racing decals that adorned the back. But something else caught my eye; in the upper right corner was a 4 X 6 inch, black and white photograph of a very pretty girl lounging on a couch. "Pretty girl," I offered in passing, noticing that the only thing the girl had on was a sofa pillow covering very little of her lower abdomen. "Yeah! My girl sent it to me," he offered in explanation, "she said it would remind me to come straight home." I took another peak at the girl; it had been a long time. Wow, did she bring back stirrings in my loins that I thought were long forgotten. "Definitely Cool," I agreed, "Joe you going straight home?" I asked. "Yeah! I think I'm gonna do that." And so I let Joe just stand there with a shy grin on his face, and his clip board held tightly in his hands. I envied him, and I wished I was a short timer too. What I really wished on

104

that cold night was to have a girlfriend that would send me a picture of her wearing nothing but a pillow, and a note for me to come straight home. I wished real hard.

Below Zero

After the New Year we finally got serious about going to Germany. Along with the New Year came the first snows of winter, the temperature hovered several degrees below zero, and with the wind chill factor it got to minus 60 at times. It was sheer joy standing outside in this kind of weather. Waiting to be admitted for a meal in the mess hall, or performing some menial task while assigned to a detail, it was most rewarding. The worst was night guard outside around some building or Army vehicle park. On night guard time dragged and you had to keep moving or you would be a frozen icicle before your guard tour was over. I took to wearing every stitch of clothing I could put on and button or zip closed but still I froze. At the mess hall I and my peers spent innumerable hours, with backs to the wind, hopping up and down trying to keep warm while the wind cut right through you. On guard duty you just froze. Anything, even the Vietnam War had to be better and warmer than this.

The date for our departure for Germany approached, and a lot of us looked forward to this with excitement and anticipation. Finally the Army was going to give us some of that world travel they had promised us when we enlisted. Preparations were done in a fever pitch, to mark, stencil, check haircuts, store, check haircuts, secure, and check haircuts. Then one day just after Christmas Bigbelly made an announcement as we stood shivering in our morning formation. We were going to Germany, and he was going to stay behind. Some of us almost cheered and I am sure that a few wept.

Chapter 6

Germany

At the beginning of January we packed our field gear and all our warm clothing into our footlockers and duffel bags for the trip to Germany, and we stacked them ready for shipment in the unit's day room. In the middle of the night the outside temperature fell to 15 degrees below zero and a water pipe in the day room's floor ruptured. The pipe was directly below our pile of footlockers. Guess whose foot locker was sitting directly over the break in the pipe?

After an emergency trip to the Fort Riley post laundry and few hours with an enormous clothes dryer I was once again ready to go.

We were taken to Germany complements of the United States Air Force, in their C141s, "The Star Lifter" aircraft, an enormous jet transport plane. Air Force transportation was not like anything I had experienced so far in air travel, it was functional and definitely not frilly. We were loaded into the plane in two single files. We walked down the plane between two rows of seats made up of nylon straps, sagging like cheap lawn chairs, running down the length of the plane's body, two rows facing out board from the center aisle and two rows facing in board. Things were packed in rather tight with pack and harness under your seat, helmet on your head, your knee between the knees of those opposite, and your rifle between your legs. This wasn't bad for the first four or five hours, we were all young and healthy, but life got more interesting as fatigue took over.

Someone would nod off to sleep and his head would drop left or right causing a loud dull "CLUNK" sound as the sleeper's 2½ pound steel helmet struck their neighbors helmet or something else of the person beside them. If someone fell asleep and their head fell forward, his helmet came rolling off, to the sheer delight of those opposite, helmet and sometimes rifle landing into the laps or knees of those opposite. This brought immediate thanks in the form of a kick to the groin with an Army boot, and severe curses. The result of this was instant awakening and renewed vigilance on the part of the sleeper. At the very front of the plane there was only two rows of seats and no center aisle this was reserved for the officers and NCOs. It was also the position of the bathroom for 100 plus men. This was a square porta-potty type box, and the front of the plane also had the only two windows available to all the passengers. For us in the rear of the plane, all in all a very boring trip with no windows to look out, and no one getting much sleep, except in extremely short cat naps.

The real excitement of the trip came when the Air Force Crew Chief wanted to get from the front of the plane to the back or visa-versa. He would walk along the top of the frame for the center seats, attached to which was the oxygen lines and masks for emergency use. Every trip by the Crew Chief back or forward would result in the disconnection of one or more oxygen lines, while we troops looked on in dismay at his clumsiness and the fact that he never stopped and re-connected any broken connections.

We stopped at McGuire Air Force Base, New Jersey and were marched off the aircraft to be fed. The Air Force I found out had a different outlook about food than the Army. While the Army made dining an adventure, the Air Force made dining an event with tasty food, well prepared and served in aesthetic surroundings amenable to good digestion The Air Force gave us real china plates to eat off of. This was novel as all we ever used in the Army was divided steel trays, just like the penitentiary. At last here at McGuire we were not regarded like prisoners. I don't know why the Army used divided steel trays to serve food on, the aim of the cooks was lousy, and they always got the peas in the gravy which was two compartments over. If the Army had given us plates like the Air Force our cooks would have slopped our gravy onto our elbow. So a steel divided tray worked for the cooks and us.

We were served a meal that was instantly recognized by us as an Army favorite, probably served to make us feel more at home, creamed chip beep on toast (S.O.S.). S.O.S. was known in polite circles as "Something on a Shingle," and in not so polite circles as "Shit on a Shingle." This Air Force version was recognizable only by sight, and though wary of product served by the Army. All of us dove into this Air Force version and we found that it tasted marvelous; we all wolfed it down by the plate full and eagerly hustled back for seconds. I thought better of asking for the recipe, as our cooks never took kindly to suggestions from the other side of the steam table, and besides it was probably a well-kept Air Force secret. At my table we talked about the difference between the two versions of the meal provided. The four of us sharing the nice clean Air Force table agreed that the Air Force must have REAL cooks instead of the food criminals who prepared what we ate. We also agreed that the Air Force cooks did not torture the food before they prepared it.

Mid-flight we were given a box lunch, passed down the aisle in a never ending stream, from the narrowness of the space between knees there was no way a cart was going to come down the aisle, like they would in civilian airlines. The box and the contents definitely resembled the box lunch given to me on my way from the induction center to Fort Ord when I had been drafted. I was immediately sure that the Army and not the Air Force had provided this meal. I regretted not having a window to heave it out of. I was dead wrong about the box lunch; it was an Air Force treat.

The whole trip took over 12 hours from Topeka Kansas to Frankfurt on Rhine, Germany, and the fun came when you had to finally give in and go to the bathroom. The Air Force had provided one Port-A-Potty for our use and it was parked at the very front of the first class passenger compartment. To get at it you had to step gingerly between legs from your seat to the line snaking away from the toilet. Your progress on a trip down the aisle was followed by the comments of your fellow fliers on your grace in avoiding their shoe shines, shins and toes. Emergency cases were handled on a one to one basis by the individual in trouble pleading with those in front of him in line, or how well the needy did the potty dance. Some troops were lenient some were not.

While standing in line for the bathroom I noticed that there was a window in the fuselage of the plane opposite my position in the toilet line, and it was right behind the C.O.s head, (rank does have its privileges). It was now daylight and every now and then I thought I could see something like land outside the window. I would lean over craning my neck to see out behind the C.O., and the C.O. would think there was something worth looking at. He would immediately whip around in his seat and peer out the window trying to see what it was I was looking at. There never was anything visible between the broken clouds beneath us, but every time I made a move to see the C.O. would jerk around. It got to be fun baiting the C.O. into turning around. He fell for it every time.

Landing in Germany was like landing at any other air force base, runway, buildings, Military Police, it was all there. The C.O. wanted us to march off of the airplane in formation, as he wanted to make a good impression. We were the vanguard of the 24th Mechanized Infantry Division, and what an impression we made. It made a great impression to see 100 plus soldiers in column stepping off the cargo ramp of a C141 transport onto six inches of snow and ice in near blizzard conditions. There was no one there to impress and after the troops had picked themselves up off the runway and the helmets and rifles were all collected up, we were allowed to march off single file at our own pace.

First Glimpses of Germany

Within hours of landing we were moved from Frankfurt south to Mannheim to pick up our equipment for the maneuvers. The 24th division was a former NATO division whose equipment had been stored in Mannheim after the division returned to the U.S. It was rather novel for an entire U.S. Army division to have two sets of equipment. Tanks, trucks, radios everything duplicated.

Winter was definitely with us, and the snow followed us wherever we went. There wasn't much of Germany to see from the Autobahn, and even less to see from inside a canvas covered Army truck. I being the eternal optimist I craned my neck to see the sights as the canvas flap over the back of the truck flipped this way then that way.

Like winter in Kansas Germany appeared all black and white with grays and the occasional beige to break the contrast. The country side was flat farm land, and the only difference between Germany and America was the architecture of the buildings. The German ones looked very German, large box like brick structures with slate roofs, but not very picturesque. I did not see any blues, greens, or reds everything looked beige. Everything was set off against a background of opaque white from the mist that shrouded everything. Those picturesque German villages with the red tile roofs must have been restricted to the tourist postcards.

Look Out Below

In Mannheim we were put up in a pre-World War II German barracks, we were the guests of the unit in charge of storing our equipment so were given the place of honor, the barracks attic. The attic was four floors straight up, stairs all the way, and we had to get our footlockers and duffel bags up there. The German barracks were an enormous affair, four stories above ground and two plus below, with five huge buildings forming a square, and the center of the hollow square was the parade ground. This is what the Army called a Kaserne. Moving in was strenuous, but after only one night we were told to move back out. We repacked up our equipment, and took our bags back down stairs. Some of our more inventive members of my company decided to short cut the trip back down stairs. Why not avoid the effort part and toss things out of the fourth story window, and let the snow on the ground break the fall? (Just like myself, our soldier's motto was, "Make everything fun," or "Put fun into everything"). So some of us did just that, being differently creative myself I rode my footlocker down the stairwell, all eight flights of it, like a bucking bronco, I had trouble though successfully negotiated the turns on each landing of the stair wells. I enjoyed myself except for the stop at the bottom, I ran into a traffic jam of soldiers and footlockers trying to exit out of the barracks door.

Once outside I was able to view the results of the flying baggage, canvas duffel bags were sticking out of the snow split open like over ripe fruit. Clothing and other personal items littered the ground around the impact zone, and still other luggage continued to descend in this way. It was a classic case of tossing good after bad; the results of the first attempts were not visible at the top because the window they were tossed out of was hidden from the ground by the roof line. So what seemed to be a good idea was continued, with the contents of the first bags cushioning the fall of the latter. I wondered what would have happened had the G.I.s who had tossed their duffle bags out the window had also tossed their wooden foot lockers too. It probably would have probably been like dropping bombs.

On the Road

Once all baggage was gathered and stacked, we were formed into platoons and the C.O. decided to try it one more time, and gave the order "Forward march." He wanted us to march to the vehicle storage area wearing full field gear, pack, galoshes, helmet, and carrying a rifle, in cold weather clothes, over a road with three or more inches of solid ice on it. With the echo of the word "March" dying away the movement of the troops was like bowling on a large scale. The C.O. and his retinue marched down the shoulder of the road where it was snow and not walking on ice, while we four abreast made the brave attempt at carrying out his command. One soldier would fall down, and one or more would trip over him, or a soldier would fall down and drag one or more with him. It was total disaster. A little over 100 yards later and word came down, "Route Step," in other words "Every man for himself."

Lucky for me I was assigned to drive, but those unlucky ones riding had to make the entire trip in the back of a freezing truck. These lucky guys got to ride along with frozen freight, frozen spare parts and frozen food. I got to drive in canvas topped cab with no heater; at least I had something to do to occupy my time.

All the vehicles heading for Grafenwher, (pronounced Graf-en-Veer), were formed into several vehicle convoys containing all five companies of the battalion left Mannheim in succession. I drove a truck and trailer as part of a 100 plus truck convoy, and with a demented Sergeant from my platoon riding in the cab with me as a passenger. He kept singing and whistling, (the Army does not provide radios in their vehicles), and he refused to share with me any of his smokes after my own supply of cigarettes had run out. We ended up 12 hours later on the other side of Germany leading only two trucks and no convoy in sight.

An M.P. was supposed to have been stationed at the off ramp we were to take from the autobahn. However, no M.P.

was visible at any off ramp we came across, and this is where the entire 724th Maintenance battalion began to fall apart. Convoys started taking off ramps everywhere. There were convoys going up the autobahn passing convoys going back down the autobahn. With convoys crossing over the autobahn at every over pass for miles. My passenger Sergeant Fred was beside himself with glee, besides being in control of all the cigarettes, he was now in control of our destiny.

Sergeant Fred informed me that I was not to worry. He had been to where we were going before and was quite confident that he could guide us onto the right German trail to our destination. I, to say the least, was skeptical, and in need of a smoke.

Two hours after getting separated from our original convoy we caught up with another convoy and we found out that this convoy was led by a warrant officer from our company leading only three trucks. Originally he had been the leader of another 100 plus truck convoy and he now had six counting us.

That night I learned how a 2 1/2 ton truck pulling a trailer could really drive in heavy snow, off road, over road dividers, or in heavy snow across front lawns. Needless to say our new leader was now desperate as he took us through village and town looking for our destination. Things were so screwed up that night that there was part of a convoy from B Company that turned around ON the Czechoslovakian boarder. Any enterprising Commie boarder guard should have raised the barricade and waived the whole bunch through and let the bargaining begin.

We finally stopped at a hotel and bar for directions; while the warrant office went into the hotel Sergeant Fred and I went into the bar. I got out my finest high school German dictionary, and proceeded to inquire from one or two of the locals which was the way to our destination, in my best high school German.

"Bitte, vo ist, ah, vo ist der. Ah... vo???

I got absolutely nowhere, blank stares and mumbled conversations from the locals among themselves were the only responses to my inquiries. My accompanying Sergeant Fred getting frustrated with me and my linguistic skills asked for directions but in English.

"Hey any of you guys know where the hell we are?"

"You are late soldier boy; we were expecting you hours ago?" They knew we were coming? The local economy definitely had its finger on the pulse of the U.S. Army. Makes you wonder if they knew we were coming from their own intelligence or from the Commies.

"How far to Grafenwher?"

"10 Kilometers straight ahead, there are signs all the way."

"Thanks, we'll be back for a beer later."

"Veedersein."

I made a mental note to throw away my high school German dictionary.

We finally arrived at our destination, Grafenwher, not far from the Czech boarder, at 10 p.m. after over 18 hours of being on the road. We made the final corrections to our course, following the directions provided by the locals. By 10 a.m. the next morning all of our lost vehicles were either found by the M.P.s, and were turned around and directed toward Grafenwher. Others of the "lost" battalion were drug out of hotels and bars by the M.P.s and were soon back with us laughing and telling tales of their adventures. To the locals it must have appeared that one hell of a large Army was descending on them from all the trucks coming from different directions, when in fact it was only one battalion.

Maneuvers Again

The Grafenwher area was set in the middle of a lush pin forest. As we drove around or walked we noticed that the trees packed both sides of the road, and were so close together that you could not see more than a few feet into the woods.

While others were at breakfast that first morning Gary and Robert had discovered a large open field between the barracks and the forest, and had decided to put it to good use. They spent breakfast stomping a huge Peace Sign into the snow. "Aircraft recognition," they called it, "For any Commie planes that fly over, they can see we're serious." The Peace Symbol must have been 100 feet across and stayed at Graph as long as we did, with Gary and Robert making a daily effort to stomp new snow into place.

The barracks at Grafenwher were crummy, one story cinder block affairs, which never got warm. They had an old oil stove in the middle of the one room barracks, and this smoky thing had to be fed daily. The oil for the stove had to be carried in a bucket from over half a mile away. Heat wasn't the biggest short coming; the latrine was in another building 400 yards away. So if the distance didn't discourage you from having to go in the middle of the night, the two feet of snow on the ground definitely would.

We were now in the picturesque area of Germany, mountains, dense forests, quaint villages, and heavy snow. Germany had 20 more inches of snow on the ground than what we had left behind in Kansas, but the temperature was at least 35 degrees Fahrenheit warmer. Instead of temperatures being in the minus degrees, they were now on the plus side of the thermometer. No artic driving wind driving the mercury in the thermometer to the negative range. This pleased me no end, I removed one layer of outer clothing and two of under. The forest surrounded us on all sides, the pine woods were dense tree trunks only three or four feet apart, with bare trunks 30 to 40 feet straight up to bushy pine tops. The trees were so tightly packed together that very little sun light made it to the forest floor, truly the Black Forest. Here there was no underbrush; the forest floor looked like it had been swept clean. The mountains added a new dimension to the beauty of the area. They separated valleys and villages, giving the area the expected German postcard look.

Taking Things Easy, My Ass

We settled into the slum they called a barracks and prepared to go into the field for exercises with the rest of the division. I promptly dislocated my shoulder, probably from the threat of having to live in another tent, in a hole in the snow, over an extended period of time. I had my feet slip out from under me while climbing onto an ice covered trailer tongue, the dislocation occurred when I didn't let go of the full can of gasoline I had in one hand or the wood bow that supported the canvas roof of the trailer, with the other. I spent the next three weeks in the rear while everyone else went off and lived in the woods and played Woody Woodchuck.

The First Sergeant took a dim view of my injury; he thought I had done it just to get out of work. He took a dim view of anything less than 100% availability for work as a crime, and considered anything less than a broken bone as a case of malingering. I wasn't admitting anything and he couldn't prove it. He did insist that I perform some form of work during my convalescence, and I was coerced into doing it with threats of what would happen to me the next time I put in for a pass. What did he devise as fitting for someone with one arm strapped to his chest? His first thought was K.P., (He really was a sensitive, feeling, and sympathetic guy), but I explained I could not mop with one arm. The next idea was the one he liked the best, and that was? Why guard duty of course. I didn't get a rifle or pistol, no whistle, not even a club. So I selected a very fine rock from the ground outside the orderly room which I kicked around the motor pool for eight hours every second day. Lord knows what I would have done had someone tried to steal a truck, and I would have probably waved at them with my one good arm.

Every day that I was not kicking my rock around some parking lot I was assigned to the damage control team for the maneuvers. Our job was to document all the unfortunate spills and chills that occurred during the exercise, so that Uncle Sam could pay the locals for their trouble. I was assigned to ride with the same demented Sergeant that I had driven across Germany with Sergeant Fred, and he was just as weird as ever. However, this time when I went along with him I made sure I carried enough smokes of my own.

I got to travel from village to village viewing the damage done, and at the same time sampling the local food and culture. It sure beat playing Woody Woodchuck. We investigated a large assortment of damage reports related to the maneuvers, some of the more bizarre were:

A driver of an M-60 tank missed a corner while navigating through a small German town and the tank rammed through the front wall of the local beer hall. After the bricks and dust had settled the driver threw open his hatch, climbed out inside the bar and yelled, "Someone better buy me a beer or I'll blow this fucking place off the map!"

By the time we arrived there were beer bottles sitting all over the front of the tank, and the drunken Germans and the crew were leaning on the front of the tank treating it like a new mantelpiece.

The U.S. Army maneuvers are a contest between two sides. The "Blue" side or "Blue Army" was one opponent, and the other the "Red" side the "Red Army." Being so close to the Communist Block countries the "Red" army wasn't the real "Red Army" but well you know!

A Blue Army tank recovery crew captured a Red Army 2nd Lieutenant snooping or lost in the woods. When they couldn't get him to divulge any Red Army secrets, his captors tied him to a tree. Not being satisfied with that they backed up their tank retriever till the tank's diesel engine exhaust poured right on their captive, and then they had the driver rev up the engine. The Lieutenant told them ANYTHING they wanted to know within two minutes, which was about how long he could hold his breath.

Return from the Field

When maneuvers were over the troops came back to the barracks, slowly, plodding along carrying their field gear as if it were the weight of the world. When the first group from my platoon entered I was sitting alone and forlorn on my footlocker in the cold empty barracks, just waiting for something exciting to happen. I arose and greeted them, barely recognizing any of them; they were five of the sorriest looking soldiers I had ever seen. Mud caked from head to toe, greasy, grimy, cold, tired, and hungry all rolled into one. They came in dropping their weapons and gear, and each collapsed on the bare steel springs of an Army bunk or a footlocker around me. They lay or sat sprawling out full length lost in their fatigue. No one said a word they just sat dejectedly and stared at the ceiling. Above our heads hung a naked light bulb, and around the bulb hovered a single civilian moth. A real moth, in mid-winter? The moth would flutter down in front of us slowly and then up to the light bulb, soon all of our eyes were following the actions of the moth. All six pairs of eyes followed the actions of the moth, down and up, up and down. The moth's rhythm never changed, up, down, up, down, with each action followed by the silent rapt attention of those of us below. The moth rose up in its flight and struck the light bulb, and then dropped straight down to ground, landing stone dead at our feet. All six of us jumped up cheering in jubilation, one or two danced around pointing to the moth yelling "Die Motherfucker, die!" It was nice that we all could let off steam in a constructive way. I have never seen full grown men act anything like that before or since.

The next group of troops in the barracks door contained my buddy Robert, someone considered strange and different by the strange and different people. Robert had a rather dramatic air about him. He could bring attention to himself in a variety of subtle ways. On this day he entered the barracks as a bug. Taking a G.I. Mummy sleeping bag he put the hood on over his head leaving the body of the bad zipped up. Instead of putting it on normally he laid the torso of the bag over his back and pulled the foot of the bag between his legs and back up to his chest. He then tied the draw strings around his neck and hood, add a pair of sun glasses and there he was. He entered and commenced to prance around the room wearing his bug suit. We laughed till it hurt.

It was with this let down from the fun of living in the field that I was shown the correct method of maintaining barracks decorum. On the second night back from the field one of the troops went out and had a few too many beers. Beer was sold in the mess hall by the bottle, from a local Grafenwher brewery. This was arranged by some local business people. They also had coin operated Pin Ball machines and Foosball games placed in the mess hall too. This drunken G.I. staggering back to the barracks, and he wanted to share his good spirits with his buddies, even though they were fast asleep. He came rolling down the center aisle of the barracks calling for his buddies, not understanding that it was past two in the morning. He was greeted first by the cry of "Shut up, dip shit," by Sergeant Andy, and then the still noisy drunk was greeted by Sergeant Andy's size twelve boot thrown very accurately from across the barracks, even in the dark. Punishment administered, case closed.

Being in Germany was not all fun and games, being so far away from wives and sweethearts caused some emotional stress. There was one Supply Sergeant who got a letter from his wife stating, "You better get your ass back over here now, or I am going out and attack the first thing I find in pants." The C.O. got him shipped back to the states on a hardship basis.

Another Road Trip

After our exercises on the Czech boarder were complete we made ready to leave and return to Mannheim. We were to drop our equipment back where we had picked it up, and then we were to return to Kansas. My shoulder had healed sufficiently that I was told that I was going to drive back across Germany. Lucky me again!

Unfortunately my vehicle was to be the lead vehicle in a convoy. My truck and trailer had a military radio installed in it for command and control, and I also had a 2nd Lieutenant installed in the cab with me for a major pain in the ass. Not so lucky me! Knowing full well that one of the most dangerous things in the world was a 2nd Lieutenant with a map, let alone a map and a radio. I took matters into my own hands. I set the radio up so that the Lieutenant could send and receive messages within a few hundred yards and outside of that range he was deaf. My electronics training was finally paying off with big dividends.

We left Grafenwher in blizzard conditions, creeping along with the road completely obscured by the snow. The snow followed us the entire way; actually it was ahead of us waiting for us. The Lieutenant complete with maps kept asking me, "Lennox are we on the right road?" "Yes sir," I would reply. I knew we were on the right road, and how did I know? The road was marked every kilometer with Army signs, you just had to know where to look.

Within a few miles of leaving Grafenwher my truck developed a few malfunctions that drove my passenger nuts. The passenger window fell down inside the door and refused to come back up. To solve this problem the Lieutenant hung a blanket over the metal window frame, keeping the icy wind off of himself and giving me a blind right side. The back window of the trucks canvas cab was missing, missing to allow the microphone from the command radio to be fed from the truck bed into the driving cab. I finally got smart and stuffed the Lieutenant's maps into the space left by an absent back window, breaking the freezing wind shrieking into the cab from that direction.

Because my passenger could not get anything but the roar of static from the radio I was told, at the first rest stop, to extend the antennas all the way up, as was Army regulations I had tied both antennas down over the top of the cab of the truck they were tied to the front bumper of the truck. I let them loose with a loud whoosh and a sharp twang, as directed. We now had about 10 feet of truck and about eight more feet of antenna above that. On the rest of the trip I cringed as we drove under any highway or rail bridge, for the antennas hit every bridge but two from there on. The antennas added a new and colorful aspect to the trip as we would "W-W-W-A-ANG" or "TW-W-ANG" across Germany each time we went under a bridge. I could just imagine some old unsuspecting German leaning over the railing of a bridge watching the world go by and getting slapped in the head as my truck went underneath. The Lieutenant eventually gave up trying to maintain communications, and was resigned to being at my mercy for the rest of the trip.

But our nightmare continued, as I came through a small German village I had to negotiate a five way intersection and make a sharp turn to the left. There was an M.P. standing in the middle of the intersection I was to turn on and as I approached he was making a violent motion for halt at something coming from the opposite direction I was to turn. I couldn't see what the M.P. was motioning to because of the blanket the Lieutenant had hung over his window, so I did the one thing I could think of in a situation like this, I slammed on the breaks. I was driving on an icy road and as soon as I touched the break peddle my truck went skidding forward on the ice past the M.P. and straight toward a brick wall. The truck continued on its slide, I sat with my hands furiously gripping the wheel while I sat back in the seat, arms fully extended, left foot cramming the clutch peddle, and my right the break peddle all the way to the floor, trying to will the truck to stop. Staring straight ahead with a stupid smile on my face, I was busy, couldn't tell you what my passenger was doing. As I neared the wall a VW bug flew between the front of my truck and the wall. The bug was so close to the front end of my truck that I could not see it over the hood of the truck. It came whizzing by my front end and never stopped. The truck came to rest six inches from the wall, with the rest of the convoy spread jack knifed all over the road behind me. I got out looked over the situation, patted the truck affectionately and jack knifed my vehicle and trailer on out of there.

The German drivers sharing the road with our convoy were their usual courteous selves. In a country that advertises "No Speed Limit" on stretches of its roads the Germans were not pleased when encountering a string of U.S. Army trucks doing only 35 miles per hour. There driving manual must say something like, "Be sure to leave one car length distance between each vehicle for every hundred miles per hour of speed." The Germans would come screaming by my vehicle doing a deceleration from light speed, trying to make the next off ramp. The result of which, more often than not, would be that they usually hit a patch of ice and would then go careening off the road. Their maneuvers either landing them in the ditch at the side of the road, or their running them up or down the road embankment. They must have thought that this was great fun as car after car tried the same maneuver with usually the same results.

Finally we made it through all the snow, the ice, the freezing cold, and the help of my Second Lieutenant, we got back to our vehicle park in Mannheim. It was still snowing and my windshield wiper had long since crapped out. With the snow blowing directly at me I crept into the parking lot which was nothing but a white carpet of compact snow and ice. All I could make out were the dents of the ditches on either side of the road, but the truck just didn't want to make that first turn. Through sheer force of effort and my brilliant driving skills I dumped the truck, trailer, and 2nd Lieutenant sideways into a ditch. I had made another conquest with my driving ability. I would have given a month's pay to have been able to see the look on the Lieutenant's face as we slid into the ditch.

The Lieutenant ditched me, grabbing his maps and blanket from the window frame and got into the cab of next vehicle in line. I got out and waited for the wrecker to come and put me back on the road again. In the mean time I admired my handy work, I noticed the state of my radio antennas, one was bent over at a crazy 90 plus degree angle and the other was shredded and looked like a straw broom.

Back in the Attic Again

We were back in our attic home in Mannheim, and I ended up back on sick call. I had my shoulder re-taped for another four weeks, which sent the First Sergeant into epileptic fits, for he was sure I did it just to spite him. He had the basic concept of "No Work, No Eat" as his golden rule of life. My doctor and I had the basic concept that a profile was a profile, and I did do any work.

Now that we were back to normal barracks routine I made note of the fact that Army served you one day's meals a week of the now notorious "C" Rations. This was an improvement over eating "C" Rations everyday as we had every day at Grafenwhcr. I guess they wanted to use up all the 1940s and 50s vintage years before they got too old, and so they had a stock rotation once a week. The reason I make note of this event was by the way the rations were served.

Our company was very fortunate as we had a very unique Mess Sergeant, Sergeant Kookwell. Kookwell was a man of simple pleasures, simple tastes, and as we guessed a simple mind too. Being limited in his outlook Kookwell struggled hard to go beyond the Army daily menu, and provide us with a "C" Rations meal that was hard to beat and yet had the Kookwell trade mark on it. He would take a 32 gallon Army trash can, and into it he would empty all the "C" Rations it would hold. Not all the rations went in, the cigarettes, gum, coffee, sugar, and other such commodities went else were. We suspected they went down town to be sold, but none of us could prove it. Kookwell would then add water to the concoction, salt and pepper to taste, and then heat and serve. We called it Kookwell's Wild C-Ration Surprise.

The cooks would dollop it onto your trays with the same indifference they dolloped every meal. It was indeed a surprise on what you would find on your tray. The occasional unopened can, but usually it was the bits of fruit cocktail swimming with the Lima beans, the bread floating like dumplings in an indescribable soup, or the scrambled eggs and ham floating in great greasy congealed lumps. It was dining to remember, you could fill up on this stuff just as fast as you could un-fill. We thought of it as a great laxative, but it was all we got so we ate it ravenously.

On a dreary Monday afternoon, I sat in the freezing basement mess hall of our barracks, facing another repast of Kookwell's specialty. I sat facing my tray of G.I. food toying with what swam in a toxic pool in its middle, and trying to figure out was it trying to escape by slopping over the dividers of my steel tray. I wondered, "Do I really want to eat this stuff." A cry rose from across the room. A lone soldier stood up from his seat at a table, noisily knocking over his chair, holding his tray of food out before him. The soldier looked down at the trays contents and dropped the ray to the table with a clatter that stopped everyone in their tracks. All heads in the mess hall turned toward this action, only the noise of the cooks slopping more swill onto GI trays could be heard. "And they expect me to Re-up for this shit," exclaimed the soldier and with that statement he stomped out of the mess hall. The silence from the surrounding tables followed him to the door, where his exit was greeted by scattered applause from the rest of us.

Weekend Passes

Now that we were back in barracks we had weekends off, and taking advantage of the local customs I went into town with my buddy and got royally drunk. I had been promoted from

PFC to Specialist 4th class, a dubious title. I wanted to celebrate and another new specialist, Specialist my buddy Robert, who was promoted at the same time as I, we went on a pub crawl through the local Mannheim beer halls and sampled as much of their wears as we could hold and still remain vertical.

Robert and I became very proficient in our German language abilities, and I can still today mumble the few words that I mastered fluently while in Germany, "Swei beer, bite." (2 beers please). It was all the German I ever needed, or ever used. That along with "Peterstraighn, Al Peterstraighn."

Robert and I walked back through town to catch the street car, (Strassenbaum), back to our barracks, and on the way to the street car stop we crossed the Necker River that runs through Mannheim. Half way over the bridge Robert stopped and he took off his coat and handed it to me. I stopped and stared at him in my own befuddlement, and then watched as Robert kicked off his shoes and climbed up on the guard rail of the bridge. The German auto traffic came to a screeching halt as my old buddy Robert jumped off of the bridge screaming "Geronimo." This is in broad day light during late February, and the spring thaw had just set in. The river ran cold and black beneath the bridge, and bits of ice could be seen floating in the water.

As soon as Robert leapt from the bridge a large crowd of Germans gathered along the bridge railing around me peering at Robert below, they pointed and talked to me in rapid fire German. I shrugged and acted like I knew what they were talking about. Buddy Robert was swimming around in the icy water waving up at the people gathered above him. I was surprised, no dead body floating by, if I had thought quicker I should have extended my hand for a collection for the show. So the crowd dispersed leaving me to walk to the end of the bridge, down the embankment, and greet Robert as he came out of the water.

I gave him his shoes and coat, and he was really quite pleased with himself, teeth chattering but pleased. I asked him, "Say buddy Robert, you feeling alright?"

"Sure am, wadda ya say we go getta beer?"

I had meant it in a mental way. "Uhm, Robert... I think we should just go home."

"Awe come on, I've never had so much fun."

"FUN! Old Buddy Robert, why did you do that?" All I got in reply was a big grin.

I convinced Robert that he needed to change clothes before he caught a cold, and we grabbed the street car on the corner and rode it back towards our barracks. The conductor threw us off half way back because Robert's condition had created a large puddle on the floor, the water rolled up and down the aisle in tiny rivers, pushing the dirt out of the floor grates. The conductor was furious with us, he yelling at us in German and English, and he fined us 10 German Marks, (2 and a half U.S. bucks), for pissing on the floor. The language barrier was too steep and there was no way to explain why Robert was all wet, or what was on the floor, so we paid our fine and ended up walking.

Robert went on sick call the next Monday feeling a little worse for the wear, and ended up in hospital for four weeks with back problems. Hospital let Robert avoid the next month or so of heavy labor, and everyone including the First Sergeant was sympathetic to his condition. They all thought he had been hurt in the line of duty, and I sure as hell didn't tell them any-thing different. I often asked Robert why he did it, to which he would reply, "Because I was there!"

Last Minute Jobs

With maneuvers over the division was to return to Fort Riley. The last task of the division required that all vehicles material and other Army stuff be returned to storage for the maneuvers next year. The bulk of the job of preparing and checking most of the division's vehicles for storage fell to the maintenance battalion of which I was part. I was turned instantly from an electronics technician into a truck driver, a truck mechanic, or a clipboard escape artist. Being as adaptable as some of my veteran instructors I learned very quickly that the easiest and best way to avoid dirty jobs or manual labor of any kind was to carry a clipboard. (You could buy a clipboard at the P.X.). A clipboard gave you importance, In the Army's eyes you had to have a clipboard for a reason. The Army wanted you to do something important so the Army gave you a clipboard, and so whatever someone else wanted to you to do, you showed them the clipboard, the importance of the clipboard took precedence. It was a very important weapon. Just flash it at a Sergeant and make a vague statement about your assignment, let a Sergeant see you walk around the outside or inside of a barracks making notes on your clipboard. Counting windows was good for killing time. And you were free; no Sergeant in his right mind would question the authority of that clipboard.

Having been caught without a clipboard I was assigned to a new detail. Much to the protests of those who knew my driving reputation and to the dismay of the Army I was once again to be that prince of the open road. An Army truck driver.

For one of my assignments I was to drive a truck and trailer from Mannheim to Stuttgart, using the Army's patented method of navigation; follow the truck in front of you. By some fluke of luck I actually got there successfully, truck, trailer and load intact. There was a down side of all this success. The trip was supposed to be a one day excursion, all Army expenses paid, drive a loaded truck to Stuttgart then drive an empty truck back. However, when we arrived at our destination no one was willing to off load our trucks, and by phone we found out that our C.O. wouldn't let us return to Mannheim still loaded. We became unwilling pawns in one of the Army's internal games of chess.

This wouldn't have been at all bad, Stuttgart can be quite lovely, but every one of us was broke as it was five days before payday. So for the first night we struggled up eight flights of stairs to another dingy barracks attic, we slept on borrowed bedding, and tried not to gaze out the windows at the flesh pots of Stuttgart below.

The chess game took four days to finish and the decision of a Colonel before the Army was through playing out its little game. In the mean time we lived in the same dirty clothes we had arrived in, and we all pooled our money and bought a razor at the P.X. The C.O. had sent word to us to return to him clean shaven, or not to return at all.

On the fifth day of our captivity we were given our trucks and trailers back, empty, and told to be on our merry way. I followed the same navigational aid given to me on the way to Stuttgart, but for some reason my truck just couldn't keep up with the rest of the convoy. I kept falling further and further behind as the convoy raced down the autobahn back to Mannheim. Finally after several miles I pulled into a road side rest stop to see if anything was seriously wrong with my truck. I climbed down from the cab and immediately found the cause of my vehicles sluggishness. There were two black lines following me into the rest stop from the highway, and they were created by the tires of the trailer my truck was towing. The air brakes on the trailer were locked, and the tires had been acting like two giant crayons.

I had only driven about 20 miles yet everything about the trailer was HOT, steaming HOT. So hot that the brake drums were on fire as a matter of fact, and flames licked out from under the wheel hubs and along the trailers axle. The first thought into my head at this time, "Well, you've done it again." I was just getting over the ridiculing from my last truck driving episode. I immediately released the air line connecting the truck and trailer, and the escaping air gave off a loud crack which was followed by a very loud bang. The release of the air pressure was the crack, and the bang was the trailer's brake lines exploding. When the lines exploded the spray of brake fluid put out the fire. So far so good.

While I sat and waited for my world to cool off I took a large Army sledge hammer out of the back of my truck, and give each brake drum a slight tap, as if to tell them to open up or I'll kill you. It worked; the brake shoes inside the brake drums released their hold, and gave a loud thud as they did so. While I waited another Army truck pulled into the rest stop behind mine, I put away my brake loosening instrument and walked over to see if someone had come to help a motorist in distress. The truck was driven by Corporal Wilson a mechanic from my own company, and his truck was having its own troubles. "Say Lennox what's going on?" "This sucker won't get up to speed, just dogs along." I neglected to say anything about the fire, and the two black lines; not wishing to offer a target for future ridicule. Corporal Wally Wilson tinkered with my engine for a few minutes, while I made sure that I kept myself between him and the trailer at all times. Wally showed me where the engine governor was, and then he showed me how to disconnect it. A little piece of information I filed away in my memory for future reference. "It won't slow you down now Lennox," Wally said adding, "You don't seem to have much luck with trucks do you? You sure you're from California?" I ignored the reference and the question.

I rolled my truck back and forth a few times to make sure everything was working to my satisfaction, and then took off leaving Wally to fix his own problem. Wally had been right about that engine governor, that truck and trailer screamed down the autobahn, as if nothing was holding it back. With the governor installed on the engine the truck would never go faster than 45 miles per hour, without the governor light speed was a possibility. I was going so fast that I even passed a few German civilians to my own and their amazement.

Not having a road map or any navigational aids to follow left me with a new problem to solve. Where was Mannheim, and what do I do after I found it. I did find Mannheim just by following my nose along the autobahn to the next big city, to find my barracks was a different matter. The overhead road signs on the autobahn helped. The one that said "Mannheim Ausgang" helped the most. Luckily Mannheim is as flat as a board, and the one landmark near our barracks was a left over massive concrete World War II bunker sticking above the landscape. I drove my truck and trailer in a zig zag course through the back streets and quiet residential areas of the town, keeping the bunker in sight at all times. I found home without a hitch, outside of ignoring protests from one or two Germans as I snaked truck and trailer through some tight twists and turns. I drove right through the front gate of my barracks compound, and without stopping to check in I carefully drove right to the motor pool. I parked the truck and trailer in the back row, behind all the other identical Army trucks and trailers. I walked to the motor pool office, and acting nonchalant I left my log book on a desk with a pile of others when no one was looking and then I faded into the woodwork.

Beer Hall Pushing

It was in May that we finally running out of trucks to do things too and it was now almost time for my company to return to Kansas. In the last few days that I was in Germany I had managed to take a week-end trip to Heidelberg, one of the cities in Germany virtually untouched by the Second World War.

Outside of tourism I and my fellow members of the 724th had spent many happy hours touring the local German beer halls trying to drink the country dry. On one such outing to a local beer hall slash restaurant with long wooden picnic tables. A very large and very drunk German decided to show us how to have a good time. This guy was six foot six and weighed in around 300 pounds, and his idea of a good time was to toss people around in the bar. The owner was having none of this and called the German police. The local German police took no crap off of anyone soldier or civilian, and after entering and inquiring, "Vas ist loss," the policeman attempted to throw the boisterous giant out. The big guy was having so much fun that he didn't want to go, and instead he now wanted to toss the cop around the bar. The policeman took out his knight stick and with one mighty blow, hit the giant square on the forehead. He hit him with such force that German cops feet raised one foot off of the ground, and the force of the blow caused the knight stick snapped off at the handle. The broken end sailed off into space, only to clatter to the floor in an empty part of the bar four or five minutes later. The big German stood there in front of the cop and made an animal grunt and shook his head. The giant then started to slowly advance on the German cop. The cop became a little alarmed at this, and so did most of us in the bar. I had my back to the wall would have backed up further, but I run out of places to back to. The cop, breathing heavily, started to back-peddle to the front door. All the while he was trying to find his pistol which was somewhere on his belt but kept eluding his grasp. The big German started after the cop, faster this time, but after taking two giant steps he reached up one hand and wiped his forehead where he had been hit. Looking at his hand as he pulled it away, he discovered it was covered with his own blood, and he then fainted into a giant pile on the floor.

Finally with all the trucks put back in their storage areas, and all the local beer joins supplies seriously dented it was time to return to Fort Riley. Courtesy of the U.S. Air Force and on their C-141s again, the same way we arrived. We headed back to Fort Riley; at least they didn't want me to drive back.

Pictures 1

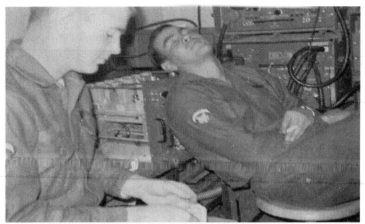

Figure 1. Cliff showing his ability to sleep on equipment. Author's collection

Figure 2. "The Bug" Barracks entertainment. Author's collection

Chapter 7

War with Bigbelly Continues

It was mid-May when we arrived back at Fort Riley Kansas, and the weather was just like the first time I had arrived, dreary. Though it was May the trees had not even budded out, and the grass was still yellow from the frost and snow of winter. Being a kid from California I expected to see flowers blooming in May. I had a lot to learn about Kansas and any other place outside of my home town. We were the last unit of the division to return, and we were all both happy and sad to be back. We were happy, because a long hard job was over and sad because we were reunited once again with our dearly loved Sergeant Bigbelly.

Bigbelly had spent his time well in our absence. He had a list of little jobs he wanted done already written out in his fat little notebook, and another list of who he wanted to do them. With my returned to Fort Riley I faced other good news and bad news. "OK so what do you want to hear first?" The good news was that I had orders getting me out of Fort Riley, the bad news was, and the orders were sending me to Vietnam. I had volunteered for it and I was ready, ready to get away from the clutches of Bigbelly. I was ready to finally go and do what the Army had trained me to do, to repair stuff not paint it, wash it, sweep it, or guard it. I was ready to do pots & pans in Vietnam.

With the division's maneuvers over there was no need for a lot of the extra men that had been poured into the division's units prior to their departure to Germany. A lot of these men were now considered excess, and quite a few of them were slated to be shipped to Vietnam with me. First things first, all of us with orders to go to Vietnam were to be put through training that was supposed to prepare us for what to expect in Vietnam.

Vietnam Simulated

Within five days of my return I was informed that our Vietnam familiarization process was to begin the next day. A group from the 724th maintenance was trucked off to join a much larger group in a backwoods area of Fort Riley. It wasn't Vietnam but it would have to do. We had simulated jungle fighting, simulated booby trap training, simulated patrols, tactics, and we simulated being ambushed. The training was simulated but the bruises, scrapes and other contusions incurred during these exercises were anything but.

To make the training as real as possible the Army had special troops, "Aggressors," ambush, harass and make our lives as uncomfortable as possible. On a truck convoy these "Aggressors" ambushed us in their favorite place, the middle of a field of stinging nettles. We all dove off of the backs of trucks, right into the undergrowth for cover, and immediately swelled up like balloons. It was miserable. The first thing done by the "Ambushed," us, was to return fire. We pop- pop-popped away with the 20 blank cartridges we had been issued. Once we realized we were in a field of nettles we collectively screamed obscenities at the "Aggressors." All that was left after some rocks were hurled in the "Bad Guys" direction was to itch and scratch. The most outraged of our group continued with the rock throwing long after the "Cease Fire" had been ordered. By the end of a week of training most of us were covered by a bright red rash, head to foot.

The weather cooperated with our training. It was absolutely crappy! The rain poured down and turned the landscape into quagmire, just the right consistence for training troops for jungle warfare. So we were indoctrination in how to slog through ankle deep Kansas mud, lay in it, sit in it and come back the next day in clean clothes and do it again. Kansas mud was not as bad as mud I would find in Southeast Asia. The Kansas variety had no booby traps in it and no poisonous snakes or enemy soldiers in it either. Also, this wet weather was to be a great incite on what was to come in Vietnam. I was to find out about the wonderful world of the Vietnamese monsoon, on a first hand basis, but that was yet to come.

Training was not all slogging through the mud we had two days of lecture after lecture in a big theater on main post. We were introduced to poisonous snakes, (The legendary Two Step Snake), machine guns, sucking chest wounds, booby traps, mines, strange kinds of venereal disease, and a whole host of other things that could kill you quick. Each of these lectures was designed to grab your attention, and that is exactly what they did. Most of us were on the edge of our seats entranced by things that could do you in.

During all this training several things kept coming back to me. Little items I had heard said to me in different associations I had had since my induction in the Army. These were reminders or statements that veterans and NCOs had said to me at one time or another. These utterances that kept running through my head had one theme: "You better get this right shit head, or when you get to Nam, Charlie's gonna fry yo' ass." This had been the anthem sung by many of my past instructors; it was a constant reminder that one screw up is all it took. One mistake would cost you your life and possibly the life of a buddy. In Basic Training this threat thing seemed an acceptable training method, as more than a majority of those of us being trained were bound for Vietnam. The same training methods continued into the Signal Corps, even while learning to repair equipment. The usual exclamation to a missed question was,

"Yo' betta get your shit together boy! Yo' ain't gonna have time once they ship yo' ass to Nam."

Of all the reminders, admonitions, songs, threats, or simulated training there was no feeling of reality. I took it all in seriously while others considered the training as laborious chore and by others as a game. The reason I took the training seriously was because of an incident I experienced before I even got into Basic Training. This one experience really hit home about the dangers of Vietnam. This event was offered to me in my first week in the Army. It was a bare truth for us new guys in bright green fatigues trying to figure out what was next in the Army. I and a group of we freshly inducted were taken to the base hospital for medical screening, and in finding our way down the miles of wooden covered walkways we found that some of the halls were lined with wounded G.I.s just returned from Vietnam. As we reverently walked past one gurney after another, one soldier, his forehead and chest wrapped in heavy gauze bandages, suddenly sat straight up and got off his gurney. He yelled to imaginary men, "There goes Charley," and raising his arms as if to fire a rifle and yelled, "Got the Motherfucker." As we stood in shock and at a complete loss to help this man, he ran off at a terrific pace down the corridor in the direction we had just come. Without discussion, we all stole quickly down the corridor in the opposite direction.

For the first time seeing the end result of war sure changed how I perceived things in Vietnam. From that day onward when anyone who made any mention of Vietnam, I sat up and paid attention to what was said. I wanted to make sure that I had everything I needed to be able to come home better than that guy on the gurney.

I kept this thought of survival, even when I came to Fort Riley. Here was the first time that I came into one on one personal contact with veterans of the Signal Corps from Vietnam, on a less than formal trainee/trainer basis. Unlike the veteran Sergeants from Basic Training and Signal School training these individuals were not interested in voluntarily telling me what to expect once I got there. From all my military and civilian exposure I knew absolutely nothing about Vietnam, outside of the fact that it was somewhere in Southeast Asia. I spent the months between November and May trying to find out what went on over there. I had to ask basic questions, "What was the name of the place where you were?" "Was it dangerous?" The extent of the information the veterans would offer was brief at best, but the data I was able to gain gave me the one thing I needed to know about Vietnam and the war. The basics were you lived on a base camp somewhere, and Charlie lived outside. You went outside the base camp perimeter wire you were in the front lines, period.

The Wait a Minute Blues

With my one week of Vietnam preparation over I was stamped approved, and considered as ready, willing, and somewhat able for duty in Vietnam, Republic of. I was handed the papers that allowing me to process out of Fort Riley. Well the Army didn't have to tell me twice, I was finally going to get out of Fort Riley and away from what was referred to as "Stateside Mickey Mouse." I was thrilled especially about finally getting away from the dirty details I had been on, and to go where I could really use my training. It was also thrilling to have something legitimate to have on a clip board. I was sure that any dirty details I was assigned after leaving good old Fort Riley and good old Fat Bigbelly would be pure pleasure. In no time at all I was packed, shot full of vaccines, had said all my good-byes and was ready to process out in a few hours after being given the word.

I was dead wrong about getting out of Fort Riley, for the time being that is. I had gone through all the processing out of Fort Riley. I had all the shots, picked up all my records (health, pay, clothing, etc.), and I was down to the last item on my check list. The one on the list just above the one marked give Bigbelly a great big smooch good-bye. I found out to my dismay that I could not clear my personnel records. Why? The Army's explanation: "You are an alien." Well I knew that, and the Army surely knew that, I had filled all those forms out before basic. The Army's reason was, I was missing papers from my personnel file, my alien good guy report was missing, and I had to have that to be allowed to leave Fort Riley. I asked, "How long would it take to get one?" The Army's reply was, "A few days, that's all, just a few days." "Check back in a few days." These were "Famous last words."

Well, a few days turned into five and a half whole months. In the mean time I had all my records stashed in my locker. I had not signed out of my company so I still had a place to eat and sleep, but I couldn't get paid and worst of all I couldn't leave Fort Riley.

The first thirty days I was stranded were not bad, I still had money in my pocket, and I had a plane ticket I had bought with my travel pay. I was optimistic about the outcome of my dilemma, and I would show up at the personnel office every week and hang around till I was told there is nothing for me and I was told to go away. However, back in the company, my name began to reappear on the duty rosters for guard duty and K.P., more and more frequently. The word had got around to the dirty detail guys; Lennox was available for work and therefore vulnerable. But I was "Checking back in a few days."

But since our return from Germany to Fort Riley things had begun to change in the old platoon. Bud then Barry and finally Cliff all left, their time in service finished. Others left too, but the one that distressed me the most was when my boss Wash left. He opted to join the Air Force over staying in the Army with Bigbelly. My buddies Robert and Roger went off to Vietnam leaving even less guys around for Bigbelly's details or the K.P. and guard rosters.

During my second month without any resolution to my predicament I began to wonder if K.P. and guard duty were going to be my fate for the rest of the time in the Army. My name showed up on the duty roster every five days for guard

138

duty, and it showed up for K.P. at least once during the four days between guard tours. Things were getting so bad that I expected to come off of a two hour guard tour and have to hustle to the mess hall to catch up on pots and pans.

With this as incentive I began to show up more frequently at personnel, with still the same results, nothing. "Check back in a few days."

I finally realized that I had to do something to get myself out of Fort Riley. For as sure as God made O.D. Green apples I was the only one who was going to do it. So in searching around for a solution to my problem, it came to me that if I was no longer an alien I no longer needed the papers missing from my file, and therefore my troubles could be over. I immediately filed papers applying to become a U.S. citizen.

My parents had become citizens when I was still under 18, and I was supposed to have become a citizen automatically on my 18th birthday provided I didn't have papers missing from my file. I was now long past that milestone in my life, and had never paid any attention to my citizenship until entry into the Army. Now every day when I looked in my shaving mirror instead of seeing a soldier's face an alien face looked back at me.

With the paperwork for citizenship completed and sent in I sat back and waited to see which wheel of government turned the fastest, the U.S. Army or the Department of Immigration and Naturalization. I would have to "Check back in a few days," of course.

Denis & Dan

During my time in the 724th Maintenance battalion I had acquired several good buddies, Specialist 4th Class Denis and Specialist 5th Class Dan were just two of them. Actually I had more than these two friends, but it was with these two I got into the most trouble with. Both of them had the same surplus status as I had in the company, but they weren't going to Vietnam.

We inevitably ended up on a lot of dirty detail together, complements of Sergeant Bigbelly. This is not the only reason that we became friends, Dan and Denis were both from the same home town in Pennsylvania, and had been buddies long before I met them. They heard through the barracks gossip that I was born in England, and they, being in need of diversion, decided to pick on the skinny kid for amusement. Whether their treatment of me was a holdover from their school yard behavior, or something to fill up a slow day, they would provoke me mercilessly. Dan was a 6 foot 4 inch giant who weighed in at around 240 pounds. He had blond curly hair but a boyish almost angelic face, which hid a very sinister mind. He had been a telephone lineman in civilian life, and now he was one of the most frequent used supervisors for any dirty job Bigbelly could find for him. Denis was a compact 5' 10" at 180 pounds, with red hair and millions of freckles. He had the mercurial temper of a carrot top. He had once been a Golden Gloves Boxer, and he made no bones about using his fists if the need arose. He was quick witted, as well as tempered, quick with his fists, his feet, and also his tongue. He was almost bald, but not vain about it for his 20 years. Obviously neither one of them took any shit off of anyone, but they loved to dish it out.

Denis would sneak up to my bunk in the middle of the night and whisper "Fuck the Queen," in my ear till I woke up. He achieved his goal, starting fights, shoving matches and yelling contests. It wasn't the "Fuck the Queen" garbage that got my temper up, it was the being woken up in the middle of the night. I wasn't foolish enough to get seriously into it with either one of them because they could have easily mopped the floor with me. I did end up with a few fat lips and an occasional black eye, but I gave as good as I got in the fist to the face department. If I was to add it up to see who won, I would say that it was me who walked a little funny from having my butt kicked regularly.

Eventually I gave up trying to fight them, and just agreed with the derogatory remarks they made about just about anything. I hoped they would get tired of their game, as I was tired of being on the receiving end. They finally realized that their "humor" was lost on me and allowed me to join in with them with the option of picking on someone else.

Prisoner Escort

I was still hung up at Riley as summer approached and the weather grew warmer our outside activities increased and so did the dirty details. One of the details that Sergeant Bigbelly took great pleasure in assigning Dan, Denis and I to, was stockade guard. We were taken to the prisoner stockade on the main post of Fort Riley, and there our job was to provide prisoner escort duties. We were to take the Army's criminals any place they needed to go. To see their Army Lawyer, to see an Army Doctor, or to see a patch of Army leaves that needed to be raked up. To be doing bad time in the Army you had to be stupid or insane, it really wasn't worth it as it just lengthened the time you stayed IN the Army. One look at the stockade and you had to be crazy to live in the primitive conditions there. Thank goodness the guards stayed outside while the criminals stayed inside and inside they regularly kicked each other's butts.   This Army jail was a hot bed of racial unrest, and hate and discontent was the attitude of the prisoners we were to escort. The Army only provided their prisoners with the bare essentials of life inside the stockade, so prisoners got a cot, three meals a day, a place to wash in cold water, and clothing with a big white letter "P" on the back. If they destroyed or ruined these they did without. The requirement to join this exclusive club was that you had to be a criminal to get there, or insubordinate or injurious to a superior. My time being a prisoner guard proved to be a very short but very exciting time.

The post stockade was where those who have committed Army crimes of a serious enough nature are kept before and sometimes after trial. Army crimes are identical to civilian crimes, but in the case of the Army crimes the difference was that Army crimes are colored O.D. green.

Our job as a prisoner escort began with arming us with a loaded, (No round in the chamber), 12 gauge Winchester pump shotgun. It was a cannon compared to my standard issue M-14 rifle. Our job was to move prisoners where we were ordered to, and then to bring them back to the stockade again. The shotgun we carried was not the type that you went hunting with, but a shorter barreled trench version. This cannon was a very lethal weapon. At first this was one of the more nerve wracking assignments I had ever been given, but after three or four times of being assigned this detail we all got rather nonchalant about the whole affair.

At first I was intimidated by the threats from our governing NCOs. They stated that if one of your prisoners escaped while in your charge, it was you who would have to finish out the escaped prisoners sentence. From the very first time every prisoner I ever escorted asked me and every other prisoner guard, the same two questions, "If I run would you shoot me?" The first time I was asked this I stammered and stumbled around for an answer, perplexed I mumbled, "Face front and shut the fuck up." After finding out the finer points of prisoner guarding the answer to the same question was usually a nonchalant, "Take off!" The other question from a prisoner was, "I bet you wouldn't be so big if you didn't have that shotgun?" To this there was never any real response someone of my physical size could make. Dan however, on a leaf raking detail, took time out from his busy day to put down his shotgun and beat the crap out of his prisoner to finally once and for all satisfy the prisoner's curiosity.

The rules of the stockade were that when you picked up or returned a prisoner at the stockade you were both inspected by the officer of the guard. The prisoner stood on a yellow painted square on the ground outside the guard room, separated from the stockade compound and the outside world by a ten foot high chain link fence with triple coiled concertina barbed wire on top. The guard stood on an identical yellow square five feet

142

behind the prisoner, or within clubbing distance with a rifle butt.

On the day that Dan returned his beat up prisoner to the stockade, the one who had inquired as to Dan's size without his weapon. I was being inspected on my yellow square with my own prisoner. Dan's prisoner was slightly worse for the wear, his face was battered and bruised, and his clothing was a little disheveled. When the prisoner finally staggered to the correct yellow square and Dan presented himself standing ram rod straight with shotgun at port arms, the prisoner tried to tell his troubles to the inspecting officer. The officer of the guard was a Lieutenant of M.P.s who took a dim view of some of the antics of us amateur stockade guards. "He hit me," the prisoner complained through split lips. The prisoner definitely looked like he had been run over by a MACK truck. The inspecting officer, walked around the prisoner to the tune of "He hit me." Not waiting to drag a SIR out of the recalcitrant prisoner the Lieutenant turned to Dan. The officer next inspected Dan, not a mark on him, and asked, "What happened to your prisoner Specialist Dan?"

Dan replied, "He fell down and hurt his face, Sir."

"He hit me," was the plaintive cry once more, but louder this time.

"Specialist Dan, did you strike your prisoner?" inquired the officer.

"He fell down and hurt his fucking face, SIR" was Dan's reply.

The prisoner was taken away by another guard and disappeared inside the stockade to the trailing sad refrain of "He hit me! He hit me!" The word got around and Dan was never challenged about how big he was again.

I had my own misadventures performing this unsavory task of taking criminals from place to place. Prisoner guard is one duty I would never volunteer for, it is too nerve wracking, and way too dangerous. Every time I got assigned to this duty I would try and trade it off, or to get out of it some other way.

Those I tried to trade with were wise to guarding the stockade and wanted no part of it. I had a feeling that something bad was coming my way and the prisoners were bringing it.

One day in late June I was marching a prisoner from the fort stockade to the Judge Advocate Generals' office, for the prisoner to confer with his lawyer. I was walking my charge down the middle of the sidewalk, on main post, at the required five foot interval between us, and with my shotgun at port arms. It was a lovely sunny spring day, with many people out and about paying more attention to the sunshine than where they were going. A Second Lieutenant walked out of a nearby building as I and my prisoner were passing, and instead of waiting for guard and prisoner to pass, the Lieutenant proceeded to walk between us. It was the number one rule from the 20 minute prisoner guard school that you never, NEVER ever let anyone, "ANYONE!" get between you and your prisoner. Instead of anticipating the Lieutenants actions, I was taken by surprise and reacted to them. I swung my shotgun from port arms and laid the shotgun barrel across the Lieutenant's chest by a quick extension of my left arm, just as he came abreast of me. To my great surprise I hit him a little harder than I should have because the Lieutenant fell backwards on his butt onto the grass lawn. All this happened in the blink of an eye, and as the officer hit the ground I gave the command, "Prisoner halt!" I instinctively knew that I was in trouble. In the Army I never had to look for trouble, it was always right there waiting for me in the morning when I woke up. The Lieutenant jumped up and began to berate me for striking him.

"Soldier, you struck me!" my prisoner tried to turn around to see what had happened.

"Prisoner, eyes front," I ordered.

"SOLDIER, YOU STRUCK ME!" screamed the Lieutenant, becoming very red in the face.

I did my best to ignore the Lieutenant and the developing situation, but things were getting out of hand.

"Well, I've done it again," I thought to myself.

"SOLDIER, I'M TALKING TO YOU," yelled the Lieutenant pushing his face and body close to mine. But from the side this time, not between me and the prisoner.

I fended off the Lieutenant with my own body weight and with a little help from the shotgun I was wielding.

A crowd of curious officers and other ranks formed around us and as the scene continued to build, so did the size of the audience.

"Sir, you are interfering with my prisoner." This had no effect, the yelling continued.

"Prisoner, push up position, MOVE!"

This brought a loud protest from the prisoner, but after a little insistence from me and my shotgun he got down into the prone supported position.

At last help arrived in the form of the post Provost Marshall himself, followed by two M.P.s, they came out of another building from across the street and made their way through the crowd of several dozen people surrounding us. At this point I expected another rendition of "He hit me, he hit me," with the Lieutenant playing the part of the injured party. The Provost Marshall took command of the situation. In seconds the crowd was dispersed, the Lieutenant was being escorted into an office to be educated about prisoner and guard etiquette by the Provost Marshall, and I and my prisoner were on our way back to the stockade. I and my prisoner made it back to the stockade without further mishap; we made it safely because I had the two M.P.s walking right beside me every step of the way.

After inspection and depositing my prisoner back inside his cage I had my shotgun removed and my butt chewed first by the NCO in charge of the guards, then the officer of the guard, and finally by the Provost Marshall himself. Apparently the Provost Marshall had seen the whole thing from start to finish from his office window. The Lieutenant had been admonished for walking between a guard and his prisoner. I had my butt royally chewed out for using excessive force where common sense would have served better. "Excessive force and Common sense," I had a great deal of trouble distinguishing between the two while in the Army.

I was sent on my way back to my unit that same morning with a note pinned to my butt by the boot of the Provost Marshall that said, "Never, ever darken my door again." I was out of the prisoner guard business for good. At last!

Paying for My Sins

By the time I arrived back at the 724th word had gotten around my unit about my final episode as prisoner guard, and to say the least Sergeant Bigbelly was none too pleased with me. So by the next morning he had decided how to make me atone for my misdeeds. Bigbelly's punishment was having me mow the parade ground grass all by myself.

The parade ground was a brick yard of stumps and old broken masonry over grown with grass and surrounded by a sea of tall weeds. On top of that it was about a mile square. Bigbelly called my name at the next morning's formation and instructed me on my next important military task. He told me to go get a lawn mower from the post lawn mower agency and to get to work.

I had marched around this parade ground for many a happy hour, accompanied by a lot of other people. It was too easy to painfully turn an ankle on some of the half submerged debris hidden in the grass. And it was just as easy to trip on some exposed tree root, and have half a platoon pile up on your prostrated body.

I knew this parade ground for the obstacle course it was. It was the same parade ground that we were marched out to on regular occasions at 05:00 a.m. to greet the sunrise. These 05:00 a.m. excursions were the occasions of command reveilles, attended by the entire battalion. Nothing was more stirring than too see over 900 young, healthy soldiers lined up in straight lines, standing at ridged attention in total darkness.

On the first one of these nocturnal military rituals, it began to rain heavily before the bugle blew, and the only people who had ponchos with them were the officers. Here were 900 men standing at attention with 885 of them soaked to the skin, and when the call for the salute was made a loud sucking sound was heard from the ranks. The "Thhhssssssoooooooookkkkk!" sound that was uttered by the involuntary voices of 885 soldiers raising their right arms in salute which brought their 885 freezing rain soaked shirts into contact with their warm and dry lower backs.

But here I was Army mower in hand; facing a very disagreeable chore, that I was sure was going to take to way past dinner time. Now what was I going to do about it. Though I didn't show it, after two months of "Check back in a few days" my morale had begun to sink at this point, and the outlook of having no way out of having to mow the parade ground did nothing to raise my spirits. I didn't want to do it, in fact I even have second thoughts about mowing my own lawn today, and I have spent a fortune in bribing neighborhood kids or my own kids into relieving me of the responsibility.

Bigbelly's office was across the street from the parade ground and this gave me an idea. I figured that right in front of Bigbelly's office window was the logical place to start. He was going to want to keep an eye on me, and so I gave him a leg up on the job. On my way to my chosen starting point I stopped at the most out of the way water faucet I could find and there I added a squirt of water to the gas tank of the mower. As I said, I really didn't want to do this. I parked my mower directly across the street from Bigbelly's office and pulled the cord starting the motor. The engine caught right away and ran for about a minute before the water fed in to the fuel system and the engine died. I stood there for a while and scratched my head, and jerked the throttle controls around. Then I yanked on the starting rope for a good while, and as I knew it wouldn't or couldn't start I kept pulling on the rope. The engine never fired once. It took at least 15 minutes of this strenuous effort before

Bigbelly finally got curious enough to come out of his office to see why I wasn't doing my job.

Sergeant Bigbelly had one failing that sucked him right into my clutches, he was a home handyman. I am sure that he had fixed his share of recalcitrant machines in his home work shop, and that the sound of a non-working engine was a challenge to his home owner's mechanical ability. It was this training that was his undoing.

Bigbelly came over to see what my difficulty was and proceeded to take over the situation. He asked me what had I done, and after my explanation said "No wonder." and gave me his usual 'aren't you stupid' look. I gingerly stepped aside as Bigbelly got down to work and started fooling with the throttle setting and pulling on the starting rope himself.

He fooled around and around with it, and I stood invisibly by and let him. Bigbelly had me get cups of gasoline to wash parts or prime the carburetor or spark plug. He took it apart, he put it back together. This went on for three hours until lunch time came around. "Gotta eat!" he told me as he left to wash his hands for lunch.

After lunch and a period of time I assumed was spent on a nap Bigbelly reappeared. Together we spent more time working on the "MY" mower's problem, and Bigbelly was now becoming very instructive. He would show me all the intricate workings of this or that feature of the mower, and I would pretend to be genuinely interested. I would repeatedly pull on the starter rope on command and get more tools or gas when needed. However, with all this effort on both our parts we never got the mower working. Around mid-afternoon Bigbelly finally gave up and sent me away to get another mower. On the way back to the post mower shop, and out of the sight of Sergeant Bigbelly, I stopped and emptied the contents of the gas tank on the ground. I spent the rest of the afternoon in hiding, and the next day it was back on K.P., I never did mow the parade ground.

Scrounger in Training

Now it was late summer and by this time I had been waiting for my missing papers for over three months, and my morale had really started to slip further into the black pit. This was partly from the fact that I was hung up in transit and could do nothing about it, but mostly because I couldn't get paid. The continuous dirty details, guard duty and K.P. didn't help any either. I was so down trodden by all the dirty details that at times that I began to refer to the 724th Maintenance Battalion as the Punishment Battalion, (Fort Riley was the home to a battalion of punishment troops. These were guys who had committed deeds not serious enough for a court martial, or as a second chance to clean up your act as a soldier. The troops in this detachment were given extra basic training, and work details so they would work their way back to being good soldiers. If not straightened out they went to the stockade), or as the First Offense Fusiliers.

So I figured out that I needed some diversion to take my mind off of my troubles. I really had enough to do each day, I just figured I should find myself a form of occupational therapy that would keep my mind occupied, and keep Sergeant Bigbelly thinking that I was doing a dirty detail at the same time.

A day or two of looking around and asking questions provided the answer. The decrepit building that was home to the repair shop that the Electronic Maintenance detachment worked out of needed new work benches. I suggested this fact and immediately got the job of building new work benches almost in the same breath. But first I had to overcome a small handy cap, complete lack of tools and material.

I began my new task by asking a few simple questions.

"Sergeant Bigbelly, do we have any wood to build work benches with?" I asked after accepting this new job.

"No," came the monotone reply.

"Do we have any tools?" I next asked.

"No," again with the negatives.

"Do we have any nails?"

"No Lennox, you better pull your head out of your ass and get on with this job instead of asking all these dumb assed questions." This exhibition of eloquence and leadership settled matters for the time being.

Well, I saw immediately what my first task was to be, I had to go out and steal a hammer.

As to the material needs of this project I would attend to them after hours. I would have to steal the wood I needed. So while I walked my guard duty post at night, rifle slung on my shoulder, and hammer in my belt, I would size up the structures I was guarding. There were lots of structures to choose from some of them were collapsed or collapsing on their own, long forgotten and long without purpose. Other structures were just shelves that held items that could easily be stacked on the ground instead of on valuable wood I could make use of. In the middle of the night I would tear something apart, and then one by one I would throw the pieces of dismantled structure over a fence as far out of sight of Army prying eyes as possible. In the morning, off of guard and back on duty, I would show up to my former guard location with an Army truck, belonging to some unit, I would steal that too, and pick up the pieces.

This would be the start of a remarkable new Army carrier for me, that of a scrounger, and it would serve me well later on when I eventually went to Vietnam. After two or three weeks and after collecting piles and piles of lumber I began trading some of it for other things I needed, such as nails and other tools, for "MY" project.

Word had gotten around about who in Camp Funston had all the lumber, and behold a lot of people now came to trade. This was a new world for Sergeant Bigbelly; he was now what seemed to him to be very popular. He never had so much attention from his peers before, and he now thought of himself as a very cleaver trading Czar. I kept quiet while he beat his gums with his cronies, hoping that he wasn't giving away the farm, and then I would go and make the deal I wanted on my own.

Soon Bigbelly supplied me with my own truck to make pickups and deliveries, and he gave me my very own driver, me. The truck was a brand new 2 1/2 ton, (deuce and a half), with only 39 miles on it. The result of only 39 miles was that the truck suffered from a dead battery, and to go stealing I either had to get a jump start or tow the truck with another stolen truck. The reason the truck had a dead battery was it had never been driven anywhere. It had spent its military carrier in the motor pool sitting in one spot and never being driven. Yes good old Sergeant Bigbelly had given me the queen of the motor pool. What else could I have expected? The only activity it had ever had was being started every morning so that the oil and battery could be checked, a year or more of doing nothing but that had used up what power was ever stored in the battery. Anyway, it was my very own O.D. Green truck. Not knowing whether the Army had forgiven me my past driving sins I was not going to inform them that I even had any sins to be checked up on. Either that or Bigbelly had not yet heard of any sins associated with me.

Bigbelly would occasionally send me on scrounging missions for things other than lumber. In these cases if there was anything I couldn't barter for I would wait until it was dark and no one was around and then I would liberate it.

One day I was sent to get one aluminum framed window, with unbroken glass, to replace the broken one in our barrack's front door. I thought it over for a few minutes and then considered the huge block of identical barracks buildings I lived called Camp Funston. Each barrack had an identical front door to ours and an identical window in that front door. I took my clip board, one or two screw drivers and a hammer and walked east four rows of identical barracks buildings. This put me into another battalion's living area of the Camp Funston. There I entered one of the barracks as if I owned the place. In all Army barracks, during the day, one or two men were left in each

151

barracks usually to clean the place up, and if not that at least to loaf around giving place the appearance of habitation. This was supposed to cut down on theft, provided those left were not tempted to try their hand at criminal activity. There was a barracks orderly there when I walked in, so I told him I was there from Post Field Maintenance to fix the broken window in the door. The soldier not knowing me from the man in the moon, told me to go ahead and fix it. I set down my tools and went to work, jerking the window up and down in its frame for a few minutes while the barracks orderly paid me little attention. I then announced that I was taking the window back to the shop to fix it, and with the approval of the orderly I popped the window out of its frame and took it with me. My job there was done, Problem solved! Somewhere in the Army there is probably still a requisition waiting to be filled for a replacement window for that barracks.

Bigbelly Gets Cold Feet

Life under Bigbelly's thumb had become amusing. In the mornings after being sent out to scrounge by Sergeant Bigbelly he would always be greedily waiting to see what I had procured, and he would examine everything and ask me where I had got it. God he was dense! I would try to help him to understand the ways of the world by dropping hints, and at the same time admitting nothing.

"Where did you get this?" I would respond "Get what, Sergeant?"

"This stuff!" Trying not to admit to any wrong doing I would try, "I don't know what you're talking about."

This never seemed to make a dent in him.

"Oh! This stuff, I got it from the supply depot."

Once I tried the invisibility ploy, but even that failed to crease his thick skull. "I don't see any fucking stuff, Sergeant."

"You must be mistaken this is our stuff," wasn't very helpful either.

I stopped short of "Listen you dumb son-of-a-bitch..." Knowing instinctively that you got more with honey than vinegar, and I was also very well aware that Bigbelly could easily have me thrown into the post stockade for theft.

Life was not a bed of roses now that I was more or less doing the bidding of fat Sergeant Bigbelly. Bigbelly liked to shove me into some sort of shitty detail at least once a week just so I knew who was in charge. On the other hand, if I couldn't find some way to weasel out of the dirty detail I could usually managed to screw it up so bad that I was dismissed or sent to do something less complicated.

Everything went well for my scrounging operations until one of Bigbelly's Sergeant Cronies showed up demanding to know how come Bigbelly was in possession of a power saw that belonged to him. I managed to stay out of sight while fat old Bigbelly sweated bullets trying to convince his peer that he had no idea of how this power tool had turned up in Bigbelly's shop. Also, that the rash of equipment disappearances had affected him too, and he was sure the C.I.D. and the M.P.s would catch who was responsible.

At this point I figured that maybe Sergeant Bigbelly just wasn't to be trusted. I had actually figured this out on my first meeting with Sergeant Bigbelly, but I had not openly stated it till this time. Indeed this turned out to be the case for after this episode of the power saw Bigbelly had the nerve to tell me to take some of the swiped stuff back.

Once all the wood, tools and other accessories needed were amassed I began to assemble work benches during my non-K.P., non-guard duty, and when not doing my regular Army job. Having no real carpentry experience outside of wood shop in school, I was at a real loss on how to go about building work benches. I did manage to hammer and nail up something serviceable, but it was generally too heavy, too shaky, or too amateurish to pass for a usable work bench. In any case my efforts pleased Bigbelly, you wanted work benches, and so I gave them to him in wobbly quantities.

153

One day after I had set upright one of my first attempts at wood butchering, I decided that it looked so comfortable that I climbed on top and lay down full length on my back. (The prone unsupported - as it was called in the military). I was about to close my eyes when who should walk in while I am doing this? Yes, you guessed it, Sergeant Bigbelly.

"What do you think you're doing Lennox?" He asked in his best supervisory voice.

"Sergeant Bigbelly, I just put this bench together and it kind of wobbles, (they all wobbled), and I am just distributing my weight over the top of it so that the joints will seal better and take the wobble out." I explained with a straight face.

"Well, you learn something new every day," said Bigbelly as he walked off.

The three others in the shop thankfully waited till Bigbelly had closed the door behind himself before they burst out laughing.

Month Three

It was now entering the third month of my inability to leave Fort Riley, and I had finally run out of money, I was a little short of patience too. The Army wouldn't do my laundry so at night I would wash my clothes in the barracks shower and hang them in the latrine to dry overnight. Buddies in the barracks kept me in cigarettes, but I more or less quit smoking so as not to wear out my welcome.

My morale was getting to the "I don't give a shit" stage. I no longer took pride in my appearance, sure I shinned my boots and brass because I still had shoe polish and Brasso, but that's about all I would so. My uniforms looked like I slept in them. The only creases in my fatigue uniforms were from where I balled them up and threw them in my locker.

The most ironic thing that was going on at this time was one of the guard posts that I was assigned to on several different occasions was the division finance building. Finance is where

154

they kept ALL the Army payroll money. I was walking around an uninhabited building, in the middle of the night, and I had a loaded rifle in my possession. I imagined that one very lonely evening I should go into the building, remove what was rightfully mine, and being a nice guy, leave a note:

"Sorry it had to be this way; I took what you owed me. I live in barracks T-2011."

But not having any money was soon to be one of my minor problems. One morning in August, while standing in the mandatory morning formation minding my own business, and nonchalantly ignoring Bigbelly, I received the usual dressing down from Sergeant Bigbelly in front of the rest of the platoon. The usual consisted of a few caustic remarks about the state of my uniform, the fact that I needed a haircut, and my general unmilitary bearing. All at once Bigbelly's eyes became real big and his jaw dropped open, and at the same time I felt a very heavy hand fall on my shoulder from behind. Before I could turn around to see who or what was holding me I heard "come with me boy!" uttered in my ear.

When I turned around to see who had me in his grasp, my heart dropped into my boots, it was the battalion's Sergeant Major. The same old fear first felt way back in Basic Training reared up inside me and grabbed me by the throat. "Oh God! Not again," was all I could manage to think.

This large and beefy hand moved down from my shoulder and circling my upper arm, and I was lead out of the formation in this manner by our large and beefy Sergeant Major. His grip seemed to lift me off of the ground I was standing on. The other soldiers around me dispersed from our path, as if by magic to make way for the Sergeant Major and his catch. I knew that I was definitely alone in my plight, and there wasn't a hell of a lot I could do to resist being propelled down the company street towards the Sergeant Major's office. At his office I was propelled up the steps, through the door, down the corridor, and into his office all without my feet seeming to touch the floor. The Sergeant Major put me down in front of his desk, took off his cap, and sat down facing me. I did my best imitation of someone not about to piss his pants. I dreaded what was too come.

The Sergeant Major had been walking behind our formation and had noticed me right off, the state of my uniform, the need of a haircut, and my general unmilitary bearing. He now told me all about myself while I stared at his wall full of framed colored scenes of military carnage that were on display behind his head. "Obviously battles the Sergeant Major had been engaged in," I thought, though I didn't think him old enough to have fought alongside Andrew Jackson. He proceeded to tell me what a slovenly, dirty, disgraceful, crappy, disgusting, and fucked up looking soldier I was. He then told me that he intended to have me thrown into the stockade for messing up his nice and tidy formation, for that is where I indeed belonged. Having been to the stockade as a guard looking in, I had no desire to be one of those on the guarded inside looking out. My stomach flipped over with mention of the stockade, and my bladder immediately gave me a couple of nudges that suggested that this may be it, we may be bailing out. I pulled in what reserves of self-control I had left and nudged back, telling my insides to hold together just a little longer. By the time he was finished reading me off he was slightly red in the face, and seemed like he had rather enjoyed himself. I had been read off by Bigbelly many times, but without the same imaginative choice of words or the threatening, bullying effect the Sergeant Major had. This guy was obviously a practiced master at instilling fear and respect. My knees were the consistency of jelly, and I definitely needed a few minutes in the latrine.

I have never liked Sergeant Majors because of the bullying and intimidating manners they seemed to use, not to mention their towering physical size. This Sergeant Major was no exception. I was definitely uncomfortable; I was quaking in my boots, but after the first few moments of being yelled at it dawned on me why I was in there in the first place. I was a victim of the Army, but right at the moment I was more a victim

156

of the Sergeant Major. This was definitely unjust, I should be the one doing the yelling, but the Sergeant Major was certainly not the one to be yelled at. Some of his harangue passed by unheard as I concentrated on my counter attack, and before he was finished ripping my military bearing apart I was ready.

"Yeah, but....." I started.

"Asshole, don't interrupt," he said.

"Sergeant Major I....." I tried again.

"Sloppy looking, poor excuse for a soldier," he continued.

"I can ex......,"

"I told you to shut the fuck up!" he went on.

I got the message and waited till he got it all out. I stood there at attention, wondering if it was going to be words or fists and words. I didn't have to wait long to find out. He looked at me with disgust and rose to his feet placing his paws on the top of his desk and leaned into my face. "Now just what the hell do you have to say for yourself, young soldier? Standing in my formation looking like a Goddamned tramp and needing a haircut, you Goddamned Hippy?"

"I haven't been paid in over four months," I blurted out, "I couldn't pay for a haircut if I wanted one." His sneer, changed instantaneously to a look of surprise and he asked me to explain further. I went into the entire sad episode of the missing papers from my file, and the "Check back in a few days" treatment. As the story unfolded he seemed to take more interest, and as soon as I had finished he sprang from behind his desk and grabbed his cap. The same beefy hand that had propelled me into his office now propelled me out. Down the company street we went at a terrific pace, and off we strode to the division finance office.

Once there the Sergeant Major administered a sizzling tirade to the poor pay clerk in charge of my company, and I watched in awe as this poor clerk wilted before the Sergeant Major. I was sent scurrying to my barracks to retrieve my pay records, and within 30 minutes I had 105 dollars in my hand and was on my way to the nearest barber shop.

Later that afternoon the Sergeant Major showed up at the Electronic Maintenance shop, and had a little chat with good old Sergeant Bigbelly, behind closed doors. From what I was told by ease droppers, the Sergeant Major `tore Bigbelly a new asshole' for not taking better care of his troops. I remember it made me feel kind of warm all over when I heard about it.

The Sergeant Major never did solve the problem of my missing papers, or help in any way I knew of to get me out of Fort Riley. He just showed me he knew how to make the system work when it had to, or when he wanted it to.

Chapter 8

Barracks Humor

My morale had improved by being paid, but my foul mood was not cured by a long shot. Boy, I never met a payday, even a partial payday, I didn't like, and what a shot in the arm cold hard cash is to a soldier. Being paid was not the complete solution to my dilemma. The Chicken Shit continued and Bigbelly continued to be Bigbelly. My availability for his list of dirty jobs went on. But barracks life at Fort Riley had its lighter moments, and soldiers have been known to make their own fun.

The Dance of the Flaming Feet

All the married men in the company that had their family living on or near Fort Riley generally lived off of the post with their families. These family men didn't eat their meals in the mess hall, but would bring their own lunch in a brown paper bag. During lunch time they would spent this period someplace warm and cozy. They would nap in the barracks during lunch time. A `brown bagger,' as we called them, would choose someone's bed and lay down on top of the blankets. They were always considerate however, and instead of staining the blankets with black shoe polish from their boots so they would

159

hang their booted feet over the end bed rail. Coming into the barracks during lunch time I would find two rows of boot soles facing each other, sticking out into the aisle between the two rows of beds.

Coming back to the barracks after my lunch meal I found that I had no bed of my own to lie down on. So for some fun I walked down the center aisle of the barracks with a can of cigarette lighter fluid. I squirted a little on to the sole of each boot as I passed, and when I reached the end of the row I ran back down the row with a lit cigarette lighter touching off each boot as I went. By the time I got to the door of the barracks the room was full of dancing men trying to stomp out the flames on their feet, while yelling obscenities at me.

Perverse Humor

Living close together in a barracks produced some very strange situations, just about anything would be done for a laugh. I contributed my fair share to this form of irreverent entertainment.

One evening I had taken my usual shower and was standing naked in the latrine brushing my teeth when a rather perverse idea came to me. I marched out naked into the first floor of the barracks, where the usual pinochle marathon was under way. With my penis in my hand I yelled "Hey!" for attention. My mouth was covered with toothpaste froth from cleaning my teeth, and my overall appearance definitely turned some heads. A naked man was not unusual when you lived one on top of the other as we did. Once I had received the attention I thought my performance deserved I announced to one and all, "I was cleaning it and the dammed thing went off by accident." This brought shouts of indignation and groans from others as I marched back into the latrine.

Mandatory Formation

On a Saturday night late in June five members of the motor maintenance platoon who were AWOL, got themselves thrown in the local civilian jail for raiding a junk yard. The C.O. had to leave the comforts of his comfy home very early on Sunday morning to bail these criminals out of the local jail, and boy was he pissed. The C.O. was so angry that upon delivering the junk yard raiders back to the company that he decided he would have everybody in the company up that Sunday morning. The Captain decided to have a company roll call right then and there, to find out who else was absent without leave. Also, just to show all of us just who was boss? Because the C.O. had to be there he made sure that all of the Platoon Sergeants and other NCOs were there, and at 8 a.m. on a Sunday morning we were all called out of our barracks and ordered to form up in platoons on the company street. With the sound of the whistle I rolled out of bed and appeared as demanded in uniform and stood half-heartedly in the ranks waiting for my name to be called so I could go back to bed. My buddy Dan made it too, but not in such grand shape as I. He had been out on the town that Saturday night before and by the look of him Dan had had, as usual, a great time.

I turned around in my position in the front row to see who was there with me. Amongst the bleary, sour, and blank faces I couldn't miss Dan's. I smiled when I spotted his tall lanky frame that Sunday morning, he was standing unsteadily in the ranks with the rest of us, but he was completely in the nude. Later he told me that no matter how hard he had tried that morning he just couldn't find his clothes. Sergeant Bigbelly saw Dan about the same time I did, but Bigbelly didn't roll with the punches at times like these. Bigbelly's face went white when he saw Dan, and he came running over to where he stood, hands fluttering at his sides. Rushing down the ranks of dejected soldiers and up to Dan, standing in the third row, he gasped, "WHAT ARE YOU DOING?" Dan looked back at him through half opened and very blood shot eyes. "WHAT ARE YOU DOING?" gasped Bigbelly again, Dan blinked twice, very slowly, and his tongue slid out of his mouth and wet his lips. Dan reached out with one hand and offered something to Bigbelly with a croaked "Here Sarge." It was Dan's balled up dog tags and chain. Bigbelly looked at the proffered articles and his jaw worked up and down like he was trying to say something but no sound came out. "Here Sarge," said Dan again as Bigbelly stood before him staring at his offering and his nakedness.

"I quit!" said Dan.

The dog tags jangled as they rotated at the end of their chain that Dan now offered Bigbelly the chain suspended from one of Dan's fingers.

Snickers from the ranks.

"You can't quit," replied Bigbelly. His tone changing from shock to something more rational, but still excited.

"Hey Sarge, if I have to put up with this bull shit, this jobs not worth having," said Dan thrusting his articles back at Bigbelly.

More snickers from the ranks.

"You can't quit!" Bigbelly said almost pleading.

"Come on Sarge, this is Sunday my day off," explained Dan in a complaining voice.

It took Bigbelly some time to come up with the right answer. To help matters along someone in the ranks offered, "Hey Sarge, how about we all take our clothes off, then we'll be in uniform with Dan."

Dan kept things going himself by saying, "where the fucks the latrine, God I got to pee," and he turned left and right looking for a place to relieve himself.

Near panic was in Bigbelly's voice as he uttered the solution to this dilemma, " D-Dan-uh-Dan, you just go back in the barracks and lie down, I'll just count you as here," said Bigbelly.

162

"Hey Sarge, I'll go and lay down too," came a voice from the last rank.

"Stand fast there, this only applies to Dan."

Grumbles of preferential treatment came from the troops.

It was lucky for Bigbelly that the C.O. never got a glimpse of what was going on at our end of the formation.

Dan slept all Sunday and on Monday morning Dan was his same old self once again.

The Kid from Cape Cod

August arrived in Kansas, hot and muggy, complete with tornados. I was still doing the "Check back in a few days" routine, and with the same negative results.

With August the Kansas State Fair came to Fort Riley and pitched its tents just down the road from Camp Funston. Why? I don't know, but that is where the fair set up. Several members of my platoon went to the fair on that Saturday, and one of them was a young man from Cape Cod, Massachusetts. This kid of 19 lived on my floor of the barracks, directly across the aisle from me. He had the bottom bunk right next to my buddy Dan. The kid went to the fair with the idea of having a good time, and in the process of doing so won an enormous Teddy Bear. Then the kid made his first mistake, and brought the thing back to the barracks.

I had not gone to the fair, but had spent my usual Saturday, hanging around in the barracks, broke as usual. I spent my time writing letters, reading or just laying around waiting for Monday to happen. The kid from Cape Cod showed up with his prize and a `Big Winners' smile on his face. This broke the monotony for me. After fooling around with the bear for a while the kid propped it up on his bed and went off somewhere. I spent the rest of the afternoon watching the bear, while the bear watched me from the kid's bunk. The kid came back and sat on his bed next to the bear and read for the rest of the afternoon, the bear was pink and cuddly, and nobody paid much attention to it except to ask, "Where did the fucking bear come from?" That is until Dan came back, bouncing into the barracks, and like everyone else he immediately spied the bear. Dan walked up to the Teddy Bear, grabbed it off of the kid's bed, and hauled it and himself up on to his top bunk and there he began humping the bear.

The kid was shocked. I was shocked. The rest of those in the barracks were shocked. We all stood by amazed and amused but unwilling to rescue the bear from its bed spring squeaking fate. Dan paid no attention to those around him, but went at the bear with a will. We all knew Dan to be a real crazy animal, but this was a bit much.

When Dan finished with the bear it didn't look so good. It had a bent and broken arm and leg hanging from its body by threads, its head was half off, and it just didn't look cuddly anymore. Dan pitched it down to the kid, who really wasn't thrilled, so the bear lay around the barracks for the rest of the weekend while people came and went asking, "Where did the fucking bear come from?" Unloved and unwanted the bear hung around the barracks with us until Monday morning and someone put it into an empty wall locker next to Dan's bunk. The whole thing seemed forgotten. That is until the next Saturday when the C.O. came around with Sergeant Bigbelly in tow on this unusual Saturday morning inspection. This was unusual because we never saw the C.O. come around on inspections. He sent his other underlings to check on us. We never saw the C.O. do this. No matter, everything was going well with the inspection. The Army liked to make sure that we didn't have stolen weapons, women, or wine stashed in the barracks. Oh, and they were also interested that the place was kept reasonably clean. The C.O. entered the barracks and went about checking out the men and the barracks. After doing my side of the aisle he started down Dan's side, but for some reason known but to him, he started opening the empty wall lockers as he came to them. A couple of low comments were made to Bigbelly who dutifully noted them in his note book, and the inspection continued. Another unlocked locker was checked, three more and I realized that the C.O. and Bigbelly were going to find the bear. With three to go the C.O. didn't miss any he was drawn like a magnate to these empty wall lockers. A whispered "Oh Shit!" went through the barracks as some of others all at once realized what we had forgotten. The C.O. did not let our suspense go unrewarded. He opened that next empty locker, and there at the bottom, staring crookedly up, was the kids abused pink Teddy Bear. As if this sight greeted him every Saturday the C.O. turned calmly to Sergeant Bigbelly and asked, "All right, where did the bear come from?" (We of the lower ranks all knew that officers didn't use obscenities. Officers get special schooling before they become officers on how not to say naughty words. They leave swearing to the people who know how. That's one of the reasons that I never became an officer, I wouldn't give up cussing for anyone). Bigbelly looked at the bear, Looked at the C.O., at the bear again, at the C.O. once more, and it was the first time I had ever seen him with nothing to say. The bear was pulled from its hiding place and held up at arm's length by Bigbelly, "Who owns this bear?" he asked.

Silence greeted his inquiry, "Who owns this bear?" he asked louder this time.

From across the aisle I could see the reddening face of the kid from Cape Cod, and I thought to myself, "Lookout he's gonna blow." And blow he did! The kid from Massachusetts could stand it no more. I guess the pathetic state of the bear, and the traumatic memory of its ordeal was too much. He broke down in tears, "ITSMINE, IWONITATTHEFAIR, AND-(gasp)-AND DAN RAPED IT!" came rushing out. All those present were stunned into complete silence by this revelation, the only sound in the barracks was of the kid gently sobbing and the C.O.'s eyes clicking as they rolling heaven ward. I could tell by the look on the C.O.'s face that this was the first time he had encountered a raped Teddy Bear in a locker. Bigbelly turned to the C.O. and translated what the kid had said, "He said

165

that Dan raped it Sir. Ah, that, ah that's a court martial offence sir," offered Bigbelly. It took a few seconds for the wheels to turn smoothly once again in the C.O.'s upstairs, "Thank-thank you Sergeant. Which-huh-which one is Dan?" Bigbelly obligingly pointed him out with an outstretched pudgy arm and finger, and the C.O. turned to Dan who was standing at attention, trying to act like he knew nothing about what was going on. "Well?" asked Bigbelly, sensing instinctively that this was his moment, as he directed his enormous belly menacingly in Dan's direction. "The C.O. and I are waiting for an explanation Dan." Dan stared at the ceiling rafters as if the answer to the question was printed somewhere up there. The kid sobbed on. Finally I couldn't take it any longer. From my vantage point across the barracks, the tableau before me was comical. From where I stood it reminded me of the painting of "The Last Supper," everyone frozen in place, all beckoning toward the central figure. This time however, it was Dan in the center. A giant staring at the ceiling, a fat man holding a damaged pink Teddy Bear staring menacingly at the giant, an officer in somewhat shocked disbelief, and a kid sobbing his heart out on an adjacent bed, surrounded by fatigue clad troops craning their necks to see what was going on. I did the only thing I could do, I burst out laughing.

The tension broken immediately as the rest of those in the barracks joined in, all but the kid, who was having difficulty gaining control of himself, and big fat Sergeant Bigbelly who was completely at a loss because of our hysterics. The C.O. regained control of himself first, wiping his eyes with a white handkerchief that he had pulled from his rear pocket, and turning to Bigbelly smiling said, "Sergeant Bigbelly, if this is an Army bear get it to sick bay and have the M.P.s deal with him, pointing to Dan. If it's not an Army bear get it out of my company area." With that the C.O. turned on his heal and left, the inspection was over. Sergeant Bigbelly trotted dutifully behind the Captain as he followed him out the barracks door holding the pink Teddy Bear out like it was distasteful for him. Smiles followed both of the out the door.

The kid and Bigbelly never forgot or forgave Dan, and the rest of us made sure Dan never forgot. From that day onward Dan was referred to as "BF," which stood for `Bear Fucker.'

The Shakedowns

Inspections in the Army are to be expected. They inspect for cleanliness, readiness, and combat efficiency, and they inspect just because it is Saturday and that is what is done on a Saturday. As I have said inspections were frequent in the Army and usually not really strenuous to prepare for. But there was one form of inspection that did not sit well with any of us who were the inspected, and that was a shakedown inspection. This inspection was an out and out search.

The Army was continuously loosing things, tanks, guns, ammunition, nurses and the like, and for some silly reason those above us, those in charge of us seriously believed that all these missing items would be hidden in our barracks. I guess the reasoning from above was that, "Hey! Where else do these soldiers have to go to hide stolen stuff?" So a Shakedown Inspection could be called at any time, day or night. So it was, at any moment someone would announce it's a shakedown and that was it. You went immediately to your bed, stood beside it and waited. Yep the entire world of the entire company A of the 724th maintenance battalion waited in anticipation of the next command of "The Shakedown is Over."

An officer or NCO, usually a stranger to us, but to us in the barracks most officers and NCOs were strange. This inspector would come and have us stand at attention, by our bunks, usually under pain of death for moving or talking. The inspector would then crawl over and through everything. Everything involved all your personnel possessions, every square inch of the barracks, and depending on how big the article they were looking for was, our bodies and what we were

167

wearing was inspected too. We would stand around for hours while the search was carried out, and if we were allowed to talk to one another we would pass the time forming theories on where the stolen or missing article might be.

"How can they be missing a gas mask, who in his right mind would take a gas mask?" I asked one Sunday morning.

"Someone needing a Halloween costume," was the only answer we could come up with.

The usual barracks banter started shortly after the first five minutes of the inspection. About the time that boredom usually set in.

"Hey Denis, I have an idea," it would start.

"Lennox if you have an idea you stole it, you ain't had an idea of your own ever." said Denis.

"Hey, I'll bet I know were all this missing stuff goes."

"OK bright boy, where?"

"Those off post brown baggers take it home in the evenings in their empty brown bags. Just so they can show their wives what they do in the Army." That was a theory I offered.

"Lennox you're a real fucking mental case," retorted Denis.

"Do you think your everyday common soldier, even a brown bagger wants anything to do with this Army shit when the day is done? I think it's the officers and NCOs that take the stuff."

This comment usually raised some objections from the inspector.

"Yeah, I think they takes it and sells it on the black market outside of town, just so's they can support their habit."

I bit, "What habit is that Denis?"

"Why their addictions to shoe polish, brass polish and Chicken Shit of course," and we would laugh uncontrollably at our own wit.

No contraband was ever uncovered in our barracks or any other barracks in company A, but the shakedowns still continued.

Denis and I saw a need to brighten up these boring mindless sessions of watching a stranger prowl through our living area. Denis was the owner of a portable tape cassette player/recorder, and so we made this the vehicle for our deliverance. We spent one weekend creating a tape of homemade sound effects, and just in time for there was another shakedown inspection called that next Wednesday.

When we were marched into our barracks and told to stand by our bunks, Denis popped the tape into the tape player, turned it on and left it on his bunk.

Our inspector was greeted with a few lively minutes of bed springs squeaking rhythmically, accompanied by loud falsetto shrieks and guttural utterances like "Ooooh baby! Yes baby, Yes!" This was followed by our latrine glee club singing a selection of the dirtiest songs. In addition we had a Hollywood style fist fight, done in the grand style of old time radio broadcasts complete with splintering furniture. In all there were many different and weird skits included on the tape, all that Denis and I could imagine to fill a slow weekend in Fort Riley Kansas. The real crowning achievement of the entire tape was a recording of someone with a simulated 55 gallon bladder urinating for what seemed forever. This individual piece of audio magic lasted for more than three minutes, and was punctuated by a very appropriate sigh of relief at the end.

The effect of the tape was immediate on the troops in the barracks. It definitely brightened up their otherwise boring day. On the many shakedown inspections that we endured together there were many requests to replay all or certain portions of the tape. The real benefit of the tape was that it really disrupted our inspector's concentration, and on several occasions the inspection actually stopped while the inspector paid more attention to the sounds emanating from the tape recorder than his job.

Fort Riley is situated between the burgs of Junction City and Manhattan, Kansas. Junction City is a soldier's, town sure it had residential areas and stores, but hock shops, bars, and a bus depot were the main points of interest. While on the other end of the spectrum and the other side of Fort Riley, Manhattan sported a state university complete with young college women, sororities, women's dormitories, and women. However, no matter what the female population of Junction City or Manhattan was, unless she was a hooker, no girls wanted anything to do with any of us. There was one exception to this female dilemma surrounding us, a place where women did want us even though we were in the Army. It was a real den of iniquity.

Denis and I along with four others from the barracks found out about this place one Saturday night completely by accident. Joe had a car and with the offer of gas money a free drink or two Joe had been persuaded into chauffeuring us around. After checking out all the local G.I. bars for female companions, we found our way to the local VFW post. No sooner had we walked in the door than four dames who strongly resembled my grandmother came over said "Hi, here for a good time?" and then drug, more like firmly lead, four slightly drunk soldiers onto the dance floor. There the four were forced to perform various interpretations of dances they knew nothing about, to music that for them could have been from a foreign land. Denis and I had been missed during the selection process by being last in the door, so we enjoyed ourselves by yelling encouragement to our comrades from the side lines. The four old birds didn't let our pals go for three dances, talking their ears off as they struggled by, doing their best to coach their new partners into the intricacies of the fox trot, two step, or whatever. Released from the clutches of these grand dames, Denis and I were swept aside by our pal's eagerness to get out of the door. "Don't you guys even want to stop for a beer," I yelled after them, and followed them out in hot pursuit as the old dears spied fresh meat and headed in my direction.

More Bad Decisions

Denis and I found ourselves scheduled for guard duty on a Saturday which thrilled us both no end. Guard duty on a Saturday consisted of 4 hours of tedium on guard and a break of 8 hours of tedium before the next 4 hour tedious tour. Since Denis and I ended up on the same guard shift we had to decide what to do for our 8 hours off. After short deliberation and checking the contents of our pockets the problem was solved by going down town for a drink.

This was strictly taboo as far as the Army was concerned. You were required to be available at all times while assigned to guard. So instead of telling the Sergeant of the guard we were going down town for a drink, we told him we were going to the library. Just like telling Mom or Dad when we were kids.

We had till 2 a.m. to show up on guard so we went to our favorite bar the Oasis and had a few drinks. Then because we had a whole 8 hours to kill we had a few more. One thing led to another and we ended up missing the last bus back to camp. It was after midnight and we were feeling no pain what so ever, and since it was a balmy summers evening we both had the brilliant idea to hoof it on our own. The distance was at least 10 miles.

Things went well for the first two or three miles, but Denis knew of a short cut and I went along because I didn't even know where I was. We climbed over a six foot high stone wall and headed off in what I assumed was the right direction across a rutted bare piece of ground.

We were in an open field when all at once we realized we were not alone, from behind us came the pitter patter of many heavy large feet, and the snorting of heavy breathing. As we stood still to listen the pitter patter became a steady pounding, and without a word to each other we both took off as fast as our legs would carry us. Denis had led us into the middle of the post buffalo coral, and they were coming after us.

"You dumb fucker," I yelled, "Look what you've gotten us into."

"No shit, Sherlock," was the gasped reply.

Several dark, large hairy beasts the size of small busses circled us at a gallop, snorting all the while, and from time to time one or two dodged in our direction as we sprinted and dodged drunkenly into the darkness. (Let me explain something, young men have the ability to sprint and to dodge drunkenly, while older men can trip, stumble and fall drunkenly). There had to be an opposite wall to the one we had originally climbed over and after what seemed hours there it was. Denis and I both flew up and over this six foot wall in two bounds, planting a foot in the middle and grabbing the top and over we went. Those bastards were huge, and for their size could move with amazing speed and agility. It was either that or I was too drunk to move very fast and they were actually very slow. Whatever the case I never went back to find out which was which?

We were lucky. On the other side of the fence was the main road through Fort Riley and a post taxi happened by as soon as we had caught our breath. No matter the cost it was worth it to get back to the barracks in one piece.

We made it in time to strip off our civilian clothes, throw on our uniforms, and stagger outside for the ride to our guard posts. I was really, in the vernacular of the soldier, "shit faced" by the time I arrived at the motor pool which was my guard post, I picked up my rifle from the relieved guard and strolled off on the first round of my post.

At 2 a.m. in Fort Riley Kansas there is absolutely nothing to do, and no one to bother you unless it is the officer in charge of the guard, himself bored and with nothing to do but check on his troops. There is one exception to this last statement, and that is Coyotes. They were around all night, howling and prowling, and all you had for protection was an M-14 rifle.

You had the rifle but no M-14 bullets. With this in mind I strolled on into the night, determined not to get caught shit faced on guard or as a meal for a prowling Coyote.

The motor pool of our company was no small affair. It was a barbed wire fenced block of eight acres of land. This barbed wire fenced ground was the parking area for trucks, trailers, Jeeps, and other assorted O.D. Green painted vehicles. Not to mention several one story buildings full of spare parts, tires, government paper work and the other accumulated wealth of the United States of America. The surprising thing about the motor pool was that it had one entrance in and out, but there was no door or other barricade to close the gate. Vehicles could come and go as they pleased if I was walking guard on the other side of the area.

It was around this block of fenced material I alone marched, guarding it with my empty gun, against all enemies foreign and domestic. To help my disposition it started to rain. It started sometime during my guard shift, I remember it rained because I was wet and it woke me up, I had fallen asleep while perched on a paint locker. Sleeping sitting up was a new one for me. So much for my determination! I put on my poncho, the one that foamed when it got wet, it foamed because one of its previous owners had washed it with laundry soap and I guess the poncho liked to relive the experience, and I headed, foaming along, alone on my appointed rounds.

I spent part of the night leaning up against a set of duel tires belonging to an Army 5 ton truck, asleep. Asleep standing up was a new one for me too. Usually I stayed awake on guard and walked my post in the prescribed military manner, but tonight I didn't seem to care. I did care though when I woke up and saw by the moon light, the light colored Jeep tire marks in the damp sand of the motor pool. They weren't there when I had begun my tour, and I couldn't miss them as they went right by where my leaning form had been. The fog inside my head meant that I still wasn't quite sober and I spent some time following the tire tracks around the motor pool wondering how they got there, and mumbling "Oh Shit! I'm in big trouble," to myself.

Finally the light bulb went off over my head. I said to myself, "Either that's the driver of the guard and everything's OK, or those are from the Officer of the Guard and I am in deep, deep, really deep shit." Not a very pleasant choice, so I followed the tire marks some more to see if they happened to end up at the rear end of a Jeep. Fortunately for me they did not, the tracks disappeared out of the one and only motor pool gate, leaving me to ponder my fate.

By the time 6:00 a.m. rolled around I was sobering up but with my head pounding, I was once again promising God and everybody that if I lived through this situation I would never, NEVER, ever do it again. (Get drunk while on duty, not get drunk). At 6:00 a.m. precisely I was relieved in many ways. The tire tracks, I found out, had been made by the kid from Cape Cod Massachusetts, who was the Driver of the Guard, coming to see if I needed any coffee. I did, but in my condition I would have probably spilled it all over myself.

It was with great relief that I handed over my empty rifle and climbed into the Jeep. The kid from Cape Cod and I went to relieve Denis at his guard post the supply depot. On arrival we honked the horn and yelled, no Denis appeared. I opened the gate to the depot and an empty metal five gallon can took off across the depot grounds clattering loudly as it went. The can was attached to a spring loaded reel off cable and the can noisily banged into the cable drum when it was finally wound itself up. Still no Denis appeared. We eventually found him asleep in a tent. Denis and I both went back to the barracks and died for the remainder of the weekend.

Bad Decisions Downtown

Chasing women in Kansas was futile, especially if you didn't have a car. No self-respecting American women from Kansas would be caught dead going on a date via city bus, so as

174

a soldier in a soldiers' town the prospects for romance were extremely limited.

On several occasions Dan, Denis and I had had the conversation of where was the best place to find women. Church was offered as a sure thing, but I explained my endeavors to that end in Georgia. Dan maintained that the local college campus was the best place to find eligible women. We questioned him about what ratio of success this method brought, but Dan was very noncommittal, he just smirked knowingly. Denis stayed with the Oasis bar, but I put forth the theorem that the best place to find women was in any ladies room.

The only time I ever got lucky in Kansas was on a week day in downtown Junction City. I had been given the day off. The reason I had been given the day off was I gave it to myself. There were certain things in the Army that you just couldn't wait for the Army do for you. The Army was responsible to provide three square meals a day and a place to sleep. Many of the other social amenities you had to get for yourself. I figured that I deserved a day off so I took it, and after making up some excuse to be out of the company area I left. To get out of Fort Riley was easy, busses to town came by camp Funston on a regular schedule and so it was a matter of getting on one. No M.P.s at the bus stop or entrance to the fort ever stopped a bus to check passes.

On this day I took a bus into Junction City to see what the place looked like in day light. I spent the 10 minutes needed to look at the sights of Junction City, and then decided to have a drink. It was either that or head on back to camp, and I wasn't giving that thought much consideration.

In Kansas if you wanted a drink you first went to a state owned liquor store and bought a state owned bottle of booze. Then you took your bottle to a private club, where you would be served drinks out of your own bottle for a price. This seemed the wrong way round to me. This system sort of reminded me of the saying, "Carrying Coal to Newcastle," bringing booze to a bar. This was indeed what is called a

"Fool's Errand." It didn't make much sense to me but it must have made sense to someone.

It was just past 11 when I got to the Oasis Bar, and had my drink. The place was deserted except for a young, blond, mini skirted beauty she was playing pool by herself at the other end of the bar. She was a soldier's dream. She was female, a lone female, a good looking lone female with long shapely legs, and she didn't seem to mind being undressed by my eyes from across the room. From my vantage point on a bar stool this wasn't the Oasis bar I was in. I was in heaven, especially when she bent over to make certain shots.

Eventually she got bored playing by herself and came over and challenged me to a game of pool. She said her name was Victoria, and I liked the way that name rolled off of the tongue. I rolled her name around on my tongue a time or two it tasted great. I had never seen her before, but that was not news. There never were not many females around where soldiers hung out, but this one would have definitely been remember able. This was the middle of the day, the bar was still deserted except for the two of us, and so I didn't feel that privileged being asked to play pool. What was a good looking blond doing in a bar, all alone, in the middle of the day? This was not a question that I needed to ask. Besides, mother had never given me any warnings about women who own their own two piece pool cues. I accepted and we played a game or two, and I bought a drink or two. Well one thing led to another, and by 7 o'clock she invited me home for dinner. I didn't have to be coaxed and agreed right away. We went home to her place, a modest second floor apartment in an unassuming neighborhood of Junction City. She told me that she didn't really invite guys to come home with her all the time. I didn't dispute the point, but we never did get around to dinner. We started in necking and pawing each other as we both maneuvered for the best position while sprawled on her couch. Neither of us were drunk and so when the subject of going to bed together came up I was wide awake and ready for action. She, acting demure agreed reluctantly at first, but warmed to the idea with some further persuasion on my part. Not the monetary kind!

So we strolled from the sofa to the bedroom, and now I no longer had to undress her with my eyes, I got to use my hands. I was as nervous as a kid on a first date with the prom queen. I managed to get her down to her underwear without being too eager and ripping any buttons off. I then turned and neatly folded my uniform in a bundle on the floor, placing my boots on top, just like I had been taught since my first day in the Army. And we jumped into the rack together, and I thought I had it made. A day off, a beautiful blond, so who needs a loaf of bread.

We had just gotten under the covers and we were slowly exploring each other's bodies when she uttered those little words a soldier longs to hear, "Beat Me," she said.

"Say what?" I asked.

"Beat me," she cooed again.

"No sweat!" I replied.

As a well-trained soldier you didn't have to tell me twice, and so the hits just kept on coming. (I didn't beat her with my fists'; I slapped her, maybe a little too hard). For some reason what I was dishing out was not what she had in mind, and she deciding that she didn't like it. She started screaming.

It would have been OK if she had just been screaming nothing intelligible, but she started screaming for the police. The apartment house neighbors hearing the commotion took things seriously and called the police. As soon as I heard the sirens I also took things seriously and decided to get out of there.

Naked, uniform under the left arm boots in the right hand, and off the second story balcony like a paratrooper I went. The fall wasn't bad, but I had never done this before under these circumstances. I knocked the wind out of myself with the sudden stop at the bottom. Some fool had built a child's sand box beneath the balcony and I landed in it. With the sound of the police sirens getting closer acting as my incentive, I picked myself up and got the hell out of there. My former date was by now howling from the balcony and the combined sound of her plus the sirens drove me onward into the night. Two fences and two blocks later I was safe, safe except for all the noise my heart was making trying to tear itself out of my chest.

Enough excitement for one night, I settled for a nice quiet bus ride back to Camp Funston and the male solitude of the barracks. Arriving back at the barracks I tried the "Hey guys, you'll never guess what happened to me," statement, but my story was greeted with "Lennox you fucking liar," and other derisive greetings. I gave up trying to convince the others of the good time I almost had, but when I quietly confided in Denis he replied "Lennox you fucking liar" so I let things lie. I never did go back to the Oasis, and from that day I swore off of pool playing blondes.

Escaping Bigbelly's Clutches

Sergeant Bigbelly was on the constant prowl for people committing Army sins. Such sins would be: Avoiding assigned work, Not being where he expected to find you, sleeping on the job, not coming when your name was called, and the biggest sin of all not doing what he had instructed you to do. Sergeant Bigbelly made sure that the post snack bar, library, E.M. Club and the barracks were constantly checked by either himself or one of his cronney NCOs to see if any of his worker bees were not on the job. All of us knew the standard places that were checked, and all of us knew that some creativity was needed in avoiding slave labor.

I and my fellow worker bees knew of were very creative in avoiding sweat labor, dirty details, or any form of work. Bigbelly was too short and too heavy to look or climb into the back of a supposedly empty bed of a deuce and half truck, so a lot of guys found a spot that was safe. The back of an empty truck maybe safe from Bigbelly, but not his more agile cronnies. Sleeping out in the woods was not smart, as there were too many bugs, but some smart guys tried that but not more than once. It was a constant contest of who could avoid Bigbelly's work details, and do so in a place that you could not be found hiding,

Because of my relationship with Bigbelly I was too big a target to go missing from work, and I had to find my own ways of avoiding his clutches.

Every Saturday morning the battalion had to perform "Motor Stables" otherwise known as truck maintenance in the motor pool. For this chore I was assigned my very own U.S. Army two and a half ton truck. Not the kind with a canvas covered wagon type back. My truck had all metal tall box mounted instead of the regular canvas covered bed. My truck was to be used as a maintenance shop on the move.

The idea of Motor Stables was to maintain your vehicle. Great! My vehicle had a couple of draw backs attached to it. It was brand new with less than 50 miles on the odometer, which seemed OK, but the truck had been sitting in the motor pool for months and never went anywhere. For this reason the trucks battery was dead. Also, the lousy paint on the truck and body was flaking or chipping off daily. This made Saturday morning a real chore.

First thing Saturday morning I had to get someone with another truck to tow mine to compression start the engine. Once the truck was running and warmed up I had to keep it that way for at least 10 minutes. With the truck parked back in its usual spot I could then turn it off, and check the oil and drain the air brake tanks.

All the while I and the rest of the truck maintenance force would be checked on by good old sergeant Bigbelly, and shown where we were doing things incorrectly. I had had my worldly education by Sergeant Bigbelly, once I started performing chores for him, I had found out the one truth of the world. Which was: there were three ways of doing anything. There was of course the right way, and then there was the wrong way. However there was a third way of doing things and that was the

179

Army way. I just never could get the hang of doing things the Army way, the way Bignelly wanted things done.

I could never spot paint the outside of my vehicle before more paint to chipped off somewhere, and of course Bigbelly would point out my mistake to me. The battery terminals of the dead battery had to have a light coat of grease on them and of course my coating was too thick. This went on and on.

Since my trucks' metal body offered some interesting possibilities I once climbed on to and tried the dangerous act of sleeping up there. I escaped detection for a couple of hours but I was discovered after one of my booted feet showed itself over the edge of the truck body. I escaped punishment for dereliction of duty as I convinced the NCO who discovered me that I was spot painting. Thanks to my little pot of paint and my brush,

Since the top was no good to hide I tried the bottom. I discovered to my delight that when I was on the ground working on the underside of my truck Bigbelly and the rest of the NCOs usually left me alone. So one Saturday after the painting and the checking I crawled under my truck with a bunch of old commo wire. Under the truck I wrapped arms around the trucks drive shaft and then wrapped my arms together with the commo wire, and I found that I could hang by my arms, recline and take a comfortably and nap. Bigbelly on his rounds would see my boots sticking out from under the truck, but he was too round to bend over and see what I was up to down there. If he wanted me he would kick my boot, which would arouse me and I would fake being hard at work. The best part of this scheme is that Bigbelly never caught on.

Mike's Chevy Chase

September came and my situation had not changed one iota from the previous three months, and I began to dread the last year and four months I had yet to go in the Army. Oh I was still "Checking Back," less frequently now as I was becoming somewhat suspicious of the Army's ability to find lost papers. I was sure that I was going to spend all my time remaining in the Army right there at Fort Riley pulling guard and KP.

I entered the barracks one evening after chow, and I was greeted by Mike being picked on by a member of another platoon. Mike was a nice guy, a really nice guy. We had done K.P. together many times, as well as guard duty and countless dirty details. Mike was the kind of guy who would take your shift if you were really in need of relief. He was a great pal! I would say that feeling was pretty near unanimous for Mike from the whole company. So when I found him in the midst of a heated argument with some giant from another platoon, I was to say the least, surprised. Mike was medium in size, about 5' 9" and of average build, but the guy who was all over him was twice his size and had a reputation as a loud mouthed bully. This bully was the one used by the loan sharks to collect debts on paydays. They called him "Hector the Collector." Mike was giving as good as he got his hands on his hips, and his head back. I was very surprised to see Mike sticking up for himself, not because I thought him chicken, but because he never had a harsh word for anyone. I was even more surprised when he accepted the bully's invitation to "step outside."

Mike was a quiet kid of 19 from a small town in northern Oklahoma, with a boyish handsome face and a quick smile. He got on well with everyone. Did his job, and wasn't one to complain about anything. But I guess we all have our "OFF" days, as this bully was cussed him up and down.

By the time the argument had got to the physical challenge phase several more troops had come in the door to witness the argument loudly going on in the first floor of the barracks. As Mike walked past us, his face flushed in anger some of us tried to talk Mike out of doing anything foolish. As the bully marched past behind Mike I put in my two cents worth. I knew of this guy as did many others, he was a mean S.O.B., just plain mean, and he liked to throw his weight around.

"Come on Hector leave the kid alone," I said as the bully went by.

"Fuck off Lennox, cause I'm gonna get you next, you hear me" was his response sticking his finger under my nose as he went by.

"I'll be here Hector, but I want to warn you, you're not gonna get no cherry." Hey! I'd been beat up by guys much bigger than him.

Several of us followed them outside hoping we would not be witnessing Mike being murdered or simply being stomped into the asphalt. Mike and the bully squared off in the middle of the street, but before any punches began to fly Mike dropped his guard. Hector scowled at him, sticking his chin out he said, "Come on, Chicken?" But instead of rising to the insult Mike just stood there smiling, and then Mike said to Hector, "wait here, I'll be right back." To which the bully replied "OK, but don't try running away." The bully was left standing alone in the middle of the street while Mike disappeared around the side of the barracks. I nodded to Denis who had just shown up as Mike left, "lets stick around this ought to be good." "Yeah!" said Denis, "Hector has come to a battle of wits, unarmed." A few moments later we were all interrupted from our mutterings by the squeal of car tires and the loud roar of suped-up engine. A turquois and white '57 Chevy entered the company street from the south and accelerated rapidly toward the bully and others standing in the road. Seeing the danger the troops scattered, vaulting over the white washed telephone poles bordering the company street. This left Hector all by himself staring in disbelief at the front end of an on rushing Chevy. His own brain finally woke him to the danger and he took off ahead of the car and barely ran out of the path of this high revving machine, and dived over the white washed telephone poles himself. It was in this instant that I recognized that it was Mike at the wheel of the car as it whizzed by me. The car sped on down the street, and braked sharply as it turned the corner into the parking lot in the middle of the barracks row. The bully looking somewhat taken aback, but not really realizing what was going on peered tentatively over the telephone poles looking left and right to see if it was safe. Seeing no cars he again stepped back into the street to wait for Mike. Again came the screech of tires, the revving engine, and a cloud of dust from the parking lot. No "Hi-Ho-Silver was heard! Once again Mike's car shot out and bore down on his adversary. The bully was once again caught standing in the middle of the road, but this time he was looking the wrong way. He barely had time to turn and face the oncoming car, and then dive over the telephone pole to safety again. Mike braked hard to make the south exit. "Hey!" was the awakened bully's exclamation, "that was that little shit Mike." "Brilliant," I thought.

Mike made two more passes at his foe before he slowed the car enough to see if he had had any effect. The car came to a crawl past the now sizable crowd of interested on lookers and race enthusiasts. Mike rolled down his driver's window, and asked, "Well, had enough? I got plenty of gas." This began a verbal volley between Mike in his car and the bully standing on the safe side of the white telephone poles.

"Why don't you fight me like a man?" growled the big guy as I and some of the other spectators giggled.

"I am fighting you like a man; I think we are evenly matched."

"Come on Mike, get out of the car, I want to give you a kiss goodnight with my left hand." Said Hector, shaking his big beefy fist at Mike.

"Stand back on the road, and I'll give you a kiss with the front bumper of this Chevy."

"What are you chicken?"

"That's original," said Denis from the side lines.

"No just sensible." Said Mike.

Well the duel finally ended when Mike agreed to leave the bully alone, and the bully agreed to leave Mike alone. All this agreement was brokered at the insistence of Denis, Dan, myself and several others from the barracks.

The bully was around from time to time, but his bulling stock wasn't as high around the company as before. But Mike was now known respectfully thereafter as either The Main Street Mauler, or as Chevy Chase.

Attitude Adjustment

There were times while I was in the Army when I could recognize the look on someone's face to mean pure desperation. This was usually the result of many different elements playing their parts to screw up a soldier's mental equilibrium. There were many causes for this condition. Being far from home was one, having to deal with a ridged code of conduct, lack of personal freedom, no privacy, lack of feminine company and just being in the Army in general. A total exasperation of having to deal with a system that was as respondent to your emotional and mental needs as a pillow. The soldiers I saw in this state had the same wild eyed look of desperation found on parents who have to deal with teenage children. The only thing to do with an individual when this look was encountered was to take the person out and get him hammered, or the poor bugger was going to go off the deep end.

Denis and I were hanging around the barracks one Friday afternoon. We were hanging around the barracks on a Friday because it was at the end of the month, just before payday, popularly known to us in the Army as "The day the eagle shit," and we were as always collectively almost broke. But in truth we were generally hanging around the barracks because there isn't much else to do when you make all of 105 dollars per month. When Dan came in and started to tell us about his day, we could tell by the way he was acting that he was upset by the day's events. Dan at this time was less than 90 days away from getting out of the Army.

Denis and I knowing our responsibility got together and compared notes:

1. We had all of 11 dollars between us.

2. Dan needed a mental diversion.

3. Neither of us had a pass to get off of the post.

4. The military police were everywhere

5. Dan was not a cheap drunk.

6. Finding Dan a woman was definitely out of the question.

So what do we do, agreed, we go A.W.O.L. and get Dan drunk.

We lived in a part of Fort Riley named Camp Funston, or Tons of Fun as we called it. Funston was one mile from the back gate of Fort Riley, and the back gate was where the majority of camp followers lived. The bars, liquor stores, pawn shops, plus other assorted pond scum could be found there. So a solution to our quest was not out of reach.

We had no passes to get off of post because kind old Sergeant Bigbelly had pulled ours for some screw up or another we had been involved in. To us, no pass was no big deal; you just waited until it was dark, and made sure that you didn't get caught. Having no passes we took Dan and quietly sneaked out over the back fence and walked through the fields to the back gate and the nearest liquor store. There we bought the cheapest bottle of whiskey we could find. That was within our 11 dollar budget. We next sneaked back onto the fort.

Instead of asking for trouble and going back to the barracks with our bottle we all stopped about half way back to the barracks, and we sat under a highway viaduct over the local rail road tracks, and we listening to the cars pass overhead. This was an excellent place to hide from prying M.P.s, as it offered the best cover and concealment. We would pass the bottle back and forth listening to the cars thump thumping over the expansion joints overhead. It did take a while for Denis and I to fulfill our goal, but Dan was very cooperative consuming most of what was offered. The scene was reminiscent of skid road/Bowery movie, three reclining figures hanging around under a highway overpass passing a bottle back and forth. The cars thud thudding overhead.

It was quite late by the time Dan's mind was finally off of his problems. All Denis and I had to do now was get a large drunk back to the barracks without an encounter with the M.P.s.

We started out walking back to the barracks with Dan staggering along behind. At the end of the viaduct some fool had left a car parked. "Let's not walk when we can drive," announced Dan, and unfortunately for Denis and I the car had been left unlocked. Dan crawled in behind the wheel and thank God for us there were no keys in it. "No Goddamn keys," he announced and not satisfied with that Dan decided to hot wire the ignition and crawled under the dashboard to show us how it was done. Denis and I standing outside did a double take when we saw him, something that big, disappear under the dashboard of the car, and we dove in after him and drug him out by his ankles. After some argument and protesting on Dan's part we had him back on two feet and we continued on down the road.

At the end of the road there was a fire alarm telephone box attached to a telephone pole, (a little red box with an emergency telephone inside and a red light on top). As we coaxed Dan onward toward the barracks, the red light suddenly disintegrated with one blow from a mighty right hand.

Once again Denis and I got Dan on the move, but at the next intersection was a stop sign attached to a steel fence post. Dan spotted the sign and no amount of persuasion could have deterred him from having a wrestling match with it. Denis and I looked furtively around for some sign of the police or interest from some passerby, but luckily the street remained deserted. No amount of grunting, panting and other animal sounds coming from Dan attracted any attention. Denis and I untangled Dan from the sign and fence post after he had twisted the sign three times around and had it bent down and parallel to the ground. With some persuasion we got him to leave the sign and once more all of us headed for home.

Denis and I led Dan into the final stretch, the barracks area, and we hoped that our luck would hold because Dan didn't seem to have tired any from his destructive efforts so far. As we

186

passed each row of barracks I counted each mess hall, (The last building in each row of barracks was a mess hall), and calculated how much further it was until we would be safe. Our barracks was five rows along from the mangled stop sign. Denis and I felt that there were no more temptations in our path that would attract Dan's attention, and so we continued on down the street walking slightly ahead of the staggering Dan.

We walked down the street passing the mess halls as we went. All of a sudden there was one God awful racket going on inside the mess hall we were next too. Denis and I turned to make sure of our charge, but there was no Dan to be seen. We both scrambled to the back door of the nearest mess hall, while the din from inside grew in magnitude. The back doors were standing wide open, and lights were coming on in some of the surrounding barracks we dashed through the doors.

Mess hall tables and chairs were strewn haphazardly about the dining room, but there was a clear path where Dan had plowed down the center of the room. The crashing that had been going on stopped as suddenly as it had started, as Denis and I raced to the opposite end of the building. There we found a glistening wreck, bordering on major disaster quality, of the steel divided serving trays and their tipped over rack. On the way out the door we passed a tipped G.I. stove. Denis caught sight of Dan first and running after him yelled for me to follow. There was now activity outside some of the surrounding barracks as the curious came out to see what was going on. Dan was staggering toward our barracks down the middle of the main street, a five gallon steel thermos dangled from one hand and an electric clock by its cord from the other.

Denis and I ran up to him and knocked his trophies out of his hands, yelling at him, "come on, come on." We drug Dan by the arms just as fast as his condition would allow, and we safely made it the remaining blocks to our own company area. Up our company street we ran and into our nice quite, dark barracks. The lights in the bottom floor came alive as Dan couldn't find his bed and needed illumination. Bodies stirred out of their sleep began to descend on the three of us with angry questions. Denis and I tried to calm the angry pals and buddies there but something caught my immediate attention. A large 4X8 foot sheet of plywood shot past us. This was a fixture in the barracks, a board to block the winter blast that blew through the door anytime it was opened. The plywood was mounted on its edge on skids to make movement easy. You only needed this thing in the winter months. Dan was propelling the board down the center isle of the barracks at a dead run. Dan was blitzed out of his mind so his aim wasn't that great and the board slammed loudly into the wall that was the corner of an alcove to the back door of the barracks. Dan still running flashed past the board, on down the alcove's alley and through the back door, and landing in the grass and dirt outside. "Shit!' was all I said as Denis. "Double shit! Was his reply. We went and picked up the befuddled drunken Dan, and helped him climb up and into his upper bunk. Once in bed he gave no more trouble, and Denis and I removed his boots and tucked him in for the night.

Our job at last completed, and no M.P.s pounding on our front door. Denis and I said good night and we and the whole barracks went to bed for the night.

It hadn't been the wildest night of my life, but it certainly had been one of the most destructive. Dan after sleeping it off and was his usual self from then on until he finally left us. Thank God I never had to perform this exorcism for Denis or anyone else, as I didn't really want to find out how a Golden Gloves Boxer like Denis would react getting rid of his frustrations.

Helping George

Things were continuing to change in the barracks, oh it was still full of characters, but there were less and less of them. Robert and Roger went off to Vietnam. Like me they had volunteered, tiring of Bigbelly and the constant Chicken Shit details. The platoon I had joined last year was now down to less than 20 people. One of these barracks denizens, George, was the barracks only known alcoholic, a lifer with 19 years and six months in the Army, and hoping to make it to retirement. Unfortunately for George, he was as much on the way down as he was on the way out. He had been a top soldier but the booze had gotten to him and he was now a Specialist 4th class.

Life with George was always interesting. One evening coming in late from guard I discovered George drunk and asleep on his bed moaning and crying out "Oowww! OWWW Ouch!" in his sleep. He had fallen asleep while smoking and his cigarette had burned down between his fingers, and was burning him.

George would spend the sober part of his day doing whatever jobs were handed out to him or writing letters to congressmen trying to make his retirement status fire proof, and the drunken part of the day he spent avoiding Bigbelly. This was necessary as his drunken part of the day definitely put his possibility of reaching a pension in jeopardy. All of us in the barracks knew George and found him, drunk or sober; to be one of the smartest, most articulate people we had ever met. We would go out of our way to shield George from Sergeant Bigbelly, who had a particular axe to grind for a Sergeant in disgrace.

We got George out of his burning bed one night, and then disposed of his burning mattress and then found him a replacement in the middle of the night so no one would know. We covered for him when he missed formation, and we kept quiet about his drunkenness on duty. George had more than one soldier pulling for him to make it to retirement. He Commanding office, the Captain was looking out for him and we knew through a clerk in the company office that the Captain squelched a number of Bigbelly's attempts to torpedo George's retirement.

Bigbelly Strikes Again

Sitting around the barracks on a weekend was a way of life for the low paid and carless soldiers that we were. Going downtown offered no joy as the prices there were too high, and we had seen it all before.

Denis, Dan and I were pretty much alone in the barracks on a Saturday afternoon, I was writing letters and Denis and Dan were shinning their boots. One or two other guys were there but we were not conversing with them. Denis had bought a six pack of beer at the P.X. and had brought it back to the barracks. This was a strict no no. We were not supposed to have alcoholic beverages in the barracks period. We had not forgotten this rule, we just ignored it. A couple of beers were all anyone of the three of us could afford, so we shared the six pack while the day passed.

Out of nowhere appeared Sergeant Bigbelly and the C.O. They just walked into the barracks without announcement. Saturday afternoon was after normal working hours, and having the C.O. and our Platoon Sergeant walk in on us was a surprise. They were both in uniform, and seemed to be checking who or what was going on in the barracks. When they walked in the three of us were immediately in full view, and so was the beer.

The C.O. acted like the beer wasn't there and came over to the three of us and made small talk about why we were in the barracks on a beautiful Kansas Saturday afternoon. We all three stood out of respect for our Captain, but Bigbelly decided to make his brownie points and picked up one of the cans of beer and held it up so the C.O. could see it. Bigbelly then started in, telling us of the illegal act of having beer in the barracks, and that it was a definite crime and punishable with an Article-15 and a reduction in rank. Bigbelly seemed rather pleased with himself as he stood beside the C.O. and contemptuously held out the can of beer.

Our Captain listened along with the rest of us as Bigbelly droned on, and the C.O. waited till Bigbelly had hit a flat spot and stopped talking.

"So men, what have you got to say for yourselves?" The Captain asked.

Denis, ever the smart one piped up, "Sir," he started.

"The governor of Kansas has stated that he does not consider 3.2% beer to be an alcoholic beverage." This came out of Denis' mouth.

Where the hell did that come from? Was the only question in my mind at that time? How does this guy know this stuff?

"Is that right," was the reply from our Captain as he turned to Sergeant Bigbelly.

"If that is good enough for the governor, then that is good enough for me," said the C.O. and he walked toward the door of the barracks.

Sergeant Bigbelly taken completely by surprise quickly put down the can of beer and trotted off after the Captain.

"How do you know this stuff?" I finally got to ask Denis.

"Oh! I heard it on the local radio the other day. Us barracks lawyers have got to stay well informed you know," was his reply.

Month Number 5

October finally showed up with its cold winds and falling leaves. Our daily vigil outside the mess hall waiting to be fed produced some shivering and chills, so anything was accepted to get you in and out of the cold. I arrived at the mess hall early for diner one day and as usual had to spend my time standing in line with the other troops waiting for the mess hall to be opened. As usual this was the time to socialize with soldiers from other platoons, tell jokes, cut up or air your bitches about the Army or whatever.

The head cook "Harry" finally opened the door and explained the reason for the delay. The person in charge of head count was late. In the Army a Sergeant was responsible to count each person coming into the mess hall to be fed. Along with counting the heads of each person, the Sergeant was also responsible to make sure that each person signed his name before being fed. I guess the Army didn't trust any of us.

The head counter for this day had been one of the married Sergeants "Brown Bagger" who lived off of the post and it being dinner time he had naturally gone home to dinner. Since I was first in line at the door Harry took one look at me and said, "Lennox, you're gonna be head count today." "Harry," I protested, I had been on K P so often that we were on a first name basis, "I ain't no Sergeant." "Big fucking deal," responded Harry, "you're the fucking head counter."

So I became the head counter, I sat there hungry, dejected, counting the heads coming through the door. The head count was a source of amusement to us below the rank of Sergeant. To us the Army was divided up between "Juicers," those who drank, and "Heads," those who used drugs. So to amuse my buddies coming through the door I would point to some known "Head" and click my head count clicker and announce, "there's a head," point to another and repeat the process. Some called it "Horse Play" I say it was all to the entertainment and amusement of myself and those in the chow line.

Well after 50 minutes of this my stomach was doing flip flops, demanding that I put something in it. I had been counting "Heads" and non "Heads" till no more were available. It had been several minutes since anyone had come through the door, and to me it looked like dinner was over. The aroma from the steam tables was distracting, my body demanded something, and even Kookwell's Wild C-Ration Surprise would have been welcome.

Finally I could stand it no longer, and I asked Harry, "Hey Harry when do I get to eat?"

"How many names you got on the chow roster Lennox?" Asked Harry.

"I got 90 names Harry, 90 names,"

192

"No good Lennox you don't eat till you get 125 names," I was dismayed.

"125 names, Harry chow's over in 10 minutes," I replied.

"I don't care, Lennox you don't get to eat till I get 125 names," I was exasperated.

I thought a minute and asked, "Harry do you care whose names you get?"

"No Lennox, I just want 125 names."

So several Disney characters ate, movie stars, prominent political figures, sports figures, cowboys and Indians, and several other persons of notoriety ate also. Everyone I could think of came to dinner. I got to eat and went away satisfied, maybe not happy but satisfied.

A few days later I passed Harry in the company street, and he yelled over, "Hey Lennox, they found your chow roster. Watch your ass." Enough said, I immediately looked up Denis and we went into a huddle, Denis was my barrack lawyer.

Sure enough "They" were after me, right after lunch word was passed that the First Sergeant wanted to see me. Next to having a chat with the Sergeant Major, the prospect of an interview with the First Sergeant thrilled me no end. Lord how that made my day.

The First Sergeant was big, he was mean, he was ugly, and he was on my case. First Sergeants were just like Sergeant Majors, but were still learning the ropes on how to properly bite troops in the ass. I was shown into his office and not pulling any punches the "First Shirt" started right in on me. Court-Martial was mentioned along with prison, fraud, forgery, federal crime, Article 15 with a fine, and he threatened to have me on K.P. for the rest of my natural life. He had the signature roster with all the "fun" names rolled up in his hand, and he would shake his fist and the roster in my face as he yelled at me.

"I want you to explain this to me?" he demanded. I thought it was pretty obvious. I asked, "Is this an official investigation?" This stopped the raging bull dead in his tracks, and I could see by his expression that it also confused him somewhat, maybe I was wrong and he wasn't out to shove the chow roster in one of my body orifices.

"No, this is not official," he replied. Good I thought, now anything I say at this time will be between him and me.

"Lennox did you think this was funny?" he asked. "Well yes Top, I thought it was funny. Don't you think it's funny?" I asked in return.

This caused the First Sergeant to stop and think. I could tell he was thinking by the puzzled and then pained expression that came over his face. I do remember detecting the faint smell of burning rubber, which may or may not be significant.

"Yes I thought it was funny," came his reply, but the puzzled expression remained. "I want you to tell me why you did this?"

"Well Top," I began, "I am a PFC (Bigbelly had had me busted back for P.F.C. for talking back), and Harry the head cook is a Spec. 5, Harry told me I had to have 125 names on the roster in order to eat. I asked Harry if he cared whose names were on the roster, he said no so that's why I put those names down."

Once I had got it out I felt enormously better, the situation until now had been very one sided. I had all the facts on my side, and the First Sergeant had the U.S. Army on his.

The conversation now continued in a more moderate tone of voice, the first shirt having spent his venom was now trying to digest what he had bitten off. I for once in my life kept my mouth shut and let him mull it over for a minute or two, (again the burning rubber smell).

The First Sergeant sent me on my way with a warning, and with the statement, "I'm gonna check this out with Harry and I will be talking to you further."

Nothing ever came of it, but I was always passed over for head count whenever an emergency head count had to be assigned. For some unknown reason I also spent extra time on K.P. for the next two weeks.

194

Leaving Fort Riley Behind

I actually did get out of Fort Riley, but it took the influence of a very important person. I had been stranded there since May, and it was now the end of October five months later. It had been a very trying experience. What finally got me out was not the inevitable arrival of the replacement of the missing papers from my file. It was the arrival of the Inspector General, and his power over the system to see that truth and justice prevailed where before only nastiness and inequity had existed.

The Inspector General was not just a man he was retribution all in one pair of pants. His arrival on post struck fear into the hearts of officers and NCOs alike. A good report from the Inspector General (I.G.) would go a long way in perpetuating a career, while a bad report could end one. So with the announcement of the impending I.G. inspection, mayhem broke out in the ranks as officers and NCOs brought pressure on us to have everything well prepared. This was the one inspection that the officers and NCOs would jump through their assholes to pass.

Under the heading of "Justice for All" the I.G. would listen to all gripes, bitches and complaints, and then take any appropriate action. He was the one true justice we lower ranks could bring a grievance to without fear of reprisal from above after he had left the area.

I took the opportunity of the inspection to request an audience with the I.G., and used the time to explain to him the situation I found myself in. I found that the I.G. was indeed sympathetic to my plight. A volunteer for Vietnam, an alien with papers filed to become a red, white and blue U.S. citizen, (no matter what the motive), and I had been waiting patiently without complaining too loudly for five months. The I.G. promised to look into the situation. I should check back in a few days.

Within a week my orders were re-issued allowing me to leave Fort Riley without the required but missing good guy papers in my personnel file. One week, I was relieved, I was astounded by this one man's power, and I was amazed. The I.G. was indeed a lower ranks savior, he could indeed move O.D. Green mountains, and uplift the down trodden. I was Free!

The Jungle Telegraph of we lower rank G.I.s began to click as soon as my orders were announced as being forwarded from the Pentagon. The guys in the company who worked at headquarters knew me and knew what I had been going through were luckily on my side. The word came down to me from friends at Brigade Headquarters that my orders would be cancelled when they hit Battalion Headquarters because I was the only one in the battalion that had the military occupation that I held. I didn't know there was a military occupation designation for 'Pot and Pan Scrubber Par-excellence.' This was a much needed skill by the powers that be. The jungle Telegraph troops at Brigade Headquarters picked up my orders at that level and a buddy handed the orders to me. They were handed to me by a smiling buddy with theis admonishment, Now you can say FIGMO, McNasty," (FIGMO was an acronym that stood for Fuck It, I Got My Orders, F.I.G.M.O). The next sentence from my buddy was a warning. "Now get the Fuck out of here," were his exact words, and that is exactly what I did. Within 15 minutes I was packed, signed out of the company and was on my way to the local airport. This way the orders never got to battalion and I just disappeared before they knew I was gone.

At last I was out of Fort Riley, in signing out of the company I was handed my personel file, so I finally had ALL my records in my possession, and I had my orders to Vietnam. I only lacked one thing, a ride to the airport. Mike agreed to drive me. With that arranged I said my farewells to Denis and the others and off I went.

What I really said good-bye to was K.P., guard duty, dirty details, but not before I blew Bigbelly a kiss.

As I drove out of Camp Funston for the last time I felt that this event required some statement to symbolize my frustration and relief from frustration. I ask Mike to stop at the back gate, and I got out of the car to make my peace. I spent a few minutes thinking about what to say or do. At first I wanted to whizz on the back gate, but there were too many cars around and the M.P.s in the guard shack would not have taken this act in the spirit of which it was performed. So I picked up a rock from the ground and threw it at Fort Riley. With that out of my system I went home.

Chapter 9

A Detour on the Way to War

Going home was easier said than done. Once my joyous exit from Fort Riley was accomplished I made my way to the Manhattan City Airport and cow pasture. Mike dropped me at the one room terminal, and I thanked him and said my good bye to a good buddy. The most interesting thing about the Manhattan Kansas City airport was the ticket seller. It was a one man show. The guy who sold me my ticket was the same guy who guided the three hour late propeller driven plane to the terminal building by waving two red flashlights. He was also the guy who loaded and unloaded the baggage, and the same guy who sent the three and a half hour late plane on its way. This guy must have had stock in the airline, may have been in a salaried position, or he had a terrible union.

Once in Kansas City I had to find a new flight to Los Angeles four hours later than I had planned. I stood, having missed my connection, at the airline ticket counter in the best uniform I owned, a rumple set of summer khakis. (All my Class "A" green uniforms had been turned in in May on my assignment to duty in Vietnam). I was no longer the proud, squared away soldier I had been on my way to Fort Riley. I had enough of K.P. Guard Duty, Bigbelly and missing papers in my file, I really didn't care. The only reason I was wearing a uniform at all is because I had a military standby discount ticket and the airlines won't let you use it unless you're in uniform. This regulation I found highly ridiculous. They don't require student standby passengers to fly in school clothes do they?

I was leaning against the ticket counter trying to make arrangements for my flight to Los Angeles when up to the counter came another soldier. He was a Private, (with no stripes on his sleeve), dressed in Army Class A greens, bloused trousers over his boot tops, (but no jump wings), spit shinned jump boots, a blue infantry rope on his right shoulder, wearing every bit of military tinsel the P.X. sold including marksmanship badges that dripped in a ladder down his chest from his breast pocket, and he had a teenage blonde of amazing proportions dripping from his left shoulder. There was not a combat award on this guy, no shoulder patch of unit service, so I don't give him a second glance. The girl friend, however, was another issue.

I stood there in my rumpled suit that was a size too big for me, and the only piece of Army paraphernalia that I was wearing was a round "U.S." collar brass along with branch of service insignia and nothing else. The Signal Corps insignia consisted of two crossed signal flags propping up a torch.

The Private saw to his own needs ignoring me, and while he was doing that his blonde girlfriend detaches herself from his left shoulder and walked over to me. Having already noticed her ample proportions earlier, I now availed myself of a second helping at close range. She must have been new to soldiers and soldiering because I was just concluding my own business and had picked up my papers when she asked me, "How come you don't have any medals like my boyfriend?" I smiled savoring the moment. She wasn't bad looking, and there was a certain something about the amount of cleavage she was showing. I swore I could see her naval. It had been a long time between conversations with female blondes or views of cleavage. "I'm a soldier honey, not a playboy," I replied and headed off to the passenger waiting room.

With my delayed flight into Kansas City my arrival into Los Angeles was even later. I was very enthusiastic to be there and looking forward to a long leave with time to forget Kansas. The one negative to my feeling of elation was, would there be anyone waiting for me. I had spent the big money phoning home from the Manhattan City airport and had been assured that my younger brother would be at the Los Angeles airport to pick me up. My younger brother was known to wander off, generally to a bar. I hoped that the lateness of my plane would not foul my arrangements up, but at least I knew what to expect.

Getting off the plane in Los Angeles I was indeed greeted by my younger brother Alan who had managed to arrive on time to drive me home. Unfortunately for me Alan was four hours late like the plane, having spent his time waiting for me in the airport bar.

I picked up my canvas duffle bag and my brother and headed out to the airport parking lot to get the car and go home. "I don't re-remember where I parked but I have this lil' red ball thing on the antenna so the car it'll be easy to find," he said. On reaching the parking lot what should greet my eyes but a sea of red ball things. Apparently they were very popular.

My brother's car was a sports car, which made it harder to distinguish in the sea of red balls. I spent many anxious and tiring minutes walking up and down the rows of cars, with a duffel bag on my shoulder and a curse on my lips.

Sailing to Citizenship

When I was still at Fort Riley and announced my decision to apply for citizenship it is surprising just how congenial and downright helpful complete assholes like Sergeant Bigbelly could be. I didn't know if it was a twinge of patriotism, or what, but I was given every bit of assistance I needed to get my papers filed, the use of a U.S. Government ball point pen and a flat surface to use it on. But Bigbelly did complain about how much time I spent filling in the forms. There was a limit to his benevolence. I spent three days, dragging out every possible moment, moments that I could not be put on detail, because Bigbelly was offering me "every assistance" possible.

To get the papers on their way I was photographed in vivid black and white, and finger printed like a common criminal at the post Provost Marshall's office. My Military Police experiences at Fort Gordon were coming back to me; I knew exactly what to do when it came to mug shots and finger prints.

Now that I was on leave in California, six months later, I had almost forgotten about my application, now that my need for it had diminished, and I was reclining at home when the letter arrived instructing me to appear to take my test. Test, I have to take a test! I immediately gave up my slothful ways and submerged myself in American History and Government at the public library. These immigration guys certainly didn't make it easy.

While at Fort Riley I had promptly and properly applied to become a citizen; I reflected on all the hard work my parents had done in their quest to become citizens. They had put in months of night school and self-study, but I figured for me it would be a snap. After all I had had all of that government and history stuff in high school, so I thought, "Yeah this will be a snap." I had sent in the citizenship papers from Fort Riley and I expected the citizenship certificate would be sent back in return mail. After all the U.S. Army must have some clout with the U.S. government. I was wrong as usual. From start to finish the whole process took six months.

Now that I was out of Riley I still intended to follow through with my intention and actually become a United States Citizen. I never wanted to be caught up again in the same dilemma I had faced at Fort Riley, all dressed up with no place to go because I had papers missing from my file.

I studied hard on my refresher course on how the U.S. Government works. I did not want to give the Army a second shot at screwing me up.

On the appointed day I showed up in uniform, I figured if I didn't get the right answers, maybe a good impression would do the trick. So I appeared at the Federal building, located in the same dismal down town Los Angeles neighborhood as the Induction Center for the Army. This time I was not alone, as I was required to bring two personal witnesses who could swear to my good character, as instructed I had both of them with me. They were going to have to swear that I was of the right material to make a good citizen, even though I had papers missing from my file. I had searched high and low for the right two witnesses It was too late in the game for mistakes. My sister-in-law was one witness for me and the other an old high school pal Gene, who was now a U.S. Marine also home on leave, Gene was like me also on his way to Vietnam. My sister-in-law said she was doing it to keep harmony in the family, but my Marine buddy was hung over from a lot of beer I had pumped into him the two nights before. He was in such bad shape from our pub crawl that he would have agreed to anything if I allowed him to crawl off and die.

The night before my order to report for citizenship test Gene and I were out having a great time, and we were having this grand time somewhere downtown. Running out of things to do and half drunk, we ended up at a movie house. Not the skin flicks mind you, but some "B" grade murder mystery. We were there because it was late, raining, and neither of us had a steady girlfriend, so we were just killing time.

There we sat sharing a half pint of something or other, and paying no mind to the two dozen patrons of the theater. On the screen the heroine of the picture had just found the body of a man shot and lying on the floor of his black and white, Film Noir office. The dead person had been shot by a mysterious "gloved hand holding a pistol that was mysteriously extended through dark curtains." The girl had just picked up the smoking gun dropped by the mysterious hand. To the first person in the door the girl said, "Oh! What shall I do?" To this my seemingly asleep buddy Gene pipes up in typically loud

Marine Corps fashion, "Police up your brass, and move up to the 500 yard line." The place broke up. The theater was crowded with servicemen at loose ends for something to do, just like us.

As we walked from the parking lot to the Federal building my Marine buddy and I paid no attention to the surroundings, or the local denizens of the area, having seen it all before. My sister-in-law stuck very close to us walking from the car, any closer and she would have been inside one of us. Definitely a Fraidy Cat, how did she get into the family? I wondered.

After winding through many floors and offices we arrived at the appointed place for my test. As with every government office I had recent memory of, the office buildings walls were all painted the same pukey two tone green colors. Also, in each government office I looked into as we passed, the furniture matched down to the chipped paint and huge padlocks. The Federal government did all its furniture buying at the same prison, where they produced the same bad taste in mass quantities. I was eventually ushered into a small room containing the usual desk, filing cabinet, chairs, and male civil servant. In this case a very plump, jovial, and gray haired individual with a brilliant smile and very intelligent eyes. He put me and the members of my party right at ease with a hearty handshake and an explanation of what was going on.

Unlike the test given my parents hours of oral and written exams, and a lengthy personal interview. My test was to be entirely oral, I wilted at the proposition of having to think on my seat and come up with an intelligent, let alone the right answer, and then pronounce it in understandable terms.

Sending my witnesses out of the room we began. The test consisted of only three questions:

Question 1. What is the law of the land?

A pregnant pause followed while I stumbled around in my mind. Seeing my dilemma along with the blank look on my face, the examiner took pity and offered the answer, "The Constitution."

Question 2. Who is your representative to the U.S. House of Representatives?

Not being from California at the present time but from Kansas I didn't know. Again the same pause, the blank look, and the answer being given to me by the examiner. At this point I got worried, why had I spent so much time studying obviously the wrong information.

Question 3. Who is buried in Grant's tomb?

This one I answered without help, and this seemed to please my examiner no end.

My two witnesses were next ushered back into the room and they were each asked if they thought that I would make a good citizen, even though I had papers missing from my Army personnel file. Furtive looks between my sister-in-law and the Marine were exchanged before either answered, which caused a moment of anxiety on my part as to what were they going to say. My sister-in-law answered, "Yes," and the Marine uttered something that the examiner took to be an affirmative answer. My examiner then shook my hand as heartily as he had when we arrived, and he congratulated a rather perplexed soldier who didn't fully understand that he had passed.

Two days later I was back in the same building standing before a federal judge this time, being sworn in as an official U.S. citizen, and a week after that I was winging my way to Vietnam. Who says that justice is not swift?

De Tomaso's Bar & Grill

Knowing that their brother was going off to war my two brothers, Alan and Stu, decided that the least they could do was to take me out for a hearty meal before I went off to Vietnam. So it was decided on my last Saturday night of my leave. To round out the event they brought along our Marine Corps buddy, Gene, the same Gene who had sworn to my good citizenship. We all knew each other from school days and had for years. All of us loading into Stu's 56 Ford, and we faced the first dilemma of the evening, where to go. Gene and I were wearing civilian clothes as trying to appear as not-in-the-Army/Marines as possible, even though our short haircuts gave it away. "I know a great place for steaks," piped up our Marine friend. "It's a little place just off P.C.H., (Pacific Coast Highway)." So we went for a streak.

We ended up at De Tomaso's Bar & Grill just off Pacific Coast Highway. It was so far off of P.C.H. almost tucked under the viaduct for the Terminal Island Freeway. It was set back off of the highway, but you could see the lights of the place, they were in the distance through the tall weds. From the outside De Tomaso's looked like a dump, just another road house along a busy highway, on opening the door my thoughts were confirmed. We went in and as soon as the door opened we were hit by some raucous country western song blearing full tilt from the juke box. The only thing visible through the darkness, smoke and the music was the glare of neon advertising different brands of beer, but there was a delicious aroma of steak coming from somewhere in the dark.

It took several moments to become adjusted to our dank surroundings, and once we could see past two feet I noticed that the place was crowded. Figures sat in every booth, hunched over beers, and a mumble of conversation could be heard whenever the juke box stopped to change to another CW record. "This is the place," said our Marine buddy, "ain't it great." All three of us turned and looked at him in disbelief. In one of the breaks between songs, as I looked around, brother Stu had found the bar, found four bottles of beer, and found us a table by the dance floor.

I sat, but still couldn't put two and two together, I looked around, but all I could see were men, no women. "Say what kind of place is this anyway?" I asked. "Oh don't worry, this ain't no queer joint, and the steaks are great," Gene told everyone. A "Mama Cass" look-a-like was serving this night, complete with Moo Moo dress. We ordered more beers and "Miss Cass waddled off. A little light conversation over the music and we each ordered a steak from the round hall of a bar maid.

I turned around from admiring the decor and was greeted by a short blond kid in a sailor suite, his white hat perched on the back of his head, leaning on one corner of our table with a beer bottle clutched in one hand.

"What ship" he said.

"What do you mean?" asked Stu.

"Aah said, What ship?" Drawled the sailor.

Gene jumped in.

"We're not from no ship," said Gene.

"Well what the fuck are you," said the sailor pointing at my buddy and his short military haircut.

"I'm a Marine on leave."

"And what's him?" He said pointing at me.

"I'm in the Army," I offered.

With this the sailor turned his head around and said loudly to the bar, "Hey boys we got us a Doggie and a Jar Head, What ya' all thank of that." There were murmurs and laughter through the smoke and music. I leaned over the table to our Marine buddy, "Gene, what the hell is this place?" "I come here all the time, I love it." It was then I noticed the little red cloth patch sticking out of the sailor's jumper cuff, it had four white stars on it, and then I knew. We were in a southern sailors bar.

"Hey Doggie, you gonna bark for us?" asked the sailor.

I ignored him. "Come on Doggie, just a little woof," said the sailor leering at me.

"Hey, buddy, fuck off will ya," I said smiling at him and then turned toward Gene.

"Yeah, fuck off," Gene added.

"Screw you Marine," was the menacing reply.

I knew then that it was going to get ugly and that all these other guys I couldn't see in the bar were going to help it get real ugly. I had been in fights before, and I wasn't afraid of being hit. Hey! What were two brothers for, we were each a punching bag for each other. By a quick count of heads at the table and from what I could see around the bar, the odds were not exactly favorable. I knew my brothers could and would fight; we had been fighting with each other all our lives. Dad had once been a professional a boxer; we had been taught how to mix it up pretty good.   I had spent at least 14 years learning how to take a punch, and how to throw one.

My two brothers were Alan and Stu, Stu older and Alan younger. Both of them were not little guys, not tall and skinny like me. Stu was 6' 2" and an Olympic rated swimmer, with the bulging look of body builder. He was in his junior year at our home town state college, a jock who liked to spend his off hour's weight lifting. When not lifting iron weights he hoisted heavy duty blonds and 12 ounce beers. My younger brother Alan was still in his teens, 5' 10" but wiry and lean. Alan was a rebel who would rather fight than eat. I had seen him choose a fight with some real knuckle dragging monsters and come away the winner. Bloodied but still the winner.

At this moment a beer bottle sailed out of the dark and crashed in splinters on the dance floor in front of our table. And as if as one we all stood up and moved from behind our table. We all faced the direction the bottle had come from, because we all had a sense of what was going to happen next. I looked quickly around, I could see heads bobbing in front of the neon signs, and our southern interrogator had disappeared. Another beer bottle came flying through the air and bounced harmlessly off of Gene's chest with a hollow thud, to go crashing somewhere in the dark. Gene rubbed the spot then picked up the chair he had been sitting on and hurled it in the direction the bottle had come from. And the fight was on.

I have never been in a brawl like this before or since. It was a nightmare performed in dim light with chairs, bodies, bottles and fists flying everywhere. I caught a guy in a sailor suite running at me in a crouch with his arms spread wide like he was trying to tackle me. I side stepped him and nailed him in the rear with my left foot, that sent him crashing into a table and chairs after he ran by. Someone grabbed me from behind, around the waist, and lifted me bodily off of the ground. We collapsed on the bar floor in a heap, and I was pulled to my feet by Alan, "You OK?" It was more of a statement than a question; he had tackled my assailant knocking us all over. More bodies appeared out of the dark and Alan and I started throwing punches more or less back to back. We were surrounded by several swinging bodies; some in sailor clothes others, like us in civilian dress. Fists were landing all over me as I did my best to counter punch, but there were more of their fists than mine, they were winning. Suddenly a group of those that surrounded us went crashing to the floor, brother Stu on top of them. Alan sent one of the surprised but still standing bodies sprawling across the dance floor on its chest, with a round house to the ear. Big brother Stu jumped up and lunged past me sending three more sprawling in a group with a cross body block, he landing on top of them punching and pummeling. "Say he's pretty good at that stuff," I remember thinking admiringly. The crowd around me was now dispersed down to one or two who backed off. Seeing my own chance I reached down and picked up, one of the first batch knocked down by Stu, by the hair and popped him in the up turned face with a right. I was knocked down, punched, kicked and then got up and did the same to many others in the course of the next few seconds. I was staggering to my feet to get back in it once more, when a big burly arm grabbed my forearm and a voice said, "Come on!" I was propelled to the end of the bar and the exit sign by Stu. On the way we jumped over a prostrate body, and then made it through the door. Outside the cool night air hit me in the face like a brick wall, I gasped in clean air, "wait here," I was told. Back through the door went Stu, and he came busting back out within 30 seconds with a gasping brother Alan. "Let's get the fuck out of here," said Stu. We turned to go, but I remembered something "what about Gene?" I asked. We all stopped in our tracks "Yeah your right," gasped Stu. With bruises now going from numb to sore, blood dribbling from my mouth and our clothing ripped we all turned and ran back into

208

the bar. The place was a mad house of noise and motion. Glass shattered and broke on our left, gasping and groaning came from all sides. As the Navy duked it out with themselves. We could make out one big mass of bodies all crowded around one area of the bar. "There" said Alan pointing at the mass. We ran over Stu grabbed an arm and pulled the body it was attached to from the mass, I popped the jaw of a surprised face with a right, the body went limp. "Hey, just like in the movies," I said to myself. Another body and a left sent this one spinning off into the darkness, then it was my turn to grab arms, and brother Alan had a go. In seconds we had found Gene he was backed into a corner booth fighting this mass of sailors for all he was worth with the legs of a broken chair. There were two or three out cold sailors lying in the booth with him, so at least he had not been idol. On seeing his rescue he came diving out of the booth onto two more of his attackers, knocking them down, and we pulled him and the rest of the mob off of him. Shouts of "Let's go!" went up around us and all four of us headed for the door, The sailors still had a lot of fight still in them, I ran behind Alan, he dodged around a dark figure in a sailor suit standing in his way. The figure lunged for Alan with his arms, so I stopped and kicked the figure in the groin. He jack knifed over in agony. I ran on jumping or dodging other figures, both standing and prostrate.

We made it outside, gasping for air, and ran around disoriented for a few seconds, trying to remember where we had parked the car. The night air felt great as I gulped down great lungful's, trying to clear my head from some of the blows that had rained down on it. "Over here, over hear," I heard Stu calling, there was a strange sound in the air, a wailing, "Oh God, the Police." Within seconds we had piled in Stu's now running 56 Ford and we were wheeling it out of the parking lot. Sailors were coming out of the bar throwing rocks and bottles at the car as the tires spun on the loose gravel, then gripped and we sped away. We made it onto P.C.H. and headed back the way we had come, turning around I could see out the back window, the red lights of several Police cars coming from behind us, but still some way off. We turned off the highway at the first side street, turned off the lights and parked quietly.

"Jesus, that was something," said Alan.

"Christ, what was that place?"

"A southern Swabby bar," I explained.

"Gene, how did you find out about this place?" I asked.

"Oh, hay! I go there all the time, the foods great."

"You don't go there alone, do you?" I asked.

"Oh no, I go with some buddies from the base."

"All Marines?" I asked.

"A groan went up from the other two, "You ever have a fight in there before," asked Stu, menacingly.

"Oh sure, lots of times."

More groans.

We stopped at a gas station and cleaned up and cleaning out the bathroom of its paper towels to bath our wounds. Then after dropping Gene off, we had to wait outside our house till our Mom had gone to bed before we got to sneak inside and get rid of our torn clothing. After doctoring our wounds we ended up going and sitting in the waiting room of the emergency ward of the hospital. Brother Stu had broken his hand, and the rest of us were banged up pretty good. For all of our bruises and pains we had received, none of us couldn't remember when we had ever had a better time.

Fire Bug

My leave finally came to an end; I had spent the last 30 days trying to forget that I was ever in the Army. I left home in December and I traveled to Fort Lewis in Washington State for shipment to South Vietnam. The closer I got to going to War the more apprehensive of what I would find, and what I would be doing there.

Getting to Fort Lewis was no problem I was now a well-seasoned jet traveler, and I was now a lot calmer about air travel. There was only one small problem I encountered on the trip. Because I was leaving in the middle of the week I was dropped off early in the morning at the Los Angeles airport, so that my Mom could avoid some of the early morning rush hour traffic. We said our good-byes and then I settled down to wait; I had more than two and a half hours to kill before my plane left so I decided to get something to eat. I found a 24 hour cafeteria in the middle of the departure terminal, and decided it was the only place to dine as indeed it was the ONLY place for me to dine. I was served a breakfast of bacon, eggs, toast and coffee on a Styrofoam plate, which I placed on my Styrofoam tray next to my Styrofoam coffee cup and my plastic knife and fork.

I sat down and ate my breakfast at an empty table where some other traveler had left a copy of the Los Angeles Times. I began to read the paper to help pass the time. Finishing my food I lit up a cigarette with a paper match as my Zippo cigarette lighter was out of fuel, and I then casually tossed the match into the ash tray on the table and went back to reading my newspaper.

After a few seconds I noticed that something was going on behind the newspaper. Through the newspaper I was reading I could see a motion of dark shadows moving up the paper. I quickly shut the paper to see what was happening. My meal on the table in front of me was on fire. The paper match I had tossed into the ash tray had actually landed on my Styrofoam place setting, and the tray and plate were on fire. The fire was sending up great clouds of greasy black smoke with tiny bits of black stuff floating in the smoke, while the fire consumed the remains of my breakfast and the plastic silverware. I reacted in the only way I knew how, I took my newspaper folded it in quarters and in both hands began beating on the flames. Greater clouds of the dense black smoke billowed forth and the flames leapt higher with every direct hit my paper made. My imitation of Smokey the Bear caused some of the surrounding patrons of the cafeteria to get up from their own tables and head for the nearest exit. I managed to get the fire out in a matter of seconds by flailing franticly with the Times, but by then my newspaper was now ruined. It was smoldering in spots and covered with black soot and melted plastic. The table looked like a war had been fought over its surface with small pieces of blackened plastic stuck to the table top. Spilled coffee, salt and pepper and the remains of bacon and eggs mixed with the burnt debris on the table and floor. My breakfast was a total loss so I left everything in place, ignoring the stares from the remaining customers that followed me out the door, and headed for a far corner of the departure lounge to have a cigarette in peace while I waited for my plane.

Being alone, in uniform, and having hours to kill gave you three strikes against you. This I had discovered in my short career as an airline passanger. At an airport alone you are a target for panhandlers, religious zealots also panhandling, and "very strange people." Being in uniform did give you some association with other traveling servicemen, if there were any, but the general public seemed to shun anyone in uniform. Also, having many hours to kill gave you a problem as well. Your mind tended to wander.

The Los Angeles airport was a marvelously busy place, with many hundreds of men and women passing you every minute or two, or so it seemed. Being single I would take a brief peek at any of the more attractive females walking by my station outside my departure gate. Any more than a glance would get you categorized as one of the "very strange people." It seemed wonderful that mini-skirts were in vogue and the shorter the better. It was during these few hours of mini-skirt watching that I formulated my first ever Lennoxism. My brief observations lead me to formulate that: "If you were watching any particular attractive woman, and she was within 30 feet of you, no problem. However, if you were watching a particularly attractive woman at any distance past 30 feet then within 10 seconds of your spotting the woman someone, (usually some stupid idiot with nothing to do but stand there), or something will get between you and your desired object of observation.

Also, within 30 seconds of the same spotting then two or more people, (again stupid people with nothing better to do but stand there), or objects will get between you and what you are trying to get a view of.

I sat and proved this "ism" to myself over and over, and the "ism" was also true for observing males as well as females. Amazing! So I decided to give my Lennoxism a name, and I called it "Bob's 30 foot, 30 second Geek rule." Not bad for one morning with nothing to do.

Back in the Army Again

I arrived at Fort Lewis Washington with the standard Army "Hi, how are you! Take a number, sit and wait," greeting, "Your number is 5012, now serving number 7." I then got a special greeting of a more personal nature when the Captain in charge of the Replacement Depot, after he got a look at my appearance. I was wearing my one and only formal Army uniform, my very rumpled khakis that looked like they were a hand-mc-down from my big brother, and which I had just slept in on the plane. Besides the uniform I had shown up a day later than the date specified on my orders. It had been a common practice in the Army for troops on leave to arrive a day late allowing an extra day for travel, sort of a day of grace. Unfortunately this was not the case with people shipping to Vietnam. If you took a day of grace the Army took a piece out of your ass, (a very nasty chewing out), and if you were two or more days late the Army took a piece out of your pay check and a bigger piece out of your ass. I was given a very strong chewing out from the Captain for my rumpled appearance, and not setting a good example for the younger troops. I had to agree with him, after 30 days at home I didn't feel like being very military, or setting a good example for anyone. Besides I still had a black eye and two healthy bruises on my face from the brawl at De Tomasos's. After getting raked over the coals I was then told, "Get the fuck out of my office, and go and get a military haircut," he didn't like my hair do either. I was hustled out of his office so some other soldier could be hustled in. One more body from what seemed to be a never ending line of lolling soldiers outside his door, all waiting to receive similar treatment. We enlisted men were considered by some as totally disreputable and an undisciplined lot.

After the traditional brief Army haircut I had to fill out the standard three miles of Army paper work, (firstnamecommalastnamemiddleinital), and found myself in the standard replacement barracks. For the next three days I, along with several dozen other sullen and sodden troops were marched around day and night, from warehouse to warehouse, while we were issued new jungle fatigues, boots, additional haircuts for those who didn't get it right the first time, shots and the indifference of those handing these things out.

It had been almost seven months since I had my first orders sending me to Vietnam. I had had gotten all my overseas shots when I first processed out of Fort Riley, and I found out to my dismay that my overseas shots were no longer valid. I had to get the whole series of shots before I could continue my travels. What this entailed was seven new shots to bring my shot record card up to date. Crap!

The medic who pointed all this out to me was very eager to give me all needed shots right then, and right there. "Well," I said to myself, "Might as well go ahead and get them." The medic took me to a back room and closed the door, and he seemed to beside himself with glee. I didn't see why he was so happy about I was the one getting all the shots. The medic lined up all the needles and asked me "Which arm I preferred?" I said to just stick them in as I turned around, and that is exactly how we did it. I had never met anyone who enjoyed inflicting pain with a needle before, we got my shot record up to date in 15 minutes and I didn't pass out from the process.

At Fort Lewis I found the Washington rainy season celebration was in full swing, and each day we were all greeted by a daily down pour of cold rain. The rain never seemed to stop, and the sun never shined not for the entire time I was there. I found this dreary weather of Washington depressing, especially when I compared it to Southern California's sunny warmth I had just come from. The skies were dark and overcast all day long. The short day light hours during the fall months, plus the rainy weather made for a dismal experience. Traveling from barracks to mess hall was challenging to keep from getting drenched if you had to line up outside for very long. Even smoking outdoors was a challenge, after lighting up a cigarette it could turn to mush or be put out before it could be finished. None of us had a rain coat or a poncho to keep us dry, because those garments had been turned in to supply during the processing in. Beats me why, we could have used them.

Standing outside a warehouse one rainy afternoon, while standing with a bunch of soaked through G.I.s I came to a conclusion. I turned to a Buck Sergeant who was shivering in the down pour like me, and I said to this total stranger:

"I'm from Southern California and I haven't seen the sun since I got here," I said in way of introduction.

"I'm from Florida, and I haven't seen the sun either," replied the Buck Sergeant.

"Is it us or is this the Army's way of misery?" I asked.

"The sun may go by but I bet it's wearing a poncho," said the Sergeant.

"I would give 10 bucks for a poncho right now," I added.

"This building is probably full of nice dry ponchos," said the Buck Sergeant.

"If I survive Nam and come home I am going to find a girl, settle down and get married,"

The soaked G.I.s around me nodded and acted like they agreed, so I went on.

"After we get married and settle down she is going to get pissed at me for something."

The Buck Sergeant asked, "So, ain't that normal, what will you do then?"

215

"When my wife tells me to 'Kiss her where the sun don't shine! I'm gonna take her to Seattle." I said answering my own question.

"I'm with ya there buddy," said the Buck Sergeant, "Cause the sun sure don't ever shine there."

Rain continued to run off us in rivers and we shivered outside until we were let into the warehouse where an NCO got mad at us for messing up his nice clean warehouse floor with puddles. Go figure.

On top of the rainy weather there was nothing for waiting troops to do but wait. We hung around the barracks sleeping, reading, writing, and getting acquainted with those we were most likely to be going to war with. Here was another mixed bag of troops, all different ranks, different jobs, and strange and different personalities. For the most part all of us waiting shipment to Vietnam were, as usual, strangers to one another; some of us however had recently buddied up in the reception barracks. Personal tastes, similar Army schooling or prior acquaintanceship were usually the deciding factors on who you paired up with. I ended up with two guys because we started telling dirty jokes while we lounged around one day, and the three of us kept them going amongst ourselves. One of the guys was an Infantryman, a "Grunt," the other a boat mechanic. The boat mechanic was a returning veteran from the delta area south of Saigon. He was part of the "Force Riverine," the "Brown Water Navy," he was a "River Rat." I being from the Signal Corps and Fort Riley had no exciting metaphor such as theirs to describe my branch of service. So instead of saying, "Hey, you fucking Grunt," or "Hey, you fucking River Rat," to punctuate a statement they had no means of identifying me with the Army. So with this dilemma they would refer to me as, "Hey, Mr. no fucking body."

High Flying

After three days of moving from one place to another at all hours of the day or night in a rain soaked apathetic trance, we were assembled, counted and pronounced ready for shipment. My joy was boundless! At last I could leave this moss covered country and go someplace where the sun shone and it is warm. In the middle of the night we were transported to McChord Air Force Base in a fleet of Army busses. I knew they were Army busses because the gears ground on every shift, and they were painted O.D. Green outside and in. All of us were then herded aboard a McDonald Douglas DC8 (stretch version). This particular air plane was owned and operated by Flying Tiger Airlines. I could tell by the words "FLYING TIGER" painted on the side of the plane. I had seen their planes at other airport, and they were known as freight haulers. I thought "These guys fly freight around," I wasn't far wrong for here we were, and what were we anyway. But at last I was beginning my trip to South Vietnam. There were nothing but G.I.s in jungle fatigues on the flight, officers up front followed by senior NCOs, and the rest of us in the cheap seats.

My new friends and I boarded our plane together along with what seemed, and was, hundreds of other O.D. Green clad individuals. We claimed three seats together to enjoy our own company on the trip, and I readied myself for the trip over. All of the other soldiers around us looked exactly alike, all in their late teens or early twenties, clean shaven, looking very young and very vulnerable. After becoming acquainted with our new surroundings Flying Tiger Airlines seemed just like any other commercial airline to me, the plane had a few miles on it and so had the stewardesses. The decor was the same, the seats the same, even the bathrooms the same, but the big difference I noticed right away was that the attitude of the stewardesses was not the same. Apparently these women had made this trip before, and from the reception they gave us, "sit the fuck down, will ya, and shut the fuck up," they had made this trip many,

many times before. It was evident that they had seen many, many plane loads of soldiers, and that they already had had all the soldiers' fun and frivolity that they could stand.

The one thing that I immediately appreciated about the trip, and those around me concurred was, it was now no longer raining, and this pleased the majority of us. Dinner was served a few minutes after take-off, and this is what tipped me to the above observation about the stewardesses. The meal was standard airline fare, but the fact that one of the stewardesses came down the aisle during the meal with a crate of milk under one arm, and tossed each of us a carton with the same mono syllabic comment of, "Here," "Here," "Here," as she went by. The milk was followed by dessert, a crate of apples delivered to each of us with the same technique.

The stewardesses were attractive, they were female. They must have been in their late twenties or early thirties, but no matter what we appreciated anything female.

First stop was Anchorage, Alaska, a very uncheerful place in December, in the middle of the night, in the middle of a snow storm, and in the middle of nowhere. The plane did not pull up to a passenger walkway so that we could go into the airport terminal in comfort and warmth. The plane parked out on the ice covered asphalt, and the door was thrown open and left that way. To survive the shock of snow and 30 degree below zero weather blasting in through the open door we had to run over the snow and ice to the terminal. Jungle fatigues were useless for warmth at that time of year in Alaska, and there were not enough blankets on board that plane to keep out the kind of cold blasting in through the open doorway. But the jungle boots proved useful with enough traction to speed our flight to warmth and hospitality of the passenger terminal. Since there were orders not to serve any Army personnel booze we stood around in the terminal waiting for the refueling to be completed warmly drinking coffee and soft drinks at the snack bar, and then we braved the weather on the return trip to the plane. Leaving the door open had turned the inside of the plane into an ice cave and setting fire to the seat cushions was one suggestion floating around to warm things up. It took a lot of heavy breathing on the part of a hundred or so G.I.s to bring the inside temperature of that plane back up above the freezing mark.

The stewardesses continued to treat us with indifference all the way from Alaska to Japan. My two new friends and I continued our joke telling all the way there adding some fun and creating some participation from the fellows traveling with us. This all helped to pass the time as the view out of the windows was perpetual night, clouds, night and clouds or clouds, night or just clouds and night. By the time we arrived some hours later all of the late teen, clean shaven, and very young looks had turned into that of dirty wrinkled, rumpled boredom. The four letter words now flowed freely from both the passengers and as well as the stewardesses.

We landed in Japan, (I never found out the name of the city), and like in Alaska the word was that all Army personnel could not buy booze. There were standing orders not to serve anyone in those funny looking O.D. Green clothes in the bar or the duty free liquor shop. My "Riverine" friend and I had both been in the Army well over a year, and both of us knew the score and some of the ropes of how to get around certain regulations. So with a few bucks we conned an Air Force Sergeant, we found hanging around the terminal, into buying a bottle of Canadian Club Bourbon whiskey for us, it was the cheapest in the store, and we smuggled it back onto the plane.

From Japan to South Vietnam we drank our doctored coffee, and enjoyed ourselves even more raucously than on the trip from Alaska. Anyone around us could share our fun and our bottle, and this brightened an otherwise long and tedious trip. Even one of the stewardesses forgot her misgivings about soldiers and came back and had a belt with us and contributed to our jokes and our other frivolity. She explained that she couldn't even buy booze in Japan because of her association with the Army. The fun was cut short however. Word had got passed forward to some of the senior NCOs and officers on board, and one of Sergeants came back to our seating section and tried to commandeer our bottle. He threatened us with jail time and other hideous punishments if we didn't give up our bottle. Next he tried cajoling us with friendly words of advice. Cajoling with a smile from an NCO was useless; we were feeling no pain and were immune to his inducements. We were wise to the "Lifers" ways. We had some anxious moments passing the bottle under the seats to strangers, but those around us knew that sucking up to the officers and NCOs was not the way to impress new friends in the enlisted ranks. Our superior gave up and went back to his part of the plane empty handed.

My first impression of Vietnam was that from 30,000 plus feet, while we descended to 2000 in about a minute. It was a "Lame Duck" landing, that's what the pilot called it, used to avoid attracting the wrong kind of attention, that of the enemy. Peering through the cabin window I thought that the land was very picturesque, picture postcard or calendar quality scenes appeared on every vista. Mist shrouded mountains overlapping each other, marching out to meet the sea. Expansive plains, a patchwork of colored fields, together with brown rice fields, there were little towns and villages dotting the landscape, in some ways beautiful. My impression was to change once we got off the plane.

Chapter 10

"Stupid F.N.G."

By the time we landed in Cam Ranh Bay, (Pronounced Cam Ran Bay to us non-native speakers), I and my new friends were feeling no pain, of course we had been feeling no pain 30 minutes out of Japan. It was morning in Vietnam, but the blast of hot air that shot through the air-conditioned comfort of the airplane when the door was opened was like from an oven. This sobered me up at once. There was no joy in Mudville on landing, all of us on board were subdued at our first sight of the air base, and we filed quickly down the center aisle of the plane. I stood for a second in the open door, the hot sun felt good on my face, and I took a moment to look around. I gazed at the flat expanse of the concrete air field before me; the only things moving were the heat shimmer, and two or three slim whirling dirt devil tornadoes. A shiver went through me as I knew that I was really here. There were no other planes in sight, no troops except those from my own plane moving down the steps to the concrete, I was as if we were the first ones to occupy this place. I really woke up when at the bottom of the stairs two airmen were handing each of us a steal helmet from a huge pile. There were no smoking ruins, amongst the few buildings I could see, no shell craters, or the sounds of battle to be heard or seen. Just an eerie silence greeted us while several black columns of smoke rose to heaven off in the near distance. Some of us stood and watched them rise until we were told to move on Were they the results of a recent enemy attack or the result of the shit burners' art? (The "Shit Burner" was someone who burned up the crap from the latrine. The crap was taken care of usually by the application of a large quantity of gasoline, diesel fuel, and a match). This question and several dozen more in my mind were unanswered as no one was around but other new arrivals like me. So these questions remained on my mind as I stood on the ground of South Vietnam, while the sun baked down on me and reflected off of the concrete runway and the tops of lots of steel helmets.

We were ushered to waiting Air Force busses and boarded in single file. (Air Force busses were painted Air Force blue inside and out, and the gears did not grind between shifts). The buss had heavy gauge wire mesh over all the windows, and I thought to myself, "They must not want us to climb out and run away." It was later explained that the wire mesh was there to keep hand grenades from being thrown through the windows by the natives. It was then that I first felt the fear of traveling in this country, and understood how vulnerable we were even on our own bases.

Cam Ranh Bay, outside of the air base and at close range, was a plain of flat land that was a lush green in color. It was a patch of flat sandy land bordered by steep hills on one side and the sea on the other. Through the lush green color of the countryside were cream colored patches of sand dunes and the cream colored ribbons of sand where paths had been worn. These green areas were the bordered by the black lines of roads. Sand is what everything seemed to be built on. The sand dunes disappeared westward into the foothills, which climbed steeply away. Everywhere there were gray one and two story wooden buildings with tin roofs scattered about. They were there by what seemed to be the hundreds, some in a pattern of a few rows, but mostly each one was situated on the top of its own sand dune or in the valley between. Barbed wire fences were strung out everywhere, and there were sandbag revetments around most buildings and low hump backed bunkers could be seen between many of the buildings.

The busses drove along the roads through the cream colored sand dunes and I could see curious looking civilian women in funny clothes of shinny silk. Long flowing gowns with skirts split up the sides to the waist showing long silk pants beneath. Almost all of these women wore conical straw hats. "Why they are Vietnamese," I thought to myself, "and this is a U.S. Army base." It puzzled me that all these civilians were allowed to walk around unescorted, like they owned the place. Of course in one respect they did own the place.

The sights and sounds of Vietnam were new and exciting, but my most lasting impression I have of this strange land is of the smell. Something was burning, somewhere! The aroma that assaulted my senses was not like anything that I had smelled before or since, a mild bitter sweet but nauseous odor that was present everywhere in Cam Ranh Bay and I was to discover it elsewhere in Vietnam. Something was there in the air, part of it was the smell of burning wood, burning charcoal, maybe food, but the rest I couldn't quite put my finger on. The smell could have been a byproduct of the shit burner's art, but as this was all new to me I wasn't sure. Each place I went in Vietnam had a different variation of the same aroma, and the production of it was anyone's guess.

The bus trip ended with us being deposited near a large group of these gray, tin roofed buildings. I now found myself in another of the U.S. Army's replacement barracks. At the replacement barracks, we and our belongings are laid out on a patch of the ankle deep sand in front of one of the single story gray buildings of the 22nd Replacement Depot. We were inspected, counted, filed, re-counted, filled out some forms (firstnamecommalastnamemiddle-inital), and were told to stand by. This was the month of December and it was as hot as hell. Our collective sweat stained our duffel bags as we lay on them, in the available shade, waiting to be processed in. South

Vietnam was hot, damn hot, and compared to Georgia and other places I had been it was Goddamned hot. I first thought that I was in an oven, as the heat pressed down on me. But the heat was bearable, what really made life uncomfortable was the extreme humidity. Sweat soaked our brand new fatigues for the first time, leaving great black patches under the arms and down the fronts and backs. When our fatigues could hold no more moisture, the sweat ran down our bodies in rivers soaking the pants and even our socks and boots. Vietnam was the only place I have ever been where it was so hot that your legs would sweat along with the rest of your body. A most unusual thing to happen.

Once the Army had us all herded together, they lined us all up and removed all of our stateside money. Our dollars and silver change was replaced by paper money only good in Vietnam M.P.C Military Pay Certificates. A different color and design for each denomination of currency, in my hands I now held a rainbow of money. Purples, reds, greens, all emblazoned with pictures of people I did not recognize, and scenes of South East Asia. We now had paper coins; it was foolish to carry a pocket full of loose change jingling into combat, so the Army had remedied that for us. They did let us keep one reminder of our stateside ways, they let us keep our pennies, and there were no M.P.C bills for pennies. Finally by the end of a very long, hot and boring day we were each told to go and find a bed in a barracks, any barracks we were then fed and told to go to get some sleep.

The barracks I and my new pals had picked as our temporary abode wasn't the usual temporary World War Two wooden structures I had come to expect from my experiences in other replacement depots. This was a temporary Vietnam War structure, a concrete slab surrounded by flimsy wood and bug screen sides that is a good description of the structure. The barracks in Vietnam were a one or two story buildings with one thin layer of wood between you and the outside world. The walls went only four and a half feet up from the floor above that was wire screen. The whole structure was capped by open rafters supporting a peaked tin roof that was held in place from high winds with sandbags every few feet. Surrounding each barracks was a wall of dirt filled 55 gallon drums side by side, set on their ends with sand bags on top and between. This barricade of drums was called a blast wall. All this did not leave you with any sense of permanence or personal safety.

This type of construction was identically repeated all over Vietnam, and was similar to what I was to find with the majority of military buildings in Vietnam. The one real shocker however, was the latrines. Here the Army had reached a new low in low cost construction. Outhouses were the norm for Army personnel in Vietnam, the navy and air force maintained flush toilets for the comfort of their men, but the Army was content with the primitive outdoor approach. The Army's idea was a breezy one room affair with up to 16 holes on two facing banks, with ample room to hold a spirited but stimulating conversation with your neighbors. Room was also provided between holes to place the ubiquitous C-Ration toilet paper, or in the worst case a copy of the Stars & Stripes newspaper. Various copies of the Stars & Stripes or Army Times newspapers were cast about the seating area and floor, not as an opinion of their news content but for the convenience of the troops who had a lack of TP with them.

For relief that did not require a seated position there was a stand up area latrine. Several empty, metal, 55 mm artillery shell shipping cases in a row, shoved into the ground or a gravel pit in a row at a 45 degree angle. These were the proverbial "Piss Tubes," the ones everyone talked about everything going down. This facility offered the minimal amount of privacy for users, a canvas screen stretched around this area, a one or two feet above ground. This only covered the user from waist too knee. This screen shielded passer's by from viewing the actions of the latrine occupants, but as all passer's by were all male members of the Army little protection was required. What protection that was required was from the smell from the open trench or gravel pit with served as the receptacles for the urine from what must have been thousands of users. A sign posted in the latrine by some wag stated, "Flush hard it's a long way to Hanoi." This said it all.

Sleep did not come easy that first night, a lot of us sat up watching our first sun set in Vietnam, and I waited to see if the war we had heard of really began after dark. Troops with an infantry MOS (Military Occupation Skill) were drug off to perform guard duty on the distant base bunker line, visible along the crest of the first set of foot hills. They were the first to get a closer look at the war. With the setting of the sun the heat and humidity did not disappear all at once, it continued on like it had been stored up by the ground to be re-radiated at night. It was too hot to sleep so many new arrivals like myself stayed up watching Vietnam for the first time. Within our view as dusk settled in and slowly changed to full dark the distant U.S. camp perimeters became visible. There were strings of lights appearing all over our horizon, and each one was a separate American installation. More camps were visible as these chains of lights, appearing on the distant hills. These were flood lights, illuminating the perimeters of these camps. The night calmness was only occasionally disturbed by the appearance of parachute flares rising slowly from one camp or another, into the sky, arcing over in flight and then lazily falling to earth. This was all the distinct visual effects of war I had come to expect, but without the audio, no crashing of artillery and small arms.

Next Stop?

In the morning of the next day it dawned bright red from the ocean and the temperature rose with the sun, and this was immediately followed by the rise of the humidity. In both cases they did their best to rival the levels set the day before. For most of the morning we all lounged around in the sand outside an office. As the temperature climbed more and more people tried to find any sort of shade to sit in, some were even content to sit in the partial shade offered by another soldier. We waited for someone to come and tell us where we were going. My name was called out during our morning assembly, apparently my trade was in demand, as I was to be shipped out immediately and I said so long to the two comrades who had traveled so far with me. I was taken back to the same air base at which I had arrived, and was flown by Air Force C-123 up the coast to Nha Trang.

This was my first trip in an Air Force propeller driven airplane, and the Air Force certainly made it an interesting one. The trip was only 40 or so miles in distance, but the pilots made it extremely exciting. The plane was crowded with G.I.s and ARVN soldiers, A.R.V.N., (Army of the Republic of Vietnam, abbreviated to ARVN and pronounced Are-Van), all of them but I carried weapons, ruck sacks, helmets and other field gear. We passengers who were lucky enough sat on nylon webbed seats down the sides of the plane, the others sat with the baggage on the floor of the aircraft. The flight started by parking the plane at the end of the run way and revving the engines up to full brain screaming throttle with the brakes full on, the engines revved until I thought we would take off straight up or explode. Then the brakes were released and we seemed to jump into the air at a frightfully steep angle after running down the run way for only a few seconds. The Air Force had a most disturbing way of explaining their emergency procedures before the plane took off. Someone yelled out to us "If the alarm bell rings three times, that means we are about to crash." I was already a little nervous about the shakes and groans of this aircraft, and this announcement really set my stomach to churning.

There were only two windows in the fuselage of the plane, one on either side, up forward ahead of the wings. These had no covering so the wind screeched through them while we ducked for cover behind the shoulder of our neighbor.

The pilots flew the plane inside a cloud most of the way, I am sure they did this out of perversion, just to confuse and terrify me and some of the others. The plane groaned and rattled from start to stop, and left me with a very insecure feeling about U.S. Air Force. I'm also sure that the pilots took great delight in prolonging the flight with detours and sharply banked turns to heighten our experience and confusion. Looking out at nothing but an opaque whiteness for what seemed hours was unsettling, but when we finally did see the ground the scene I saw looked exactly the same as what we had left behind. And it was coming up to meet us very rapidly as the pilots made a steep landing in Nha Trang.

Nah Trang, (pronounced Naa Tra-ng by us G.I.s) under closer inspection, was more beautiful than Cam Ranh Bay. Instead of a sprawling military base surrounded by rural farms and villages Nha Trang was a city of some size. I learned later that Nha Trang had been a French resort, used primarily by vacationers. Up close driving from the air base to another reception barracks I was able to get a glimpse of some of the palatial villas that lined the beach front, and spacious tree lined boulevards that ran through the city. I glimpsed all this from the front seat of a ¾ ton truck as I was being driven from the Air Force base to wherever I was going.

Driving through the city also gave me my first glimpse of Vietnamese traffic, their version of vehicular mayhem. Busses, bicycles, motor scooters, carts, taxi cabs, cars, peddle cycles, pedestrians and dogs all competed for the same piece of roadway at the same time. Traffic seemed to go in all directions at once, and at the same direction at once. It was very colorful with the gaily painted cabs and busses, but very confusing for someone used to following rules of the road. Even someone with my driving reputation marveled at some of the confusion and near misses, followed by loud horn honking and the tinkling of bicycle bells. (The Vietnamese government was saving a fortune in tax payer money by not painting lines on the roads. No one in Vietnam paid any attention to rules of the road anyway). The sole point of sanity or control was the Vietnamese policeman standing nonchalant on the sidewalk in his white covered peaked hat and Khaki uniform. He and his pistol were, as I was later to find out, judge, jury and executioner on all traffic disputes. The Vietnamese National Police were known to us as the "White Mice", and they were not to be trifled with.

Civilians walked down the sidewalks in their silk pants, shorts and white shirts, while women in their colorful split sided national dress and conical hats were interspersed with the other pedestrians in western attire. Street venders abounded with little carts, and as you passed you drifted in and out of different smells. ARVN soldiers in O.D. Green, passed by in both directions, the Americans in other trucks or Jeeps would whistle and hollered at the younger, prettier Vietnamese girls on the street. The girls that got the most attention from the soldiers were the ones who wore tiny, backless, high heel shoes that "clipped clopped" against the girls heals as she walked. All this traffic and street noise was a background to the sing song sound of the Vietnamese language. There was one distracting piece to this street scene, trash and other scrap paper was everywhere. It clung to the gutters, stuck to the fences and hedges, and sat about every square yard of weeds, vacant lot or other open space, drifting and playing in the wind.

An air base surrounded by other military compounds, a patchwork of different wire stockades, interspersed with civilian areas, could be the best description of the general layout of the Nha Trang military area. Each compound, civilian or military, U.S. or ARVN were each separated by roads, flanked on each side with high cyclone fences topped by scrolls of concertina barbed wire. The fences and the wire had been there for some time as they were rusty and shreds of paper trash had collected along their bases, but the fences still served as formidable barriers.

I had been picked up at the air base by the duty driver of the outfit I was being assigned to, and I was then taken to one of these fenced in compounds, the one belonging to the 21st Signal Group, part of the 1st Signal Brigade, and there I was deposited in their replacement barracks. I thought that Cam Ranh Bay was bad but the 21st Signal brought military comfort down to bare bones and a new low for the Army. My new home was an ancient mattress on the concrete floor half laying in a stagnant puddle of water. This was on the first story of a two story gray barracks. The other new troops that had arrived ahead of me had taken all the better places, the ones less submerged in the puddle. Both the mattress and the water had been there for some time, as they were both smelly and filthy. There were no mosquito nettings for the beds, and no mosquito repellant or bug spray handed out. To protect myself I slept underneath my only blanket, it was dirty and well used but it was all I had. I roasting in the heat and sweated the whole night long, as without the blanket the mosquitoes buzzed around my ears.

After the first sleepless night I thought about complaining about the living conditions in the replacement barracks. I am glad I didn't as I learned later that a soldier who arrived in country after I did refused to sleep on the filthy mattresses. He received an Article 15 and a 30 dollar fine for his trouble. All of the troops on this base did not live in the squalor that was ours. The bad conditions were not a result of the war but of disinterest or non-attention to the needs of G.I.s just passing through. I could see from the surrounding barracks that the permanent troops at 21st Signal lived in a much greater comfort than we. It was no wonder that someone had hung a hand painted sign over the door of the replacement barracks that said, "Dog Patch," the name fit.

Here is where I was introduced to the Vietnamese Black Market, and had my very first conversation with an honest to goodness Vietnamese. You might say that when I arrived in Vietnam I had my morals and all my other senses assaulted at the same time. It seemed to me that ours as well as all of the surrounding military compounds had their civilian employees and the South Vietnamese civilians more or less could walk around as they pleased, no G.I.s followed or supervised them in any time. As I went around my new compound I had seen through the fence men and at times women civilians standing beside the roads in full view of traffic, urinating against the compound fence posts. (The rusting wire now made more sense). G.I.s did this too, but those in charge of us really got after anyone American peeing in public. Vietnamese Women squatting in groups along the shoulders of the roads and picking lice out of each other's hair. Once found they would crack each insect between their teeth. Some of the Vietnamese men passed by holding hands as they walked down the roads together, passing between compounds. All of these caused me to stare at this strange behavior, but I found out all of these are quaint Vietnamese customs.

One of the female Vietnamese civilians, working in the compound, found me sitting alone outside the barracks, on my second day there. I was sitting in heap of sweating exhaustion from my full day of efforts on behalf of the replacements task master. This woman was of an age somewhere between 30 and 50 years old, it was hard to tell exactly. To me Vietnamese women over 50 generally looked very old and used up, but under 30 they are quite tempting. In between they look well-kept but over worked, or half way between leathery and cuddly.

She asked me in her best English, "G.I., you go fee Ex, baiy mee ceegarre an soa a fee Ex."

Now this was not easy to understand especially when it was spoken through brown stained teeth with three gold caps visible. It took her three or four tries repeating her request before she was able to get an indication from me that I understood anything she said. A little light bulb came on over my head.

Roughly translated she wanted me (G.I. you) to "buy her cigarettes and soap at the P.X." She wanted to pay for it with something called, "Boom Boom," which I also found out later was a little afternoon delight on my filthy mattress. I hadn't yet had my ears tuned to the local customs or language, despite all the pamphlets the Army handed out. No pamphlet mentioned

"Boom Boom" as any means of monetary exchange. None of my pre-Vietnam Army training had covered how to conduct yourself when approached by the Black Market, and all the little phrase books given us were in Vietnamese not Vietnamese Pigeon English. The Vietnamese language to me was a lost cause, but Pigeon English and I had a chance and I was now catching on fast. However, I wasn't yet ready or willing to take on this female charmer. Her female charms, stained teeth and leathery complexion just didn't turn any part of me on.

I wasn't incensed and outraged by this attempt at corruption, just disappointed at who had made the offer. I don't know what I would have done had she been much younger and prettier. After my encounter I felt that most of what I had read or heard on TV before coming to Vietnam had been a load of bunk. The Vietnamese did want us there in their country, they wanted us there to buy them "ceegarre an soa a fee Ex."

There wasn't much lounging about to do at the 21st Signal replacement barracks, the NCO in charge of replacements filled our days with work details under the broiling sun. I had joined a group of other Signal Corps troops on their ways to various units in Vietnam. Together we discovered the joys of manual labor, filling sand bags, painting, stacking and re-stacking equipment. Having only been in country a day or two I was already working on a great sun burn. Those in charge just wanted to see how red this new boy could get. The one nice thing about work in Vietnam, at least we could remove our shirts or roll the sleeves of our light weight fatigues up, which offered some coolness. In the states, your shirt stayed on and the sleeves remained down at all times. It seemed to me that the Army used any means to keep us busy and out of the clutches of unscrupulous Mama-sans, and out of the Fee Ex.

Gone were the needless "keep the troops busy" dirty jobs. Every task over here had new purpose and meaning for me. There was no grumbling or bitching about having to work all day and part of the night. I as well as most of the others realized that the jobs we did were essential for our own and others protection, as well as comfort.

By the third day at the 21st I was an old hand. I was on a last name basis with the boss of the work details, he knew me by sight, I was the bright red one, and was now used to some of the sights and sounds around me. I and my fellow replacements were assigned to nailing siding to a building being erected. In the middle of the day the NCO in charge called us together and read out the latest troop shipment notice, as had been the routine for the past two days. My name was the only one called from that mornings shipping roster, and the announced destination was Pleiku. I had heard about Pleiku before, back at Fort Riley and Fort Gordon, from some of the returned veterans, and what I had heard was not good. Pleiku was deep in enemy territory.

What first came to mind was an odd marching ditty I had heard while at Fort Riley:

Victor Charles in Pleiku,

Threw a hand grenade at you

(Victor Charles was the name the troops used for the enemy, the V.C. Viet Cong).

The rest I had forgotten, but the tune and the first two lines kept rumbling around in my head for the next several days.

After the announcement the first comment I heard from my group was, "Hey, you're going to Pleiku. No Shit! There's a war going on up there," apparently the rest of the group had also heard of Pleiku too. This brought a response from our boss of, "Tough shit," and I was told I was shipping out after lunch.

Packing for the trip was not a problem as we had all of our worldly possessions with us at all times. They were kept in a truck while we worked, as we could be shipped out at a moment's notice. Leaving our possessions lying around the barracks unguarded while we were out was just too much temptation for others hanging around the barracks.

Pleiku is a town sized community located in the central highlands about 100 plus road miles from the coast, and 30 to 40 miles from Cambodia. One major highway leads in from the coast, QL19, and another one runs north and south through Pleiku, QL14. It definitely was way out on its own with no other cities or towns close by.

Some of the clerks in the depot of the 21st had also heard of Pleiku, and they had obviously heard the same things as I had. I was handed my shipping orders with the comments of, "Keep your shit together man. There's a war going on up there," and "Be careful, it's `Indian Country' up there." But for the first time I heard, one of the clerks say, "Hey man, it don't mean nothin'!" A standard phrase I was to pick up later in my own speech, as an expression for 'whatever happens' in your life and times in Vietnam. To say the least they were very sympathetic. After their solicitude I was apprehensive, if not a little scared. "Tough Shit," was the comment passed around by the rest of the replacements as I and all of my possessions were deposited at the entrance to the Nha Trang U.S. Air Force base for my trip to Pleiku. "Good luck man," was yelled from the back of the truck as it drove away.

The Nha Trang air base was crowded a large crowded place. Several aircraft hangers and other buildings all surrounded by a flat expanse of concrete, with planes of different shapes and sizes parked at different angles as far as I could see. There were Vietnamese civilians, ARVN soldiers and G.I.s all going somewhere. I checked in at the American military counter, gave them a copy of my orders, and was told to take a seat. I looked around; there weren't any, so I sat down on the floor on top of my duffel bag. Three hours later when my name was finally called I was given a seat on an U.S. Air Force C-123 to Pleiku.

The trip to Pleiku was identical to my trip from Cam Ranh Bay to Nha Trang except that it took four times as long. We flew for what seemed like days. Same type plane, same noise, same weather complete with heavy clouds, and the same disturbing disclaimer about the alarm bell ringing three times to indicate we are going to crash. The plane was crowded with soldiers but none had to sit on the floor. I sat in the usual uncomfortable nylon strap seat facing inward. This time I sat within two or three feet of the open window, and I dozed or kept to myself, as there was nothing to see out of the window. There wasn't much conversation because of the noise, and no one seemed interested in talking.

Pleiku

As the plane let down on the way into Pleiku Air Force Base I unbuckled my seat belt and stood to get a look at what it was like. I got a quick glimpse of the local countryside, the place looked uninhabited. Brown rolling, straw colored hills, with large dark green clumps of trees covering some of the hills and valleys. The hills undulated westward. There were high dark green mountains here and there shooting out of the dense green foliage clumped around their bases. But no rice paddies "Could this really be part of Vietnam?" I asked myself. I was amazed on how much the country around Pleiku resembled that of northern California, if it wasn't for the occasional military compound with its cleared off perimeter and the red color of the exposed soil I would have sworn we were flying over the Napa area in Northern California. We came in to the north of Pleiku. Circling over a large dense patch of green something went PI-IING inside the plane. I looked around and noticed the panicked looks on the faces of those around me. Some of them were looking up at the ceiling so I did the same, there was a little hole in the roof, where I hadn't seen one before, and I could see sky. The PI-IING sound came again almost within a fraction of a second of the first PI-ING and a little cloud of dust rose from the floor in front of one of the G.I.s across from me. Another hole appeared four feet behind the other in the roof. "My God, were being shot at," I thought. The G.I. across from me reached calmly out with his left foot and gently covered the hole in the floor in front of him. There was murmurs and excited talk from the rest of the troops on board, and realizing just how vulnerable I was. I tried to make myself as small and inconspicuous as I could inside my nylon seat. I did like the others on the plane; I grabbed my duffel bag off of the floor and held it between my legs, hugging it to my chest. I figured that my dirty laundry would have some mystical power to protect me from what was happening, what the others thought at this moment I have no idea. The announcement about the "three alarm bells" was recalled from memory and went rattling through my head, could this be IT! "This can't be it, I've just got here," I told myself out loud, but no one heard me from the howl of the wind through the windows and the noise of the engines. I squeezed back in my seat and closed my eyes dreading what was to come next. I could hear something that sounded like praying from somewhere around me as the plane droned on. "Say one for me," I whispered. My eyes were still shut tight when I heard the tires screech as the plane touched down on the runway.

Landing, I was visibly relieved and exited out down the ramp on quaking legs. No one had been hit by what had PI-IINGed through us, and I was especially relieved to have survived another shaking, quaking propeller driven Air Force trip. I smiled weakly at the Air Force Crew Chief as I passed him. I couldn't resist looking once more at the two holes in the roof of the plane; I glanced around but couldn't see any more holes where what had caused them had come through the floor or walls. I stepped off of the plane onto the Pleiku runway, and thanked my luck that I was once more on firm ground. I had a million questions I wanted answered, but my most immediate need was to get away from that plane. I marched to the terminal building with others off of my flight, and dumped my duffel on the concrete. Looking around the area from the terminal building I discovered that there was no town of Pleiku visible in the nearby surroundings, all that could be seen beyond the air base perimeter wire and guard towers was the thatched roofs or rusted tin roofs of a village or two nearby. Each village was set off amongst broccoli shaped trees, and dark green bushes with the occasional bright green splash of a banana tree. Off by themselves were one or two large red roofed white stucco buildings. But the area wasn't as hilly as it had appeared from the plane; this was a platcau with far off mountains to the north and east. Having spied out the surroundings I sniffed the air around me. There was still that smoky smell to the air I had noticed when I first set foot in Vietnam, but at the same time I noticed the air I also noted that it was considerably cooler in the central highlands than it had been on the coastal lowlands. The humid, constricting, stagnant air I had come to expect in Vietnam had been left behind in Nha Trang.

The Forty Third

I had orders assigning me to the 43rd Signal Battalion and as I expected there was no one there to greet me. I hung around the air base terminal building wondering if anyone knew of my coming, but after an hour I resigned myself to the fact that I had been the only one to have known of my arrival. It was now getting close to five and my stomach told me, "Feed ME, FEED ME!" I was the only one left hanging around the terminal, except for the occasional Air Force person. I would just have to phone the 43rd and announce my own presence. Try as I would I just couldn't find a pay telephone at the Pleiku air base, and I finally had to ask for the use of a field telephone from the local Air Police, very nicely I might add. I also asked the Air Police, "Hey, what's the telephone number of the 43rd Signal Battalion?" I was shown a pair of hunched shoulders and a pair of hands showing a lot of open palm as a response to my query. There was no Pleiku telephone directory, there was no information service through the telephone it was just me and a black piece of plastic to solve one of life's many riddles. What kind of place was this anyway? I was about to find out.

I picked up the field telephone and cranked the handle several times and waited for an answer, a mysterious voice came on the other end of the line, and the voice said, "Dipper Switch!" I had found the operator.

"Please connect me with the 43rd Signal Battalion," I said.

"This is the 43rd Signal Battalion," came the reply.

It made sense to me; telephones definitely had something to do with the Signal Corps.

"I - I need someone to pick me up at the airport."

"So what do you want me do about it?"

One word broke the silence on the phone, "Working?"

"Working!" I said into the handset. If I hadn't the line would have been immediately disconnected. This was the Army's way of checking that there was someone on the line. This was something I had learned in Germany, and I was proud of myself for remembering this little bit of Army know how.

"Well I need to be picked up at the airport," I persisted with the operator.

"So?" said the mystery voice.

"Say, how about putting me through to the 43rd's orderly room?" I asked, finally getting wise.

"Well why didn't you say so the first time?" Said the operator.

A Jeep arrived an hour later, I said "Hi" to the driver as I threw my stuff on the back seat, and climbed in. The driver was wearing a helmet and flack vest, and had his M-16 rifle clipped to the Jeep's dashboard for easy access. I felt conspicuously unarmed as we left the security of the air base. We took off on my first trip to the 43rd Signal, and the first thing I saw outside the air base was a better look at one of the large two story stucco buildings that I had seen from the air base. This building had two giant one story red Roman Numeral "I" above the front door, painted in the center of a giant white circle. "What the hell's that?" I asked my driver. "That is the ARVN II (2) Corps Headquarters," he replied, "The local target for VC rockets," the diver added. I nodded my head as if I knew what he was talking about.

The II Corps HQ was the center for control of all military activities in the central portion of Vietnam. This caused the white stucco building to be crammed with American and

Vietnamese officers at all times, and that is what made it the prime target for the enemy. The II Corps building had a huge grass lawn in front of its sweeping circular driveway, and there was an even larger field of punji stakes surrounding the lawn and the headquarters building. As we drove on past the HQ building we came to an ARVN road block consisting of a barbed wire and log drive around barricade in the middle of the road. This forced the driver to slow down to a crawl to negotiate the tight turns around the obstacle, and this action brought us full view of the South Vietnamese soldiers guarding the road. The center point of this road block was a World War two M-8 U. S. Army Grey Hound armored car parked by the side of the road. But something peculiar caught my eye as we drove by this armored car. The armored car had a belt of .50 caliber ammunition draped over the barrel of the armored cars 37 mm cannon. The barrel of this cannon was not the place for this kind of ammunition, and there was no .50 caliber machine-gun anywhere visible. My peculiar feeling was heightened even more as I got a look at the four guards at the road block, four ARVN soldiers in tightly tailored fatigues and shiny black helmet liners, lounged on the sides of the armored car. None of them paid any attention to us as we passed. They were deep in a sing song conversation, and hardly glanced in our direction. I thought that at least the US guards I had seen so far were wide awake, even so all the ARVN's did was to give us a wave of an arm as we drove by them. This left me with a less than secure feeling for II Corps Headquarters' and for myself.

All day, since the announcement of my departure from the 21st Signal I had been excited about my new assignment. I was more excited and relieved to be out of the 21st Signals filthy replacement barracks, but when my driver let me off at my destination I found myself in front of the 43rd Signals own filthy replacement barracks. The big difference between the two was that the 43rd's filthy mattress was suspended off of the concrete floor by a steel Army cot, a small thing, but I appreciated it at the time.

Again I processed in under the watchful eye of the company clerk, filling out the same paperwork I filled out at all my previous stops, (I was well versed about the firstnamecomma-lastnamemiddleinitial, Army requirements). All this paper pushing had worked me up into a healthy appetite and as it was now past dinner time. My papers in order I was told to go get fed.

On my way into dinner in the 43rds HQ Company's mess hall I was accosted by the large Sergeant head counter, "sign your name, it ain't free." Yes Army traditions continued even in a war zone, even here you had to sign for you meals. I finished signing my name, dropped the pen and started toward the smell of food. The large red headed Sergeant with the biggest set of arms I could ever remember seeing, who sat at a desk in the entry way to the mess hall, he reached over the table and grabbed me by the forearm with his right hand. Holding me firmly he poked me in the upper arm with his left index finger. "Take your god-dammed pill," he demanded. I recoiled from his reach in fright and responded with a sheepish grin. Before the Sergeant sat a large bowl of little white pills, and an even larger bowl of enormous orange colored pills, this was the first time I had ever seen either since arriving in Vietnam. (At Cam Ranh Bay there had been no bowl of malaria pills when you signed for meals). "Take your god dammed pill," he demanded again. He released his hold on me and I relaxed long enough to say, "Huh! Oh sure Sarge," and I gingerly reached into the small bowl and selecting one of the small white pills. The head counter watched me with a menacing look as I popped the pill into my mouth and downed it without water.

This was my first, but not my last encounter with these malaria pill medications. They were supposed to protect you from contracting malaria, that is, provided you slept under a mosquito net, used bug repellant and prayed regularly. You will notice that I said that they would protect you, not prevent, they wouldn't prevent you from getting it. While in the central highlands of Vietnam the white pills were to be taken daily and the big orange ones weekly. I personally took my malaria pills regularly, and I never contracted malaria. But I cannot say that they prevented or did not prevent malaria. I do know that they certainly prevented constipation as they were one of the most potent laxatives I have ever taken. On Mondays, within three hours of taking the large orange pill I would be heading for the latrine, pulling my pants down while at a dead run, and hoping there would be a vacant hole for me. The same trip would be made the same way several times a day and several times a week over the next 12 months I was in Vietnam.

Odd Jobs

Bright and early the next morning I was drug in front of the battalion's Personnel Sergeant for his inspection of what fresh meat had been deposited on his door step. Being a "Fresh Bod" in the battalion but not a "Fresh Fish" from school the Sergeant omitted the standard lecture on morals and sent me to work until the higher ups decided where to put me. My first job was to join a work party and string barbed wire on the battalion's defensive perimeter.

The 43red Signal seemed to have it pretty nice. They had a wooden latrine and several two story barracks for the enlisted men, and a clear field of fire on the perimeter. Wooden boardwalks connected each building with its neighbor, and with the latrine. At the junction of any boardwalk and building were 55 gallon drums half full of sand. These drums were placed in the ground at 45 degree angles, and each barrel had a neatly lettered sign above it stating, "DISCHARGE ALL WEAPONS." I wondered what that meant. The barracks were of the usual construction complete with the 55 gallon barrels and sand bagged blast walls.

The officer's quarters, mess hall and the majority of all the other buildings used by the 43rd were several hundred yards away from the enlisted men's barracks with the motor pool and several service shops in between. These other buildings

241

consisted of the white stucco red tile roofed variety, left over from the French involvement in Indo-China. These stucco buildings were quite a change from the standard American wooden construction, as they were quite a bit cooler inside, and certainly more solidly built. No blast walls were need here.

The 43rd Signal HQ was one of several American military units sharing space on a huge base camp, part of which included the "II" Corps HQ. The 43rd battalion's area was directly behind the "II" Corps headquarters building, separated by a road and then a high wall that was impossible to see over. The 43rd was a buffer between II Corps HQ and the base camp perimeter. This seemed like a neat arrangement, provided you were with II Corps HQ, the enemy had to go through the perimeter wire and the 43rd to get to them. This fact I was to discover later in my tour in Vietnam. If the enemy used rockets or artillery to get to the II Corps HQ they would generally use the 43rd's compound as the place to land the first round and then they would march their fire through the 43rd till they reached their intended target. Not good, if you were a member of the 43rd.

I walked down to the perimeter with the other troops; I was immediately distinguishable from the others in the work party by my bright shiny new green jungle fatigues. All the others had torn, brown stained and faded fatigues, faded almost grey. They also wore jungle boots that were stained the red color of the Pleiku soil, and they had not seen a lick of shoe polish in months. All of the other members of the work party avoided association with me by talking amongst themselves and walking as far away from me as possible. For this party we were all unarmed, but there were guards armed with machine-guns visible in the watch towers above the defensive bunkers.

There were several belts of barbed wire in place at the perimeter, tangle foot, concertina, and a combination of both. These were the primary obstacles in front of a spaced row of defensive bunkers and a trench line. I had never seen a trench line in my life and I was fascinated by this trip back in time, back to the era of the First World War. This was a deep red, chest high, gash in the ground, running the length of the 43rds perimeter, but connecting each bunker in the battalion's several hundred yards of perimeter. It had a sandbagged parapet, with firing positions notched at intervals. This did make me feel uneasy about what type of warfare had gone on here in the past, and what may happen in the future.

I went to work with the others removing rusted out and collapsing wire in the third belt from the bunkers and replacing it with nice shiny new razor sharp stuff that cut and nicked my hands. It was hard work and as the sun rose higher in the sky I sweated freely staining my new but sweat smelling fatigues more. We each enjoyed the suns warmth, some by removing their shirts. I was still red from the sunburn I had gotten in Nha Trang, but what the hell it felt so cool to get out in the open, I worked in my O.D. Green t-shirt. Outside the last strand of barbed wire could be seen rolling grass hills with a few huts of a thatched roof village visible in two or three places. Banana palms grew close around the huts, and the broccoli shaped trees and the dark green underbrush grew in clumps along the hill sides. In the distance was a line of higher more rugged hills with very little vegetation visible on their slopes or crests. I enjoyed the panorama of my new surroundings, standing erect to ease the strain on my lower back. I would listen to the wind rustling the brown grass, and hear a bird chirping as it perched on the wire. I wondered were the war was, this was too peaceful.

After two hours sweating in the hot sun, I had gulped down my canteen of water, replacing what I had sweated. And feeling the need I took time out to relieve myself against one of the metal steaks that held the wire in place. Out of nowhere an angry bee whizzed by my head, and it buzzed through the air at a tremendous rate. "Boy they sure got big bees here," I thought to myself. My companions disappeared immediately as one man, while I continued to spend myself enjoying the feeling. Another bee whizzed by and I heard a whispered cry of, "Hey, hey you new guy, hey new guy!" caught my attention. I looked around and spotted one of the others lying prone a few feet from me, "get down new guy, GET DOWN!" someone else yelled. "Huh!" "What?" "What for?" I stupidly replied. An angry bee sent up blue sparks and an angry PI-IING as the bee collided with the barbed wire near me. "They're shooting at us you F.N.G...... GET DOWN!" came the warning. I realized the danger but was so caught up in my pleasant past time that I turned back toward my enemy and whizzed back in their general direction. Finally relieved, I dropped to the ground to the resounding praise of my companions, "Stupid fucking new guy!"

In the three days that I spent at the 43rd's replacement barracks I learned many things, things to add to what I had learned about Vietnam since arriving. I learned that the weather here in the central highlands was milder than it had been along the coast. The daily temperature was at last 20 degrees cooler, and for that my sun burn thanked me. I also learned that life in Vietnam was no picnic, the living conditions were poor, the food bad, and dirt and filth were everywhere. I also had learned that a normal work day was at least 14 hours, but I didn't mind. For the first time my existence in the Army had a purpose, and the work I performed had meaning. I learned to take my daily malaria pills daily and my weekly's weekly. Plus I had learned that I had a lot more to learn. I was indeed a S.F.N.G. "Stupid Fucking New Guy!

After two days of sweat labor I was assigned to a company of the 43rd Signal battalion, and I was relieved that I was finally going to find a home. All of the 43rd Signal battalion was not stationed in this one group of barracks. This was only the headquarters and the "A" company of the battalion. There were three other companies dispersed at different base camps in the II Corps area of Vietnam. One company was at Kon Tum, 40 or 50 miles north. One company at An Khe, half way between Pleiku and the coast, and the third at the 4th division base camp 20 miles south of Pleiku. I was being sent to the latter, the 278th Signal Company at Camp Enari.

Chapter 11

Still a "Dumb F.N.G."

The day after I was given my orders to my new unit, and as if by magic or intuition a truck arrived from the 278th to collect me. The truck was also collecting spare parts, two other soldiers, and I taking us and all our belongings south. The driver a non-committal Spec, 5 from supply had a bored demeanor, like he had made the trip a million times before. Our driver had, along with his steel pot and rifle, a guard with an M-16 riding shotgun with him. It was here at this moment that I began to take this war very seriously. Having recently been shot at and missed at long range I hoped I wasn't going to find out about close range on this trip. We were going to make the trip to Camp Enari by driving through the center of Pleiku.

The truck was a beat up 3/4 ton with no canvas covers on the cab or the back cargo compartment. After tossing our gear on board we passengers rode off facing backward, leaning on our luggage and the supplies the driver had picked up before picking up us. My two companions, a couple of Spec. 4s had been around a while. I could tell by the way they tossed a wave to the gate guard as we past his post. One of my companions quite was tall with glasses and the other short and stocky with red hair. These two I was riding with wore the faded fatigues of guys who had been in country a lot longer than I, so I asked

245

them "how come you're going to the 278th. "We're being exiled," came the reply from the shorter one as we jolted along. My curiosity was immediately up. If they were being exiled, was I?

"Why for?" I managed.

"We complained," said the tall one.

"You complained," the smaller one interrupted.

"About the chow once too often," continued his big pal,

"Top is sending us to the 278th so we can see how good we really had it," said shorty.

"This idiot has a big mouth; he's always getting me in trouble," retorted biggy.

"You do it ALL the time," said shorty.

"You don't need no help from me," said the bigger of the two.

"Sounds like he's got a sense of humor," I added, this brought nods.

"Don't mean nothin'," said the short one.

As we passed along our way new and different sites and sounds caught my eye. The road was a two lane black topped affair, and we followed behind an old Jeep with full canvas covers making it look like a boxy sedan. "AVRN officers do that, it's their private car." I was informed. Just before we got into Pleiku proper there was a large fenced compound off to the right. It had a 10 foot chain-link fence around it with barbed wire at the top and bottom of the fence and guard towers every 100 feet. Inside the fence were hundreds of brown Vietnamese men squatting on the ground or just milling around, they were wearing strange purple uniforms. "P.O.W.s" was all the explanation needed.

As we drove along I became acquainted with my fellow exiles, John and Barry. A couple of Pennsylvania Dutch boys who it appears had a "Mutt & Jeff" relationship; they went everywhere and did everything together. We exchanged home town information and other standard G.I. small talk.

246

Pleiku was a dump, a hodge-podge of flat roofed stucco buildings with peeling paint, or no pain at all. The blocks of stucco buildings were interspersed with run down wooden shacks, vacant lots and huts of flattened out tin cans and cardboard. The town of Pleiku was centered along the one paved road we were riding on, and like other towns I had seen in Vietnam trash littered main road, the drainage ditches, everything around it and blew around in the vacant lots. This highway we were on was known as QL 14, though no signs were posted. Other local roads cut across this main highway, but they were but mostly dirt strips. Along these thoroughfares strolled Vietnamese soldiers in their near skin tight tailored O. D. Green uniforms, civilians and a new sight Montagnard villagers, (The Montagnards were the natives of the central highlands, the hill people of Vietnam. The name is French for "Mountain Men," pronounced Mont-en-yards), in their native form of dress. The women Montagnards walked around in black dresses with black shirts both trimmed with embroidered cloth and the men wore loin cloths and the same black shirt. Each villager carried a basket on their back. On the dirt sidewalks of Pleiku the Montagnards competed with the black silk pajamas, white flowing gowns, conical straw hats, and Army fatigues of the Vietnamese. And all of these colors competed with the red, greens, blues and whites of the merchandize hanging in the open fronts of the shops that lined the main road.

Shops may be a misnomer here, cells is more like it. The shops were a usually one cell of a string of what I would describe as a string of concrete garages. These garages resembled the type of garages that are found at apartment buildings in the U.S. Each garage was one shop. If there was a door it could be rolled up and the shop proprietor would live there with or without family. The wares would be hung or laid out inside the doorway, and even a car or a motor scooter would be parked inside as well. To top it off a sign in Vietnamese with or without a picture of the service provided could be included. The shops were almost entirely identical.

We slowly drove through town amongst the bicycle and motor scooter traffic, and encountered a new vehicle I had never ever seen before. It was a tiny, flimsy, three wheeled affair with an open back containing seats for maybe six people, all surrounded by a lattice work of metal to form a cage. They were visible everywhere, put-putting along the side of the road with lumber or baskets of fruit tied to the top. These cabs had once been a one or two passenger motor scooter, and the cab thing took the place of the back seat. The whole thing was propelled by the tiny motor scooter engine, and the cab could manage a forward speed of between five or fifteen miles an hour. This was depending if they were going uphill or down. Even with this population of cabs Pleiku's traffic was small potatoes compared to Nha Trang. The only full size cars or trucks on the road were military; U.S. or ARVN, and the civilian motor scooter taxi cabs judiciously avoided obstructing the military traffic.

The reason the civilian cabs avoided U.S. military traffic on the streets of Pleiku was explained to me as we rode along. It seems that the American 4th Division soldiers had a habit of taking care of their own traffic congestion problems. How to make civilian traffic doing 15 mph stay out of the center of the road blocking military traffic doing 30 plus mph was the problem. (In Vietnam the U.S. Army imposed a 35 mph maximum speed limit. A figure rarely agreed with or complied with by G.I.'s. You could get a ticket from an M.P. for exceeding the speed limit). If a cab took up too much of the available paved roadway, and obstructed a 4th Division convoy. A 4th Division truck would pull up alongside of the struggling cab and either the driver would either push the cab out of the way with the trucks bumper or run the cab off the road into the ditch. There was an alternative method of road clearing. The G.I. shotgun guard would lean out of the truck's cab and kick the taxi over onto its side.

Once trough the other side of Pleiku we were into open country. Just rolling grass hills and fields. The underbrush had been cut back from the road for 100 yards on either side. It was pleasant and quiet, only thing we passed were Montagnard villagers going to or from Pleiku, walking on the dirt by the side of the road. One difference I noticed right away, out in the open country the Montagnard women walked around topless, young and old alike.

After several miles we turned off of the main road and continued along another paved highway. Here on this stretch of road the military traffic became heavier, more U.S. vehicles and less ARVN with their distinctive yellow numbers visible on the front bumpers of their vehicles. Getting closer to our destination one feature of terrain began to dominate our vision. A huge cone shaped mountain with a flat top, rising several hundred feet above the surrounding country, indeed the highest point for miles around. I was informed that this was known as Dragon Mountain. The mountains sides were covered in straw colored grass, burned brown by the sun, with a few clumps of dark green bushes here and there, but buildings were visible on top among a forest of radio antennas. This was pointed out to me by my companions as a U.S. Army radio relay sight, and was maned by some of the men from the unit we were going to be joining.

Camp Enari, was a sea of red dirt surrounded by barbed wire, and as such Camp Enari turned out to be an "A" typical U.S. base in Vietnam. Several different bands of barbed wire entanglements encircled this massive perimeter, also behind the wire barricade sat squat bunkers and tall observation towers evenly spaced along the perimeter. Gray painted barracks, all one story this time, with tin roofs sandbagged in place were everywhere, row after row, and signs everywhere indicating unit after unit. It seemed so immense, so permanent, and so American. As we drove through the gate of Camp Enari I looked with interest at the sandbag bunkers and the other fighting emplacements at the main gate, which itself was a ponderous affair of four massive gates of barbed wire and wood.

We drove onto the base after the vehicles log book was checked and we and the cargo were inspected by the M.P.s at the gate, and off we drove into this maze of buildings. After a few hundred feet the asphalt road ended and we began driving on dirt roads of red powder. The trucks tires threw up huge chocking rooster tail of fine red dust that turned into billowing clouds that followed us along the road. In the back we were covered in this talcum fine dirt, from head to toe, baggage and all. Not only were we covered, but we left a distinctive rooster tail of red dust for more than a hundred feet, as we rolled along.

The Two Seven Eight

But we were here at last, and jumping down I began to beat the redness from my clothes and gear with my baseball cap. I was finally finished with all the travel and sleeping in swamps and sties. No more living out of a duffel bag, and most importantly, no more state side Mickey Mouse.

John and Barry went off together arguing about something as they went, I finished kicking the dirt off of my duffel and went and found the orderly room. I checked in glad to finally have a home, and was assigned a barracks, a bed, and a roommate all with a hearty handshake. I was relieved at this as I was expecting another filthy night in a filthy replacement barracks. I was next marched to the supply room where I was assigned several items of field gear, an M-16 rifle, ammunition, a helmet (brain bucket), and an armored corset called a flak vest, amongst other things. The First Sergeant of the 278th gave me the day off to get my gear in order and to get acquainted. Unlike the barracks in the states, these barracks were divided into two and four man rooms, a pleasant change from the one main room for all men.

Coming late to the "choose your roommate" party had not paid off; I was assigned to the room with the company idiot intentionally so that I was to take charge of this guy, but I sensed the real reason. Nobody wanted him, and nobody wanted to be responsible for him. Besides, that reason this was the only bed left open in the barracks.

My new roommate's name was Willie and he was a military orphan. He really didn't have a regular military job. Everyone he had worked for had fired him. Willie had nothing to do all day except what the First Sergeant could dream up for him to do. After his chores were completed Willie would spend his time sitting in our barracks room and grinning. When I was there he would grin at me from across the room, unnerving at first, as I didn't know if his grinning face was camouflage for the brain of a mass murderer or maybe a nuclear physicist, or a brain surgeon. After two weeks with Willie I was ready to climb the walls, or to sit and grin at them. (Unlike the grinning Orr of "Catch 22" there was never anything behind this grin of Willie's. His face did not hide a sinister master scheme on how to screw over the Army and all others around him.) He was a goofy looking guy, with a dark stock of uncombed hair that stuck out at all angles, and a long pointed nose that almost held up his ugly G.I. glasses. He had other pointed features, chin, head, and little eyes that sort of stared through you. He was short and skinny and reminded me of a cartoon weasel I had once seen. What conversations we managed to have together were strange and disjointed, it seemed to me at the time that Willie could have been talking to me or a pin-up picture on the barracks wall, take your pick.

My new roommate was indeed a simple kid, and I did do a little managing of him as the NCO's had planned for me to do. Willie did follow my example. He got up in the mornings when I did, and I made sure he stayed up. Willie had a lot of non-conformist in him, and after getting himself dressed would sit down on his bed and then lay back down. Unless I got him going again and got him off to breakfast. I also got him off to the morning formation in time, and I left it to someone else to propel him off to work. Getting him to the latrine to clean up I

251

considered above and beyond the call of duty. Willie and I got along well but I remember sleeping with one eye open a lot.

Willie had done our room over, before my arrival; he had changed the decor from early Army plywood brown to cheap Vietnamese blue silk. It was quite a change from the bare wood that I was now used to, but a nice change. Maybe there was hope for Willie as a decorator or a set designer in Hollywood. I added to the decor with my personal collection of pin-ups (Nothing like a pretty girl to brighten a room), and we got along very well for the first few days.

To my surprise I was assigned a Mama-San by the barracks Mama-San broker. The broker was an NCO who handled these delicate transactions. He also supplied Mama-San K.P. help to the mess hall. My new Mama-San was a local Vietnamese woman who would come in five times a week and wash my laundry, shine my boots, and clean our room. I was not her only customer and after a few weeks I swore that she was supplying a lot of the local population with my missing G.I. socks. Life in the Army had suddenly taken a turn for the better. The Mama-San I was assigned was the twin sister of the Mama-San who had propositioned me in Nha Trang. She had the same black baggy silk pajama pants, the same tight fitting blouse, the same conical straw hat, the same brown stained gold teeth, and the same leathery complexion. This one also demanded P.X. privileges from me this one wanted "Soa an sho polsh from fee Ex." Which translated into "Soap and shoe polish", for her work, and she wanted them in advance. This time there was no offer of "Boom Boom" for services rendered.

When I got around to asking my Mama-san "Why?" she had to have "Soa and sho Polsh" I got my second lesson in Vietnamese and Pigeon English.

"G.I. no good, beau coup cheap cha-li," this came out in the clear along with, "You no buy, you number 10, du Miami G.I."

I instantly understood that I was being cussed at, but somehow it didn't seem so vehement in Pigeon English.

Of course I didn't catch on at all to what "Cheap Cha-li" or "Du Miami" was until later in my Vietnamese language career. As these two words depict a Cheap Cha-li was someone who did not part with their money or pay their bills, and "Du Miami" was a form of calling you a son-of-a-bitch. So I stood and listened as this litany of abuse continued to be heaped on me in Mama-san's best Pigeon English.

"G.I. all same, all same same, all numba 10, all G.I. numba hucking 10, All Numba 10 cheap cha-li."

I found out that in Vietnam all things were gauged on a scale of between 1 to 10. Number one being the best and 10 being the worst. Of course there was "Hucking 10" which was below the lowest of the low.

I was sorely tempted to add, "Aw Ma, leave me alone Ma," during this one way conversation. I didn't argue back as I was un-armed in this conversation, and I believed that this would have prolonged the lecture I was getting.

But in this first conversation I got her drift. From what I could gather from her shrieking and arm waving, I was a no good cheap son of a gun, and like all G.I.s I was the lowest thing on God's Vietnamese earth. That about covered what she was trying to tell me. Well, I broke down, I made the long trek across the base camp, and got her some "Soa and sho polsh from fee Ex," and I stopped trying to figure out why this stuff was so important.

Communications with any of the Vietnamese people, I was to learn, was not that difficult. A little kindness and patience would go a long way in either party getting across what they wanted understood. However, when I arrived in Vietnam I was one of those people who believed that if you spoke English to anyone, be they deaf, dumb or blind, loud enough and slow enough, even an idiot could understand you.

Other Decorations

I moved into Willie's room and got organized. I checked out all my new field gear and weapons, all of it had been well used before it was given to me. There were red stains from mud over every bit of it and the poncho and flak vest had tears in them. The previous owners of the helmet and flak vest had left their mark on them. Several inked names, dates, places and pictures decorated each item.

In Vietnam decorating you "War Gear" was a popular pastime, and it was always interesting to see what the other guy had written or drawn on his. This was a G.I.s version of nose art. We didn't have a plane so we used the surfaces of what we had to express our selves. There were some standards on display, Peace signs, middle-fingers; large FTA letters, names, dates and short timer's calendars were the most popular on helmet covers.

On Flak vests there was a lot more area to work with, and so the creations were bigger. There were drawings of Hells Angels motorcycle gang colors across a back, a set of airborne wings on others or the concentric colored rings of a big target. Artistic presentation was not criticized, as not many of us were artists, most of those had gone to the Peace Corps or the peace movement. As far as writing on flak jackets there were some standard sayings printed on vests:

"Yea thou I walk through the valley
of the shadow of death
I will feel no evil,
for I am the baddest
Motherfucker in the valley."

"DOW" SHALT NOT KILL (a reference to the DOW Chemical Company the maker of Napalm).

Kill them all,

Let God sort them out

VC for lunch bunch

Short round (for the little guys)

WARMONGER

BORN TO KILL

Short Timer

Don't Fuck with the Kid

FTA (Something I has seen scrawled on vertical surfaces since I had joined the Army. The Lifers referred to it as "Fun, Travel and Adventure." We lower ranks knew it as "Fuck The Army").

Signal Sucks

My all-time favorite thing to see written on Army gear was:

Make Love Not War

There were many more, but the drawings and the sayings made them personal and colorful, and all enlisted men wanted to show their individuality even in the Green Machine. I customized my own flak vest after I had spent time seeing what others had on theirs. Not being an artist I settled for some writing.

"The contents of this container are sealed under pressure, do not puncture container. For best results, store container in a warm dry place." I was very pleased to be sporting this one around.

Flak jackets were indeed a wonder. They weighed at least 20 pounds, and were made of plastic armor. Once the flack vest was put on, it was surprisingly light weight and comfortable to wear. They were very light especially during an enemy attack. Outside of that they were a cast iron corset that was a real load to drag around. In your locker they didn't stack well, and you certainly could not hang one on a coat hanger. In your locker if your flak jacket was at the bottom of your locker you would pull half of all your other gear out when you yanked out your flack vest. When not on the flak vest seemed to be always in the way.

Getting Acquainted with My Surroundings

Looking around my immediate area there were several bunkers near the barracks, and during my indoctrination into the company I was encouraged to make note of where they were. This I did willingly, remembering my past lessons and stories from other Vietnam Veterans I had met. "You have to know where to go when the enemy sent their calling card." In Fort Riley I had several veterans tell me of the importance of bunkers and what thickness of sandbag would protect you from what types of "Incoming" enemy rounds. Aside from the bunkers, each barracks was surrounded by the now usual "Blast Wall" of empty 55 gallon drums filled with dirt and barricaded further on top with sandbags; this was to protect the contents of the barracks from near misses. This caused my first thoughts about Pleiku to run rapidly through my mind again, "There's a war going on up here."

The 278's section of the base camp was up against the west facing perimeter right against the wire. Upon further examination I noticed a general lack of creature comforts. Running water at Camp Enari was not something you could find by turning on a tap, nine times out of ten there wasn't a tap there when you wanted it. The showers, and mess hall were the only two buildings with plumbing, and all of their pipes ended up at two water towers, made out of two 55 gallon drums welded end to end. The water was heated if someone remembered to fill the gasoline tank of the G.I. heater inside the home made tanks. One of these blackened creations was sitting in all its soot coated gasoline fired glory, high up in 12 foot tower, behind the shower building. The other black thing was erected behind the mess hall. The water to fill these water towers had to be trucked in several times daily from some mysterious place where the Army issued water.

What first made me aware of this water phenomenon was the white cloud of dust raised by one of two U.S. Army tanker trucks frequently driving around and through the barracks area one with the words "Potable Water" and the other "Non-Potable Water" printed on the sides of their twin water tanks. I had heard of water that was salty, hot, cold, and crystal clear, but I had never heard of "Potable" and "Non-Potable" water before. As it was explained to me Potable water was the Army's way of saying that this stuff was OK to drink, or possibly that it was OK to put in a pot. I suppose that the reverse was true for non-potable water. The non-potable must have been the stuff we showered in, but no matter it tasted OK when or if it came out of the pipe but despite the look of having a fire going under the tower the water was always cold. The heating system for the non-potable water heater consisted of a gasoline supply dripping slowly onto a piece of armored plate suspended under the metal water tank, and the dripping gasoline was set alight by the already flaming gasoline on the plate. More drips more fire, less drips less fire and less hot water. This was simple but effective. The water heated in this way had to supply over two hundred G.I.s and a dozen or so civilian K.P.s, shit burners, and general laborers. By the time I ever got off of work and under a shower head the water, if there was any left, was tepid at best.

A Recon Replacement

The 278th had one thing that was unusual compared to the 43rd, the 21st Signal, or any U.S. outfit I had been with to date, the 278th had its own reconnaissance team, a Recon Team, conducting patrols outside the base camp. I had come to Vietnam without the idea of entering combat, that is unless I had to, but the fact that the 278th had a patrol and was actively seeking new members, something within me snapped. It happened during the First Sergeant's "welcome to the 278th," speech, he must have struck some patriotic newly minted citizen nerve in me. Before I knew it I was volunteering, floating on a cloud of national sentiment, and being welcomed with a hearty hand shake and a large pat on the back. The First Sergeant had made me feel 10 feet tall, and all because I was going to do my bit for my new adopted country, and the 278th. It never occurred to me to ask any questions about recent engagements or casualties. I have the sneaking suspicion that this former First Sergeant now sells bridges from New York City for a living.

The First Sergeant was a monster of a man, well over 6' 3". He was neat and trim for someone who looked to be in his middle age, but he had a Special Forces shoulder patch on the right sleeve of his fatigues, showing that he had been in combat with that outfit. He was impressive, a pleasant smooth faced man with a toothy grin. He was a refreshing change from the First Sergeants I had had contact with at Fort Riley. This guy seemed to care about the troops and the unit instead of just caring about the piece of paper that was his "Morning Report."

I was immediately accepted for duty on the recon team by the First Sergeant and the patrol leader who happened to be in the orderly room at that time and was immediately introduced to me. "Here's a new volunteer for the recon team, I think he'll make an excellent replacement radio man for you." A big grin and a hearty handshake from the patrol Sergeant, Top and he smiled at one another. "I-I've, I don't know anything about reconnaissance, and I've never been a radio man," I offered. I had a rough idea of what a radio man in a reconnaissance platoon did, but they assured me that I would pick up radio communications procedure in no time, as we went along. I shrugged off my own second thoughts; I figured that recon couldn't be much worse or any less dangerous than anything I had done so far in the Army. "But why do they need a `replacement radio man'," I asked myself.

KAA_BA_A_ANG!

Along with a recon team, the 278th had one other unique feature that made it distinct from the other signal outfits I had been with. The 278th had three 155mm and on occasion three additional 8 inch self-propelled howitzers 50 feet behind the company's barracks, and they fired directly over the barracks area night and day.

Cannons that big and that close, firing directly over-head caused some very tense moments for guys like me, guys very, very new to large unexpected explosions. An unannounced brilliant flash of light, which was a sudden jolt to the body's nervous system, (Sort of stiffened you right out. Vertically or horizontally), followed immediately by a deafening KAA-BA-A-ANG! The sound was a roaring like the end of the world was near, and the closeness of the blast has enough force to lift you off of the ground. These were the instantaneous effects of close range artillery; the after affects were a choking, suffocating, revolting, and blinding white cloud of noxious gas which drifted slowly through our living and working quarters. My first few experiences of this kind made me glad that I wasn't on the receiving end of these monsters. These effects were the same whether the cannons fired over you or away from you.

Artillery was so new to me that it shocked me with each round fired. I was surprised so much that I would jump several inches from each sudden explosion. Each time a cannon was fired off over me it took me several seconds to calm down, and several more seconds to get the stench of gun powder out of my nose. Eventually I got so used to the firing that when the artillery didn't fire at night I would lie awake on my bunk waiting for it to fire, and would not get to sleep until it did fire.

Do It Yourself Entertainment

That first night I made sure I found out what there was to do for entertainment at the 278th. The answer was not much to next to nothing at all. You could listen to the radio, but of course you had to HAVE a radio. I did not. You could play your own recorded music, but of course you had to HAVE something recorded. Of course I did not. There was a shack that served triple duty as Enlisted Men's, NCOs, and Officers Club. That may or may not HAVE anything to drink, and there was also an occasional outdoor movie. That is if the company HAD a movie to show. The company did not have a movie. So not interested in losing what little money I had by entering into a poker game with strangers. I spent my first night writing home, not because it was the right thing to do, I wrote home because the bar was dry.

The barracks was anything but quiet at night, and anything but private. Troops came in and out after work and a variety of radios and tape players blasted out several different beats from assorted music. Troops coming in and out stomped their boots, and talked loudly to one another. There was no way to shut out the noise, as none of the rooms had a door. Mine like most of the others had a door of colored plastic strips hanging to the floor, while others had strands of plastic beads, and others had no covering over their entry way at all.

The day after my indoctrination in to the 278th by the First Sergeant, I was marched over to the motor pool and there I was issued a brand new Army drivers license. I didn't say a word, I was never asked if I could drive or if I wanted to drive, the license was just issued to me like any other piece of gear. Apparently the Army never kept track of the past driving records of any of its troops, or what seemed to me was that the Army never cared to pass along the evidence of my past driving screw ups from post to post. Being in a war zone I was both hot and cold about the possibility of driving, I would just have to accept things as they came.

Repair Shop

After what had been many months I was at last back in the repair business, I was assigned to the 278ths Electronic Maintenance Section, (E.L.M. or ELM for short). The company had been without repair people for some time, and the First Sergeant seeing my qualifications sent me right to work. I could go on patrols later. The only problem was that I had managed to forget most of what I had learned in school. That time spent doing K.P. and guard at Fort Riley was finally paying dividends, and I had to spend a great deal of time re-familiarizing myself on how to do my job. But I was not alone in my mew surroundings, when I walked in the door of the repair shop building designated as the "ELM Shop" that first morning of work I was greeted by that famous fighting duo, John and Barry. I had not asked them their jobs when we rode over in the back of the truck, as it turned out their jobs were the same as mine.

I was now officially a Newbie in the unit, an F.N.G. to all other members of the 278th. That designation meant "Fucking New Guy" in all Army circles. In getting acquainted with both my new surroundings and my peers I encountered a certain amount of hostility. The first hostile thing I discovered was the fact that we were in the 4th Division area of operations, the town and all local "female entertainment" was OFF LIMITS. This was by decree of the 4th divisions commanding general, as by his order we were to remain pure and chaste while in Vietnam; one way or another.

Secondly, outside of John and Barry most of my peers were not willing or eager to welcome newcomers with open arms.

For whatever personal reasons they had I found most veterans were generally closed mouthed and antagonistic toward me and the other new guys. I found out that these things such as acquaintanceship took time, and that the veterans were assessing you to see if they wanted to have anything to do with you. To say the least they seemed a rather choosey bunch.

When I walked in to the Electronic Maintenance repair shop for the first time I was amazed. I was amazed that you could stack broken equipment up that high, and that this company had that much equipment to stack up and still remain operational. It was as if the First Sergeant had shoved me in a room full of junk and had said, "Here Lennox, spin these into gold."

The repair shop had not had a repairman for some weeks and everything was in a mess. It was to take many days and nights to clean it up and to get some of the equipment back into service. It felt great to be back in the saddle again. I was beginning to understand some of this electronic stuff after all.

Guard Duty

With my return to repair came my return to the wonderful world of guard duty and K.P. Within three days of my arrival I was sent out to join the nightly vigil along the bunker line of the base camp. Camp Enari was surrounded by a defense perimeter of bunkers, watch towers and barbed wire. Not to mention trip flares, mines of various types, tear gas and explosives. These weren't the dilapidated thrown together bunkers of other units I was to see later in Vietnam. These bunkers had been carefully crafted from steel plates, sandwiched together and filled with earth to several feet for protection and were monsters of defense armed to the teeth with weapons I had only been told about until now.

The bunker I was assigned to had seven separate lines of barbed wire entanglements in front of it, with a field of fire stretching 180 degrees from left to right, and the clear field of fire reached out over bare ground for 200 yards. This bare ground extended for at least 100 yards past the outermost barbed wire entanglement. Along with barbed wire there were Phou gas barrels, (Pronounced FOOH gas - barrels filled with jellied, soapy, gasoline, set into the ground to through their contents at a 30 degree angle and all detonated by an explosive charge in their bottom. When the charge was set off the gasoline exploded out of the barrel as if it was coming out of a shotgun barrel), tear gas throwers, claymore mines, and trip flares. A shield of chain link fence across the bunkers firing slit mouth that shielded the occupants from lucky hits by R.P.G., (Rocket Propelled Grenades), rounds. The bunker was a fortress unto itself, into which three of us carried an M-60 machine-gun, a Star Light night scope, three M-16 rifles and all the ammunition we could stagger under. To get all the equipment and ammunition that we required took three trips from the 278th supply room to the bunker line. I was pooped after this effort.

Through the weapons slit of my bunker I watched a spectacular peach colored sunset, as I wondered what the night would bring. This was only the first of many such sunsets I would spend my time at a bunker mouth admiring. Vietnam produced some of the most colorful sunsets I have ever seen.

This was an entirely different guard duty that what was performed in the U.S. No motor pool or building to march around, and no one was excused the duty because their shoe shine was better than mine. Everyone scheduled for guard duty stood guard. All I had to do was to stand up in the gun slit of this monster bunker and defend my portion of the flood lit perimeter against all enemies foreign and domestic. The really hard part was that I had to stay awake all night long to do it. After working all day I did four hours on and two sleepless hours off until dawn. I didn't mind defending my assigned portion of Vietnam, or having to go back and work all day after guard duty. What I did object to was the officers and NCOs of the guard sneaking around in the dark trying to catch us sleeping on duty. Being wide awake and scared as hell, I and

263

my fellow bunker guard members could usually hear anyone coming from some distance away.

On my first tour of guard duty a new acquaintance "Gordo" showed me how to stop snoopers from sneaking around outside our bunker. When we heard someone outside approaching our position, they were never EVER very quiet, Gordo would crank a round into our M-60 machine-gun and yell out, "Are you coming in or is something coming out?" This brought the repose of, "Don't shoot, don't shoot, this is so-and so." Even in the pitch dark we could see each other smiling.

I did my eight hours of guard, and then won the drawing as the newest guy in the company's guard for that day, and so I was rewarded with another eight hours of guard duty, commencing right now. Instead of going off to breakfast and back to work I got to climb up the 100 foot guard tower and sit behind a machine-gun for most of the day. I was pooped, I had spent most of the night jittery awake, and now I had to stay alert and protect my post in a military manner. I was provided with a canteen of water and two C-Ration meals to make my stay more enjoyable, and the encouragement of all to do a good job and stay awake.

From my high perch in the guard tower I had a first-class view of most of the western facing bunker line, and a sweeping view of the country to the west. There wasn't much else to do. You couldn't bring a book or write a letter, you were on guard. So I guarded! The hours dragged I caught myself dozing off on several occasions, but I made all eight hours of tower guard without taking a false step and making that long trip down from the tower to the sudden stop at the bottom.

I finally climbed down from the guard tower at four in the afternoon, just as the next guard shift was reporting in. I had spent much of the afternoon trying to ignore the suffocating heat, and watching the dust devils playing about the camp. Other than that it had been completely uneventful. By the time I got back to my barracks and put away my gear I was dragging, and I decided to skip dinner and hit the sack early that night, I had had a very full day. I laid down and fell asleep instantly in my sweat soaked fatigues. I slept but a short while, and when I woke I still felt hot and uncomfortable, and so I got up and went to take a shower. I waddled off to the showers wearing my shower shoes and a towel. Half way to the latrine I heard someone calling, "Hey You! HEY YOU!" I looked around and for the first time I noticed that it was dark and there was no one else around. I did a 360 scan, shuffling my feet in the red dust and kicking up a small cloud, but could not see where the voice was coming from. So thinking nothing of it I walked on, and again there came, "YOU, HEY YOU!" I spun around again and still no other "Hey You" was around, only me. "Hey Stupid," I stopped once more and brought my index finger up and pointed it at my own chest. "Yeah you, come here stupid." This time I could see an arm beckoning to me from one of the company's sandbagged bunkers. I walked nonchalantly over to the waving arm; it was attached to one of the company Sergeants. As I got to within arm's length of him his hand shot out and his hand looped around my neck and I was drug in through the door of the bunker. Looking around in the dismal darkness I noticed a crowd of G.I. helmets with G.I.s under them all carrying rifles.

"What the Fuck do you think you're doing, boy?"

"Sarge, I was going to take a shower."

"Listen stupid, you don't go and take a shower during a rocket attack."

"Rocket attack!" I exclaimed.

I spent the next hour getting dirty by lounging around the inside of the bunker trying to go back to sleep while leaning my naked flesh against the bunkers leaky sandbagged wall. All the while listening to the lilting strains of "Fucking New Guy, Stupid Fucking New Guy," from my bunker companions.

Odd Jobs

My new repair job was not a bed of roses, sure there was a lot of equipment to fix, but at the same time there were other jobs that came up during the day that someone in the Army gave a higher priority for completing before anything else. Several times I was taken away from my daily repair duties and put on special details. One of these details was to off load soda pop or beer for the club from the back of a supply truck. The shop was right near the club so we were a natural first pick. Soda or beer arrived in whole pallet loads, two each to the bed of a deuce & a half truck. Whoever did the trading, requisitioning, or purchasing of the stuff we off loaded sure was one sorry son-of-a-bitch, for we off loaded some real sorry loads.

Going over to help off load the soda or beer shipment we were usually excited about what lay under the trucks tarp. And we would loudly state our preference of brand we would like to see. What new delight might be in store for us?

"I hope its Budweiser, good old bud." This hope was joined by someone else's wish.

"Yeah me too man! It's been a long time between buds."

"Hope there's some 7-UP been too long for a 7-UP."

Our hopes were usually dashed when the tail gate of the truck was dropped noisily and the canvas flap covering the rear was flipped up. There before us was some off brand something that was going to be ours all ours. It seemed that we all thought and said the exact same thing when we spied the contents of the truck. "Where did they find this shit?"

The beer that appeared in the supply trucks was a steady stream of "Carling's Black Label Beer." It would arrive with the cardboard cases of the outside pallet layer rotting and sun bleached. Some of the cans in the cases were exposed and showed various rust marks like they had been exposed to the elements for some time. The steel bands that held the whole pallet together were red with rust, and nearly fell apart in our hands.

No matter what the contents of the truck was, we drank every bit of it. We swilled it with gusto and relish. We drank it ALL!

One day I had the privilege of helping to unload a complete truck load of off brand "Grape soda." As I was handing down case after case of this stuff I asked myself, "Christ, is this all he could get?" But the troops who visited the club each night swilled it down like water; grape soda went for 5 cents a can. After 2 weeks of nothing but grape soda I gave up and went to drinking only beer, permanently. There was more variety, and it tasted one hell of a lot better.

The reward from the supply Sergeant for our off-loading efforts was a proffered FREE can of grape soda. Taken and swilled down grudgingly, after all it was ALL there was. I couldn't tell if our potbellied old supply Sergeant "Pop" was a fool or a scoundrel from what he procured for us.

As far as beer was concerned there was a never ending supply of Carling's Black Label, punctuated periodically by a pallet or two of Pabst Blue Ribbon, referred to as Fabst because of the way the Vietnamese pronounced it, or once in a great while we got a shipment of Schlitz. On Schlitz days the crowd at the bar was three deep, and we drank and drank till it was all gone. Once the Schlitz was gone the next shipment would arrive, and sure enough Carling's again.

Many years after getting out of the Army I ran into a guy who admitted to being the SP4, (Specialist 4 Class, E-4 or imitation Corporal), in charge of beverage dispersal for most of Vietnam. He was stationed in the beer and soda capital of the world, Cam Ranh Bay, for the same period of time I was in country. The reason an SP4 was in this loft position was the officer and NCOs nominally in charge had better things to do.

This ex-SP4 maintained that he gave out what he had as best he could and never got paid for special favors. At first I called him a Fucking Liar, but he must have told the truth, I would certainly have never bragged about something like that.

A Truce

The very next social event that occurred for us was the arrival of the Christmas truce, and with this event came Christmas, my second Christmas in the Army. This one was announced by all the media and formally proclaimed by military order as the great Christmas truce, with suspension of hostilities on both sides as the main attraction. During this truce I couldn't help but notice that our local cannons still boomed out their greetings day or night. I got the sinking suspicion that the newspaper, Army and radio advertised "Truce" was not all it was cracked up to be.

Because of the Christmas truce all of the civilian K.P.s and Mama-sans got a few days off, and so we G.I.s had to fend for ourselves. I ended up at my favorite military pastime K.P., and found out that things were done a little differently in Vietnam. It was primitive. There was the lack of a mechanical dishwasher, the intermittent presence of hot water, and the niceties of stateside hygiene did not deter us from our chores. I found that trying to mop a rough concrete floor with a cold mud soaked mop was very strenuous work. The floor never got clean; I just pushed the mud from one place to another. There were not too many spuds to peel in Vietnam; if there were any you did them by hand as there was no electric spud peeler, besides most of the spuds were instant. All in all I spent a good part of my time on K.P. sitting on my butt smoking and chewing the fat. This duty was nowhere near as demanding as state side K.P. and I certainly enjoyed it a lot more.

For Christmas the Mess Sergeant Grayson went out of his way to put on a clean apron and T-shirt to show how much he cared. There was a hot turkey dinner for us; instead of the usual stew or S.O.S. that he was so fond of serving. All of us trooping through the chow line were appreciative and complimentary of his efforts, the cooks and K.P.s who served it. It was nice to see such camaraderie, and such appreciation for culinary efforts in such crappy surroundings. The meal was hot and it was tasty which was a novelty for our mess Sergeant.

During the truce I was informed by the First Sergeant that I was to go on my first recon patrol after the Christmas. I looked forward to it with mixed feelings of fear and excitement.

Chapter 12

Recon

There were 12 men in all assigned to the company's recon team, a Patrol Sergeant Akron, two radiomen, two grenadiers, a machine-gunner, five rifle men, and a medic. I knew none of the other eleven patrol members by sight or by name, but they were very familiar with one another. I felt a little conspicuous meeting them for the first time. Each of us was as different from one another in personality and appearance as night was from day, but the one thing that we all had in common was that we were all volunteers.

Two days after Christmas I prepared for my first recon patrol, in the early morning hours I assembled with the other members of the patrol at their supply point, a Conex container. (A Conex was a corrugated metal shipping container, it had a hinged steel door that could be locked, and they came in various sizes, this one was 6x6x8 feet). From it I was issued one aluminum framed rucksack, one canvas bag containing 20 M-16 magazines, and 2 square plastic 2-quart water canteens, hand and smoke grenades, and other equipment. We were also issued food by the patrol Sergeant simply dumping the contents of 2 cardboard boxes onto the ground in front of the team. When it came to the selection of food there was a choice of green canned "C" Rations or of brown packets of dehydrated rations called LRRPs (Long Range Recon Patrol and pronounced LURP), rations. I was too polite, not knowing anyone, and I stood back and let the others select theirs first. This was a big mistake; I ended up with nothing but Chili Con Carne LRRPs as my rations for the next three days breakfasts, lunches and dinners. This was a really BIG mistake on my part as I could have soaked those beans in water for a week and they still would have sounded and tasted like I was eating gravel. I learned fast, and the next time I went on patrol I wasn't so polite.

Here were 12 men with very diverse tastes in what to wear out in the boonies. I sat around checking out my gear before this first patrol and watched camouflage fatigues, Tiger striped fatigues, (Tiger striped fatigues were not U.S. Army issue, but were acquired from the shops in any town in Vietnam), cut down t-shirts, and other different "Macho" attire being sported about. The most diverse part of dress was in the choice of headgear. I was stuck with my sweaty old baseball cap, but there was an assortment of floppy, wide brimmed, engineer hat called "Boonie Hats," Vietnamese versions of the same thing, U.S. Ranger cowboy hats, and a wide assortment of colors and modes of camouflage. On top of all this was how some of the troops folded, bent, and mutilated their hats to get it to look "just right."

I was relieved to find out that I wouldn't have to wear my flak vest on patrols. This armored contraption weighed over 20 pounds and was made to protect our upper torso from flying grenade or artillery fragments. Wearing this piece of hardware through the woods would have been the same as bringing a Swedish Sauna bath with me.

After I was loaded up with all I was supposed to carry I could barely stand up. In my pack I carried a poncho, blanket, food, trip flares, trip wire, a Claymore mine, Det. Cord, (detonation Cord, a plastic tube filled with explosives that would explode along its entire length when set off electrically), a 1 pound block or two of C-4 explosive, two pairs of clean

271

socks, an bag of 20 magazines of M-16 ammunition and an AN/PRC-25 (known as a Prick 25) radio. Strapped to my body and the outside of my pack were 2 two quart bottles of water, 10 magazines of ammunition in bandoliers, four hand grenades, two smoke grenades, a field dressing, a steel helmet and an M-16 rifle. The pack and equipment weighed a ton. I estimated that the pack alone weighed about half the weight of my skinny body. Whenever I took this stuff off the only way to get it back on was to lean the pack up against a tree, get into the pack straps in a sitting position and back or shimmy up the tree until I was back on my feet. Once in the erect position I had to lean slightly forward as the weight on my back made me feel like I was being pulled or falling backward.

I had carefully checked each item given to me. I filled my 2 two quart canteens, checked every M-16 magazine for a full load and made sure that the black electricians tape was secure around the pin and safety spoon of each grenade I had. Next I strapped that 20 pound monster of a radio to the rucksack frame so that the control knobs and antenna stuck out of the top of the pack for ease of access. I wrapped my extra socks around my load of trip flares, or extra batteries so they wouldn't rattle, and said I was ready. That's when the patrol Sergeant had me jump up and down with this water buffalo size of a pack on my back, and then I went back and repacked everything because everything rattled.

For personal hygiene I followed the suggestion of my Sergeant and I carried two tooth brushes, one in each boot. I slid the tooth brushes down the top of my jungle boots for easy access. The left one for my teeth and right one for my rifle, but what the hell, after two days in the bush they both tasted the same.

After packing our back packs with all that they could possibly carry we got to go and play around while wearing them. This was for training purposes, and whether it was for a new guy or a refresher course for the old hands we spent the next hour doing nothing but reaction drills. Fully loaded we simulated a patrol. We learned our interval between each of us, and how to maintain it. "Don't bunch up. One round could get you all," was the old saying. We practiced what to do in any given emergency situation. Ambush, being shot at, running into an enemy on a trail, Sergeant Akron tried to put us through as many situations as time would permit. I learned my place as a radio man, and what I was supposed to do in each situation. Drills over tired and sweaty we loaded up the truck for the trip to the boonies and the real thing.

On my first patrol I found out that teeth were only brushed dry while on patrols, or only brushed with water no tooth paste was used. If you brushed your teeth the regular way the enemy could spot the white tooth paste blotches on the ground where they had been spat out, and by following the blotches from place to place the enemy could possibly predict your route or destination. Surprise to me I never thought that the enemy might have their own recon patrols out looking for us. This was a very rude awakening there.

The medic arrived from a medical company somewhere on the base camp, and most of the patrol knew him by name. They called him "Speed" because he always ended up lagging behind. He wore a strange get up. A parachute pack of medical supplies strapped to his chest, and still he carried a rucksack for his other needs on his back along with an M-16 rifle. That's right our medic went armed, at first glance it made me thing that something might be up. This seemed more eccentric than what I had seen so far. In general the equipment carried by our recon team was not extravagant, but reduced to only the essentials we could carry on your backs. The extras we carried were two 15 foot whip antennas, survival axes, 50 feet or more of rope, extra radio batteries, and machine gun ammunition if we were bringing along an M60 machine gun. These extra loads were shared out by the entire team. But this medic's parachute pack of medicines was something he was going to have to hump all by himself; I wondered how he would lie down in a fight, probably on his side.

Once we were assembled and packed ready to go, the usual routine was to take us out somewhere and leave us. We were trucked out about 20 or 30 kilometers from Camp Enari, always to the south, on highway QL 14, toward the Ia Drang valley, to a starting point and dropped off. We were usually deposited by our convoy at an off road location, after we left QL14. Usually the side of a hill or on the top of one of the numerous brown, grass covered hills.

The area around camp Enari was rolling grass hills that were burned brown during the dry season by the sunshine, or burned brown by defoliation efforts any other time of the year. There terrain was not all bare ground there were small groves of trees on some hills, and larger forests of trees and bushes covering many of the valleys of the country. Several Vietnamese villages were scattered along the main road, but the majority of the area was mostly inhabited by Montagnards. The Montagnard villages were larger, better organized and more frequently encountered in the wilds of the area. Because of the Montagnard habitation of the area it was not unusual to find terraced fields of rice running through some of the valleys. Other times we encountered groves of cultivated fruit trees on hills, and plowed fields for ground crops were found almost anywhere. Depending on the time of year the rice paddies could be flooded and planed with a crop or dormant and dry, but any fruit trees we encountered were always flourishing. In many of the plowed fields we came across out in the middle of nowhere were small bamboo traps, bamboo bows strung with wire or string, used for trapping birds or small animals, to the Montagnards food was where you found it. I never knew or found out if these cultivated areas were friendly or enemy we just came upon them marked them on the map and moved on. This was the same type of country I had seen flying into Pleiku, and the same rolling hills continued further south through much of the central highlands.

The pace of patrolling through the bush was murderous, hauling 60 or so pounds on your back, of food and other essentials up hill and down dale in circumstances of extreme danger is hard work. For my own part I really enjoyed the physical exertion, as it challenged me to keep up with those with more experience. At the same time I was learning a new trade, that of the infantry soldier, and that of the radio operator.

I was told that the other members of the patrol were not prone to carry anyone along who could not pull his own weight, and some of them were quite vocally brutal about it. There were murmured comments and expletives about F.N.G.s sent in my direction, some were of a playful nature, while others were aimed at provoking a reaction. These other members of the patrol wanted to see what I was made of before they offered any advice, encouragement, or acceptance. Dumb Asses, Pussys, Cry Babies were not welcome on patrols, neither were Mama's Boys, Wimps. If you measured up you were slowly initiated into their small select group of fellow volunteers. To the group's way of thinking this sort of selection process was not cruel, not harsh, but it was necessary.

At first I was very naive about life in the Vietnamese bush, especially on my first patrol, and my new comrades let me make some real bone head mistakes with my field gear. I am sure that they let me make them for their own entertainment. The biggest mistake I made was to tie my steel helmet to the top of my packs aluminum frame by its chin strap. This was a painfully bad mistake to make, every time I hitched my pack up onto my shoulders the 2 and ½ pound helmet swung around the side of the pack and banged into the side of my head with a very painful clunk. The first and last time I hitched my pack up more violently the helmet swung over the top of the pack and clunked me more painfully on the back of the head. I was sure that I saw stars when I tried this move. After two or three vicious thumps on the head I found a new and less noisy way of tying my helmet to my pack.

From this experience of being knocked on the head, I learned that one of the most important tools a soldier could take along was extra boot laces. This is what you used to tie down any "loose" gear you had attached to your pack; you also tied laces around your legs just below your pants large cargo pockets so they wouldn't sag below your knees when loaded.

This was the central highlands a hundred miles from the coast but the heat of the highlands still bore down on me like I was back in that oppressive heat and humidity of the coast. This was a burden bigger than my back pack. Sweat streamed off of me in small rivers, soaking my fatigues, underwear, and my socks and boots. Before the first day was through I had removed my underwear, and never wore them on patrol again, preferring the breeziness of life au-natural. Truly Commando style! This was much more preferable than being sawed in two from the groin upward by sweat soaked drawers, (officially known as drawers, men's O.D. in Color), and to being chaffed raw by the sweat soaked elastic waist band. I swore off wearing my G.I. issue underwear after this first patrol, the only times I put it on was when I knew I was going on guard at the top of Dragon Mountain and I knew there I would need the warmth.

An O.D. Green G.I. towel draped around the neck and under the shoulder straps of the pack helped to ease the cutting effect of the pack straps on the shoulders. Also it served as a handy sponge for some of the perspiration being generated.

Up and down hills we trudge, sometimes on trails sometimes not, down valleys and across streams we traveled. We moved through various kinds of vegetation. On some hills it was grasslands with the occasional broccoli shaped tree scattered about, and the going was easy. Here you were easy to spot, so we moved fast and got into the trees as soon as possible. On other hills we walked through woods, and had to pick our way through the undergrowth, trying to make as little noise as possible. This was a dangerous time because you couldn't see more than a few feet. Then there were huge bamboo groves, and probing through these areas was like walking by a fence and trying to see through the cracks, these were dense forests of hundreds of bamboo stalks. These bamboo groves could be 60 or more feet in height, and the grove would give off clacking or creaking sounds by the bamboo being moved around by the upper breezes. The woods and the bamboo groves would be interspersed by patches of tall grass and weeds, some as tall as a man, but mostly the grass had been burned down to brown stubble. The hardest most dangerous going of all was in the valleys, here we struggled and staggered through a jungle, triple canopy in a lot of places, of bamboo and vines growing up around the trees. The light of day was shut out from most of the under growth in the floors of the valleys, and the going was dank with a heavy stench of rotting vegetation. No breezes penetrated the valley floors through the tangle of tree limbs above, so the air below seemed stagnant, and was very heavy to breath. The jungle canopy though giving us shade did not keep the heat out, it kept it in soaking every part of your jungle fatigues with your own perspiration. Here in the valleys we could see no more than a few feet, and the possibility of ambush was most severe. This increased our alertness, our avoidance of making noise, and to our perspiration. Through these types of terrain we walked 20 to 30 kilometers in two days, always on the alert, constantly aware of our surroundings. From my exposure so far, Vietnam was the strangest collection of plants, bugs, people and animals God could have assembled in one place. I moved through this country scrambling to keep up behind my patrol leader, trying to keep my balance with an ear glued to the hand set of the radio to listen for any messages coming through was a serious challenge. For someone of average agility I wasn't doing too bad, one hand on the radio hand set and the other on my rifle pistol grip, keeping my footing was as difficult as walking a tight rope stretched over a deep defile.

The maneuvers with the radio were a ridged routine. On clear or hilly terrain use the short antenna. Bend it left over your shoulder so that you can grab it going through trees and bushes and you won't get hung up. Go down into a valley and put on the 15 foot whip antenna, this one you had to keep letting out to its full height and then retract every few seconds. Then hopefully you didn't miss any message traffic. Walking around with that whip antenna strapped on you sure felt like a conspicuous target. Indeed you were a target, a BIG target. It was explained to me that the enemy liked to target radio men. Knock out the radio guy and the rest can't call for help. This little bit of knowledge made my day when I found it out; maybe this is why they were needing "replacement radio men?"

This was a man's job and it required a man to do it. Hollywood movies made it all look so simple, but a Hollywood movie barely lasted 90 minutes. Humping a back pack in the boonies was an all day and an all-night job. It was the toughest thing I had ever taken on. So much to learn and learn right in a very short span of time, and so much physical strength required to do the job. I was discovering that these guys I was with had legs of iron, and I had better get them too and fast.

Rivers and Streams

Of all the terrain we covered rivers and streams were the worst, here was real danger, and is the reason the patrol carried 50 feet of rope. Plus whether they were wide or narrow, shallow or deep they were a bitch to cross. You were vulnerable at all times, the only time you were safe was when all of the patrol was on either one side or the other. The water could be no wider than a foot or two but they could be waist deep or deeper to cross, or they could be a rushing torrent many feet wide and only a foot deep. The water would be ice cold compared to the air temperature, and that brief instance of immersion would all but take your breath away. After this initial rush you could relax and enjoy the feeling of cooling off for a few minutes. You were going to get wet no matter what happened, sometimes all of you sometimes just part. You crossed the water one at a time, while the rest covered you from both banks. The degree of wetness you suffered depending on the depth of the water, its swiftness and your own personal agility. These determined whether you took a whole bath or half a bath. It didn't matter about getting wet; it was keeping that radio dry and your weapon dry that was important. Getting the rest of you wet didn't matter, a dry radio that was important. Get across and the first thing to do was pull back on the bolt of your M-16 to make sure there was no water down the barrel, next you made a muffled voice commo check on your radio. Your Army jungle fatigues would dry in minutes while you walked around in them, but your boots or boots and socks if you wore socks, sometimes didn't dry for days. All these experiences would occur with an intense pressure on you for security, security, security. It would be tough to find cover waist deep in a stream, and it would be just as tough to cover your buddies while they waded through. River crossings scarred the hell out of me, not for the fact that you got wet, but because you were so out in the open and vulnerable.

Rest breaks were a welcome respite from the pack and its biting shoulder straps, taking it off for a few minutes left you with a feeling of relief, I was floating on air. At a rest break I learned to try and accomplish three things. Water was the first need on any break, and I consumed large amounts washing down several salt pills. The consumption of food and water never seem to reduce the weight of my pack, and putting my rucksack back on after a break was always a challenge. I could never stand erect, grab the pack by its straps and swing it up and onto my back. The first time I tried this I ended up down on the ground in the weeds six feet from where I had started. This is when I perfected my backwards shimmy up a tree routine to get my pack back on. After water, and if I had time I would check my rifle by extracting the round in the chamber and making sure I hadn't clogged the barrel with dirt in my struggles up and down hills. After my rifle I changed my sweat or river soaked socks and hung the wet ones on my pack straps to dry. This was depending on how wet my spare socks had gotten, if I had taken a bath in crossing, made a difference in if I changed socks or not. Removing wet socks after two and a half days in the woods I would find bits skin stuck to the sock.

Water

Water was the one commodity that you couldn't carry enough of. I carried two 2 quart water bags attached to my rucksack, and that was never enough. After two days hiking and sweating all of us were carrying canteens that were either very low or completely empty. To replenish our supply we had to forage for fresh water in one of the valleys. The patrol Sergeant using his map would direct us to a source of water, (a blue line), which was usually deep under triple canopy jungle. We would all climb down and when the stream was found one or two of us would climb into the stream while the rest of us formed a perimeter around them. A two or three foot length of green bamboo was cut and used as a hose. One end being inserted into the running water and the canteens filled from the flow out of the other. Our canteens were handed in and out by the water party until they were all filled. Purple Halazone water purification pills were dropped in each bag or canteen which gave the water a bitter taste like Iodine, but it was better that than the possibility of getting dysentery from drinking contaminated water. The only thing that helped the tasted of the purified water was to dump in a little Cool Aide, if you had any Cool Aide. They didn't sell Cool Aide in the P.X. someone had to send it to you from home.

A Nutritious Snack

On my first patrol, when I experienced LRRP rations for the first time, I also discovered the first humanly inedible morsel that I had encountered in the Army. It was a little brick of compressed cornflakes; this caramel colored delight was the Army's idea for a nutritious candy bar. This item of food was to be the one and only thing that you couldn't give to a Vietnamese kid, if you tried they would throw it to the ground and spit on it, and you, if you hung around. Plus you would be heaped with abuse, in Vietnamese and broken English, by the kid and all the other kids around. If you tried to toss it out of a passing truck to a group of kids, it was likely to be tossed back along with a hand grenade. My first taste of a corn flake bar convinced me that I never needed to taste another one, and I never did, besides tasting rotten it was very hard on your dental work.

Silence

When humping in the boonies there was not a great deal of words spoken between any members of the patrol. Silence was a way of life out in the wild; no one went on a patrol with loose metal objects on them or a transistor radio. No one called out to their buddies to get their attention, hand signals were given to indicate what was needed, and when signals were given you had better keep your wits about you. These hand signals were rudimentary, but they got the message across. If you misunderstood a signal or didn't pay attention as I later saw a couple of individuals do, the signaler, who usually was the patrol Sergeant in these instances, grabbed the person not paying attention by the pack straps and silently shook the individual or drug them to do what was wanted done. The patrol Sergeant did this while silently pounding a finger into that individual's chest.

I did all right on this first patrol, I kept up, I didn't screw anything up but I didn't make any new friends. I did become familiar with a lot of new faces and a lot of strange names. But at the same time no shots were fired in anger, and no one was injured or killed. I did get invited to come back and go on the next patrol, so I at least hadn't done anything to piss anyone off. On this initial time out in the woods I had discovered a few things about myself. I could clamber up a near vertical slope with a monster rucksack dragging on my ass and with a rifle in one hand at the same time. Through fear of screwing up royally, the enemy, other members of the patrol and the unknown I could stay awake at night for my two hour turn at guard. This was remarkable especially after hauling my tired body around the woods for 14 hours. I also discovered I was tougher than I thought I was, and that it wasn't too hard to be a radio man under trying conditions.

Back to Work

So with my first patrol under my belt we were trucked back to Camp Enari from our rendezvous point. This was on the third morning I had been away, and once back at the 278th life continued as normal. Getting off the truck I was greeted by Sergeant Threctour, the guy in charge of the repair shop I was given an hour to put my gear away, get a shower, a change of clothes, and get to work. The normal routine for patrol members was, after each patrol we were taken back to Camp Enari and given the afternoon off, but things were still stacked up at the repair shop, and as he said, "I had had enough fun for one day."

The normal patrol activity was three days out and two days in, but the two in camp were spent as normal work days. Work days included guard duty and K.P., and extra work that I had missed by being off playing in the woods. It was the first time in my military adventure that I accepted all this without grumbling.

It was now the "New Year's Truce" and once again we were to take a break and leave the bad guys alone.

Coming back after my first patrol I found myself assigned to guard duty for New Year's Eve. Being on guard duty on New Year's Eve was depressing enough for me. It wasn't that I had been invited to a party, or had something more exciting to do. I wanted to see what went on in the base camp and maybe participate a bit. To add insult to injury, word was passed down the bunker line that anyone firing off a weapon at mid-night would be court-martialed. This made us all ecstatic. "Now what are we to do with all those parachute flares we hauled to the bunker?" Was my question! Mid-night rolled around and the entire base camp erupted in loud yelling cacophony accompanied by gun fire, tracer bullets, red and NVA green arched into the black night, artillery and mortars boomed out their welcome, flares arced out form the camp, and all other types of military pyrotechnics were set off. All the yelling and firing came from inside the base camp's bunker line, the bunker line sat in silence. All of us in the bunkers watched the show for a short while, it was very gay and colorful, and then sadly turned back around and did our duty. In the morning I and my bunker buddies made several trips between bunker and barracks, hauling back all the flares and military pyrotechnics that we had taken to the bunker in anticipation of letting off our own fireworks display.

Back on Patrol

I went back on patrol after the New Year's Truce ended and being aware of what was out there and what the routine was I found life out in the woods not as difficult as it was on that first trip. The first trip all we had done was hump around the boonies and look around. This I discovered was the true essence of reconnaissance. By our patrolling, and the patrolling by the other U.S. units we kept the enemy from using the areas close to Camp Enari. We were Camp Enari's early warning system. Wow! This was heady stuff to think about. We were not out in the woods to fight the enemy but to deny the enemy the use of the territory. The fighting was to be done by the 4th Division and its units. We were to find people for them to fight. I felt like a cog in a big wheel when this was explained to me by Sergeant Akron. I had a whole new purpose. I was now an RTO, (Radio Telephone Operator), with a mission; I was helping to spot the enemy. For me each trip I made outside the perimeter wire of Camp Enari was a learning experience, and after each trip I felt that still I had a long way to go and much more to learn. Patrolling had a wide and varied number of tasks that we were to perform during any one patrol, and it took

283

ueveral trips to the woods to become any way near proficient in accomplishing what and when to do what was needed done.

On some patrols we were required to search the abandoned villages we came across. Abandoned villages were usually sites with little or nothing left of the living structures, (hootches). Either from decay or the need for building materials in the neighboring villages, the buildings had completely disappeared. What remained were the banana trees in over grown gardens, and the bare ground of the hootch sites. Each home in a village would normally have an underground shelter to hide the inhabitants in time of danger, and along with enemy activity these hiding places were what we were to search for and destroy.

Spider holes, caves, bunkers, covered pits, or holes in the ground, they all had to be found, explored and then destroyed. When we found a hole in the ground one of us had to go in and investigate it. Patrol Sergeant Akron kept a revolving roster for this hazardous duty and we all took turns. You would be inserted into the entrance head first up to your hips, holding a flash light in one hand, a .45 automatic pistol in the other. When it was my turn to be put down the hole I went into the darkness head first, like everyone else. Praying and holding my breath was the usual way I was put down one of these holes. You were inserted in this way by a patrol member holding on to each of your legs, to give them leverage for keeping you from falling into further into the deeper holes, or to pull you out in case of trouble.

You were never sure what you would meet down there, strange animals, the enemy, a family hiding out, anything. Entering these holes was the most dangerous part, for some of the older, longer abandoned, shelters had been taken over by insects and other critters. Several times I watched men being put into the hole, and within one or two thousandths of a second of insertion the body would go completely ridged, and next the legs would start churning, pulling and pushing those hanging on all over the place. A muffled "PULLMEUP! PULLMEUP!"

could be heard, while those above ground struggled to extract what was attached to the squirming legs. It was like pulling a cork out of a bottle.

Spiders, snakes, and other animals shocked us all at one time or another, but if nothing was in there waiting for you, you went deeper. A real nasty trick of the enemy was to hang "Two Step" snakes, Bamboo Vipers, by their tails from the roof of the bunker. If you didn't check the roof they would be biting you on the back when you went in. Other times there might be Punji stakes hidden inside. The Vietnamese or Montagnards were ingenious in their construction of their hiding holes. Two or three room underground homes were not unusual, and logs, sandbags and steel engineer stakes were sometimes used in the construction. After admiring the construction effort in building the hole you often wondered, "Where do the find this stuff?" What we were looking for most was hidden enemy or weapons. Each hole had to be searched and then destroyed by explosives. A well placed block of C-4 explosive would usually blow them in, but if the number to be dealt with was too large or for the really large bunkers. We would call base camp to have more explosive delivered or to have some engineers join us.

Guys were put into the holes head first so that they could defend themselves if someone happened to be down there. Tricks of the trade like this had been learned the hard way by other troops, and we certainly made use of their knowledge. If there was a Vietnam primer on "Do it yourself" techniques to use in exploring holes, tunnels etc. It was never known to me, I was just happy that I wasn't one of the guinea pigs that developed the methods we followed. For me a G.I. flashlight could never shine bright enough for me when I went down. I wanted a lot more illumination than the light than I was getting out of a couple of "D" cell batteries.

No one refused when it came to their turn to be stuck down the hole, we all took the same chances. Reluctantly, but we took them. There was never any argument about whose turn it was the Sergeant Akron kept the roster, and your turn was your turn. It took a lot of courage to stick your head into the dark unknown.

Finding, exploring and destroying holes in the ground were a regular part of our patrol duties, and no matter how many times we covered the same real estate we always found more holes. Exploring the unknown was never dull or routine to any of us, but this is what we had all volunteered for. We were recon and we were proud to be able to say that we had accomplished our missions.

Fortunes of War

I was finally getting to know some of the guys I patrolled with. At base camp meals or on guard together we had that chance to talk that was not allowed out in the bush. Other times, while out on patrol some of them handed me items or silently swapped food or gave me pat or an arm squeeze, but they were letting know that they were human. There was "Neon" a short, compact, cocky kid from Ohio who alternately humped an M-79 grenade launcher or the M-60 machine-gun. He had a case of some mysterious clap that he was trying to hide from the medics back at base camp. He was hiding because if they found you with this type of infection they kept you in hospital until it was cured. Neon wanted to make it home; he had 60 days to go.

There were all kinds of rumors about the clap in Vietnam, but one of the most frequently told was of those with the incurable cases of the clap or syphilis. There was supposed to be a boat load of G.I.s with incurable social diseases sailing the South China Sea. They were to remain out there until they died or were cured. Needless to say, we troops were weary of reporting the wrong kind of social contact that resulted in some form of Gonorrhea, especially a dose that had weird symptoms. The symptoms were not the real worry; it was the Article 15 and the fine they gave you for getting a dose of the Clap that you wanted to avoid. Getting a case of the clap was supposed

286

to the crime of "destruction of government property." I often wondered how they figured that one out.

Of the other members there was "Kingpin," a hard ass from Ohio, who didn't say much, except when you screwed up, and then he let you know about it. He was a pole lineman by military trade. "Dingus," a quiet kid, again from Ohio, and was the "B" team radio man. His job back on base was with the transmitters. Wally, also known as "Blondie" for his mop of blonde hair, worked in the communication section. "Chico", a Mexican American form Nevada, who's fondest dream was to make the recon team on a permanent basis so he could get off the K.P. roster. An Ohio transplant "Howdy" who was now an ex-beach bum from LA, also from the communication section. We had "Keyman," another kid from Ohio. There were others, like "The Mummy" who only went out every third or fourth patrol because their job back at base would not allow them to be gone too long. All of the guys had names I could read stenciled on their shirts, over their right shirt pocket; this was not always the name that they went by. More often than not the proper mode of address was to use their nickname, like "Speed" the medic or "Blondie" almost everyone went by another name than they're own. Mine was F.N.G. for the present. They weren't written anywhere you just had to remember them.

On patrol, not all of our jobs were searching for the enemy or enemy activity. Occasionally we would be called on to sit in place and relay messages from other recon assets that were too far out of base, or in too hilly an area to be heard back at base camp. We would sit on top of a hill and relay word for word what was said by the recon unit to base and visa-versa. On other occasions we discover things, like large caves, on our searches that would get others involved. Or we would get a call from base that would instruct us to wait and observe something coming our way. This was the real work for Recon, observing and reporting. No matter the task, whether it was people moving in the area, which more often than not were

Montagnards walking around, or some other patrol in trouble. We had to be ready to respond to a variety of circumstances.

On some of these instances we waited hidden in the bushes for whatever was happening to happen. Being on the radio I was party to the instructions that came through. The other members were completely in the dark and only got instructions on what Sergeant Akron wanted done. I or Dingus would be parked behind the Sergeant keeping the channel open just sitting and listening to a one-sided conversation.

Getting Help from Home Base

Sergeant Akron was busy one afternoon calling in artillery on suspected enemy troop movements nearby. The rest of the patrol formed a circular perimeter around us, while I sat like dog on a leash. The Radio on my back made me the dog, and a cord, (the leash), from there leading to the radio handset at the Sergeant's ear. Sergeant Akron using map and plastic template adjusted the artillery fire to precise locations. All at once the artillery fire erupted on the hill top across from ours. The crash of the incoming rounds was sharp and the yellow, red and black flower like eruptions of the rounds could be seen plainly. I looked at Sergeant Akron with a question on my face. As soon as the rounds had started coming in they stopped, without Akron having to say anything into the handset. The artillery started falling again two hills to the south of the first. Sergeant Akron looked at me and shrugged, "ARVNs" is all he said. "ARVNs" I repeated. "Yeah, doing artillery adjustment with the US Army is not bad, but doing this with ARVN artillery has some real potential danger to it." Apparently their math wasn't as good as our math, and occasionally (let's say most frequently) a few artillery rounds would go astray. Astray being, somewhere behind you, somewhat near you, and the ever popular around you, etc. So the word was if it was an ARVN fire mission either give them coordinates near Timbuktu or get the hell out of the area.

On the radio you got to listen to some very strange things going on around you. The radio frequencies that we used were also used by other people, and a lot of the other people did not speak English. People speaking what I assumed to be Vietnamese would come blasting through the airwaves, taking over the frequency for quite some time. Minutes would go by when all I could hear in my handset was something like, "Gleep Gleep Gleep unintelligible words, words, words, words." This made me wonder just whose side they were on, and if they were not on our side, did they know our location? The people speaking in this foreign language could be so loud that it was like they were right next to you yelling in your ear. This left very little choice in communications. Yelling at them to get off the net was not allowed. Neither was asking them, besides they probably didn't speak your language. You either had to wait till they finished or try the back-up frequency, but chances are they would be there too.

Point Man Gets O.J.T.

Up until this point artillery was the only form of combat action I had seen, both theirs and ours. I now had five or six patrols under my belt, and was ready to try some new and different things. There were two new people coming on patrol with us so Sergeant Akron gave me a break from schlepping the radio, and asked me if I'd like to try point. I said sure, I was feeling rather salty with all the new experience and knowledge I was getting I could do anything. So I got a quick five minute indoctrination on what was involved from a current point man and I figured I was good to go.

Point man was a rush, it was exciting, almost a continuous adrenaline high, trotting ahead of the group instead of plodding along with the group.

On my first try at point we were off and once on the move we picked up a well-used trail and decided to follow it for a while. Trails were tricky; there were booby traps to look out for. I was walking rapidly down a lane parallel to the trail, the trail passed into a small grove of trees. I turned a sharp corner to follow the trail, and ran smack into a giant Boa Constrictor hanging down from a tree. I hit the snake with my chest and a huge watermelon size head turned toward me, and a three foot long forked tongue licked at me. In a fraction of a second someone right beside my ear screamed, and I jumped at the same time, at least six feet in the air, backwards, and I emptied the contents of my M-16 magazine into the surrounding trees and bushes before I hit the ground. From my vantage point, on my back on the side of the trail the snake was trying to eat me whole. My shaking and fumbling fingers were trying to prevent this by reloading and firing my rifle as fast as I could. I emptied two more magazines in the direction of the snake before help arrived.

The others had gone for cover at the first sounds of gun fire and the scream, and some of them had moved forward to see what was going on. When they caught up to me, I was still sitting off the trail, and had just finishing shakily removing the third magazine from my rifle and was fumbling for another in the bandolier tied around my waist.

"Lennox, are you OK?"

"The first man there pumped a magazine from his own rifle in the direction I was firing. I didn't know who it was.

"Lennox take it easy man, what happened?"

"S-S-S-S-SNA-S-S," was all they got out of me.

I stopped fiddling with my rifle as the rest of the patrol came up and someone went and explained to Sergeant Akron what had happened.

The snake was a butchered mess of red flesh and scaly skin hanging limply from an over- head tree limb. I was told that the estimated length was between 12 and 18 feet long. The reason for the estimate was because the snake was missing certain parts, like its head, after being chewed up by the mass of lead I was putting out at close range. There were little bits of snake meat all over the place.

The snake was a mess, my pants were a mess and my nerves were a mess. The snake I had met had screwed up my entire day, and I had really screwed up the snake's. I was absolutely useless for the next two days, but most of all right then I needed a change of pants. I was so shaken up by this encounter that Sergeant Akron seriously thought about sending me back to base camp on a re-supply or Med. Evac. Helicopter, but I lasted the rest of the patrol as far from the point position as I could get. Drinking anything from a metal canteen cup was risky for the next several days, because of the risk of chipping my teeth with my trembling hands.

After this particular patrol there were several nicknames considered for me. In Germany and Fort Riley I had acquired the name "McNasty", due to my perceived sharp wit and a tendency to let people know it. After the snake incident several new names were tried on me for size, obviously "Snake" was the first, and that was followed by "Headless" "shaky" and "Rock and Roll." The later name for the way I had dispatched the snake, using full automatic on my M-16. However, "Snake Killer," or other manly names were not mentioned, and thank goodness "Pant Shitter" or "Nasty Pants" were never thought of. One other nickname was given to me by one of the grenadiers from the patrol, and that was "Scotty."

Of all the nicknames that were tried the only nickname that stuck on me was "Scotty." I was called that either because of my ancestry or as an add-on to the Fort Riley "McNasty" moniker to produce Scotty McNasty. For whatever reason, once the name was applied it stuck. Even after the snake story had got around the 278th, the story didn't change the name chosen for me, I was known as either "Scotty" or "Scotty McNasty," and to members of that outfit I will be known by that name for the rest of my life.

Snakes of All Kinds

Snakes were not uncommon in Vietnam, and the following statement is how we had been warned in pre Vietnam training all the way back in Fort Riley. As the Sergeant Instructor told it, "There are 100 types of snakes in Vietnam, and 99 of them are deadly poisonous. The other one is not poisonous it will simply crush you to death." Actually Vietnam had 140 varieties of snakes and only 37 of those were deadly, but that was more than enough deadly ones to go around. The one I had run into was the one that would CRUSH me to death.

On patrols we had at times seen snakes or seen traces of them. Creepy shed skins of various lengths, and snake crawl or slither marks on the ground, and at night you always wondered just who or what you might wake up with in the morning. On my first patrol while walking through a lengthy stretch of knee high grass a very familiar head reared its self 20 meters in front of our patrol leader. I spied this shape from my position right behind Sergeant Akron as his faithful R.T.O. It was the head of a Cobra, (Don't ask me what kind. It was a Cobra, and one looks just as deadly as the next), and the worst part was that the head stood at least half a meter taller than the grass. If this was not disturbing enough as a second head appeared right beside the first head. The whole patrol, every man of us, stopped dead in our tracks, and we stood all wondering how many more are there. Rifles were raised, and I had mine on a shakey bead on the lead deadly. Without a word Sergeant Akron raised his right arm and pointed in a 90 degree direction, and we silently went the way opposite of the snakes.

Then there was the fabled "Two Step" snake, the most deadly of them all. As it was told to me the "Two Step" snake was as big as a number 2 pencil, light green in color and had a 2 inch in diameter head. This description did not indicate any form of deadly reptile to me, but the rumor was that if this thing bit you you were dead within two steps. A chilling description if there ever was one. What was being described was the

Bamboo Viper, and it was deadly, but only if it bit you 47 times. We ran into this little green bugger when walking through bamboo groves, or entering some underground bunkers. The snake would be inside the bunkers hanging by their tails from the roofs. In the bunkers they were put there by our hospitable opponents to give us a nice warm welcome. This Bamboo Viper was small, and it was poisonous, but it would usually discharge its venom into your loose fitting clothes if you got to close. In a bamboo grove they were nearly invisible, and so moving through bamboo was a slow methodical process. Not because of the snakes but because of the noise from the dry leaves and bamboo, and then there was also the snakes.

A Reminder of Home

After the snake incident I took the next two patrols off to get my sanity back, plus to catch up on the mountain of equipment that still resided in the repair shop. One of the repairs required some wire, and in the signal corps that stuff is everywhere. However, I could not find any in the supply room. In search of some wire I went hunting for a small quantity of wire in the junk that littered the fields and buildings around the shop. In my wanderings around the junk yard like area behind the shop I discovered a long forgotten item lying under a heap of scrap lumber. It was something I had not seen for many months. It was of all things, that wonderful invention of Thomas A. Crapper, a genuine flush toilet. It had been dumped for obvious reasons; there were no plumbing in our Part of Vietnam or any other flush toilets at Camp Enari, unless they were in the general's trailer. I pulled this treasure from its hiding place and mounted it over a drainage ditch by cutting a hole in an abandoned wooden pallet I had also found. To finish the job I mounted a sign on it. "Cambodian Flush Toilet, Monsoon season only." In Vietnam entertainment was where you found it.

Necessities of Life

I found that there were many lessons for me to learn from patrolling. It had taken me several patrols to become accustomed to the physical hardship of the job, but the hiking, the heat and the pack straps never got to be easy. The way to tough it out and endure was a matter of applying my Basic Training, and following directions of my patrol Sergeant and other seasoned patrol members to the letter. One of the first lessons I learned was that "C" Rations or LRRP rations needed some help and improvement in the taste department. I began carrying a bottle of Tabasco sauce in my pack and I would exchange shots of it with others who carried ketchup or steak sauce. Your meals or personal comfort were only restricted by how much extra weight you were willing to strap on your back.

Being on patrol and getting used to life at base camp as well as in the woods I realized that there were three things needed by any G.I. to get along well in Vietnam, and all three were not hot meals. First was a P-38 C-Ration can opener. Several were supplied with each case of Cs. Nearly every G.I. had a P-38 hanging around his neck on his dog-tag chain. Either that or they had it on a key ring, in a wallet, or in a pocket. You didn't leave home without it. Those "C" Rations cans were tough and they didn't open themselves.

The Second thing needed was a spoon. The most common type was the white plastic spoon found inside individual C-Ration meals. These were most common because there were never very many spoons to be found anywhere, even in an Army mess hall, they were never available in the supply dumps, knives and forks were plentiful but not spoons. Rumor had it that the Vietnamese K.P.s would take them home with them and were using them to tunnel back onto our base. If you look in any photo album from a G.I. who spent time in Vietnam you would find photos with the white C-Ration spoon in evidence. Hundreds of G.I.s have had their photograph taken in Vietnam displaying the little white spoons sticking out of their top fatigue shirt pockets.

The third item that a G.I. needed was a church key bottle/can opener. Why? Because the Army did not supply beer or soda pop in the civilian style easy open pop-top cans. We got the good old heavy duty steel ones. So if you were looking to quench a thirst you had better be prepared to open your own can the hard way. Sitting out on the bunker line at night with a warm case of good old Carling's Black Label beer, you had better have what it took to get at it before it became much warmer. Because your buddies weren't going to play bar tender for you, and a church key wasn't supplied WITH the beer.

Incoming Friendly Fire

On patrol I became used to the physical hardship, the constant vigilance, the sweat and strain, but what I didn't become used to was being on the business end of our own Artillery. When we were humping through the boonies or lying out at night we heard, heard and felt, or heard felt and saw our own artillery rounds land. If you just heard it, the sound was a "W-whuummp" somewhere in the distance, if you heard it and felt it, then it was a louder "W-WHUUUUMMMPP" and a vibration was felt through the earth under your feet. When you heard, felt and saw it the "W-WHHUUUUMMMMMPPPP" was right next door and you could see the red and black flash of the explosion, and the earth would rock violently. The artillery fired H & I, (Harassment and Interdiction), fire to preselected targets around the countryside. The artillery planers were trying to catch the enemy in the open or along known trails as he moved around. The artillery supposedly knew our current location, but when we heard, felt and saw artillery land we became nervous and where not exactly sure about the artillery's intentions. The shock of living with outgoing artillery rounds buck ut base camp was no way near as violent as living with the incoming rounds out in the woods.

Defoliation

The countryside we patrolled through was the weirdest collection of plants, animals and people that God could have put in one place. Some of it looked same from hill side to hill side, valley floor to valley floor. What stood out about the vegetation was the shortness of most of the grass we walked through. There were some stands of six to eight foot Elephant Grass, but the majority of it was three and four inch stubble. It looked like it had been mowed. There were areas where the ground beneath my feet was completely bare of any growth, and in these places the ground was blackened from fire. The fire I witnessed for myself some time later. On a later patrol while we lay in the grass eating our noon meal I noticed an Army single engine plane swooping low over and adjacent ridge line and dive into the valley beyond. After two or three twists, turns and dives over the same spot the plane pulled up and headed away from us, it was being followed by a huge sheet of red and yellow flames licking at its tail and an expanding cloud of black smoke. The plane, it turned out, had been dropping incendiaries to start the fire, to burn off the grass, and leaving the enemy with very little foliage to hide in. Seeing the flames coming our way we saddled up and put a couple of blue lines between us and the fire.

A Night to Remember

At night we camped in at pre-selected map locations either as part of a planned ambush, or trail watch plan, or as part of our patrol routine, and this gave base camp a known map reference point should we need help. The twelve patrol members would form an all-around perimeter at the night location and place our Claymore mines and trip flares at points advantageous to our defense. A radio watch was kept all night long to monitor radio traffic to and from base camp, but also for our own protection. The radio watch was also responsible to guard us all from intrusions at night. So one of us was awake at all times.

On one night we were just camping out in the grass lands when we got a call from base camp over our radio. The Army's ground surveillance radar site at Camp Enari had picked up something moving on the side of the hill we were on. (To us this was very unusual; being technicians we knew that the Army's ground surveillance radar, one of the wonders of the universe, wasn't that accurate at the distance we were away from the base camp). We were all alerted to the danger, and sure enough we became aware of noises of movement around us. I waited lying on the bare ground, fully awake while my stomach tied itself in knots, what could it be? I was tense and scared as I lay there in silence. Alone but not alone there were 11 more scared individuals close by. I scanned my area of responsibility, the area in front of me, unable to see anything, but waiting and wanting to hear any sound that would give me the direction to fire at whatever was approaching. Each of us watched and guarded our area of the perimeter, waiting for what would happen next. I began to wonder about our not being dug in, no fox holes. None of us could see any of the movement, or who or what was making the noises going on around us. We all waited for the firing to start, and the anxiety to end.

Our patrol Sergeant called back to base camp, he whispering over the radio.

"Joker One, Joker One this is Seven Eight, over."

"Joker One, Go!" Came the voice back through the rasping squelch noise of my handset.

"Joker One, request Illum., (an illumination round, a parachute flare. Sent either by artillery or by aircraft), over our position, A-S-A-P. Joker One acknowledge! Over."

There was a long pause before any acknowledgement was received, "Seven Eight, this is Joker One. Hold one for Illum."

A pause and then the announcement, "Round Out." A short pause and then "One on the way, wait!"

Our normal patrol area kept us well within our own assigned 155mm support artillery range, but this night we were out deeper than normal. We were outside the range of our 155s and so heavier artillery was employed, and this is was where we had a failure to communicate. A neighboring artillery unit from our own was employed to fill our needs using 175mm cannon. (The 175mm was the biggest damn gun the army had. They put an 8 inch shell in a gun with a really long barrel). However, there was one small error made, the artillery men mistakenly sent us a HE (High Explosive) round instead of an illumination round. There was no doubt in any of our minds as to what it was when we could hear it coming in our direction. The noise was like a freight train chugging along, and so word was whispered around from man to man amongst us to "Take Cover."

The 175mm HE shell has a 100 meter bursting radius; this is something I had learned in Basic Training. With this in mind I crawled around like a frantic alligator, while feeling my way around the place where I had lay prone on the ground. "Take cover!" Where? I heard some of the others also scrambling around. There was no place to go, and no place to hide except under your helmet.

The shell came on and on. To me the oncoming shell sounded about the size of a house with an attached two car garage as it rushed toward us. The shell went on over us, but no flare appeared in the heavens. There was just the sound of this monster descending to earth towards us. I heard a muffled "Jesus Christ," and I placed my arms over my head. The world around us erupted with the sound of a thunder clap when this monster crashed into the ground; I was engulfed by a flash of white light, and felt the air pressure sweep over me as the concussion of the explosion reached me. All of us were lifted off of the ground by the shells impact, and tossed back to earth which was still violently bucking. The blast from the shell left me gasping for air, as it slightly knocking the wind out of me.

Pieces of flying metal filled the air around us, whizzing and cracking as they took pieces out of the nearby trees.

Once the echo of the explosion died away there was no longer any sounds of movement from my group or from whatever had been around us, and after we had all calmed down from the delivery of our requested "Flare," our patrol Sergeant got back on the radio. In whispered words he got back in contact with base camp.

"Joker One, A-h Joker One, t-this is t-this is ah Seven Eight, over"

"This is Joker One Go,"

"A-ah, Joker One, A-ah thanks...thanks for the Illum. Joker One, we-ah, we won't need further assist, over"

"Roger Seven Eight, Joker One out"

Next morning we swept the area around our night location trying to discover what had been moving in the night. There were no bodies lying about, no blood or drag trails, and we were all both relieved and disappointed by these results. We spent some time in examining the shell crater which was only 200 yards from our night location. "Artillery sure is good about installing holes in the ground," was one comment I heard. "Yeah, and they don't mind where they put them either." After inspecting both the size and the nearness of the shell crater we all agreed it was good to be alive. I dug an inch thick chunk of our wayward artillery shell out of a tree trunk, and put it in my pack for a souvenir. After I had packed away my metal memento, I made a little mental note to work on my own personal communications skills, I should pray more often.

Chapter 13

Orosz and Big Jon the Adventures Begin

It was shortly after my joining the 278th and I had completed several patrols that I had a real surprise coming my way. It was a bright sunny morning, and I found myself standing outside our company mess hall after a breakfast of the usual powdered eggs and greasy something. I was lingering over a cigarette before I went to the shop and to work, and as I stood around the exit to the mess hall I saw a rather familiar face. The face belonged to my old pal, Orosz. Orosz came out of the mess hall with an "I'll be damned, (Insert dirty name here) Lennox. What the hell are youse doing here?" Orosz and I had known each other somewhat peripherally while we were both stationed at Fort Gordon, Georgia. Peripherally meant he was either standing next to me in a formation or right beside me during K.P. We had both lived in the same barracks and attended the same signal school there, but were not close buddies. We had even put in some quality time together, on Guard duty together before we went our separate ways.

I hadn't seen Jerry Orosz in over a year, and here we were together again. Orosz had spent all this time right here with the 278th, and had just returned from 30 days leave in the U.S. of A. There he stood in as much civilian attire as he could get away with, a pair of bell bottom pants, a tank top, and several strands of love beads. He definitely looked like he was out of place for the O.D. Green Army he was part of. He had been in the states for extending his tour of duty in Vietnam. We talked about his home, Ohio in "The World," a place that was very far from where we stood that morning. "How the hell is youse, Lennox? I haven't seen youse in a dogs age." We caught up on each other's less than illustrious Army doings over another cigarette or two. "Yeah I lives in dat old, dilapidated, abandoned VC chicken coop over there," he said pointing out his barracks. "Youse should come visit some time."

Orosz was a well-built guy of 5' 10" and a solid 165 pounds. He had a great stock of straight jet black hair, long from being on leave, but combed and parted neatly. Orosz had two dark brown eyes set in a handsome face that also supported a great black brush of a mustache. It was an irreverent bush, an anti-regulation bush, one that was way beyond military limits. He talked to you in a "hey youse guys," type accent, and when he explained something to you he was very slow and deliberate, choosing his words carefully for their effect. He also used his hands and arms for exclamation points about what he said.

I explained about where I had come from and the "Hell" I had getting out of there and the "Chicken Shit" during my time at Riley. I told him what I was doing both at the repair shop and on the recon patrol. "Oh yeah, I used to go out on dem patrols too." I explained about my recent encounter with the snake and my new nickname "Scotty." "Oh yeah, Scotty huh! I can go along with that. But youse is lucky Scotty they could have called you Dumper Man or Mr. Dump or something like that there. From what youse laid in em pants of yours." I agreed I was lucky.

Orosz refreshed my memory about himself. Most recently he had been one of the guys stacking up broken equipment in the repair shop. But Mr. "H", (also known affectionately as Old Double H or HH to those who knew and respected him), the warrant officer in charge of both the repair shop, motor pool and the recon patrol, had shuffled him off to an administrative job. Orosz now handed out drivers licenses and checked and assigned vehicles in the motor pool. He had just extended his tour in Vietnam by six months, and for that commitment he had received a 30 day leave.

Orosz was another Ohio native, (the 278th seemed to be overstocked with guys from Ohio), and from my own personal recollection, had the reputation of being able to out drink, out cuss and out pee any man in any battalion. I don't know what Orosz had done prior to entering the U.S. Army, but whatever it was he was well prepared for any military challenge that came his way. He had all the skills a soldier would need to get along anywhere. Orosz, you might say was a military enigma, he had already mastered all his required military skills before entering the Army.

We had finished with our after breakfast smoke, but not our conversation. So here Orosz and I still stood outside our mess hall continuing our conversation. It was 7:30 and the mess hall had just closed and the rest of the troops had trickling out some time ago. We were taking our time about getting to work when a strange screeching sound filled the air. It was a high pitched scream, a shrill whistle, that kept getting louder the longer we waited, and as I looked around to see where the sound was coming from I couldn't help but notice that Orosz was no longer standing beside me, he was prostrate on the ground nearby.

While I looked down at my pal a very large explosion suddenly rent the air from close by, and sent me sprawling face down on the ground beside Orosz. "What the fuck was that?" Was my first and last question to myself? The sound had come from an enemy 122mm rocket descending on Camp Enari, it had sailed in and hit dead center on the mess hall directly across the dirt road from the 278's mess hall. Orosz and I were lucky, and had been shielded from most of the blast by having our own mess hall between us and the explosion. The mess hall that was hit was miraculously empty at the time except for one luckless G.I. on K.P., who was left incredibly unhurt except for bruises from being blown through the wall of the building. With the sound of the explosion still roaring in my ears I looked up to notice a very large chunk of something dark heading my way from the heavens. "Move Orosz, Move!" I screamed as I jumped to my feet and took off at a dead run. This black thing descending from the heavens turned out to be a large chunk of corrugated tin that used to be part of the mess hall's roof. It clanged to earth right where Orosz and I had stood.

Orosz was quicker than I, and upon seeing the danger himself Orosz was on his feet and away in an instant. Unlike me he had not waiting to see where the roof landed, so headed at a dead run for the nearest bunker, and I followed close on his heels just as fast as my skinny legs would take me. We crossed the distance to the bunker, about 100 yards, in Olympic sprint time as little pieces of the mess hall rained down around us. I was two steps behind Orosz when he reached the bunker's entrance. There was no door, just a black rectangular hole in the middle of a mountain of sandbags; unfortunately he reached the entrance at the exact same time as the 278's First Sergeant. If you remember the First Sergeant was an ex-green beret, 6' 3" plus in height and a good 220 pounds. Orosz was ten years younger 5' 10" and a measly 165 pounds. When they collided Orosz threw a shoulder into the First Sergeant, and just plowed the "Top Soldier" out of his way. I watched in amazement as the First Sergeant went up in the air in slow motion, kipped backwards and he landed on his back in the entrance way. I being right behind Orosz didn't bother to stop, and put a size 10 and a half jungle boot square on the Sergeants chest on my own way over him.

The weird part of all this was not watching the Sergeant pitch over in front of my eyes in slow motion, not the fact that the enemy only used one rocket round to hit one mess hall (dead center), but coming to an out of breath halt beside Orosz on a seat in the bunker, and noticing that he was quite calm and collected and half way through a cigarette. "What kept ya?" was all he said to me.

303

Within 15 minutes of this little episode the all clear siren sounded, and 15 seconds after that the First Sergeant had Orosz and I standing at attention in front of his desk in the company orderly room. He was doing a great impersonation of someone who was mad as hell. "You sons of bitches think it's funny to step all over me." The flat of Top's hand slammed down hard on his desk. I cringed, I couldn't see Orosz. On the whole, Orosz and I were doing our best trying to explain that the Viet Cong must have a new secret weapon, a grease seeking rocket, and we had nothing to do with that. All the while we were biting our lower lips trying to keep straight faces, and not look at the perfect red imprint of the sole of a U.S. Army jungle boot, upside down, on the front of the First Sergeants shirt. It was there for the world to see like a giant cancelled stamp on a letter at the post office. The boot print was distracting enough, but it was the deep red face of the First Shirt was the most distracting for us to see.

Orosz and I apparently were not very convincing about our innocence in the unavoidable encounter with the First Sergeant, because immediately after our balling out we found ourselves on the dirtiest job that Top could have imagined for us. The First Shirt had assigned us the task if cleaning out one of the company outhouses.

Shit Burners

Outhouse, Crapper, shitter, latrine cleaning was a daily chore liked by no one, and so several local natives earned a good living ridding the Army of its daily accumulations of outhouse deposits. This was a job that each company in the Army in Vietnam either had their own people do it or contracted for with local civilians, and the old Vietnamese man who held the contract in the 278 was known as the company "Shit Burner." This was a universal name for this universal job, as the same job held the same title all over Vietnam. So we got the dirtiest job in the company, and the "Shit Burner" got the day off. The Army had an entire field manual devoted to the care and maintenance of outhouses, and this was presented to us by the First Sergeant as he sent us on our way.

Cleaning up the crapper didn't just involve cleaning up the premises; we had to get rid of the accumulated contents as well. Each hole of the crapper had one half of a 55 gallon oil drum, on end, below it, and these had to be emptied. The normal procedure was to remove the drums from the outhouse through trap doors, and then mix the drums contents with gasoline and diesel fuel. The mixture was then set on fire and allowed to burn until the drums were empty.

The 278th's company shitters were breezy wooden shacks located at three strategic locations around the company living and working areas. The one we were sent to take care of first was behind a small ridge in the ground, visibly away from the company area by 100 yards. Camp Enari was so large that it had a pimple of a hill inside its perimeter, and this mini-mountain radiated several ridges and folds that extended outward through the camp. Our first outhouse sat alone from the rest of the company buildings, hidden from view of the orderly room and the First Sergeant by a ridge.

Orosz and I followed the trail of pits of newspaper, cigarette butts, and TP around the ridge to the outhouse, carrying buckets, brushes, disinfectants and a five gallon gas can each. Mine was full of gasoline and the one Orosz carried was full of Diesel fuel. Together we staggered under our loads and followed the trail of shredded toilet paper and other trash that marked the way to our punishment job. We arrived at our destination in a state of depression. Of all the things I had wanted to accomplish in life this was not one of them.

The shitter was a tin roofed shack, like most of the Army construction, with wood walls three quarters of the way up from the floor and the top quarter was wire screen, and all this housed the 16 holes for the convenience of all. All the outhouses I have ever visited had a distinct aroma all their own, and this one took my breath away. Before we bagin our task

Orosz und I sat down outside and up wind, and sadly pondered our situation.

If you have never experienced it let me put you in the picture. Outside the 16 holer was aromatic to say the least, but inside the stench would overwhelm you. No matter what air flow was provided for the stench inside never went away. Holding your breath upon entry was of no use the smell was almost visible, and it left a nasty taste in the back of your mouth. You learned to breath through your mouth, but that would not protect you entirely. You gaged! If you took your malaria pills regular you could do your business in 30 seconds or less and be on your way, but not everyone was conciensous about their pills. Lingering over a smoke and a quick glance at the "Stars & Stripes" news paper was not for the faint hearted. It was for those with severe nasal congestion or a completely burned out olfactory system. For the rest of us getting out of there quick was the only solution.

After a few minutes of contemplating our fate the conversation finally got around to our present dilemma.

"Do youse really want to do this?" Orosz asked.

"Are you kidding, I would rather face another snake than clean out this crapper," was my reply.

"Good," Orosz said rising to his feet, "I've got an idea. Youse wait here until I get back."

With that Orosz strode off in a direction opposite from the one we had both come from, and this left me thinking, "It looks like I am going to be the only one cleaning latrines today." Dejectedly I hung around the crapper half-heartedly picking up bits of paper and cigarette butts, and giving the appearance of working while I waited to see if Orosz really would return.

Orosz returned after a short while, pushing a big wheeled, red handled hand truck, with a large black sagging rubber object strapped to the handles. When he got closer I could see that the black object was a collapsed rubber fuel bladder, and Orosz explained, "I got it at the chopper pad."

"What is it exactly?" I asked.

"I got us a little bit of JP-4 (jet fuel) from the chopper pad."

JP-4 was wonderful stuff, anytime that I could find some I would fill my Zippo cigarette lighter. It was the one fuel that produced a flame that couldn't be blown out in high wind. Unfortunately a Zippo full of JP-4 was only good for about four lights, but each light was about four feet long.

Orosz and I set to work removing the heavy shit cans, eight from each side, and hauling them all into a group on one side of the outhouse. Here we circled the wagons, or shit cans, and here we sloshed them with the gasoline and diesel from our five gallon cans. The stench inside the outhouse was nothing compared to the oder coming from all 16 of the cans when they were brought in close proximity to each other. As the saying went, "It would gag a maggot." You certainly didm't want to look at what the cans contained, as on my first glance of the first can I removed from the shitter I thought that the contents were moving. Breathing through my mouth helped me to take the long pole and stir the contents of each can. The gasoline helped to smother some of the stench but not enough. The tricky part about stirring the shit was to first recognize which end of the stick to use before you started to do the stirring, we didn't have any gloves. This was a part of a basic military axiom, knowing which end of the stick was the shitty end when you passed the stick to someone else. After a few minutes of doing the job, as the manual instructed, we figured it was time to burn the shit. Before we set them alight we wheeled over the fuel bladder and added a touch of jet fuel to each drum. After using all the JP-4 fuel in the bladder, and being satisfied that there was enough combustible mixture to do a quick and thorough job, Orosz said, "Take the cart and stand off a ways."

I wheeled the cart back about 100 feet and turned around to watch the fun. A shimmer of fumes hung over the barrels, and Orosz stood off to one side an unlit cigarette in his mouth and his own Zippo lighter in his hand. Turning away from the barrels Orosz flicked the Zippo, and touched its flame to the end of his cigarette. In one fluid motion Orosz started running in my direction, and reached back over his left shoulder with his right hand and flipped the lit cigarette toward the drums.

The cigarette arched high in the air over the drums, and all at once all of the outhouse drums were immediately consumed in a bright orange flash. A ball of flame expanded in all directions, with a loud WOOOOOF sound, giving off a heat warmer than the sun, even where I was standing. Within a second the outhouse itself next exploded, in a loud BAA-OOOOM, in its own ball of orange flame, and most of the tin roof shot straight up in the air. I was amazed, this was great. There was one other ball of flame and that was the small one running toward me, Orosz.

I had been standing quite a ways away, and the intense heat generated at the moment when the combustibles touched off turned the front of my uniform from dark O.D. Green to a dark brown. Every exposed hair of my body was instantaneously singed off. This included eye brows, the hair on the backs of my hands and arms, and my very first attempt at a mustache.

My first concern was my buddy; his burning form still ran toward me. As soon as we reached each other I tackled him at the knees bringing him to the ground, and we rolled around in the dirt, which put out the burning parts of his uniform. While this was going on a black and orange pyre soared skyward from what used to be the 278's crapper, and flaming and smoldering pieces of wood rained down around us. In the distance I could hear the wail of sirens as the base camp went on full alert, (the second time in the last hour), and I imagined the panic as soldiers ran about madly seeking shelter or manning the base defenses. "Christ Scotty is I still in one piece? Look at me Scotty tell me I'm OK?" I looked him over. "Your OK," said, "Just a little singed around the edges." As Orosz and I lay amidst all this self-created destruction I wondered to myself, "now how the hell are we going to explain this one?"

Orosz was not burned badly, some of the fuel from the explosion had splashed onto the back of his uniform shirt and pants, and it had only burned for a few seconds before being extinguished. What helped to save him from serious injury was the loose fit of the uniform. The uniform had burned through in several places, but he only had first and second degree burns in a few spots. The outhouse on the other hand was a splintered mass of burning wood, whose roof had landed on top of the ridge in a twisted tangled mass of metal and wood.

Technically, Orosz and I figured everything out much later. We had not counted on the wind direction; a slight breeze had blown the fumes from the gasoline and JP-4 into the outhouse trapping some of them there under the peeked roof. When the drums had ignited they were not far enough away from the structure, and the fumes under the roof had been set off sending the roof skyward.

"That shit sure burns," said Orosz. As we sat and watched the flames and black smoke ascend, we both realized our one most immediate problem. Once things calmed down, someone from the company was going to come to see what had happened to us. We looked around for the jet fuel hand truck, it was lying on its side a few feet from us, and Orosz made haste to get it back from where he had gotten it, scorched bladder, paint and all.

Within 30 minutes of the explosion we were back standing at attention in front of the First Sergeant's desk, (a sorrier looking pair I'll bet he had never seen in all his military career), and this was less than two hours from our first appearance. While we were doing our best to explain what happened, Top was doing his best ever impersonation of someone having apoplexy. After we gave our rehearsed "don't know what happened Sarge," speech I could see the white froth collecting at the corners of Top's mouth while he yelled at us for being a couple of "lying assholes." His hand slammed repeatedly on top of the desk, "Now I want the truth, what the hell did you two assholes do out there." Our explanation that the Viet Cong must have a new secret weapon, "A shit seeking rocket," was not going over, it had as many holes in it as the uniform Orosz was wearing.

As I stood there in front of the Tops' desk and subconsciously listened to him chew Orosz and I out, I thought to myself, "You know I do entirely too much of this, I have definitely spent too much time on the carpet in front of this someone's desk." I had been chewed out on many occasions, and since I was not going to get a word in edge wise my mind wandered a bit. It wasn't disrespect, just boredom.

I slipped the "How to Burn Shit" field manual back onto Top's desk as I left. The top cover was almost gone the remainder was severly charred. So were the outer edges of the pages on one side of the book. It was his maual.

While leaving the company orderly room after our meeting with the First Shirt I turned to Orosz and said, "You know Orosz there's gotta be something wrong with you if you can't take an ass chewing and not walk away smiling." Orosz heartily concurred saying, "Yeah Scotty, but we gotta stop meeting like this though, it gives me heart burn."

"Yeah," I responded, "we've set some sort of military precedent. We've known each other for less than four hours and already we're back in the same shit we left a year ago."

"Fucking "A" Scotty."

"Besides, I think that that man hates us," I added.

"Fucking "A" Scotty."

After being allowed to clean up, we spent the rest of the day doing a job Top thought we could handle, burning the long grass out of the drainage ditches in the company area. This actually turned out to be fun, a mechanical stirrup pump fire extinguisher full of diesel fuel and a Zippo lighter. It would not burn hot enough to explode, so we spent the rest of the day taking turns with our home made flame thrower. There was one unfriendly part of this flame thrower game of ours. The First Sergeant had placed an armed guard on us with an M-16 rifle with a full clip, and orders to "Shoot to Kill" if anything got out of hand.

As for our arsonist tendencies toward the cleaning of outhouses, the First Sergeant couldn't prove anything, as we had

310

successfully removed any evidence of our wrong doing. The real evidence had been removed mostly straight up in a ball of flame. Even later, an investigation by the M.P.s proved inconclusive results, which meant that they couldn't prove anything either. It was all put down to spontaneous combustion, and Orosz and I agreed with that finding when it was announced. There wasn't much left of the latrine, a few charred boards and a few deformed oil drum halves. The crap was all gone though, and that was the one thing we had done right. Top Sergeant had a long memory though, and he did manage to make life uncomfortable for us for our remaining time in the 278th.

In two days I was heading back out to the field on another recon mission, and Orosz was trying hard not to be found by anyone who would mention his name too loud. I was relieved to go back out on patrol, and get away from the entire furor surrounding my episode as an arsonist. Comments of "How's it going Sparky," or "Hey! You two are really Hot Shit," had followed Orosz and I from one corner of the company area to the other for days. We didn't mind, we were "Hot Shit," and he and I still giggle about this episode today.

Montagnards

On the next two patrols we ended up spending a night in Montagnard villages instead of camping out in the open. The Montagnard Vietnamese were different from the other Vietnamese. Here my Anthropological skills developed in college come into play. The Montagnards are the traditional highland dwellers. They were darker skinned than the lowland Vietnamese, and very different in their culture, dress and language. Their culture was so closed that village or clan members very rarely married outside the village or clan. The lowland Vietnamese were a mixture of whomever had conquered the country last, (Chinese, Mongol), and they lived primarily along the coastal plains. There was a population of

Vietnamese in the highlands, but they lived clustered around the cities and towns, leaving the wilds to the Montagnards.

The Army rumor mill stated that Montagnards were once upon a time head hunters, and though not open about doing it they were still were head hunters. The rumor mill also stated that the Montagnards would as soon as lop off a Vietnamese head as the head anyone else. With this disclosure I swallowed hard and vowed to keep my eyes open, and my nose clean in the Montagnard village.

All of the Montagnard villages we stayed in were always well organized, neat, and with thatched roof hootches raised off the ground by stilts. The village was laid out in neat rows inside a strong defensive perimeter. The only untidy thing about the villages was that their warthog pigs ran around free. The pigs were big black suckers, with protruding three or four inch tusks and sagging bellies that almost drug on the ground. These pigs lived in burrows under the stilted houses. I suppose they were as good a protection as watch dogs, and they looked fiercer than any junk yard dog I had ever seen. In contrast, Vietnamese villages looked like a slum, shacks one propped up or leaning against another, all made of junk or hammered out pop cans. The Vietnamese hodge-podge and ramshackle villages looked puny compared to the Montagnard villages. However, both had their wire and bunker defenses, and both looked like they could protect themselves well.

The reason we were stopping at the village was explained to us by Sergeant Akron before we arrived. We stopped at the village to provide us with a patrol base while we searched the area immediately around the village for enemy activity. The village defense force had been getting harassed at night by snipers and enemy patrol activity, and our presence plus the village defense force was to provide a show of strength and unity.

The first visit we made was to the village of Plei Clan Ngol, (we pronounced it Play Clan Noel), about 30 to 40 miles south of Camp Enari. When we arrived we were treated as long lost sons by the village elders, and after our first sweep outside their perimeter we came back into the village for the night. We were fed and entertained royally by the village people, and hosted by the head man of the village. We shared our rations with the people, we had brought two extra cases of "C" Rations between us in case we were to be entertained, and the villages produced large vats of a potent drink, a local rice wine, for us. It was a great honor to be allowed to drink the rice wine of the village, and each of us had to squat down at one of the huge vats and drink our fill through a bamboo straw. My duty was to drink wine from the jar until the level of liquid in the jar was lowered to a mark on the straw. Several of us patrol members were crowded together squatting on our haunches as we drank with the villagers pressing on our shoulders till our task was done. I fulfilled my own part of the rice wine drinking festivities, drinking down to a notch in the bamboo straw. I felt like I had been drinking for most of the evening, or literally until it seemed like the top of my head popped off. After this experience I was allowed to go to bed.

God I was drunk, I had never been so divinely looped in my entire short career of rice wine drinking. I was truly shit faced. But, reason was still within my grasp, staggering though reason was. I had difficulty finding my ass with both hands let alone finding my bed.

Instead of our usual sleeping out on the bare ground, each of us was put up in a different family hootch for the night, and though quite drunk I wasn't quite drunk enough for what came next. I was led to my assigned bed for the night by a Vietnamese interpreter that the U.S. advisers in the village had on staff. I crawled up the log steps and into the main room of the hootch I was directed to. In the flickering lamp light I got a glimpse of Mama-San, and the rest of the family which included a girl of about 14 years. The girl was sitting on a straw mat in a corner of the room separate from the rest of the family. The head of the house hold, approached. I smiled stupidly to his unknown words. Through an interpreter I was

313

welcomed royally, and through the interpreter the headman said, "You will sleep with my daughter," pointing in the direction of the 14 year old in the corner. Every traveling salesman in the world had probably been waiting to hear those words; I blinked slowly in response, and blearily eyeballed the daughter. I was having trouble believing what was being said to me, I was having trouble focusing, I smiled stupidly, and I shook my muddled head to make sure I wasn't dreaming, and said to myself "Naaah! This can't be happening to me." I then said to the interpreter, "He wants me to sleep with his daughter?" "Yes, great honor," said the interpreter. I thought out loud, "Oh God! I've died and gone to heaven."

I had seen several Montagnard maidens and Montagnard women on my brief time I had spent in the Vietnam wilds. I had seen them walking around in their villages, and as they walked around in the back country, (from village to village or from village to town, to the market), where we patrolled. Almost all of them walked around naked from the waist up, and this offered some delightful treats in contrast to the all-male scenery of the Army. At ages 14 to about 20 the women all looked delightfully enticing, and I had had the urge at times to walk all over one or two of them bare foot. Beyond the age of 20 they all took on a well-worn appearance, and lost a lot of their luster.

This 14 year old had all of the luster any red blooded G.I. wanted. Through the interpreter I discovered what this was all about, I was having trouble getting through the fog in my brain. So the interpreter gave it to me slowly. It was a great honor to have a guest in the house, and so to return the honor a daughter was offered to the guest for warmth during the night, since the Montagnards did not have an abundance of blankets. The head of the house wanted me to honor his house by sleeping on the same matt as his daughter, and nothing more. Disappointment floated in front of me, but my stupid smile remained.

I also found out that the first time the old man said "You will sleep with my daughter," it was a request, and you could politely decline the offer. If the old man said "You will sleep with my daughter," a second time, the only way you got out of it was if they carried your dead, (probably head-less), body out of that hootch.

I was led over to the daughter, very pretty with her smooth dark brown skin, a demure exotic beauty, with long flowing black silky hair, sensuous lips and eyes, and you guessed it, naked from the waist up. The words of the interpreter echoed through my brain all night long, "you are to honor his house; she is your blanket, sleep on the same matt and NOTHING MORE." I lay awake most of the night while my snuggle mate slept soundly. It was the roughest night without sleep I ever spent.

In the morning I, like the other members of the patrol, were given a brass bracelet by the head of the tribe, as a symbol. Each was inscribed with strange and primitive symbols and writing. I was now a member of the Montagnard tribe. With my head pounding viciously from the rice wine I looked at the bracelet as I staggered to the center of the village to answer Sergeant Akron's roll call. I thought to myself as I walked, "Jesus, I don't know what I've done, but I've even won the brass ring." That 14 year old daughter was the closest thing to heaven that I had been near to in a very long time, and I was proud of myself for having the restraint needed.

We left the village that morning and went back to humping through the boonies. A week later I heard through the patrol grapevine that the tribe headman had been summarily executed by the VC, two days after we had left his village. The VC had come into the village after we left, and decided to teach the village a lesson for collaborating with the Americans. The old man was shot in front of all his family and population of the village; it was a shock to all of us. The whole time we were in the village the VC must have been waiting and watching outside. I was sad to think of the unhappiness that village was now experiencing, when they had been so happy when we were there.

Back in Base camp this information angered and enraged every one of us from the patrol, and we congregated around our supply Conex after dinner. Feelings were running high at this impromptu meeting. "Let's go back there and kick ass." Was just one of the opinions voiced that day? A couple showed up with their M-16s and demanded their rucksacks; they wanted to go back right then and there. But in spite of all the hot feelings, reason prevailed. "Mr. H," the officer in charge of the patrol showed up once he heard about his troops gathering at the Conex. He confirmed for us the rumor that we had heard, and he gave us all the gory details. All of us were silent while "Mr. H" related what had happened. After we were given the word the threats and the shouts for revenge rang out once more. It took a lot of talk from "Mr. H" to calm us down. It was a bitter pill that we had to swallow, realizing that we were not regular combat troops, who could stay out on an extended patrol to pursue the enemy. Nor were we trained for such a mission. There would be no returning to the village of Plei Clan Ngol, the old man was dead, and there was nothing we could do about it. Revenge would have to be left to someone else.

"Don't mean nothin'!." Was the only condolence we troops offered each other as the meeting broke up and troops drifted back to work.

My second time of spending a night in a Montagnard village was as interesting as the first, and just as exciting. Our patrol ended up our first day's march at a Montagnard village located in a small grove of trees, on flat ground, about two miles off of QL 14, near a Vietnamese village we knew as "Cheap Charley's." The Montagnard village was being consolidated with several others at a new village sight further east of QL 14. This was being done so that a bigger village population could provide better protection for themselves with less manpower. Engineers from the 4th Division were there with trucks and heavy equipment helping to dismantle hootches and move them to their new location. We arrived at the village and met up with the engineers, and our job was to provide security on one side of the village for the night, while the engineers guarded the other three sides.

With everything understood we set in for the night in the usual way, we were not dug in in anyway, just hiding behind trees and bushes, but this time the patrol was stretched out in a crescent shaped line 50 yards in length, on the east side of the village. We provided a guard of six men awake at all times all night.

In the middle of the night I was woken up from a fitful sleep by the sound of a large volume of small arms fire coming from the engineer side of the village. I and all of my comrades were instantly awake and alert, and with the firing my stomach did its usual flip flops while I waited nervously to see if things would get worse or completely out of hand. The engineers were firing at something out to their front, and mines were exploded adding punctuation and authority to the firing. Hand flares were popped up overhead illuminating the village and woods in eerie dark shadows that moved around as the flare floated to earth. "What the hell's going on?" whispered up and down our line from man to man. Since I could see nothing I like my buddies held my fire.

While out patrol Sergeant tried to get the engineers on the radio, we all lay glued to the ground and listened intently as the volume of fire increased and decreased as if it were waves on the ocean. While our Sergeant was still trying to get radio contact with base some of the engineers shifted fire from their front and put it on top of us. Hugging the ground M-60 machinegun bullets and tracers plus other unseen bullets ZZZZinged and PI-inged over our heads, and occasionally slammed into nearby trees and bushes.

There wasn't much to do but lay there and take it for the few minutes that it lasted, but the firing ceased as quickly as it had started. I could hear the shouts of those on the engineer side, (hopefully those in charge), yelling "Cease Fire! Cease Fire Damn It!"

317

Our Sergeant had finally got through to the engineers, but the realization that no incoming or return fire was being received had settled a lot of the engineers down. The lack of enemy fire, was one thing another was the realized fact that they had burned up most of their own ammunition. "Why don't we call in an air strike on them," offered Neon. I agreed from my position behind a spindly clump of grass. Before it became light a collection was taken up from each of us to send the engineers some ammunition that we still had plenty of, and I spent the rest of the night in blessed silence. Wide awake but blessed.

During all of this hell in the middle of the night, some idiot in base camp was heard on the radio offering to drive out a resupply of ammunition to the engineers. Thankfully further tragedy was averted; the M.P.s had stopped him at the front gate. "Blondie," said that the M.P.s should have shot him at the front gate, saving the enemy having to do it.

In the morning our patrol swept the woods and fields to the engineer's front, looking for whatever had attacked them. On reporting back our Sergeant told a Lieutenant of engineers, "Well sir, we swept all around the perimeter for 200 meters, and as near as I can tell you all were attacked by trees and bushes not Charley."

Tet

After our return from this Montagnard village relocation expedition we were ordered to rest from patrolling for a few days, in compliance with the Tet Truce. The "Tet Holiday Cease Fire Truce" was an agreement between us good guys and those bad guys up north. They were not supposed to do bad things and neither were we, but all of us near the impact zone for incoming rounds suspected something was going on. In our private discussions, in the barracks, after hours, enlisted man to enlisted man, we didn't trust "Charley", (Hell we didn't trust our own NCOs), and we didn't think he would pass up an

318

opportunity to move stuff around during a truce without penalty. The only difference I noticed between the Christmas Truce and the Tet Truce was that the Christmas one was in December and the other February.

The Tet holiday was the biggest celebration in Vietnam, their New Year, and several days were spent in observing it. To the Vietnamese it was considered EVERYONES birthday, and in celebration the Vietnamese visited family and friends. The Vietnamese dressed up in their finest, and feasted in grand style as part of their celebration.

I was happy to be back in Base Camp for a rest, and spent my time moving out of my present blue silk room with Willie, I had become bored with entertaining the village idiot. Another room in the barracks had recently been vacated by someone going home, and I took the opportunity to move in, as soon as the previous owner's foot-steps disappeared out the door. In this room there was no roommate, so the room was a lot smaller than my Willie one. However, I didn't mind, I didn't have to look at some one playing with their lips from across aisle. My old roomie Willie was so far gone that I was going to give him some band-aides to wear on his finger-tips so he would not get bruises from when he played "In-A-Gadda-Da-Vida", The "Hungarian Rhapsody," or other up-beat melody on his lower lip.

During the truce I got stuck into my repair work again. John and Barry had been hard at it while I went for my walks in the woods. Together we whittled away at that pile of broken equipment, and finally between the three of us we were making a big dent in it. We were always putting in long days and nights, it kept you busy and out of trouble. Once again I performed guard duty and K.P. as required by the duty roster, as the Vietnamese civilians K.P.s were off celebrating their holidays.

The Night Visitors

However, on one very dark and rainy night during the truce I was roused from my slumber by the company C.Q., (Charge of Quarters), NCO and told that my presence was wanted in the orderly room. I threw on my brain bucket, and wearing nothing but my O.D. Green G.I. skivvies I ran in my untied jungle boots to the orderly room. I ran getting soaked to the skin, through a cold windy night with a driving the rain coming from the west. When I arrived at the company orderly room I was told that men from the top of Dragon Mountain were coming in to get parts for some very important broken but much needed radio equipment. I was to be there to greet them and get them what they needed.

I ask the C.Q. incredulously, "Someone is DRIVING in here from Dragon Mountain?" In the short time I had spent in Vietnam I had learned one thing, you didn't drive around in the boonies in the middle of the night.

Impressed with the urgency of the mission I went and opened up the repair shop and hung around shivering, and waiting to see if anyone made it in from Dragon Mountain. After a 45 minute wait an open topped deuce and a half truck pulled up in the company area, with a lot of yelling and flashlight waving. From the beam of the headlights I could see that several people had jumped down from the back of the truck as I peered out into the driving rain from the doorway of the shop. There was more yelling and flashlight waving as the truck sat, its engine still running, headlights showing the black lines of the falling rain, and a group from the truck came toward me splashing through the puddles. I stepped back into the warmth and florescent light of the shop and waited to see what these desperate people looked like. Three very water soaked, and rough, tough and scruffy looking G.I.s entered my shop on soggy muddy boots. None of them wore ponchos or any other rain gear, and their wet uniforms clung to them. The leader was a buck Sergeant of huge proportions, and I knew he was the leader at first glance; the other two stepped aside for him to enter first. They were all soaked through and all looked dirty and unshaven with up to three days beard on their faces. All of them were wearing floppy engineer "Bonnie" hats and flack-jackets, and they looked to me like the epitome of the combat soldier with their immaculately clean weapons. Over one shoulder the leader carried an M-3 sub-machine-gun, a Grease gun, and on his right hip he carried a 12 inch Bowie knife in a black water buffalo hide scabbard. This was Big Jon, and he had a commanding presence. He and I were to become good friends later in our tours of duty.

Big Jon, I was to find out was a legend in his own time, apparently he knew everyone and it also appears that everyone knew him. Because of his past exploits Big Jon had been exiled from the company area, and he now lived with these other exiles and misfits on the top of Dragon Mountain. What misadventures that had caused his expulsion to Dragon Mountain I was never to find out.

This was a mountain of a man, 6' 2" and 250 pounds at least. Most of his impressive bulk came from a massive barrel chest supported by two tree trunks of legs. His soft "Boonie" hat rested precariously over his eyes, covering most of his dark curly hair. The front and back brim of his hat were curled up, giving the hat an old U.S. Cavalry look.

This dramatic appearance was offset by a smooth boyish face reflected his age of early 20s, but his eyes were the eyes of someone much older.

"Y'all Scotty McNasty?" he asked in a slow southern drawl.

"Yeah, that's me." Obviously my reputation had preceded me.

"Well good, I got me a dead radio on top of Dragon Mountain and I'm in the need of some hep."

"What kind of help do you need?" I asked in return.

"I-ya need some parts, and if you ain't got em maybe I need y'all to come back with me." That statement started me thinking. I didn't relish the thought of taking my chances on the

Vietnamese road after dark. Besides, I wasn't dressed for a trip. So I began a search for what Big Jon wanted.

Together we must have looked rather ludicrous. On one hand a soldier heavily armed and dressed rakishly, the epitome of a fighting soldier, conversing with an idiot standing around in his underwear.

I eyeballed his two companions; they wore a weird collection of US and Tiger Striped uniforms, and an even weirder collection of weapons. Looking closer at their M-16s, one was of the original issue with the old style open flash suppressor, and the second had a short barrel with a large cylindrical silencer attached at the end, it looked like a sawed off shot-gun with an M-16 attached. I looked at each one carefully; no bullet holes or blood indicated any mishaps on their travels from the mountain. I was somewhat amazed that they had made it at all. I asked if they had experienced any trouble on their trip, and their reply was noncommittal, like they did this every day, "none at all."

In a few seconds Big Jon told me what he needed, and I went to look for what he wanted. There was no screwing around, no negotiation, there was no barter. He had a need, and I gave him what he wanted. "Hep!"

I went looking for the parts that would get Big Jon back on the top of Dragon Mountain the quickest. He like his two companions walked around and helped themselves to whatever they saw and wanted. These two picked up and pocketed stuff whether my back was turned or not. From what they pocketed in the way of tools and parts I thought that they were pretty desperate on top of that hill. Whatever the reason I kept my mouth shut, after all they were heavily armed and I was the one in the underwear.

Half way through my search three more scruffy looking troops, like this first gang of pirates, appeared in the door and entered without a word. They then proceeded to climb on any flat surface available and lie down and sleep. These three were left alone by Big Jon and the other two, who continued on their search of the repair shop.

I found what Big Jon wanted, and called him over. Being the complete Army bookworm, I handed him his parts only after I had filled out the parts requisitions the government required me to. "This should do it," I offered with the parts.

"If it don't," said Big Jon, "I'll be down to get you in a deuce and a half, Scotty McNasty." He said half smiling at his own joke.

Smiling at his humor I attempted to usher Big Jon and his five other companions out of the shop. The three prostrate figures were roused with some effort and complaint. "The perfect Signal men," offered Big Jon, "They can sleep anywhere, on anything and anytime."

With that familiar statement I thought, "Now where had I heard that before. It must be one of the Signal Corps by-laws."

After getting what they came for they all left in the same deuce and a half that had brought them, with the same shouting and waving of flashlights. Watching them leave I did notice that there were several more men on the back of the truck than the six that had come through my door. Plus I noticed that machine-guns and other weapons bristled from every corner and side of that truck as it drove out of our company area. "Perhaps they knew what the Hell they were doing after all," was my own thought as I watched them drive away. I gave a silent prayer that they would make it back up to their mountain retreat in one piece.

Two mornings later, which was the morning the Tet Truce ended the company was called to a formation in front of the barracks, and an announcement was read out by the C.O. This was alarming to most of us as mass formations were rare due to enemy rocketing and mortaring. The announcement that was read out was even more alarming. The 278th Signal Company was to be deactivated within the next 60 days, and all of us with time left on our tours of duty would be sent to other units. All of Camp Enari was to be turned over to the ARVN forces, and the 4th Division base camp was to move to Camp Radcliffe in An Khe. We were shocked by this revelation; the 278th had become our lives and family. A murmur of protest went through the ranks with the announcement of `deactivation.' The C.O. had to yell "AT Ease" several times to calm us down.

As it was explained, this was all part of the U.S. Government's policy of Vietnamization. There would be no more patrols as our energies were now to be spent tearing down facilities that were not to be left for the ARVN.

Pictures 2

Figure 3. Bunkerline Camp Enari. Author's collection.

Figure 4. 278's Recon team. Big Jon's collection.

Figure 5. Bunker on top of Dragon Mountain. Big Jon's collection.

Figure 6. Big Jon. Big Jon's collection.

Figure 7. Dragon Mountain. Author's collection.

Figure 8. Type of patrol territory in the Central Highlands. Author's collection.

Figure 9. On Patrol Central Highlands. Author's collection.

Figure 10. Montagnard village Plei Klane Ngol, defence bunker in background. Village was close to LZ Oasis in Central Highlands. Author's collection.

Chapter 14

The Great Dragon Mountain Shoot-Out

With my part time job as a recon team member over I settled into the everyday base camp routine of going to and from work, to and from meals, and to and from bed. I found this routine lacking in the excitement department. For whatever reason the enemy generally left us alone, and very few alerts were sounded. After long hours of work there was very little recreation available, and a lot of us made up our own diversions to help pass the time. There were occasional movies provided by the Army, mostly grade B movies that never had any sexy parts in them, but they had plenty of violence, and violence was OK to show us. Movies were shown out doors in the clean fresh air, rain or shine, and the screen consisted of an eight foot by eight foot sheet of plywood made of two 4X8 sheets of white painted plywood joined together. The screen was propped up with handy sticks and odd pieces of wood. We would sit around in the dirt wearing ponchos if it rained or anything from fatigues, underwear, or parts of civilian clothing while each movie's plot was revealed to us. There was little regard given to the correct sequence the film's reels should be shown in, it was not unusual to see the ending somewhere in the middle and the beginning at the end. The projectionist, who was one of us, would be cussed and taunted each time the film broke or a reel had to be changed, and the movie would take twice as long to show because of taunting. But in general a good time was had by all.

If you didn't like the film but wanted some liquid refreshment there was a shack provided for us as a bar, a combination 278 Signal enlisted, NCO and officers club all rolled into one. A thirsty soldier could get soda pop, beer, if there was any, and senior NCOs and officers could get booze for as long as it lasted. By edict of the 4th Division commanding general only officers and NCOs above the rank of E-6, (that means Sergeant with three stripes up and at least one under), could buy booze. With this club arrangement Officers, Senior NCOs and Enlisted Men would all drink under the same roof intermingled while bellied up to the bar, but when seated you had to observe the niceties of rank and sit at designated tables. There were rules of behavior while in the club, the main rules of proper etiquette were: no spitting, no gambling, no biting, no political discussions, and no fire arms allowed. Only on occasion did things get out of hand ending with a lively brawl.

In the barracks the radio became a large part of the evening's entertainment, and Pleiku had its own AM and FM U.S. Army radio stations. This was part of the military entertainment services an AFVN (Armed Forces Vietnam) radio station, and they would broadcast rock-and-roll music day and night on the AM side. The Army's kind of rock-n-roll was always the less offensive type, the "B" side of the record type of rock-n-roll music, (sugar coated bubble gum music, as we called it). The Army's type of music was not the so anti-war rock-n-roll, or the drug tainted acid rock that was usually blasted out by radio stations back in the world. We got for our listening enjoyment, a lot of great Mo-town, but mostly it was anything that didn't mention drugs, war, sex, or the U.S. Army. The FM side of the radio played classical music and the type of elevator music our parents enjoyed, but what we heard from the FM dial was mostly classical music. On the FM side each musical rendition was accompanied by a very low keyed, low resonant and very low volume announcement that the music was brought to you by "AFVN" radio. Not many people listened to FM radio from AFVN. Back in the world, at home, AM radio is what we young guys had all listened to. FM radio was for the "Long Hairs" the "Professors" the "Long Haired Bearded Wierdos" who liked classical music.

The music was always accompanied by announcements about personal hygiene, reminders to buy savings bonds, lectures on Army regulations, and admonishments to avoid liaisons with local prostitutes. Remember to vote through your voting officer, share your "Stars and Stripes" newspaper, and all the social events that were happening in the II Corp and 4th Division areas. We listened intently, it was all we had.

Many evenings were spent listening to music other than the AFVN radio, this music had been sent or brought to Vietnam by different soldiers, and then husbanded and played secretly alone or with buddies. Guys played this music to remind them of different times and different places. These music sessions were spent in the dark just kicking back and listening, or listening while thinking of home, writing letters. The music helped in remembering good times with family and friends.

Several songs struck a resonant note with many of us regardless of ethnic, religious, or social background. "We Gotta Get Out of This Place," from the Animals was sung in loud choruses by all. That song was out anthem, our mantra, our one desire. The song "The Letter," "Homeward Bound," "Leaving on a Jet Plane," "Sha-Na-Na-Na," were all favorites of everyone, and there were very few of us who would not pound out the rhythm to Iron Butterfly's "In-a-gadda-da-vida" on the nearest flat surface when it was played. For those with the luxury of a tape recorder or record player, they would entertain their own audiences with the more bizarre troop favorites, renditions of Country Joe and the Fish playing "I'm Fixin' to Die Rag," we all learned the lyrics of that favorite and would sing out loud and true when that song was played. Jimi

Hendrix's electric mayhem in "Purple Haze," "All along the Watch Towers," or "Are You Experienced" had us all rockin'. Janis Joplin and other irreverent favorites the Army radio would not play were all to be heard as you walked down the main hall of the barracks. I along with others, "Goddamned the Pusher Man" with Steppenwolf, sat in silence to admire the perfection of The Cream, but of all my favorites, the seemingly depressing poetry of the Doors struck a resident note, and there were many others who asked those with tapes or records to play one or two songs again and a again.

The U.S.O. and the Army's entertainment service organization I seldom saw at Camp Enari, but I did see two Red Cross girls once. They were both well-built and that to us was entertainment. Just before Christmas, the two beauties drove up in a Jeep, said hello for five minutes without getting out of the Jeep, and then went on their merry way dispensing cheer to other soldiers far from home. Outside of the occasional Army nurse that you saw professionally, glimpses of American women were rare, and as they say "A sight for sore eyes." There were some unkind stories going around about Red Cross girls (known as Donut Dollies). It was said that they went for officers only, and that was for 50 dollars a shot. I didn't think anything of these rumors when I heard them, as I didn't think anyone of them was worth 50 dollars. Besides I didn't have 50 dollars, but I wished I had.

One U.S.O. show arrived at the 278th, just before we left Camp Enari; the show was a Filipino rock and roll band. They did some great imitations of U.S. and British rock groups and rock singers, but then again, if it had been a tap dancer with a singing saw we would have enjoyed it. (In fact we did have just that kind of show when I was later with the 43rd. Just the same, nobody booed or jeered, and everyone clapped when it was over. We were starving). Watching the Filipino show with closed eyes you would have sworn that Janis Joplin had sung "Piece of My Heart," or that Jimi Hendrix was there in person beating out "All Along the Watch Tower." It was amazing how

332

diverse this group was in reproducing almost the exact sound we wanted to hear.

Some people found their entertainment the hard way. One night, in the wee small hours, several people got together and they sand bagged the door of the "Lifer Hootch" shut. (The Lifer hootch unlike our barracks with a door at each end had only one way in or out). Whoever planned this escapade really did a good job, as they used enough sandbags that the door was impossible to open either in or out no matter how much force the Lifers could bring to bear. The next morning the resident "Lifers" were yelling through the barracks screen. They were threatening us, and demanding to be let out by the snickering bunch of soldiers that gathered outside. Finally, after many threats and strong demands someone went and tore down the sandbag wall penning them in.

For real entertainment there was nothing like the U.S. Air Force, and they really did it up right. I found out about this through Orosz, as usual when getting information from Orosz it was always the "Hard Way." Orosz always made getting information a real learning experience. One Sunday morning I was detailed to go and pick up Orosz at the 43rd Signal Headquarters on the other side of Pleiku. For this 20 or so mile ride I was given a ¾ ton truck and The Mummy as a driver. Two things immediately added to the anxiety of this trip as The Mummy drove like a maniac, and had caused me some very anxious moments before. The Mummy passed everything in front of him, and he didn't care who or what it was that he passed it. The Mummy usually passed whatever on the wrong side of the road, and at full speed. The ¾ ton truck was the other problem. The truck had a gasoline engine, but someone, either with a misplaced sense of humor or as an act of deliberate revenge, had filled the gas tank with diesel fuel. So, we raced in the ¾ ton truck all the way through Pleiku and out the other side without a mishap. However, we left a dense smoke screen of white smoke behind us everywhere we went. When I say dense cloud I mean a choking white cloud that smelled terrible.

I was surprised that a gasoline engine would run on diesel fuel, but it did. It did not run well, and every take off from a standing start was like taking off in third gear. The engine labored and dogged along till it got going, and then we smoked on by. I was also surprised that The Mummy could get that truck to move as fast as he did. It was Sunday morning and everyone was off the road and sleeping late. On arrival I checked in at the 43rd's HQ orderly room expecting to find Orosz, but instead I was handed a note by the C.Q. (The Charge of Quarters, the guy in charge while the First Sergeant and the C.O. were away). The note simple said "pick me up at the club at the Pleiku Air Base," simple enough, I had landed there and I knew it was not far away. The Mummy had no problem tearing down the road from the 43rd to the Air Base, but he was considerate he did slow down for the ARVN II Corps road block. Our white cloud followed us there too.

The Air Base had a club alright it was a mansion, a palace when I compared it to our shack we called a club. Inside I was both shocked and appalled by what I discovered there. The Air Force had a full blown steak house cranking out steaks for $2 each, and an EM club complete with a 40 foot bar and slot machines. The bar cranked our drinks to anyone who could put their money on the bar, and the slots paid off regularly. I hadn't seen steak in so long I had forgotten that they even existed. The very first thing inside this Air Force marvel was a sort of "Hat Check" counter, and I was greeted in English by a lovely Vietnamese woman. She took my rifle from me and gave me a chit for it, it took some thought on my part to surrender my weapon but the Air Force Sergeant standing behind the beautiful girl was very insistent. The Air Force had already had experience with Army troops shooting up the joint when they were disappointed about something. The Air Force also went out of its way to make sure that there no unhappy Army troops ready to tear up the place out of anger over poor winnings. For that reason the Air Force provided a certain number of slot-machines for the visiting Army personnel. They paid off better than the rest, and therefore kept the G.I.s happy.

After walking around this palace opened mouthed and goggle eyed I found Orosz. He was on a stool in the bar and he was as drunk as a lord. It was at this point that my education began. The bar tender explained to me that on Sunday mornings the Air Force bar put on a special. Bloody Marys' were sold for 10 cents each, and the event was called, aptly enough "Sick Call." The Mummy was with me this whole time, and told me to sit with Orosz while he slipped off and got himself a $2 steak, and I could do the same when he got back. So I sat with my bombed buddy, and made idle chatter with him. I even plopped down twenty cents and joined him in "Sick Call." I had no idea how he or when he had gotten himself to the 43rd, but I am sure that the object of the trip to the 43rd was the occupation of the bar stool he sat on and the empty drink glass in front of him. I was delighted with this new knowledge about Sunday at the Air Base. I had my steak, and then The Mummy and I picked up our weapons and Orosz's M-2 Carbine, and poured Orosz into the shotgun seat of the ¾ ton truck and headed back to Camp Enari.

I would like to say that this trip back to Camp Enari was quiet, but that would be a lie. The trip was a nightmare. The drunk in the shotgun position did not go quietly to sleep as I thought he would, oh no! He decided to be an old time western stage coach shotgun guard, and as we drove through the open country Orosz would stick his M-2 (M Duce) carbine out the window and pepper the ground with 30 caliber bullets. The Mummy driving, wildly as usual, would try and grab the rifle away from Orosz, but without success, and I being in the back of the truck was helpless to interfere. Orosz finally emptied his one 30 round banana clip and curled up and finally went to sleep. I figured that this had been enough excitement for one Sunday, but at least I got a steak out of it.

Pet Parade

To entertain myself I decided that a pet would be nice, but what kind of pet should I get. There was a pack of about a dozen mongrel dogs hanging around the barracks and mess hall night and day, and these hounds were owned by different G.I.s. Orosz had his own dog, a jet black female named Whore, who went everywhere he went around the base and slept under his bunk. She was well named, in the year that I spent in Vietnam, Whore had three litters of pups; fathers unknown.

Most G.I. dogs were content to hang around the back door of the mess hall and mooch food off of guys coming out. I never saw Whore hanging around with that mob. The very first time I saw her she was nipping the hell out of another dog and chasing it yelping out of her area. She was solid black and large like a stocky Labrador Retriever. What made her remember able was when I saw her she had the hackles standing up on her neck and looked very fierce. She could be quit vicious, and several times I had seen her take a chunk out of a G.I., a passing Vietnamese, or another dog for apparently no reason. After getting to know her it seemed that anything that tasted like a Vietnamese was her all-time favorite food. She had no love for the Vietnamese, and if a hootch maid or other civilian would walk close by where she was lying she would reach out and nip an ankle or whatever.

For the biting reason I accompanied Orosz down to the M.P. pound and visit her shortly after I had first seen her. Whore would be in the locked up for biting someone and they would have her in for rabies observation for a week or more. Whenever Orosz arrived she was always pleased to see him wagging her big curly tail, and as she was usually pregnant she would waddle up to him and slobber against him in her excitement.

Whore was really a remarkable animal, and she followed Orosz around the compound like a puppy. However, there were times that she showed her personality. If Orosz was walking somewhere with her trotting along beside, and a G.I. who knew her came by in a Jeep or truck and called her by name, she would leave Orosz for a ride without a second thought.

Orosz told me that he had left Whore by accident in Qui Nhon (pronounced Quin Yon) on the coast, about 100 miles away. Three days later she returned exhausted on her own.

Well with the motley assortment of dogs already in the compound I wasn't in the market for a dog. I thought there were 10 to many of them hanging around the company area already. A cat was out of the question, and I had only seen one in the few months I had been in country. So to be different, one afternoon I hitched a ride to a Montagnard village just outside Camp Enari's gate and bought myself a monkey. On many patrols I had bought fresh fruit from local Montagnards, and in the process I found out that they would raise dogs and other animals to sell as food for themselves or pets. Conversing with Montagnards during trade, there was a universal sign language that goes with haggling, and it amounted to pointing and holding up a number of fingers. There was also some slapping of the forehead, folding of arms, nods and other comic antics. I don't know what kind of monkey I had bought, other than it was a brown one.

I had seen one or two monkeys as mascots or pets of other G.I.s, and I thought that a monkey would be a lot more fun than a dog. The Montagnard who sold it to me didn't care what I did with it, pet it or eat it, as they would do the same if business was slow. So I figured that I did the monkey a favor.

To go and get a monkey from the Montagnards was a very involved process. First you had to get out of Camp Enari, and then back in. First you had to get permission to leave, in writing, next you had to have a vehicle with a proper log book (no auto theft to go joy riding, or hitch-hiking was brooked by the U.S. Army M.P.s). Once the proper paper work was in order weapons had to be prepared, and other military gear worn, flak vests, helmets, and bayonets. Then you had to have all this stuff inspected at the camp gate before the M.P.s would let you in or out. Sometimes you would wonder if all this was really worth it, while you waited in line behind other vehicles, which were also waiting to get out of camp.

The monkey was a cute little devil. Another G.I. in the barracks donated a collar and chain that had belonged to a now demised monkey. Now that I had my pet properly tethered I thought about teaching him tricks. I had once been told. All it would take was a little understanding, love, and perseverance and any pet would show you affection in return. This little guy responded to my kindness right away. He showed me that he could piss and shit on everything I owned and everywhere he could in my room. Monkeys, I found out, are one of the dirtiest animals around, and mine was no exception.

My monkey had a few tricks of his own up his hairy sleeve, and he showed me his first one on the second day I had him. I took him on a mini-field trip to the camp P.X., the soldier's supermarket. (Getting to the P.X. was no mean fete. It was a long way away from where I lived, and so a long walk. If you could get a ride the more the better, but getting a ride was a trick. G.I.s drove by all the time going somewhere, but a G.I. driver to give a stranger a ride and go out of their way to get you to the P.X. was not usual. You had to get lucky and hitch hike like mad). The P.X. at Camp Enari was a huge barn of a building, actually a steal warehouse, much like todays discount supermarket but without the nicety of shelves. Pallets of merchandize were laid out in rows on the floor, G.I. customers walked up and down the rows picking out what they wanted. There was a formal check out procedure with cash registers in plywood cubicles, with Vietnamese check-out girls. Outside of that there wasn't much resemblance to Sears or K-Mart.

At the P.X. there was always a line of soldiers waiting to get in, and the length of the line usually matched the line of soldiers waiting to get out. It was big, noisy, and dirty inside, but it was the only show in town, and you could kill half a day just browsing. The selection or variety wasn't much though, aside from the world's largest selection of shaving articles, shoe

338

polish, or cigarettes the merchandize was spotty and you had to be there on the right day to get something special. Like a camera, or a watch.

As I entered the front door with my monkey on my shoulder I noticed four pallets in a row each one was piled high with loose bags of M & M candy. Some of them had been broken open and some of their contents had been ground into red mud on the concrete floor. The smell was delicious, and my monkey reacted to it by trying to climb down off of my shoulder. "The P.X. is now importing luxury items," I thought to myself as I drug my reluctant charge along by his chain. I grabbed a couple of the larger bags as I strolled by, and went on about my shopping.

I spent my time leisurely walking up and down the aisles of merchandize, and while I was sifting through some items on a pallet my monkey escaped. He scurried off down the aisle dodging jungle boots and their forest of O.D. Green legs, and was gone before I could stop him. I stopped shopping and went looking, but had no luck in finding him. I had a vision of a $10 bill flying away as I finally gave up and went to pay for the few items I had picked up. At the check-out area I found the one thing I really didn't want to find, a starched and spit shinned Sergeant Major, and he is holding my monkey in one of his beefy hands.

I thought of making my own escape without the monkey, but my conscious got the better of me. So sucking up my courage I walked up and faced the bane of my existence in the U.S. Army. "Ah, Ah Sergeant Major, I believe you have my monkey," I started, smiling confidently. I noticed right away that the monkey did not look normal, its cheeks were bulging three times their normal size. I also noticed that the Sergeant Major's other hand was bulging, bulging with several bags of M & M candy.

"OK soldier," he said, "here's your Goddamn monkey, and here's your Goddamn M & M's" as he handed me both without stretched arms. I took them both sheepishly and made for the nearest check out line, the Sergeant Major called after me. "Boy, don't bring your Goddamn monkey back hey-ya again, ya hear me boy!" to which I agreed.

I was now several bags of M & Ms richer, 10 to be exact, and several dollars poorer. I had another vision this time of a $20 bill flying away, but no matter rich or poor the monkey didn't seem to care either way. However, at the same time I was relieved that my encounter with the embodiment of the green machine was not as painful as it could have been. I slunk off to the nearby EM (enlisted men's) club to console myself with a cold beer, with a firmer grip on the monkey's chain this time.

The consolation was slow in coming, and the beer wasn't too cold either. I got to talking with other G.I.s from other units, and the conversation got around to my monkey who was still packing away M & Ms from one of his many bags. The monkey was handed around from soldier to soldier and once again some butter fingers let go of the chain and the monkey took off again. This time there wasn't so many places for the monkey to hide, and after scurrying around and making some preliminary reconnaissance of the club the monkey was picked up by a perverse G.I. who sat it onto the blade of a slow moving Casablanca ceiling fan.

At this point I should explain how this was possible. The AC voltage provided at Camp Enari for running equipment, appliances, etc., was not your standard U.S. 110 volts of alternating current. This stuff in Vietnam did not come from some huge hydro-electric facility over miles of high tension wire. Our electricity came from a gas or diesel generator of dubious reliability. For whatever reasons the voltage varied dramatically, by that I mean it went from a low of 75 volts to a high in the neighborhood of 145 volts. Being a technician and interested I had actually placed a voltage meter on an electrical outlet and monitored the output over a period of time. The one devastating fact about these voltage levels was that the voltage could fluctuate greatly between the two extremes, and it would do it very quickly and extremely often.

340

Well, the ceiling fan was revolving very slowly because the camp AC voltage supply must have been at its very lowest level. The ceiling fan was oscillated so slowly that my monkey had no difficulty with sitting on the fan blade without holding on. I and my new associates had a good time watching the monkey go around and around on his perch while we all sucked down a beer and talked about the weather and the war. Some soldiers tossed up M & Ms for the monkey as he went by, making the event even more entertaining. It was very entertaining until the voltage level rose suddenly to somewhere near its top end, slinging the monkey off his perch and into the wall across the room. I went over and checked my pet for vitals, and since he was just shaken up I picked up my dazed pet and we went on home.

I've had this little guy only one day and already he has brightened up my daily existence, I was feeling rather good about owning him. My one main concern about keeping him in the barracks was not his filthy toilet habits, but how to keep him from becoming a late night snack for the pack of hounds dwelling in and out of the area; the dogs roamed the hall at night looking for an easy kill.

To prevent an untimely loss of the monkey I went to the junk yard and came back with an odd shaped piece of scrap plywood big enough to block my doorway, and tall enough to prevent the pack of marauding dogs from jumping over. I wedged this into the door and supported it with part of my bed and the back of my wall locker.

Two days after my monkeys first flight from the ceiling fan, my monkey made another amazing scientific discovery, and one that was to leave its permanent mark on him. Electricity! After work I was laying on my bunk letting the monkey wander around the room while his chain was tied to the bed frame. The monkey discovered my one and only electrical outlet in my room, which had my new P.X. radio plugged into it. Being a curious fellow my monkey began tugging on the radio's electrical cord to see what it was. He could only pull the plug part way out of the socket, and so he tried to pull it the rest of the way out by putting his hands behind the plug. ZZZAAAPPPPP! I looked up immediately.

He had made another flight across the room, and another connection with a plywood wall. He sat up right away and shook his little head, and then looked at me as if to say, "Did you get the number of that truck?" I picked him up and checked him out, all parts were accounted for, and I put him back down figuring that he had learned a valuable lesson. I got up and unplugged my radio to remove further temptation from his reach, and then I went and lay down and went to sleep. In the middle of the same night I was awakened to another ZZZAAAPPPPPP, followed by a small THUD, action followed by a reaction. I found the monkey with the beam of my flashlight; apparently physics wasn't his strong point, or memory retention for that matter. He had got his hands inside the socket, and had found out about electricity the hard way.

I picked him up again and put him in bed with me, and attempted to go back to sleep. Sometime later that night the same two sounds as before woke me, but this time he didn't survive the flight. I was sad at losing my pet and sadder still as I still had a footlocker full of M & Ms to get rid of.

Mail

Mail was important, but unlike in the states delivery wasn't regular. In a combat zone you wrote a letter, addressed it, and then wrote the word "FREE" in place of a stamp. You took your letter to the company mail drop in the company office and it was sent to the addressed person absolutely "FREE." Amazing!

Getting a letter back was not that easy. I did get mail, but some letters arrived with news that was two weeks old or older than letters I got from other people. It was not that the letter writers were slow it was the mail. The old news arrived after newer letters had been written and sent, which at first was very confusing. I felt that someone, somewhere, in charge of sending mail to us had a warehouse full of mail sacks. Sacks of mail would be pulled randomly from the warehouse to fill the space available on a plane heading to Vietnam. The remaining sacks of mail would have to wait for another plane with more room. I thus heard a bit of news about my Mom from my girlfriend a week before I heard the same news from my Mom. Confusion continued as my response to Mom or the girlfriend lengthened the time for any corroboration about the news. Let's just say that confusion was in the air and it continued for weeks on certain issues, but being so far from home it was always great to get mail no matter how out of date or confusing.

Dragon Mountain

Each night the guards listed on the guard duty roster were assembled around the supply shed. From the list of names people were selected by fad or fancy and the guard assignments were made. Some from my company were assigned to the Camp Enari bunker line, and some to the bunker line around the top of Dragon Mountain. It was a Lottery.

I had made the trip to both places on several occasions. The bunker line around Dragon Mountain was primitive and puny in comparison to Camp Enari, as the bunkers were dilapidated, only made out of sandbags and timber, and interestingly enough rat infested. Also, Dragon Mountain's summit did not have as many protective belts of barbed wire around it or as many weapons defending it.

To get to the top of Dragon Mountain you were driven out of Camp Enari before dark in the back of a deuce and a half truck, with machine-gun armed Jeep following. We covered the five miles to the base of the mountain in silence and with weapons pointing out and at the ready, even when we passed the "Friendly" Montagnard village by the side of the road. The climb to the top was via a one lane red dirt road that spiraled up the side of the mountain for two to three thousand feet. All

343

along the route all eyes scanned the road ahead for mines, and we paid close attention to the surrounding tree, bushes and ground for the presence of the enemy, these security measures didn't stop until we were inside the perimeter at the top.

Guard duty on top of Dragon Mountain was nerve wracking, and it was also freezing cold at night. Your teeth chattered for either reason. Sitting in the open mouth of a sandbag bunker with the cold wind blowing in your face, was not what the warm tropics were all about. "How the hell did it get so cold in Vietnam?" I remember asking the guy frozen next to me the first time I did guard there. Your teeth chattered while you starred down-hill for several hours at a stretch. The wind and weather helped in keeping you awake as did your shivering and shaking from the cold. This was not my idea of a fun evening. Guard duty was 2 men to a bunker, so your shift was 2 hours on and 2 hours off.

The supply pukes in the states had told us that we would not need our field jackets in the tropical paradise of Vietnam, and many had turned in their jacket. I had held on to mine and had it with me at the top of Dragon Mountain. My Army field jacket kept the top half of me warm from the strong mountain freezing wind and rain, but most of the poor guys up there in a bunker with me only had a G.I. blanket to keep them warm. In either case we froze at night, and I spent my time staring out of my bunker wondering when will the night end.

The top of Dragon Mountain was not entirely in the hands of the U.S. Army, we had one half and the ARVN had the other. For my money it was questionable who had the other half. The mountain was an old cinder cone with one side collapsed, what was left of the mountain top was flat and formed the shape of a large letter "C". The distance between the two points of the "C" was 100 yards or more at the top, where the side of the cinder cone had collapsed. This opening between the 2 arms of the letter "C" was full of underbrush from top to bottom and was an excellent infiltration route for the enemy. One arm of the "C" was manned by the South Vietnamese, protecting one of their own signal installations, and we had the other arm. The defenses on our side were suspect in their ability to provide adequate security, and we were down right paranoid about our ARVN counter parts security measures.

On my first visit to Dragon Mountain I had already heard the story about the Captain who had found one of his troops asleep in a bunker while on guard duty on top of the mountain. And how the Captain had drug this private to the front gate on the mountain, and had shoved a hand grenade into the troop's hand. The Captain had then pulled the safety pin out of the grenade with the comment, "now go to sleep Motherfucker," the Captain had left the troop outside the gate. I had vowed to stay awake no matter what the cost.

It was shortly after the demise of my monkey, Orosz and I found ourselves pulling guard duty together in the same bunker on top of Dragon Mountain, a not so fun evening of two hours on and two off. From the top of Dragon you could see for miles, and as the sun set in its usual spectacular fashion, the different military installations visible lit up their perimeters. The town of Pleiku off in the distance turned on its lights, and late cars and trucks could be seen speeding along the one and only road through the landscape that was now more picturesque than usual. We sat for a time admiring the change in scenery and amazing colors generated during a sunset in this part of the world. We forgot the war briefly as we watched our surroundings change, as daylight melted away. We made small talk about home and family, and tried to amuse each other with jokes and the exploits of our youth. We talked of cars we wanted to own, cars we wanted to buy, and cars our parents drove. Women and sex, were never discussed, such discussions were taboo. What your Mom made for dinner or desert was the topic most talked about. We hated Army food, and we loathed our Army Mess Sergeant. We talked about Sergeant Grayson, and what we had seen go on in the kitchen of the mess hall. We both had seen and heard stories of culinary tragedy, and on guard duty was a good place to share them.

345

We smoked and we joked until it became dark, after dark smoking in the open was taboo, it was also stupid. After dark Orosz lit a cigarette while sitting on the fire step below the mouth of the bunker, and holding a poncho over his head. So that the red glow from the cigarette was not visible from the mouth of the bunker, or the glow would not back light the inside of the bunker. Smoking was not permitted on the bunker line, outside or in the mouth of the bunker. The red glowing end of a burning cigarette at any distance gave any of the little guys form the other side a good aiming point.

When Orosz had finished his smoke he placed the butt between thumb and fore finger, and carelessly flipped the burning end of the cigarette in a spiraling arc out through the mouth of the bunker. I chastised him for not setting a good example for someone who was relatively new in country, and got the finger and a toothy smile for my efforts. Orosz's cigarette butt landed on a decomposing sandbag just outside the bunkers mouth, and it lay there and smoldered until it set the sandbag on fire. Sometime before I arrived "in country" the U.S. Army in Vietnam had switched from cloth sandbags to plastic ones, but our bunker was very old and had been constructed months ago, almost entirely of cloth bags. The cloth bags had seen many seasons, and were as dry as paper by the time Orosz's cigarette arrived. It didn't take long before the bag was sending off flames of an inch or two long, and once going the flames had started to spread within a few seconds. The flames ran rapidly expanding and were creeping towards the other sand bags around the bunkers base.

Looking out the mouth of the bunker the fire caught my attention right away, and I turned to my friend and said, "Hey Orosz, that butt you shot out of here has set the bunker on fire."

"Well hell, go ahead and put it out Scotty."

"Hey buddy; I'm not the fire brigade. You set it on fire you put it out."

Grumbling, Orosz climbed slowly through the mouth of the bunker, and once outside he started kicking at the fire. This action sent bright red sparks flying in all directions, and also brought a reaction from the South Vietnamese on the other side of the mountain top; they opened fire on us. I stood in open mouthed amazement while Orosz lazily kicked at the fire and the red streaks of tracer bullets flew above the bunker and around his head. The tracers were followed by the pop, pop, popping sound from the rifles on the opposite horn of the mountains. At first I was unsure as to who was shooting at us, I thought it might be the enemy, but then I saw the muzzle flashes from the bunker positions on the ARVN side. With each kick Orosz sent more sparks flying, and more bullets came flying from the other half of the mountain. Finally I got a grip on myself and leaning forward at the waist out the mouth of the bunker, I was just able to grab Orosz by his pants leg with one hand. I began tugging at him and yelling for him to get in. I was facing the ground more than Orosz and he could not understand what I was yelling. He stood there looking down at me for what seemed to be minutes saying, "Huh! What! What's going on?" Orosz screwed around like an idiot as I pulled at him, and yelled at him from below. While bullets continued to buzz overhead.

My efforts finally paid off and Orosz jerked his head around looking up at the tracers. "I'll be dipped," he said once he realized that he was in danger, he forgot about the sandbag fire and he dove head first in through the bunkers mouth. I was at once relieved, as the ARVN had adjusted their aim and some of their bullets were making a WACK, WACK sound as they struck the sandbags on top of our bunker, sending sand and dirt cascading down on us.

Orosz came to his feet and his senses at the same time, and he announced, "Hey, they can't do that to us," and with that he grabbed the receiver of our own M-60 machinegun, cranked a round in, and began spraying bullets back at the South Vietnamese. This started a general melee of shooting from all the bunkers near us and on the other side of the mountain as well. Finishing off the first belt in the direction of the ARVN,

Orosz turned to me and commanded, "Load Scotty." To which I promptly complied bringing up a fresh belt of M-60 ammunition from its box on the fire step, and I made sure that I knew where the spare machine-gun barrel was in case we had to replace one. As I wrestled in the darkness with the ammunition belts I thought to myself, "Thank God these damn ARVN have lousy aim."

Empty shell cases jangled off of the roof and wall of the bunker as Orosz blasted back at the ARVNs like a man possessed. The field phone inside our bunker clacked away in its metallic imitation of a telephone ring, but it was ignored by both of us. It was hard to hear much of anything from the loud bangs from each burst of fire from our gun and the jingling of the empty shell cases ricocheting around the bunker. I finally picked up the phone only after Orosz was about to finish off our third and last belt of machinegun ammunition, and the only reason I picked it up was I wanted a re-supply of M-60 Ammo. As I put the receiver to my ear the voice on the other end of the line said, "This is Sergeant of the Guard Kooms and I am giving you a direct and lawful order, CEASE FIRE, MOTHERFUCKER! Cease fire at once." Orosz finally out of machine-gun ammo was now ducking up and down behind the sandbags in the bunkers mouth, and popping up and plunking away with his M-16 rifle. It took me a few seconds of shaking and yelling at him for me to get through to him. The war was over.

It had lasted all of 15 minutes from start to finish, and the first person to get down to us after the firing had ceased was a huge shape with a pronounced southern accent we both knew well. "Hey y'all, what the Fuck ya shootin' at." Orosz recognized the voice right away, "Jon, Big Jon, that youse buddy?" Big Jon lumbered up to the mouth of our bunker yelling "Hold your fire, y'all, I'm coming in," and his massive form appeared in the bunker mouth. It was miraculous, his bulk fit through the mouth of the bunker, complete with "Grease" gun. My night vision was completely gone, the muzzle flashes had ruined it long ago, but through the darkness and from two inches away I recognized his voice. "Scotty McNasty, how the Fuck are you?"

The ARVN commanding officer on Dragon Mountain was miffed, his superior at his base camp was enraged, and his superior's superior at ARVN II Corps headquarters was outraged. These were the least of our worries, our First Sergeant, the one who hated the sight of Orosz and I was eventually going to get wind of this, and he was once again going to be pissed.

Orosz and I were a little pissed too; they made us pick up all the expended brass our machine gun had spewed all over the inside of our bunker.

The morning dawned clear and crisp on top of the mountain, but the base of the mountain was a sea of white. Only the tops of the highest hills were visible, Camp Enari usually off to our right was a blank white space. With the fog moved in, it would be some time before we were relieved. So with some time on our hands we surveyed the damage on ours and the other side of the mountain. We had had the far superior fire power and therefore had inflicted the most damage. The ARVN's wooden outhouse and mess hall were both sieves, while our hill side and bunkers had suffered only superficial damage. I do recall Orosz saying to me after viewing the damage, "Ya we did good, but I wish I had had a .50 caliber instead of an M-60 machinegun. I woulda really fucked up their whole day with a 50," to which I responded, "Naaaa! I would have had to work too hard lugging 50 caliber ammo around." Luckily for both sides no one was killed or injured during our fire fight.

It was late in the morning when we touched down to earth from the back of the truck bringing us back from guard duty, and there was someone waiting for us, and yes, we were summoned before the First Sergeant. On reporting to the orderly room we were immediately ushered into the First Sergeants office. Top had indeed heard about the fire fight, and had assumed the worst; he figured right away that Orosz and I were responsible for starting it. We stood at attention on the same two tile squares we had occupied once or twice before in front of his same desk, and the First Sergeant read us much the same riot act once more. As I stood there and sort of half-heartedly listened to the First Sergeant chew us out I thought to myself, "It sure was fun last night, but next time I want to fire the 60." I also thought, "I gotta find me another way of getting my kicks, cause this guy is boring me to tears."

We didn't get sent to jail, we didn't get a dirty job to do, and we didn't get a medal. What we got was a royal chewing out and a lot of threats. I glanced at Orosz as we stood there and noticed a rather resigned look on his face. After Top had let off a little steam he became more reasonable. He ended this one sided conversation by saying, "Don't ever be brought in here again, I may not be so lenient on you next time." With that he reached into his desk drawer and pulled out a .45 automatic and slammed it on the desk top. "Now get the hell out of here."

"I think your right Scotty, that man hates us," said Orosz as we left.

Big Mouth

Two weeks later the U.S. Army signal sites on top of Dragon Mountain were turned over to the ARVN, and all U.S. personnel were removed from the mountain. Big Jon and his band of cut-throats were once again part of the 278, and they were welcomed back by us as long lost relatives and prodigals. They were welcomed that is, until the trouble began.

The trouble began one night at the club, someone loud mouth decided to make an attempt at comedy or sarcasm, in a comment about our reunion, "Ya, you hill dwellers are finally back stinking up this place. I thought we were rid of you guys." This was greeted by a few people looking up from their drinks but no laughter. But then the idiot persisted, "You guys from Dragon Mountain didn't have it so bad. You were just a relay station; all you had to do was put up an antenna and then put

350

your feet up." The idiot paused and then added, "Ya lazy bastards!" On a one to one basis on the job this could be handled, but when a comment like that was said in the club full of G.I.s the fight was on. It was a good one too. Chairs, tables, and cans sailed through the air till all of us fell exhausted almost as one.

From my vantage point in a corner of the club I watched the loud mouthed comedian being hustled out the door of the club by an NCO. I decided to mix it up with the boys so I stood up and was immediately flattened by a mystery man. I had no idea of who hit me. I waited a second and stood up again, and this time I took two steps toward the action when Big Jon flattened me like I was a rag doll, I went sailing into the empty tables and chairs knocking them over like bowling pins. So from my bruised and aching position on the floor I watched Big Jon tearing around the club knocking people over like a steam train gone mad. It was like the sheriff had come to town to settle everybody down, and with Mr. Bigmouth nowhere to be seen there was no reason to punch anybody. The fight was over before it really got going due to this mad man plowing through everyone. I waited till he was done then I got up groaning and bought him a beer. In the morning at breakfast in the mess hall "Big Mouth" was sporting a broken arm. I didn't ask him where he got it, as my Mom had warned me not to talk with morons. He wasn't too communicative though, because he had to do all his talking from between his split lips.

The Glee Club

Orosz and Big Jon had been friends long before I joined the 278th, and so after Big Jon had rejoined us in the base camp the three of us would convene together after work and pass the time. We would lounge around a bunker or the club, drinking a few beers, chat or just sitting and listening to the music we could hear. One evening while sharing a beer in the club, someone brought up the subject of music, in particular a

351

favorite popular song. Orosz had a go at singing it, but he could not remember all the words. Big Jon tried and I tried but neither of us could remember the words even though we remembered the melody. We tried other songs but again we came up short in remembering the lyrics. Then one of us mentioned Army songs, and Orosz stood up and sang a few bars of the song being mentioned. It turned out that there was more than one version of this song. There was the one Orosz sang the published and recognized Army version and number two, the other, the unpublished version. The dirty Army version! I took a turn and rendered all of the lyrics to the dirty version, and one dirty song led to another dirty song, and between the three of us we had quite a repertoire of bawdy ballads.

The three of us stood at the bar amongst an O.D. Green clad group and sang our hearts out. For our effort we got the wail of a siren, and the blast from and NCO's whistle. Camp Enari was under Rocket attack. Normally you dropped your drink went to the barracks and grabbed your war gear then headed for the nearest bunker. We skipped all that, as by the time the siren went off we were several beers to the wind. All three of us grabbed our beers and just headed to the nearest bunker. There we sat on a sandbagged seat and continued our sing along. The cannons crashed outside and the enemy rounds crashed somewhere on base but we were undeterred. We sang whatever song we three agreed to sing, we felt no pain, and those in the bunker with us joined in at times. The NCOs there with us gave us some shit about being out of uniform, but we were too far gone to care. The Glee Club had been born.

So from then on whenever we were together and in need of entertainment we would sing some of our remembered ditties in the best harmony we could muster. No one in the club seemed to mind how raucous our lyrics or our singing was, and on occasion some people would offer ditties they hadn't heard us sing. We even sang everything from rock and roll to pop, even though we rarely knew all the words. We sang dirty little songs to cute songs, but we drew the line at "Show Tunes," but hell we even sang requests.

So the three of us, Big Jon, Orosz and me formed a glee club, and called it the Varsity. It's not that our singing was so good; our purpose was to entertain ourselves. We set up a rule for the club and the rule was cast in concrete, after all we felt that we had to have a rule. Anymore we felt would be too oppressive.

Rule No. 1. All club meetings were mandatory, but if you couldn't come it was OK.

When it came to singing my own personal favorite song from our repertoire was "In a cabin in the woods," complete with all the arm movements and hand gestures. This song required that those singing it perform the song with motions that depicted the words. The song was repeated several times, and each time through a line of verse was left off but the arm motions remained, until the entire song was performed in pantomime.

For those of you who don't know the song it goes:
In a cabin in the woods,
(Make a tent with your hands over your head)
Little bear by the window stood,
(Place your right hand over your eyes looking for something)
Saw a rabbit hopping by,
(Make rabbit ears held out in front, making a hopping motion)
Knocking at my door,
(Make a knocking motion)
Help me! Help me! Help me! He said,
(Throw arms up in surprise, with each Help me!)
For the hunter shoots me dead,
(Point a rifle)

Little rabbit come inside,
(Make a beckoning motion)
Safe within my arms,
(Draw a finger across throat making a throat slashing sound)

There was nothing more stirring than to enter our club and see three or more grown men perform this pantomimed song. Each one concentrating for all they were worth in case they make a mistake and have to buy a round of beers.

Drug Problems

There were drug problems to be dealt with, and daily we were bombarded with anti-drug slogans on the radio, posters on the bulletin board, and NCOs snooping around trying to find drugs or drug users. I did not understand all the fuss on base camp. Outside of the base camp you could stop anywhere in town or at the side of the road and someone would try and sell you drugs.

If you wanted drugs they were easy to find and just as easy to avoid if you were not interested. Usually people on drugs stood out a mile by their actions. Those that used drugs while on the job or on duty as we called it were asking for trouble. As I have said the NCOs were beating the bushes to find drugs and drug users.

The most obvious case of drug abuse I ever saw was in Sergeant Grayson's mess hall. One day while I and Orosz were on K.P. together we witnessed one of the cooks sitting on a mess hall chair and having a long conversation with a crate of carrots. Neither Orosz nor I could tell which contributor to the conversation was the most coherent, but the M.P.s came and the cook went away. They did leave us the crate of carrots as a memento.

Electricians

When Big Jon and his mob moved off of the mountain they judiciously went through all their barracks and removed all light fixtures, electrical sockets and switches, but they left the wire in place. This was the normal practice for troops in Vietnam, as you never knew if you were going to have such luxuries at your next place of residence. You could get wire, miles of it, but sockets, switches and light fixtures were hard to get. Our Captain was informed about this "unauthorized" removal of government property when he was visited by a full bird American Colonel, accompanied by an ARVN Colonel, the American Colonel was part of the Military Assistance Command Vietnam MACV (also known as Saigon Warriors). The Colonel to say the least was miffed.

Almost everyone in the company knew of the Colonel's visit, as visits by Colonels were rare, and Colonels always brought bad news. There was a great expression of empathy for the Captain, as everyone could imagine what he had to go through. At the time we didn't know what the Colonel wanted, but we knew that this was no social call. To us a Colonel was nothing to be ignored, what they wanted was nothing to be denied, and they were nothing but trouble.

Very shortly after the Colonels visit, our Captain caught up with me on the company's basketball court. This was a rock strewn piece of barren open ground with a basketball hoop at one end. At the other end was a place to rest your bruised body from playing a contact sport with people who needed to let off a little steam. I was there shooting baskets with Big Jon when the Captain walked up with a box under his arm. We stopped our game out of respect to the Captains rank, and as I didn't need another visit with the First Sergeant. I was there shooting baskets because I had the morning off after being the company runner all night, and Big Jon was there as he had not found a job in the company yet. With the Colonels visit the C.O. had, in a few short minutes had been presented a large problem, and hud seen the solution by looking out his office window, seeing Big Jon and I. Big Jon was registered Electrician back in the states. Big Jon knew it, the Captain knew it, but I was completely in the dark about it. The C.O. handed Big Jon the box, it was full of electrical fixtures, and said, "Put them back."

Big Jon knew the reason for this field trip, and he insisted that I come along and help him with the rewiring of the hootches. I agreed since anyone leaving camp required a shotgun guard and I could do with a ride and maybe a little excitement. So we both got our war gear and weapons and headed for the main gate to Camp Enari in a Jeep.

The trip by Jeep to the top of Dragon Mountain was very fast, and thankfully completely uneventful. Uneventful that is until we got to the main gate at the top. We had a few anxious moments with the Vietnamese gate guards, telling them in English what we were there for didn't help matters, and showing them the box of electrical fixtures just confused matters. Big Jon and I got out of the Jeep and had to physically act out rewiring, using our fixtures, before the gate guards got the message and passed us through.

The barracks that had been abandoned by Big Jon's troops were not being used by anyone, and this caused us both to comment on what the big flap about rewiring was all about. Big Jon clued me in on his Electricians background, and explained to me what we were going to do and how we were going to perform the task. We were going to do what is known in the Army as "The Quick and Dirty." Big Jon and I set to our task with a will. As usual no anti-spark boxes had been used in the previous wiring, so this made our job easy. But not being one to waste time Jon showed me how to do it the real-easy way, he would grab a fixture out of the box, put in the place it had been removed from the wall and then drive a nail through it. We would then place the ends of the nearby hanging wires behind it and move on to the next place where a fixture was needed. Big Jon was a real life trained electrician, had worked

356

for his dad who was an Electrical Contractor. He commented as we left, "this was the fastest wiring job I had ever been on."

Once we were finished we walked out the door of the hootch and took a look around, outside a few Vietnamese ARVN were hanging or squatting around but the place looked deserted. Since no one was using the hootch and both Big Jon and I didn't want anyone breaking in and stealing those valuable light fixtures, something that would disturb that Colonel again, we nailed the door shut. Not being satisfied with that, to be doubly sure that no one would break in we found some old scrap, jagged plywood and we nailed that over the nailed shut door. So to be triply sure that no one would break in I walked back to our Jeep and picked up a tin can shaped grenade of riot (CS) tear gas we just happened to have with us. I pulled the pin and holding the safety spoon down with my thumb; I shoved it up and out of sight between the scrap plywood and the door. Making sure that the safety spoon was held down by the plywood's pressure on the door. I released the grenade and stepped back and admired our work.

Our job well done, Big Jon and I climbed back into our Jeep, and headed out of the gate, back toward Camp Enari. As we drove through the gate, who to our surprise did we see coming the other way driving his own Jeep, but that full bird ARVN Colonel from MACV. "I knew that S.O.B. was coming up to check on us," said Big Jon, and I nodded my concurrence.

The first thing that flashed in my mind was, "That guy is going to get that tear gas grenade in the face when he goes to check our work." For some reason I tried to make the Jeep go faster down the mountain. Following the spiraling road down the mountain a second thought came to me. "If he gets the first grenade he is going to come after us." "Stop the Jeep," I yelled at Jon. We were about half way down the mountain, and Jon slammed on the breaks, sending the Jeep sliding in the dirt till we stopped. I explained my fears to Jon. "Hey don't worry lil' buddy," he said, "what's he gonna do, send us to Vietnam."

357

Big Jon was right, so I rummaged around in our bag of tricks in the back of the Jeep till I found what I was looking for. I knew it by its feel; it was a Baseball grenade of crystalline tear gas. This was a ball shaped plastic grenade, that when set off would discharge tear gas that would hang in the air. The gas would be visible in sun light, the light sparkling as it reflected off of the crystals that hung in the air. The gas would hang in place, around where it was discharged, until a vacuum was created, (like a breeze or a door opening), and then the gas would react like regular tear gas. A regular tear gas grenade went off like a smoke bomb with clouds of the gas billowing out of the can. We had used these Crystalline Tear Gas grenades in bunkers and holes we found on patrol. We left the gas inside as a surprise to anyone wanting to reuse what we left of the bunker.

I pulled the safety pin and tossed the grenade in the ditch by the side of the road. After that, Big Jon and I got out of there fast and didn't stop till we were off of the mountain. We drove back toward Camp Enari a short ways, till we had a good view of the road down the mountain, and then we pulled over to the shoulder and waited. We didn't have to wait long. We heard the Jeep before we saw it, and it was traveling fast down the mountain. I said to Jon, "by the speed he's going he must have got the first one." All of a sudden the speeding Jeep veered left crazily and hit the side of the mountain. "Must have hit number two," said Jon. As we watched, the Jeep careened right and struck the roads dirt bank, and then the Jeep veered left again and hit the side of the mountain once more. "Time to go," said Big Jon and he revved the engine and engaged the clutch and the Jeep shot forward toward Camp Enari.

We got back to camp and reported to the C.O. on our completed mission, but we made no mention of the Colonel or the tear gas. Surprisingly enough nobody else mentioned the Colonel or the tear gas either, ever. The Colonel never returned, and no charges were ever brought, I guess MACV put it down to "enemy action".

Chapter 15

"The Bronze Star Grayson Blues"

Daily the 278th Signal was moving closer to deactivation and disbanding, and each day there was less and less repair work to be performed, and more and more labor of packing this or getting rid of that. All of Camp Enari was going away, the 4th Division was moving bag and baggage to the base camp at An Khe half way between Pleiku and the coast. At times we could see convoys of ARVN trucks driving slowly by our barracks area; they were hauling bits of Camp Enari away with them. Trucks would pass with roof joists upside down and sticking out of both ends of the truck others had the tin for the roof stacked on the bed, and yet others hauled stuff. Camp Enari was materially going somewhere.

Ammo Dumping

Because of our wonderful relationship with the First Sergeant Orosz, Big Jon and I found ourselves on some very strange details. The three of us were given the job of getting rid of all the left over ammunition and explosives from the recon patrol, and this we were to do under the supervision of the company's supply officer Lieutenant Stockroom.

Ammunition is funny stuff, it was only good for one thing, and that was going BANG! One way or another! Once you owned it you couldn't trade it back in, and you couldn't trade it away. Every other unit at Camp Enari already had more ammunition than they needed. Many other units had their own recon team, and they were looking to get rid of their own surplus ammo. You couldn't give the stuff away, as that would screw up someone's books or create surpluses and storage problems. The one thing you really couldn't do with it was to turn it back into the Army supply system. You had to get rid of it, eat it, blow it up, so once you had the stuff, it was your problem.

The first thing to be gotten rid of were 33 cases of dynamite stored in the company's Ammo & explosives bunker. When we inspected it, before the Lieutenant decided what to do with it, we discovered how risky this job was going to be. The dynamite had been in the bunker an awful long time. We could tell not just from the dust on the cases, but by several of the cases leaking liquid nitro-glycerin. Orosz quipped as we tip toed past, "This could turn out to be a very explosive situation."

Outside the explosives' bunker once again we were informed by the C.O. that he had made a deal for someone who would accept the dynamite. The dynamite was scheduled to go to the Montagnards at a village named Plei Ping, and today was as good a day as any to do it. The three of us drew lots to see who would drive the truck, and as luck would always have it I won. I had never won anything before in my life, and I win this. How do you figure?

The Montagnard camp was 30 or so miles south of Camp Enari, down highway QL 14, and I would be driving an Army deuce and a half over a dirt road, through enemy territory, loaded with high explosives, alone. Boy, it just didn't get any better than this. The fact that the First Sergeant didn't insist of me having to do it at night had some value. After my assignment was announced everyone in the unit avoided me like the plague, it was as if I didn't exist. Poor Scotty, I knew him when.

The truck was loaded "carefully" by Big Jon, Orosz and some supply people, and since I was driving I was allowed out of the loading detail. I stood way, way off to one side, behind another bunker, with my fingers in my ears. Finally my turn came, and I very gingerly started the trucks engine and very slowly headed out on the trip. I got the truck rolling very slowly forward, and as I went along I picked out what I thought was the smoothest part of the road. Once on the move I kept rolling not stopping for anything at 10 miles per hour. At the main gate the guards waved me on through without the perfunctory inspection, after word of what I was carrying was given to them in advance. It was like driving on eggs all the way, so I never took the truck out of second gear so that I could look for bad spots in the road to avoid. This is the method I followed all the way. I had two security escorts for the trip one leading and one following, which consisted of two machine-gun mounted Jeeps full of armed men. This was less than reassuring to me as they both stayed well outside of the blast range. For 33 cases of dynamite and one truck, that was about 100 meters in every direction. I didn't really mind the job of driving explosives around, since coming to Vietnam I had become rather fatalistic. As the saying went, "it don't mean nothin'." The truck I was driving had six foot by one foot bright red signs on each side with 10 inch high white letters proclaiming the contents of the truck to everyone "EXPLOSIVES." I was praying that the Charlie couldn't read English.

It was, I think, rather challenging to drive 33 cases of dynamite around. The real challenge was to see if I could get to my destination in one piece or a million. After 4 grueling hours behind the wheel I finally made it to the destination. I made it in one piece, and I thanked the stars above that I had not become one of them. The first thing I did was to relieve myself; it had been a long day and with the excitement over my body demanded attention. I was real nervous on certain stretches of the road, and I had to take a break or two to give my right leg a rest. Army trucks were not made for smooth rides, and over a dirt road there had been some places that I was tempted to grit my teeth and close my eyes as we went over them, but all in all I was very relieved to be in one piece.

The Montagnards were very pleased with the dynamite, and I knew that they would make good use of it. I had visited this village before, and knew the camp's American advisor team and some of the civilian defense force by sight. We all helped off load the truck, "gingerly," and then I and my security force drove hell-for-leather back to Camp Enari.

Odd Jobs

The next day the same detail continued for me and my pals. Now we had to get rid of all the left over small arms ammunition. Several dozen magazines of rifle ammunition, belts of machine-gun ammunition, hand grenades, Claymore mines, and 40mm M-79 ammunition and the like. It took a three quarter ton truck to haul it out of base camp to where we were to get rid of it. The usual chocking cloud of dust followed our truck as The Mummy driving at his usual break neck speed motored us off of the base. There was a large cleared area outside of the base camp, it was still insight of the camp's perimeter wire, and it was here we set up shop. Big Jon, Orosz and I were eager to get at blowing this stuff off, but we were being hampered in our efforts by the presence of the supply officer Lieutenant Stockroom and one of his supply clerks. They had come along as the supply section was in charge of all this stuff, and would have to write up all the paper work required by the Army to account for it. They had followed us in their own Jeep, just the Lieutenant and his supply clerk, and their paper work made three. I am glad that the supply people allowed us some leeway during regular patrols, as it would have been terribly inefficient to go into a combat situation with a clerk at your elbow checking off each round fired on a clipboard.

So here we were on the unfriendly side of the barbed wire, and though we were armed to the teeth I felt a little insecure. The first thing to be disposed of was a case of dynamite blasting caps. The reason that these hadn't gone along with the dynamite to the Montagnards was they were needed to set off Claymore mines and C-4 explosives. Anyone could get explosives, the detonators were hard to get. These blasting caps are touchy buggers; any one of them could mess up your whole day, setting off a whole case at once, perhaps would mess up a week-end. Two of us humped the case 200 yards further into the clearing, so that we could get clear shots at it from our set up position. With that done we opened the festivities with M-16s firing off the rifle ammunition as fast as we could pull the trigger and reload. I am a good shot with an M-16, and I was bouncing bullets all over and around the case but without detonating it. Orosz had switched from his M-16 to an M-60 machine-gun, and Big Jon changed to a 40mm grenade launcher, while The Mummy and I stuck with my M-16 rifle. The Lieutenant was doing his best to direct our fire, while the supply clerk handed out ammunition. Big Jon, Orosz and I were doing our out and out level best to disregard the Lieutenant's directions and to happily blast away.

Orosz finally ran out of machine-gun ammunition about the same time that I gave up with my M-16. I had fired 25 magazines of 18 rounds each through the rifle on automatic and semi-automatic, and the barrel of the rifle was glowing red to white hot when I stopped. So I decided to call it quits as I was having no success, and I laid my rifle down against a tree stump to cool off. While I went to see what I could try next, along came the supply clerk. In directing his Lieutenant's attention to the condition of the M-16's barrel he emphasized how hot it was by using his foot instead of his hands. He put his full body weight on the rifle, and the barrel bent at a 30 degree angle 9 inches from its muzzle. This was a brand new M-16, just out of the wrapper, that I had just drawn from supply that morning to use on this detail. Later I had one hell of a time trying to turn it back in to the same clerk who had bent it. He was not going to accept damaged government equipment. I strongly suspect that he is currently an IRS tax auditor. It took some strong language, threats, and a lot of talking to get him to take back the rifle. I had to accompany it with a written statement about combat damage, and that's the only way he would accept it.

Finding no new weapon that I could use I watched Big Jon launching grenades one at a time at the case of blasting caps, but after three misses in a row he became very serious and determined. A look of concentration came over him, and he took careful aim with the next high explosive round. I watched it sale out from the short barrel of the M-79 toward the case, and I marveled at being able to see the flight of the bullet. This round struck the case dead center, and exploded on contact, which was followed almost simultaneously by an enormous second explosion which was the blasting caps going off all at once. We felt the concussion and blast from the big explosion at the same time we heard the BANG and saw the debris flying in all directions. Big Jon had done it. He turned back from the settling debris with a nonchalant air as if this type of shooting was his every day specialty.

Next on the list of things to go we threw all our smoke grenades, downwind so we avoided choking in the smoke. The smell of those things was awful and would gag you, not to mention change the color of certain bodily functions to the same color of the smoke you breathed. Hand grenades came next, and Lieutenant Stockroom wanted to count each bang to make sure they all detonated. There were over 100 hand grenades to get rid of in this manner, and Big Jon and Orosz made mention of the fact that we were outside the base camp and drawing attention to ourselves. No matter, we complied with the Lieutenant for a while, but about half way through we began throwing three grenades at a time.

With all the ammunition gone the last things remaining to get rid of were 17 Claymore mines, some explosive Det. Cord, plus several sticks of C-4 plastic explosive. A single Claymore mine contained one half pound or so of C-4 explosives. This type of mine was also full of BBs, and was engineered to throw the BBs in a certain direction when detonated. Hence the printing on the curved face of the mine, which stated, "Front toward Enemy." All together we had over 30 pounds of explosives, enough to make a very nice bang. Orosz and I convinced the Lieutenant that it would be a good idea to blow this stuff all at once, insuring its mutual disintegration. Besides, with the explosives gone we could get the hell out of there, as the longer we stayed there the more skittish we became. Big Jon reminded us that the more ammunition we shot off the less we had to defend ourselves if needed.

Big Jon had discovered a partially collapsed bunker behind a mound in the clearing, and suggested that we blow off everything inside the bunker. Big Jon assured us that this way it would keep the debris to a minimum. Again Lieutenant Stockroom had to agree to the idea, and once he did I set to work with a will. I crawled inside the bunker, and drug the explosives in behind me. I began wiring all of the blasting caps for the mines, and C-4 together in a series parallel wiring scheme so that they would all go off together. While I was doing this I explained to those outside the bunker what I was going to do, but somehow this didn't set right with Lieutenant Stockroom. The Lieutenant began shouting encouragement to me through the openings in the bunker, "Lennox, it's not going to work Lennox." "Lennox I told you it isn't going to work," I continued on affirming that it could and would work. Little did this Lieutenant know whom he was dealing with, I was an Army trained electronics technician, who really loved his work. I really loved it especially when it came to blowing things up electrically.

Once the wiring was finished we got together all the electrical detonator cord we had, that amounted to about 300 feet of cord, and we connected it all together. Then we laid it back behind the bunker and around the back of a small earth mound, and further back to a shallow ditch we found there. Everyone got under cover in the ditch, and when all were ready Orosz pulled an electric Claymore detonator out of his left hand pants pocket and attached it to the end of the detonator wire. He raised his head trying to make sure that everyone was down under cover, and then yelled for the Lieutenant to say the word. Lieutenant Stockroom rose up and gave one more, "it'll never work," and then gave the nod for the go ahead. All was silent when Orosz raised the detonator in his right hand over his head and squeezed the trigger. Silence! Nothing happened, Orosz pressed it again, and still nothing. Lieutenant Stockroom got up from the ditch; feeling vindicated in his assessment of my electrical ability, and stood up exclaiming, "See Lennox, I told you it wouldn't work." Paying no attention to the Lieutenant Orosz reached into his right pants pocket and extracted another Claymore detonator, and attached that to the end of the wire. Without looking around Orosz raised his arm once more and squeezed the trigger of the new detonator. The bunker exploded straight up in the air with one hell of a BANG.

Bits and pieces of bunker were now raining down on us and I turned my gaze back to the ditch and saw Orosz curled up into the fetal position, with his arms wrapped around his head. I looked up and saw a large black object heading our way, and had just enough time to cover my own head when an empty sandbag flopped down almost noiselessly between the two of us. In the distance we could all hear the plaintive wail of sirens as the base camp went on alert. As the sirens began I looked over at Orosz, and he gave me back a "well we've done it again," look. It wasn't a bad bang for 30 pounds of explosives, I guessed that I hadn't allowed for the compressing effect, a layer or two of sandbags could provide when placed on top of that much explosives. After the bang, Big Jon had looked back over his shoulder at the Lieutenant, and watched him skidding along the ground on his butt propelled by the concussion of the blast.

The Lieutenant was not pleased, his pants were dirty, but at least he knew now that it would work.

Not bad for one day's work. Wc had dusted the pants of one second Lieutenant, and put one entire base camp on alert. As I looked back toward our handiwork on the other side of the mound a column of brown smoke and debris rose several hundred feet in the air, I turned back when Big Jon came scrambling along the ditch in a crouch telling everyone "let's go, let's go." When he got to me he said, "Nice going Scotty McNasty, but now we have to get back on the base." At once I realized the seriousness of our situation, we were outside the barbed wire, and we would be facing our own armed countrymen who may be disposed to shoot first and ask questions later. Getting back on base without becoming casualties was no mean fete; it was mostly a matter of luck. Big Jon and I walked unarmed up to the gate in front of our truck waving and shouting, "don't shoot, don't shoot, we're Americans." The gate guards after inspecting us asked, "What the hell were you guys doing out there anyway?" "We were just giving Lieutenant Stockroom here a tour of the perimeter, and I'll be doggone if we didn't do it from the wrong side," drawled Big Jon.

First Convoy

Several days later I made my first convoy in Vietnam, and got first hand glimpse of one of the most deadly places in Vietnam. I rode as a shotgun guard in a truck convoy between Pleiku and An Khe, and the ride took us through the infamous Mang Yang Pass. It was really an uneventful trip, but it gave me some further knowledge of life on the planet Vietnam, and it also gave me several hours of anxiety as I rode slowly along at the end of the convoy waiting for something to happen.

Before the convoy left Camp Enari I spent my time examining the truck I was to ride in and the driver. I was very particular about my own safety, and wanted to know if this guy could at least drive. He was a lean and lank southern kid of about 19, with a definite disdain for me and the convoy.

"You ever do this before?" I asked.

"Sure the Fuck have," was the drawled reply.

"I-I'm nervous. Are you?" I asked.

"I already shit three times this morning, and by the third time I could shit down the neck of a Coke bottle without spilling a drop. That answer your question?"

"Yeah, my assholes a little puckered too." I immediately got more nervous, and then had to run to the latrine to relieve myself of my own diarrhea from the malaria pill blues. When I returned I found my driver leaning over the engine of his truck making a final check. Over the engines noise I asked, "Ya think we'll get hit today?" All that brought from him was an affirmative nod of the head. That started my insides churning again, and I had to run back to the latrine.

The rolling hills I had viewed around Camp Enari and Pleiku continued toward the pass, and many villages inhabited the hills and valleys we rode through. On the road heading east from Pleiku we passed a large lake that was surrounded by steep hills right down to the water's edge, and on a small island was a pedestal with an enormous white statue. What the statue was, or of whom didn't matter, it was a very beautiful setting, and when I asked my driver what it was, I got an "Ah don' give a fuck." So I stopped gazing at the scenery and spent more time doing the job I was supposed to be doing, scanning the surrounding countryside for the enemy.

We passed detachments of Army engineers sweeping the shoulders of the road with mine sweepers strapped to their backs. "Why don't they sweep the road too?" I asked my driver. "The dinks put most of their mines on the shoulders, and besides them engineers have giant rollers that they use on the road," I was learning a lot.

At every bridge crossing a ravine or river we had to detour around the obstacle as the bridge over it had been destroyed, and the bridge lay as so much twisted rubble now part of the obstacle it had once surmounted. These crossing points were all guarded, they were maned by either U.S. or ARVN troops, and they had built up sandbag defenses all around the ends of the downed bridges. Included in the defenses were bunkers, APCs and at some crossings tanks. The crossings itself were now bull dozed tracks down and across the river or ravine, and either a dirt path or tread-way bridge spanned the gap from bank to bank. It was distressing to see these huge concrete and steel structures broken and twisted into so much junk, and I wondered how long ago they had been blown up.

At every village we passed by, and that seemed at times to be at every turn in the road, there were little Vietnamese kids standing at the side of the road. And as each vehicle passed them the kids would raise their hands up to it with their first and second fingers forming a "V", the peace sign. "Hey!" I exclaimed to my driver the first time I saw it, "They're throwing us the peace sign." The driver looked at me incredulously, "You Fucking idiot! They want a Goddamned cigarette." All he needed to add was "You naive asshole," but that's what they wanted. I proved it at the next turn of the road; one cigarette set four kids, three of them no more than four years old, dressed in only a cast off and faded O. D. Green Army t-shirt, scrambling after the one cigarette I had tossed from the truck.

After several more months in Vietnam I was finally able unravel the mystery of how old were these kids I saw by the side of the road. I found out that there was a sort of uniform code that these kids adhered to, which made it easier. When a male or female child is born in Vietnam it is left to run around naked until it is about two years old. This saves on laundry, and on diaper service. When a kid reaches two it is given an old cast off G.I. T-shirt, as a total wardrobe. You can tell the age of kids by how the T-shirt fit. The T-shirt reached to the ankles of the younger ones, and came to just above the belly button of the four year olds. When a child reached the age of about five it was given a pair of short pants to wear, and the t-shirt was thrown away or more probably given to another kid.

369

As we neured Mang Yang pass the hill sides and the road both became steeper and much more rock strewn, dead and broken trees stuck their stubby, black and leafless fingers in the air. Scorched spots were visible on the hills and black cropped stalks of grass and twisted and blackened bushes paid tribute to the action that went on in the pass. I checked my rifle for the sixth time and peered harder at the surrounding hill sides, but nothing happened to my great relief, on both the trip there and back.

My surly driver was as relieved as I was at this lack of action, and when he got out of the truck back at Camp Enari he vomited his guts into the dirt. I stood by the side of the truck until he finished, and then offered him my canteen of water. "Thanks man," he said, "I sure am glad as hell that that's over." I didn't press it, but I was to find out later exactly how he felt.

Civilian Help

One of the biggest jobs we were given before abandoning Camp Enari was to dismantle its so many thousand line dial telephone exchange. I didn't think the base camp was that big but apparently it was. Having very little need to use a telephone, I did not know that Camp Enari did not have the usual Army field phone switch boards complete with hand cranks to ring a bell. The field phone switch board exchanges were the kind of phones where you had to keep saying "Working" about every third word of a conversation so that the switch board operator did not pull the plug and cut the line. So Camp Enari had a dial telephone exchange just like being back in the U.S., pick up the phone and there was a dial tone. I had seen the telephones on desks but I had no one to call so I never thought about them. Wow!

This was to be a really big job, and all the telephone gear was to be dismantled carefully and sent back to the states. This stuff was so valuable that the Army had sent over three civilians to pack and ship it properly. Apparently this was not going to be the standard Army hack job of dismantling things with a hammer or an axe. The "Telephone Company" had come to save the day. We met these civilians their first day in camp, shortly after our morning formation when I, Big Jon, Orosz and a few others were assigned to help them with dismantling the exchange. These civilians were in seventh heaven, all three were middle aged men, and acting like a bunch of kids. They proudly wore brand new O.D. Green jungle fatigues and boots, and they were excited to get a chance and come and see the war.

We walked together from our barracks area up the hill toward the telephone exchange, and while we were walking an artillery unit fired off a salvo from the other side of the base camp. The civilians all jumped as one, two of them landed behind the barrel wall of a barracks we were near, and the third threw himself into the ditch beside the road. All of them were yelling "IN COMING, IN COMING" at the top of their voices. Big Jon went to get the two out from behind the blast wall while Orosz and I stood over the one in the ditch, and informed him "Stand up, we'll tell you when it's in coming." Orosz and the rest of the detail headed on down the road, and Big Jon, the civilians and I had to hurry to catch them after we had gotten our charges settled down.

We worked on dismantling the gear all day; this was to be no quick and dirty job. No brute force was needed. We had to unscrew, unbolt and gently disconnect every wire one at a time. When I had a chance to talk to Big Jon and Orosz, I suggested that we invite these new guys to have a drink with us that night at our club. This was to be proposed all in the proper spirit of camaraderie and good fellowship, and as a welcome to the unit and Vietnam. I explained my real plan in more detail, and they both thought it a fine idea. Big Jon went and made the invitation, and it was readily accepted.

The shack we used as an EM, NCO, and Officers club was directly in front of the three 155mm cannons that used to fire over our barracks area. So any time the artillery fired off the bar and those inside seemed to jump off of the floor. You might

371

say the club got the worst of any artillery fire missions. We were hoping that the artillery would have a fire mission this evening. We knew the artillery men well, or the "Cannon Cockers," as we called them. They would come and drink and spend time at our bar when off duty, and so we had a good relationship with them. During dinner, instead of eating I used the time to string a telephone line and two field telephones between the bar and the artillery position. As I walked into their command shack with the field phone and line I explained my needs to the NCO in charge. All he had to do was to call us up just before he fired off any rounds that night, to this he readily agreed, especially as I promised him a case of beer for his trouble. A case of beer was a $4 expense on my part, the beer was never that good, but I figured it was worth it for a laugh.

The civilians showed up at the bar after dinner, and had a few drinks. All in the bar were now in on the stunt we were going to pull and so everyone played along in a friendly spirit of welcoming new members to the unit. The civilians had a great time swapping stories with several of the troops. My accomplices and I manned a strategic perimeter around the field phone, and waited for things to happen. Two pleasant hours were passed in this way until the bell on the field phone chirped briefly, and Orosz answered it and gave a snappy "278 Go," to the voice at the other end, and a sharp "Roger," before replacing the receiver on the phone cradle. He next winked at Big Jon and I and we all three of us turned around and rested our backs and elbows against the planks on the top of the bar. It took only a minute, and a bright white flash of light lit up the inside of the shack, and a giant explosion rocked the room and seemed to lift us all off of the ground as one. The Cannon Cockers had come through, and the three of us sprang into action. Orosz, Big Jon and I started yelling "IN COMING, IN COMING" at the top of our voices, and stood back against the bar again to watch. Some of the soldiers started to panic, but most did not react to our yelling as they knew IN COMING from OUT GOING. The three civilians leaped from their seats, and as the white cloud of gun powder smoke rolled over us and covered everyone and everything in the room, the cannons fired once more. This added further panic to the civilian's flight, as I watched the three of them jump over tables and chairs, push people out of their ways, and ran Panic stricken out the door of the bar. Once outside all three jumped off of the steel plank bridge that spanned canyon in front of the bar. They threw themselves into this six foot deep drainage ditch that ran in front of the bar. This was the same ditch that those of us too drunk or lazy to stagger the 50 feet to the latrine would use as a place to relieve themselves, adding to the red mud at the bottom. The rain water and muck at the bottom of the ditch was sufficient to make their nice new fatigues look like they had been in country for a good long while. Welcome to the 278th!

A good laugh was had by all who witnessed the show that night, and it was all at the civilian's expense. They got their revenge for our joke, as they made sure they worked us all the harder the remaining time it took to dismantle and pack the remainder of the telephone exchange. When the civilians left were had completed only one of dozens of tasks that were required to close down our unit.

As promised I made good on my $4 deal and delivered a case of beer to the cannoneers. The Cannon Cockers from next door did not get to enjoy their rewards for their part in our prank, for long. Three nights after the civilians had left one of the 155s behind us exploded, killing the crew and the NCO in charge. When we heard the unusual explosion from our barracks area and saw the fire, some of us had sprinted over to see what had happened, and if there was anything we could do. There was fire and shouting as we got closer, and what greeted us was a gristly scene that stopped us in our tracks. Blood and gore everywhere, fires from ready use powder cooking off, and five crumpled, smoking mounds that were once our friends. An NCO got us to go home; there was nothing we could do. It was days later that we found out a F.N.G. had tried to show everyone how fast a Cannon Cocker he was. We were told that he had not closed the breech block all the way before the round was fired.

The Dump

As things would happen, one of the chores that were required during the deactivation was the getting rid of unwanted or surplus material. The stuff that you were not supposed to have it in the first place, stuff that was extra or stuff that was broken and you had hung onto anyway. Orosz, I and plus another two G.I.s from the transmitter section ended up detailed to take a load of broken and unfixable equipment and other trash to the dump, with instructions to get rid of it any way we wanted. Burning, sledge hammers, whatever, but to destroy it and come back without it.

This was going to be a fun detail, so Orosz and I threw some tools and thermite grenades in the cab of the truck, and we were on our way. Let's just say that destruction seemed to be a job Orosz and I were good at, and we were always excited to be doing something destructive. I drove the truck to the dump site that the engineers had constructed outside the base camp. The dump turned out to be a giant bare patch of ground field with a deep rectangular hole in the middle, the hole had shear vertical sides. The site was set up to handle engineer dump trucks, designed so they should back up to it and dump their loads over the edge. The dump in total was several acres square of cleared flat land, all of it churned up to red mud covered by blowing trash, and the hole was well camouflaged as I didn't see the hole in the ground till I was almost on it. What I did see was the truck that arrived ahead of mine and a few hundred yards in front, being swarmed over by Vietnamese civilians as it got close to the hole.

Instead of going forward and having the Vietnamese jump on the back of our truck, I turned around under directions from

Orosz and headed back out the way we came in. Once back on the road we stopped and formulated a plan.

"O.K. let's have some fun," began Orosz.

"Scotty you drive in as slow as you can go, and the rest of us will have batting practice from the truck bed."

Our truck had no canvas cover or wood bows over the back, and so we had a clear area to swing a bat. All of us had no qualms about batting practice, as we knew that the scavengers would be all over us before we could get to the hole. Using rifles wouldn't be the solution to this situation, and just might result in unwanted bloodshed. Orosz handed out shovels, axes, sledge hammers and instructions "To hit `em where it hurts, but only use the handles or your fists."

With Orosz and the other two G.I.s in the back armed and ready we headed back into the dump, and just as we thought, as we neared the pit scavengers jumped on the truck from all sides. I kept the truck rolling in first gear, and never slowed below 10 mph. There were a few anxious moments as scavengers were batted off the back of the truck by our very enthusiastic crew, and after several Vietnamese were launched off of the back of the truck the rest got the message and left us alone.

This treatment of Vietnamese civilians may seem cruel and cold, but these scavengers made their living almost entirely off of the dump. They were governed by the some very basic rules of survival, and none of them seemed willing to listen to reason. Whatever a scavenger could grab was gold no matter what it was. I had once witnessed a 5 gallon can of motor oil fall off a trailer of the truck in front of mine while in convoy, and the can landed in the middle of the road causing me to break for it. Out of nowhere a Vietnamese scavenger appeared and held up the remainder of the convoy behind me while the scavenger picked up the can and ran off with it. To be realistic I don't think that any request by us to, "Stay off of the truck," in English or Vietnamese would have made any impression on them. We were meat on the table.

Orosz dismounted and guided my truck back slowly until the end of the deuce and a half hung over the hole. Looking down into the hole we could see several more Vietnamese picking over the mounds of smoldering refuse. The drop was at least 15 feet straight down, but it looked like a mile. I asked Orosz, "How are we going to destroy this stuff without those scavengers getting to it? I don't want to climb down there with them."

"We'll just start a fire down there and when it gets going good we'll through down the equipment and the other stuff," said Orosz.

One G.I. stood in the front of the truck bed and waved an M-16 over the canvas covered cab of the truck to keep the devious ones from sneaking up on us from behind. This gave us some room while we got down to the business of destroying stuff.

There was a lot of paper in the trash we were carrying, so that was tossed down first and Orosz threw down two or three thermite grenades on top of it to get things going. Several of the above ground scavengers again approached the back of the truck, but were warned off when one of us saw them coming and grabbed his M-16 and pointed it in their direction. The fire below began to grow and we threw down some of the damaged and broken equipment, some cables and some more thermite grenades. Some of the below ground scavengers approached our fire and no matter how we threatened them with our M-16s they still tried to drag equipment out of the fire.

Orosz shouted, "I'll fix them," and he ran for the cab of the truck and from it he grabbed two CS tear gas grenades out of our assortment of dirty tricks we always carried. He then ran back to the pit and pulling the pin on one grenade and tossed it to the bottom of the pit. The grenade immediately began spewing out a dense white cloud of smoke. The white cloud of smoke settled in the bottom of the hole and within a minute covered the entire bottom like a white blanket. It was like the scene from a horror movie, dark figures choking and moving through the white mist. The scavengers began chocking and gaging from the gas, they left our fire alone and ran to the far side of the pit to escape and began trying to climb the shear earth sides of the pit. The cloud rose in height from the bottom of the pit reaching for the escaping Vietnamese scavengers as they tried to scale the sides.

Orosz stood above the pit and waved another tear gas canister at the Vietnamese below. He yelled down, "Touch it again and you get another one." This they understood for it brought some acknowledgement in the form of waves and nods from those gagging and chocking below. Whether this bit of English language explanation from Orosz was understood or not by those below was never argued, but they got the full meaning of his statement from his gesture with the second grenade. Our fire and equipment was left to burn after that, with no further attempts to interrupt our task. We were assured that we had completed our task of destruction with Orosz sending one of the other soldiers down into the pit to insure that everything had been destroyed, after which we hauled him back up with the aid of a rope. The choice of who went into the pit was easy; all the equipment we destroyed came from the transmission section. So we let the two guys who were with us draw lots for the privilege of who would go down and inspect. Hey! It wasn't our gear, it was their gear.

Convoy into Danger

During the days left I made another convoy to An Khe as a shotgun guard, but this trip was a little different than the first one. The trip was uneventful until our convoy reached Mang Yang pass, there we were halted on the road as there was a convoy fighting its way through an ambush coming the other way.

As we waited, parked nose to tail on the asphalt, M.P.s and armored infantry troops roared past us in APCs and other vehicles, and we shotgun guards were posted as a security screen in the hills on either side of our own vehicles. Suddenly a M.P. Jeep roared up the length of our convoy, and our vehicle drivers each jumped back into the trucks and started their engines. We sprinted back to the trucks and loaded up and prepared to head down into the pass. Coming up from the opposite direction was the convoy that had had to fight their way through. Trucks and other vehicles from a Transportation company flowed past us showing no signs of damage. There was one vehicle, one of the last, of this convoy that got our undivided attention as soon as we saw it coming up the road. It was a tanker truck. This was a gasoline tanker truck. The tanker crawled up the steep road in low gear with black soot pouring from the exhaust stacks of the truck, and gasoline pouring from the bullet holes in the sides of the tanker. It looked like a crazed water truck washing the street at an unhealthy odd angle. From the bullet holes that had been shot into the tank of the truck. Gasoline spewed from the bullet holes at different angles. The driver was only partially visible through the peep holes cut in his home made shield of armor plate, and he looked white as a sheet as he drove looking straight ahead. As this truck past the other trucks in our convoy in front of ours horns were honked in salute, and arms appeared out of windows giving peace signs, a wave or thumbs up. I threw the driver a snappy salute as he passed my vehicle, but he seemed not to notice anything but the road ahead. The smell was unmistakable, gasoline all right.

Descending further into the pass we came to the scene of the ambush. There was a wrecker trying to right an APC which was lying on its top in the ditch. A huge greasy black cloud rose to the heavens from a deuce and a half as it burned on its collapsed and missing front tire. It had obviously hit a mine. We paused to navigate around these obstacles, and then went on with our journey picking up speed and interval between vehicles as we sped on our way safely.

Out for the Count

One dark and stormy night the siren's at Camp Enari wailed and the whole place came alive as we were once again under enemy attack. We were not told what kind of attack we just got up, dressed, grabbed our war gear and headed to the bunkers as the explosions started. Our local cannons roared and roared and roared, and the atmosphere inside the bunker I manned became very tense. Rumors flew around the inside of the bunker like wasps on a melon; lots of guys had ideas about what was happening outside. "It was a ground attack," or "Charlie had driven through the wire in a captures APC," "The VC were bombing us with tear gas." To say the least the atmosphere was tense with anticipation, and none of the rumor spreaders being able to see outside added to the tension.

The atmosphere became electric with the more explosions we heard. I was indeed tense, sensing that something unusual was up because of the rapid fire of the cannons outside. I like the rest in that bunker were at the mercy of our surroundings as we all sat or stood in that crowded bunker. I was at one point was wondering who or what may be coming through the door next. Orosz found me first, and squeezed into the seat beside me, and the tension immediately broke with his friendly face in that dimly lit bunker. O.D. Green sandbags did not reflect much light from the illuminated faces of the watches guys wore. Big Jon moved in next after he heard Orosz talking to me. "Hey there lil' buddy, y'all doin' OK?" was the last thing I remember. The lights went out completely.

I woke up in a well-lit strange room, a room with quiet a high ceiling, and there were curtains all around me. I was alone, and I had no shirt or t-shirt on. My head hurt, my eyes hurt from the light, and my head was wrapped in what I thought was a towel. My right ear was on fire, and sparks shot through my brain every time I moved. Once my vision stabilized I tried to sit up, but it hurt to move, and after three tries I made it. The curtains parted and a vision of loveliness in O.D. Green fatigues parted the curtains and walked through them and smiled a dazzling smile at me. It was an American Army nurse, not an angel from heaven, and I wanted so bad to touch her. I reached out to touch her as she continued to smile, but my hands would not reach her. Reality finally dawned on me and realized that this beauty was a Lieutenant, and Officer, and touching was a no. Officers did not fraternize with enlisted men. I was heartbroken by her just as soon I had been enchanted to see her. "Your back," she said. I could not open my mouth or utter a single sound or word; I just stared at her beautiful face. "You've come back," she said. Finally two and two clicked together and my mind engaged my voice and I responded, "Where did I go?"

The answer was simple I had been knocked unconscious. Sitting in the bunker with Big Jon and Orosz I had been clunked on the head by another G.I. who had been sitting opposite the three of us. I was looking the wrong way when it happened or I would have been clinked right between the eyes.

I sat up slowly while a little man in tap shoes clattered around inside my head and more sparks flew. Slowly I was gotten off the trolley I lay on, and to my feet by Lieutenant Beautiful and a male orderly who came in as we were speaking. I walked unsteadily at first, out through the curtains and into a brighter light. I ducked my aching head trying to avoid the light when I heard the most wonderful sound. "Hey there Scotty McNasty, how is you?" It was Big Jon.

I was in the medic's building at Camp Enari, and it was strange to me as I had never been here before. My two buddies had carried me to this place while 122 mm rockets rained down on Camp Enari. I was out cold when they brought me in and it had taken a good 30 minutes for me to "Come Back."

It was explained to me as we walked slowly back to the 278th what had happened. We had been sitting in that crowded bunker with my head turned toward Big Jon when a G.I. across from us went nuts and threw his helmet. That 2 and a half pound steel pot had slammed into my right ear, knocking me unconscious. What happened to the crazy G.I. was not known as several people had jumped on him. I was bleeding badly and had a battle dressing applied to my wound and then Orosz and Big Jon had carried me all the way to the medics. It was good to have such good friends.

I never found out who had thrown the helmet, I never found out the name of Lieutenant Beautiful, but I healed over time, but the First Sergeant had me back to work the next morning.

Oh! Rats!

There were three immediate draw backs in turning over our base camp to the Vietnamese that became apparent to us all. These were more social draw backs than anti-social draw backs. The first was in relationship to our neighborhood, and the second was a problem with the population of our neighborhood. The third was about employee relations, but we will get into that later.

With the announced abandonment of our base camp there began a gradual exodus of the different units that had been assigned to our base. Everyday trucks would roll by our compound carrying troops and belongings out of Camp Enari. These departures of different units bag and baggage posed a problem for those of us remaining. As units left they drove by our area sending a great never ending cloud of dust into the air, and this choked us and coated our belongings and equipment. No matter how far from the road you lived or worked the fine dust settled everywhere. The second problem caused by the unit's troops leaving was that their resident rat population had no place to go and nothing to do, and so some of them would move into quarters where humans still resided. Our rat population increased significantly each night.

Rats had been part of the way of life for soldiers in Vietnam, long before I ever set foot in that country. We in the 278th had been accustomed to our share of rats in the barracks, the bunkers, and out work areas, and like other units had regular unauthorized rat hunting expeditions to control the population. After all, those rodents bred like rats. Well, as new rats came into our area our problems with them multiplied further. Rat fights over rat territory became frequent. Rat family fought rat family for their share of the 278th.

I was lying in my bunk one quiet evening, sound asleep, when one of their airborne members landed square on my head, it had jumped from one of the over-head rafters. It was pitch dark in the barracks, and I was aware that I was alone in my room but not in my bed. I was shocked, I was surprised, and I was instantly awake and aware of that something unusual had happened. At first I didn't know of what was on my head, but it was still up there. I was scared that whatever it was would bite me. I was pissed off because my night's sleep was now over.

I awoke instantly from the impact, but I did not jump out of bed and cry out. For reasons unbeknownst to me, whether from military training, involvement with strange bed fellows, or the unknown human ability to commune with rats telepathically, I knew right away what had happened. I froze, I admit it, and I was scared stiff. I lay there on my bunk unable to move, for fear of getting bit, and let this rodent, which seemed the size of a house cat, march up and down on my skull, but I just lay there I didn't or couldn't do anything about it. I lay there with this thing perched on my ear with its scratchy claws digging into my flesh. I next felt it leaning over my face with its hairy nose, its whiskers tickling my cheek and my eye as it sniffed around.

As I lay there and felt this beast rummage around my head I said to myself, "OFF, get the hell OFF." Whishing it away did nothing, I lay there still and anticipated jumping on this rodent and clubbing it to death, but my head always seemed to be in the way. I finally settled on a course of action, but this employed mayhem which relied on the hope that the rat at some point would get off of my head. I lay there and hated this rat, I could still feel its whiskers as it paraded around my head, and as I lay there I plotted its demise.

The rat was smarter than I was; it bit me on the ear and jumped off just as I reacted to the sting of its teeth. I was left swinging a jungle boot at thin air, but the rat did not escape my attempt at murder. I got my flash light out from under my pillow, and shone the beam around trying to find my assailant. I found his beady eyes in the corner of the room beside my bed, and I nailed him with my G.I. boot. The rat squealed with the first Bull's-eye! The finest shot I had ever made with a boot, and it was one the rat wouldn't recover from. So following my Vietnam training, I didn't give him a break. "Make sure of your enemy," came back to me. It resounded in my head in the voice of my Basic Training Drill Instructor, Sergeant Jessie. I got down on all fours, and then I hammered it with the heel of the boot to make sure of it.

The next morning after work assignments had been handed out I went to sick call to report my encounter with the rodent. I arrived at the medics at the same time as Sergeant Threetours of my unit. We both had the same problem, a hickey from a rat, but they appeared that they were from different rats. As we sat and waited our turn for a medic to see us we compared stories of our rat encounters. I had managed to kill mine, but Sergeant Threetours rat had gotten away.

Sergeant Threetours got to see the medic first, and after only being in the dressing room for a few minutes he came out rather ashen looking. "Hey Sarge," I called out, "what they do to you in there." Before he could answer the medic appeared in the door and called my name. I gave Sergeant Threetours a questioned look, and he said, "They want to give me the Pasture Rabbis Treatment." That sent an electric shock up my spine, I had heard about "The Pasture Rabbis Treatment" all the way back in high school first aid class, and what I remembered I didn't like. The vivid details carried over from first aid class were of a hypodermic needle 8 inches long that was stuck into your spine through your stomach, 16 times, and I cringed from the recollection.

I swam into the examination room on a cloud, and woke up when the medic asked me, "So what's your problem?"

"I got bit by a rat," I replied meekly.

"You bring the rat with you?" The medic asked.

I looked around the room and gazed at the sign on the wall that read, `Is Grape Nuts a Social Disease?' I saw that there was no one there to help me in this, and so I asked the medic, "Bring the rat with me? You're kidding?"

"No, I'm not kidding, if you bring the rat we can find out if it has rabbis or not. No rat, you get the rabbis treatment." To emphasis his point he pointed to another sign over the door this time. This one read, `Get bit by a rat or a snake, come to the 4th Medical detachment and BRING the rat or snake with you.'

Can't you just take my word for it that the rat didn't look sick," I inquired.

"No I can't" was the warm reply. "No rat, no mercy."

I knew why Sergeant Threetours looked so distraught, and thinking fast, I told the medic I would be back with the rat. I ran off back to my barracks as fast as I could go. Once there I dug the rat out of the trash barrel, where I had thrown it after I made sure it wasn't going anywhere under its own power, I dusted it off and admired it for the first time. "My, what a handsome rat," I said to myself as I headed back to the medical area. I was lucky I had got to the barrel before the rat became a meal for one of the scavenging dogs from around the barracks. Rat in hand I ran back to the medic and presented my prize suspended by its tail. The medic was pleased no end, but he had to ask, "You sure this is your rat?"

"You think I would produce just any rat? These things are hard to get! Look at the condition of this one, I had to personally knock its brains out," I said as I held the rat out to him by its pinkish tail.

"What do you want an affidavit from the rat?" I asked.

"No, but this rat was awfully conveniently produced?"

"Believe me I'm not into re-producing rats on cue."

"I didn't ask you about your sexual habits, I asked if this was your rat."

"It's mine," I said, "see here it has my boot mark on the back of his head. See it says 10 ½ right there."

The rat was sent away for analysis, while I waited nervously but patiently outside the sick call building. The medic came out after a while and called my name. "Lennox, come with me." I followed the medic back into his dispensary, and he sat me on a cot.

"Your one lucky dude, man!" He told me.

"No rabbis?"

"No rabbis." was the response.

The medic cleaned my wound while I sat under another large sign which read, "Moby Dick Treated Here." The cleaning if the rat bite with alcohol stung, but it could not wipe the smile off of my face.

By being able to produce MY rat I was able to forgo the Pasture Rabbis Treatment, but Sergeant Threetours wasn't as lucky as I. As the days passed he would confide in me all about his treatment, as if we were medical students sharing a difficult case. His treatment consisted of 16 shots through the stomach, one a day for 16 days, and with a needle only two or so inches long. As he described things to me I was very sympathetic, but after listening to him I always thanked God that my aim with a G.I. boot was better than his.

Rat hunts became more frequent after a few more people got bitten. These were unofficial hunts, not properly sanctioned by the Army. Several of us more insensitive troops would get together with Montagnard crossbows, jungle boots, baseball bats, clubs and other blunt instruments, but no fire arms. When the C.O. and the First Sergeant heard of the nightly rat hunts they refused to let anyone use their M-16 rifles or M-79 grenade launchers in the barracks. An edict about the use of certain weapons was published on the company bulletin board that brought great resentment on the part of the troops, but the edict did not diminish the number of participants who took part in the nightly skirmishes. Each night a surprising number of G.I.s would climb into the rafters of their barracks, and wait there with flash light and weapon in hand until an unsuspecting rodent appeared for the ambush. We troops had decided earlier on that M-16s were never to be used as we deemed them too humane to use on rats.

Someone came up with the bright idea of killing the rats by using CS Tear Gas, and a group of hunters immediately liked the idea. All of the barracks members were evacuated while the gas was set off, and to our delight we found that this method was great. It was great at killing rats, we pulled a dozen or more out of the barracks. There was one drawback however. Our clothes, bedding, and other belongings stunk of tear gas for days.

Eight Legged Friends

Animal hunts at the 278 were not restricted to rats; we had occasional snake hunts when they showed up in the compound. Snakes showed up hunting after our fat and juicy rats, but the most sought after animal came on eight legs and were known as the body crab. A lone G.I. without a roommate White turned out to be a world champion collector and game keeper of body crabs, but for some reason these were not the type of pets most desired by G.I.s.

As I have told White was a little slow about personal hygiene, but White was also a slob, and all of us knew it. After he contracted a case of body crabs he let things get out of hand instead of going to the medics and getting rid of them. By the time his sin in hygiene omission was discovered he must have had millions of them. The crabs were finally noticed when they started spilling out of White's room and infecting others. Three or four guys from the barracks started complaining about how they couldn't get rid of the crabs, and after comparing notes it was discovered that over half the men in the barracks had them. A meeting was held of the infected and the un-infected, and after two and two were added all four fingers pointed to White who had not been invited and did not attend the meeting. A delegation went into White's room to confront him with their suspicions, and upon entering they confirmed all supposition about the source of the crab infestation. The joint was really jumping. You could say that Willie was like Jimmy Durante, "He had a million of `em."

After the discovery of our infestation a group of very angry soldiers gathered outside the barracks and vocalized what should be done. The crowd grew as more troops came back from work to get ready to go for chow, and a riot was brewing after this discovery and the source of the vermin. As part of the riot festivities White, his mattress, and other bedding were drug out of the barracks. White got off lucky he was given a G.I. shower while his bedding was doused with gasoline and set on fire. Several members of the "Crabs R us Club" were at the same time getting ready to give the gasoline treatment to White's room and the barracks as well, but the C.O. and First Sergeant were able to intervene.

To settle the troops down the Army's version of the Public Health Service was called in. That very afternoon the barracks and all of its inhabitants and all of its contents were doused thoroughly with anti-crab spray and each of us were given a large supply of crab dust along with a long lecture on its correct use. I never saw White after his delousing; he just disappeared from our lives in a cloud of soap suds and de-crabbing powder. White and all of his little friends were not missed.

Ridding ourselves of body crabs using disinfectants and medications was considered to be the weakling's way, by some of the older Lifers. "You bunch of Pussys, you should get rid of them little friends the old Army way, boy," I was told. "What way is that, Sarge?" I asked on cue. Sarge smiled knowingly and explained, "You shave one side of your crotch, and then you take a can of cigarette lighter fluid and an ice pick. You douse the hairy side of your groin with the lighter fluid and then set your crotch on fire. When the crabs run out to the shaved side you stab them with the ice pick." I wanted no part of the old Army way.

The Blues

Just before I left the 278th for good a rumor was going around the compound that our Mess Sergeant, Sergeant First Class Grayson was going to get the Bronze Star medal for service in Vietnam. On hearing of this I and many others who had been on K.P. and had witnessed what went on in the mess hall were appalled. To us there was never anything roasting in an oven, it was always warming in a big pot on the stove. What was warming was a steady diet of S.O.S., and Grayson and his cooks ladled out liberally. With the announcement of a medal for Sergeant Grayson were in disbelief. Those who got to eat in the mess hall regularly were outraged; you had to have witnessed the goings on behind the scenes to be appalled. We knew we were in a war and supplies were sometimes short, but Grayson's culinary ability had rivaled and partially eclipsed those of his Fort Riley counterpart Sergeant Kookwell. While Kookwell could work military wonders with "C" Rations, Grayson could only make us wonder how this Mess Sergeants had earned his stripes in the first place.

Having dined many times at Grayson's place of business I and many others considered what Grayson put on your tray to be travesty. A miscarriage of culinary justice! An assault on the senses of those who knew what good food tasted like. It wasn't bad; it was awful, continuously awful. It was awful every day, day after day. Things were powdered, the eggs, the potatoes, and whatever else could be dehydrated or condensed was done so. Re-constituted milk was a wonder. We wondered if it had ever been milk. I suppose that was a reasonable thought on our part because re-constituted milk was like chewing milk. The Officers over us didn't have it as bad as we did; they ate elsewhere, so they never really knew what we endured. But those of us who had to sample this man's efforts meal after meal were sure that if this guy got a Bronze Star medal for service then the "Fix was In," and those above us didn't care how we fared.

Here was a U.S. Army Sergeant who was literally covered in tattoos. He had spider webs on his elbows, naked girls on his forearms, and God knows what on his chest and back. Big Jon had named Grayson "Goofy Grape" because of his silly grin, and also for the way he walked. Sort of the reverse of pigeon toed he walked with his toes pointed out at a 45 degree angle. Big Jon swore there was something seriously wrong with that man, and most of the rest of us concurred. None of us were sure if it was mental or physical, but it was most likely with his cooking ability.

On one occasion a Colonel from the 21st Signal was visiting the unit and for lunch Grayson announced that he was going to serve the NCOS and officers including the Colonel, steak. The rest of us were being served a non-descript gray stew. With this announcement there was such a furor raised in the chow line that the gray stew was served to one and all. My own part of the furor was yelling questions like, "where the hell did you get steak? And is there anymore?"

I sat down on hearing of the award and resurrected a poem I had composed while with the 24th Mechanized while in Germany, and had used it to indicate my displeasure in our commander's leave and pass policy. Though never published anywhere, the poem had been entertaining to the troops at the time I written it, and I thought that it wasn't half bad for my first attempt at poetry.

All that I can remember now of the version written in Germany is the first of its four verses, and that went:

Oh Germany is the place to be
I'd love to take a Rhine cruise,
But I'd have to kiss some ass
To get a three day pass,
I've got the Lindon F. Carlson blues.

I resurrected the poem for the occasion of Grayson's Bronze Star award, and rewrote it to fit the occasion. The new rewritten version expressed the troops of the 278th chow line true feelings about their beloved mess Sergeant. I entitled it `The Bronze Star Grayson Blues', and it the verse beat gave it a tune all its own that added to the flavor of it.

I resurrected the poem from memory for this expression of our displeasure once the announcement was made about the medal for Sergeant Grayson. I wanted to share my true feeling with my pals Orosz and Big Jon, so that we could share with the rest of the 278th what was our opinion of this great cook. After a few moments with pencil and paper I was ready to share my first attempt of rewriting, and both Orosz and Big Jon declared it a masterpiece.

The Bronze Star Grayson Blues

Signals the one, it's a son-of-a-gun
But the food is really bad news
The eggs are old and the rest of it's cold
We got the Bronze Star Grayson Blues

Oh it's waddle waddle waddle
To the mess hall we toddle
Our appetites there to loose
The meat loaf is rotten and nutrition forgotten
We got the Bronze Star Grayson Blues

If it's greasy they got it
And really lots of it
Of vegetables you can choose
We know it ain't fair and Grayson don't care
We got the Bronze Star Grayson Blues

We got the G.I. Shits
And the Ptomaine fits
This mess hall really does loose
We'll be home someday, we hope and pray
Without the Bronze Star Grayson Blues

We shared this ditty with the rest of the company and the rest enjoyed it so much that several of us would gather at the entrance to the mess hall, and bellow the song at Grayson. He wasn't upset in the least and the song did nothing to improve the variety or the taste of the food. He never asked for a copy as a testimonial to his culinary ability.

This little ditty of mine prodded other troopers to get creative too. Big Jon and Orosz came up with the following that would also be sung by a chorus of G.I.s at the door to Grayson's mess hall.

G is for the Grease he serves us.

R is for the Rations we don't get.

A is the Asshole we call him.

Y is for the Yearning we have for food that tasted good.

S is for the Son-of-a-Bitch that we call him, or the Steak we never see.

O is for One day he will be gone.

N is for the Nutrition that we don't get.

Put them all together they spell Dip Shit the Mess Sergeant we all hate.

The day finally came that my job was completed and my services in the 278th were no longer required. I and several others were given orders that sent us back to the headquarters of the 43rd Signal Battalion. Not my buddies however, it was a sad day when I had to make my goodbyes to my two best friends. I packed my bags and baggage in silence and sadness that day and slowly loaded it on board a deuce and a half with the others for the ride to the other side of Pleiku. I said my good-byes to Orosz and Big Jon, we exchanged home addresses for after the war, the guys were not going with me on this trip, and our farewell was sad as we had a very close relationship with one another. "Crap, there goes the Glee Club, after we had got it going so well." I thought to myself. I waved a fond farewell from the back of the truck as it took me away, in the usual thick cloud of dust, from my good friends. We all waved so long for as long as the truck was visible, which was usually a maximum of 30 feet, and we were slit up for what I thought was forever. This had been my experience throughout my Army life. Make some good friends, have some fun together then its goodbye, and start all over again. "Crap, I'm going to miss those guys."

Pictures 3

Figure 11. Orosz at Plei Klane Ngol. Big Jon's Collection.

Figure 12. Local Sandbag emporium, bags of Vietnam for a penny and a new bag. Author's collection.

Figure 13. North end of a south bound convoy. Author's collection.

Figure 14. Road security highway QL14. Author's collection.

Figure 15. Enemy action on QL14. Author's collection.

Figure 16. Man Yang Pass. Author's collection.

Figure 17. The Peiku Dump, you took your chances going in there. Authors's collection.

Figure 18. Big Jon & Billy Badass with trading material. Big Jon's collection.

Chapter 16

Trading with the Supply Pukes

I rode back to the 43rd Signal Battalion facing out from the bed of the truck with my M-16 at the ready I already knew most of the sights between Enari and Pleiku, and we rode in silence, but keeping an eye out just the same. Even though I was somewhat familiar with the 43rd I was hesitant about joining, I had been back to the HQ and A company area a couple times since I was dispatched to the 278th, but I knew no one by sight. There several months now separating my visits to the 43rd.battalion. I did not know what to expect upon reporting in, would I be back to duty soldier only doing dirty details or would I be able to work at my military skill? What would become of my two buddies I had left back at the 278? All this ran through my brain on the jolting truck ride to my new home.

I had been in the U.S. Army for over two years and I now knew my "Ass from my elbow," as the Army saying went. I was seasoned and I wanted to make the best possible first impression upon joining these guys, as we all know first impressions should be a good impression. "This wasn't going to be tough to do," I said to myself, as I thought of myself as what you might call grungy; I now knew my way around. The truck dropped all of us off just outside the back gate to the 43rd's compound. I jumped down from the truck and helped John and

Barry, the same two I had left with so long ago, drop down all the gear.

We must have made a puny sight to anyone looking; we were like immigrants entering the U.S. at Ellis Island, a ragged bunch carrying all of our worldly possessions in sacks. It does make it hard to make any sort of impression on anyone when you and your belongings are unceremoniously dumped off of a truck at the back gate of the unit you are being assigned to. But this is how we arrived. The "Exiles" John and Barry grabbed their stuff and went off to the orderly room, hoping that they wouldn't have to beg the First Shirt to let them come. Jack I spent some time getting organized, before I made my entrance.

Being a veteran and proud of what I considered a great outfit and because of our recon work a `somewhat combat' outfit so to speak, I had put on my best bravado for this occasion. I wore my recon patch proudly from my fatigue shirt pocket. I wore my dirtiest, most washed out set of jungle fatigues, and my scruffiest pair of boots. I wore my unauthorized engineers floppy hat (my best Boonie job), and on my hip I had a machete which I had grabbed from the recon Conex before it was locked for good. This blade was very interesting as it had "War is hell" scratched on one side and "But Contact is a Motherfucker" scratched on the other. I wore my flack vest, complete with various sayings left by previous owners, and I was wearing an Army rucksack along with carrying my duffel bag. To set off this entire getup I carried my M-16 and had a newly acquired communist SKS rifle slung across my back. I thought I had just that touch of daring, that devil-may-care attitude. Unfortunately, the first person I run into as I walked through the back gate was an unimpressed Sergeant Major wearing, of all things, starched and pressed fatigues and spit shinned jungle boots. "Why Me? Why Always Me?" was the first thing that came to my mind.

This Sergeant Major was not of the same monster size of all other Sergeant Majors I had thus far encountered. He was scrawny in comparison, two inches shorter than I, and weighed

398

what looked like only a 100 pounds, soaking wet; a mere shadow of other Sergeant Majors. The only thing that he had in common with his peers was the stripes on his sleeve, a disagreeable disposition and a loud voice to do his nagging and demanding with.

This guy was out of his mind with joy when he saw me come through the gate, and he made a bee line over to me just to welcome me properly. I had been living in semi poverty for the last few months, and here is someone wearing starched fatigues and spit shinned boots. No "Hi how are you," no pleasantries of "Welcome to the unit," of any kind. The Sergeant Major just went to work on me like any other Sergeant Major, he walked round me and he pulled on each item of my equipment that he took to be un-military or unusual. He spent a minute or two holding on to each item and, describing each to what must have been an imaginary friend, as no one was there, and he made sure that anyone else within ear shot could hear what he had to say. Talking back was not in the cards I just stood there and waited till he got tired or got finished with me. "And where did we get this," he said, pulling out my machete. I saw nothing wrong with my mode of dress, I was dressed to impress, and obviously that is what I had accomplished. Unfortunately I had no desire to impress this guy.

This unfriendly person next demanded to know which unit I was with, and alludes to the possibility that "Whoever I am with, cannot possibly be an American unit; because of the way I am dressed." I thought for a minute, "If I tell him I'm with the 43rd he will be all over me like a cheap suit. He will have my name and he will then have my ass." So I lied and told him that I was with the 1st battalion of the 10th Cavalry, and as I wasn't wearing a shoulder patch of any kind there was no evidence to contradict me. I had heard of a unit called the 1st of the 10th Cav., and I knew that that outfit was part of the 4th Division. I didn't know where the 1st of the 10th was or what they were assigned to do at that precise moment. I was counting on the fact the Sergeant Major had also never heard of the 1st of the

10th. By the seat of my pants I knew that if this Sergeant major ever got my I.D. he would be like a dog with a new bone. He would never let go of my ass. So I did what needed to be done I bluffed.

"Let me see your orders," was his next demand.

"I don't got no orders. I don't got to show you no stinking orders," popped into my head.

I only had verbal orders assigning me to the 43rd Headquarters, so no written orders to show, thank goodness.

Being from a unit he obviously knew nothing about calmed the Sergeant Major somewhat, and he demanded to know "what the hell am I doing here in his compound." I immediately saw my chance to escape.

"Sergeant Major, I am visiting my wounded brother here at the 71st Evac.," I explained.

"Soldier, this isn't the 71st Evacuation Hospital."

"Why I've been let off at the wrong unit," I exclaimed in mock surprise.

"Could the Sergeant Major provide me with directions or transportation to the correct destination? No....., well I thought not.... I'll just pick up my gear and I'll get off of your earth, `scuse me Sergeant Major."

I picked up my bag and hot footed it out of the gate and down the road outside the barbed wire fence. I was sweating profusely and red in the face as I went through the gate. "The enemy must be friendlier than that guy," I said to the gate guard as I passed.

I waited down the road and out of sight until the coast was clear once again, and then I slunk back into the compound. I checked in at headquarters building after leaving my gear at the orderly room, and got myself a place to sleep. After that I hid out from the Sergeant Major. I had been wearing a uniform with no name, rank or serial number on it, and that really saved me for the next several months. Though I avoided the Sergeant Major like the plague, there were times when he did get close enough to give me the once over. He would always pull his hat off while looking at me, and scratch his close cropped head of grey hair thoughtfully while his brain tried to figure out why I looked so familiar.

I checked into the 43rd's A company barracks, a two story affair, and I set up housekeeping in one of the unused cubicles I found on the second floor. The room had enough space for a set of double stacked bunks and a shelf to keep my belongings, but what the hell it was going to be home for a while. This wasn't as bad as accommodations in the Army went, and I certainly had had a lot less, much much worse. For privacy, such as it was, there was a plastic Suzi Wong bead curtain for a door, donated by some previous owner. It didn't keep any one out, but it did let in any available breeze. As the saying went, it was so small that if I wanted to change my mind I had to go outside.

I thought that I was out of the strange detail business for a short while and back in the repair business again, being I was told I was assigned to the battalion repair section. There arose one minor difficulty. Being back in repair, I found I was in the same condition I found myself when I arrived at Fort Riley. I was excess. There were already eight repairmen with my job classification already at work in the repair unit, and like Fort Riley most of them out ranked me.

The Army operated on what was called T,O & E., Table of Organization & Equipment. Each unit had slots to fill with men to do a certain job. In my case I didn't have a slot. I was an orphan again.

When I reported for work I was told all about that T,O & E by the NCO in charge, Sergeant Fullcup. There would be a job slot available for me in the future, but I was left less than convinced, as the first job I was given was as a shotgun guard on a truck convoy heading for An Khe.

Before I left on my new work assignment I looking over the 43rds' repair shop, and I was amazed at what I saw. This was not the run down WW II three room motor pool shed that was the the home of my Fort Riley repair experience, and nor was it the one room shed I had worked out of in the 278th. This was a repair palace, a spacious hall full of repair benches and dozens of people repairing piles of equipment that was visible on every bench. I was in awe, this was the first time out of school that I had seen a repair shop that actually looked like a repair shop.

The headquarters company of the 43rd now had a First Sergeant different from the one I had worked for when I had first came to Vietnam, and this one was a little more flamboyant. He had shaved all the hair off of his head, in an effort to keep lice and other hygiene problems at a minimum. He had a large pot belly, and he liked to be called "Buddha" because of his physical resemblance to the statue. The first time I saw him I walked around behind him and did a Curly Howard Three Stooges imitation by slapping my hand on the top of his head rapidly, and letting out with some loud WOOP WOOPs at the same time. Not the right move to make however, the First Sergeant from the 278th had informed this guy what to expect in the way of my performance. What followed was several days of dirty details which let me know just how glad the First Sergeant and the 43rd Signal were glad to see me.

To my great and pleasant surprise Big Jon and Orosz soon followed me to the 43rd Signal. They arrived within a week of my arrival, and in no time at all we were on detail together, just like old times. The one good thing that happened during this time was Big Jon and I became roomies, sharing the same diminutive plywood cubicle.

Orosz arrived in camp with his usual flourish; he came into our new plywood cubical that first night waving a full bottle of Vodka.

"Hey Orosz, where did you steal that?" I asked.

"Mr. H" gave it to him as a going away present," said Big Jon following him into the room.

"A reward," offered Orosz whetting his lips,

"for faithful services rendered above and beyond the call of duty."

With one smooth action Orosz unscrewed the tin top of the bottle and flipped the bottles' top back over his shoulder and into the hall.

"Well we won't be needin' that anymore," he said with a wide grin, and the party was on.

The Glee Club Reprise

On the second night that Orosz, Big Jon and I were back together in the 43rd we immediately preceded to the EM club, commandeered some seats and ordered a beer. The beer wasn't any better at the 43rd, but the facilities were much improved. The EM club was in an old brick French building, much more permanent than we had had before. After wetting our whistle's we discussed our revolting situation, we were all orphans. To make up for this we re-activated our Varsity Glee Club, and proceeded to serenade our new comrades with our repertoire of dirty and other ditties. Not everyone was pleased to be serenaded in this way, and a few "Hey! Shut the Fuck up will ya," comments were hurled our way. We had to realize that we were no longer at the 278's rag tag club but were now in the sophisticated 43rd Headquarters and "A" company EM club. Our response to our detractors was "Get fucked!" The 43rd music haters stood up, so we stood up and the size of Big Jon settled the situation without further words. After our second rendition of our favorite tunes to the members of the 43rd within ear shot, we had several converts, who wanting to join our sing along. We screened everyone completely, we wanted fun guys, so we looking for that streak of perversion that would match our own.

We collectively agreed that for the most part we were with a "real bunch of assholes," and were going to have to break these idiots of the 43rd in to what life in the Army was all about. The three of us had found out that it was about belting beers, belting a song, belting each other, fun, and camaraderie. It was not about sitting quietly and sipping and crying into our beer in solemn contemplation of my miserable life and surroundings, and when do I get to go home. Boo Hoo!

Eventually we did add some new twists to our Glee Club meetings; we figured we would have to admit a few of these 43rd sad sacs to our ranks if we were to liven up the joint. We agreed to change our ways, in that we formalized our meeting structure. We elected officers. There were three positions open and we filled them with the three of us, by a quick show of hands. In a few minutes we had done what other organizations take months to perform; all with the help of Carling's beer suds. Great now we were formalized. What next? Now to new business and that involved new members. Nominations were Superman's Pal aka Jimmy Olsen, all agreed as it took only one nay vote to eliminate a candidate. Who else, well there was a shoe in, Orosz had a new roommate Aurley, Louis G., and since Orosz had the biggest room in the barracks we would probably be meeting there so why not. Louis "Lou" was the hairiest Italian American alive. He was a human fur ball. He could grow hair on a billiard ball, till 30 years later when he became that billiard ball. Three hands went up and Louis G. was in.

Sitting on the Bulls Eye

The best things about the 43rd were: The food was better, no more Mess Sergeant Grayson, there was a real club with real booze, and in one section of the camp there was, even that great achievement of civilization, the flush toilets. They were out of reach of we lowly enlisted men though, they were in the officer's latrine. On the other hand there were some bad things about this new home. The worst thing about the 43rd Signal Battalion, besides being home to a Sergeant Major, was its physical location in Vietnam. The battalion HQ area was on the crest of a hill, and on the downward slope of the hill, directly behind the 43rd was the very large, very White painted, and very red roofed ARVN II Corps HQ buildings. That wasn't bad enough, but besides the II Corps buildings there were two huge

100 or so foot radio telephone antennas at the north end of the battalion's compound with flashing red lights on top. These antennas were not the stick shaped radio towers I had seen at other radio stations; these two were about 100 foot square screens. There were also two more of the same giant antennas at the south end of the compound, complete with their own flashing red lights on top, but they were a little ways off. This made the battalion area an ideal target area for enemy mortars and rockets, as the Army had done all the marking off of the area for them. If the enemy didn't want to shoot at us but wanted to hit the II Corps HQ next door our area would catch any over or short rounds depending on which direction the enemy fired from. The "INCOMING" warning cry followed by the blast of high explosives and the warning siren were to become a regular event day or night.

I had been rocketed before but somehow I had felt like the enemy was not out to get me personally. I felt that at the 278th that we could do something about it, I could man a bunker with a fire slit facing the enemy and a machinegun at the ready, that's what I could have done. . Now at the 43rd it was just sitting there and taking it not just one or two rounds at a time but up to five or more rounds in a string. Here we were sitting in the middle of a bullseye of our own making, inviting the enemy to fire at us. We were just waiting, crouched in our bunkers, waiting for the one round that was going to get you.

Somehow the Army had found the perfect piece of ground with which to put a G.I. barracks on, the ground had a giant red circle painted on it, around that circle was painted a larger circle in white. You get the picture yet? Then around that circle was painted another larger red circle and so on. The Army had found perfect place to put me and the 43rd Signal, right in the middle of the bullseye.

After joining the 43rd, and after being rocketed for the third time and experiencing the accuracy of the enemy gunners first hand. Sitting in a bunker one morning at 3 a.m. I imagined what the enemy must be thinking before he sent a couple of

Chi/Comm (Chinese Communist) rounds our way. I could just see them sitting in their bunkers, on top of one of the near hills, training their gunners, "Now remember Nguyen, just drop mortar bomb between the red lights on those antennas. Yes that right, aim right in center of red and white target painted on the ground, and you are bound to hit something. Just walk them back and forth for good measure." Life on the impact zone was not fun. Don't hit the things with the red lights on top, we need them to line up our shots.

Even though we had the `INCOMING' explosions to live with, life was just not the same as it had been. Living at the 43rd I missed the crash and bang of the outgoing artillery, I didn't realize I had grown that accustomed to extremely loud noises, I had a hard time getting to sleep each night. The crash and bang of the incoming enemy rounds did make up for what I was missing somewhat.

Big Big Jon Problems

Having Big Jon for a roommate was great. He was the best roommate I ever had, and we got along great. However, there were some problems of coordination between us during rocket or mortar attacks. Big Jon was really a really BIG guy, and the problems stemmed from the fact that Big Jon slept in the bunk above mine. All 250 plus pounds of him would greatly tax the springs suspending his mattress. They taxed them so much that I had to slide into my bed horizontally beneath the bulge which was Big Jon. For fun one day I took all of the springs out of his bed frame, leaving four, one on each corner. When Big Jon got in that night I made sure that I was not lying underneath him. His mattress sagged onto mine and his weight almost caused both mattresses to touch the floor and the bed frame to bend in the wrong places. Those four springs never did pull back into shape after being stretched so far. We both had a good laugh.

When a rocket or mortar attack would occur in the middle of the night Big Jon and I would both tumble out of bed and head for the nearest shelter. Since Big Jon slept above me he did most of the tumbling, and he would inevitably land, for the first few times, on top of me. The impacts with Big Jon produced some painfully bruising results. Once out of bed and untangled from each other we would throw our clothes on, grab our weapons and gear and run to the nearest bunker. Once there we would spend a good part of the night sleeplessly waiting for something else to happen, and sometimes it did and sometimes it didn't.

After many of these occasions there was always one thing that puzzled Big Jon, and that concerned my state of readiness compared to his. We both always arrived at the bunker at the same time, but I always had my boots on and laced up, while Big Jon's laces trailed behind him in the dirt. This would drive him to distraction that I could arrive better prepared than he, and sitting in the mouth of a bunker in the middle of the night he would voice his complaint. I wouldn't tell him the solution to this mystery, and I would smugly make remarks, "that he had better get his shit together as a soldier." I finally told Big Jon the solution to this shoe lace phenomenon years later after we were both out of the Army. The truth was that after we tumbled out of bed, and I picked myself up from the floor, I would put on my pants then sit on the edge of my bunk lacing up my boots while I watched a mad man running about the inside our room trying to get his gear together. I had tried to get my own gear on once while Big Jon was running around, and I had been painfully flattened against two different walls and the bunk beds in the process. So from that time onward I decided that the effort wasn't worth the abuse, and so I sat back and watched big Jon get his stuff.

When the rockets or mortars came in, everything and everyone became frantic. A lot of people forgot we were all in this together, and became pushy and bullying in their haste to seek shelter. During one attack I watched Big Jon collar some bully by the back of the flak jacket and hold him back from running over people. "Hey, we don't do that around here. Ya

407

got that lil' buddy." Orosz met up with us in the bunker during this attack and told us a remarkable tale. Before any of the rockets had hit the ground his dog Whore almost drug him out of bed. "Yeah, I was sleeping der, and she had me by the wrist and pulled me out of bed." He rewarded her later with her favorite food, canned P.X. hash, not Vietnamese ankle. The consensus amongst the three of us was that Camp Enari was so much quieter and safer than this place.

The 43rd was the same lovely place that I remembered from months ago. The one big bonus the 43rd had over the 278th was there were no huge billowing dust clouds from passing trucks here. The roads around were all paved, and most of the compound was made up of hard packed red mud and rocks. The French, the ARVN and now the Americans had occupied the same ground for some time, and most of the soil had been packed down long ago by the tramp of thousands of boots. The top soil on the internal roadways and pathways had been worn down to rocks, years ago, and these sat half submerged, in the smooth red clay. Running across this stuff in the middle of the night, under conditions of extreme stress was dangerous. You could just as easily turn an ankle and end up sliding into your bunker like a baseball player, but with the rocks ripping your pants to shreds.

Mistakes

It was here at the 43rd Signal Battalion that I made my biggest mistake I had ever made since I had gotten to Vietnam, bigger even than joining the U.S. Army. I went to the U.S. Army dentist. I woke up one night with a tooth ache, and perceived that this was nature's way of telling me that it was time for that annual checkup I had avoided for the last two years. The next morning I walked down to the 71st Evacuation Hospital to visit the dentist.

I met some very interesting people sitting outside the dentist's office waiting my turn. The waiting room was on the dirt patch outside the dentist's part of the hospital, and I joined several soldiers, with dental problems like my own, lolling against the building's side shooting the breeze to pass the time. One of the patients was a camouflaged Ranger from the 4th Division, he had the same problem as I, but his was producing a wicked looking bulge in his right cheek. His had occurred from not brushing his teeth in the boonies for many many weeks. He invited me to come and visit his outfit stationed in one of the out laying villages. I did, and this visit produced the opportunity for Orosz, Big Jon and I to start our own trading circuit in the months to come.

Once I was ushered into the dentist's office and sat in his chair I remembered why I had avoided this experience for years. The dentist began to admire my dental work with what seemed like a very dull ten-penny finishing nail and a finger the size of a big toe. He was a big man with big hands. I was glad he wasn't a Proctologist with the size of those fingers. The dentist "Hmmmmed" and "Ooohed" a few times as he gouged around in my mouth. The vocal noises made didn't communicate much to me. He next said, "Well, you know what you are in here for," and with that he put his huge knee square in my chest and proceeded to pull two teeth. No Novocain, no "This will hurt you more than me," he just yanked two teeth. Actually he didn't just yank two teeth he jacked them back and forth in my jaw until the tooth gave up and popped out. My jaw ached for a week. From then on I preferred rocket attacks and snakes to going to the dentist.

"Did it hurt?" Asked Orosz.

"Yes buddy, it hurt like hell."

"My chest hurts were a huge knee pressed into the middle of it. My forehead hurts from where he placed his huge left hand to get leverage with his huge pliers, and my jaw hurts with him jacking the teeth out. It felt like he was pulling my toes out through my mouth.'

"So yes it hurt!"

The Easter Bunny Came

Another Easter in the Army came but with it came one of the most moving experiences I had in Vietnam. On Easter Sunday we were called to a formation, a most unusual command, as formations attracted enemy rockets, and while standing in rows and thinking about the possible consequences, each of us was handed a small cloth bag. These were affectionately known as ditty bags, (or diddy bags), a bag of personal hygiene items and other articles sent from people at home. All of us were taken aback by this unexpected show of affection, as we were very aware that the war was not popular and neither were we. It was a great gift as we definitely could use the contents. We had often felt that we were way off at the other end of the world alone, and here is a present from people who cared. Maybe we were not so all alone. Each bag contained soap, a razor, tooth paste and brush, and other personal items. Mine had some writing paper and envelopes, and each one had a small piece of paper telling us who donated the items. I wrote my own short note of thanks to whoever sent us this windfall, but it was tough to express the proper feelings.

We were thankful and all better off from what came in the bags; after all, it was a long long way to the nearest P.X. Getting there involved getting across several base camps to that house trailer full of items no one wanted to buy, it was a major expenditure of physical strength, shoe leather and sweat. To people making the pilgrimage to the P.X. with the announcement, "Hey I'm going to the P.X., anyone want anything?" I would state my own contempt for the trailers contents by yelling back, "Anything their out of, I'll take two of." Big Jon made the trip one day and returned with nothing but an arm load of pink bath towels, "That's all there was, lil buddy," he explained. The pink towels were great; we folded them in half, cut a slit in the middle, and wore them like ponchos to and from the shower. Comments were made about the color worn, but we always replied in Falsetto voice, "no peeking boys!"

Buster Brown & His Dog Tagge

The 43rd, like the 278, had its own set of eccentric characters, and I was getting to know some of them. On my arrival at the 43rd I was introduced to the supply officer in the headquarters, a Lieutenant Brown, Lieutenant "Buster" Brown from Boston, and like all good Buster Brown's he had a dog named Tagge. I was also introduced to this nasty fucking, mangy cur of a dog the hard way. Lieutenant Brown was OK as Lieutenants go, but his dog was one of the meanest hounds in the compound. Buster never took care of his dog; he just let it roam around the compound on its own. In daylight you had a chance to avoid this dog, but at night you were his meat. Consequentially, walking around the 43rd at night was very hazardous, cables were stretched across roadways, and vehicles moving around used no headlights. There was very little lighting and you were bound to run into good old Tagge somewhere any time. This canine would latch onto an ankle or nip you on the seat of the pants when you least expected it. Needless to say there was a lot of G.I.s who wanted to pay back good old Tagge. Lieutenant Buster would brook no complaints about the meanness of his dog, and neither would he keep it tied up. So those with revenge in their hearts waited. The revenge seekers waited for the one thing all soldiers in Vietnam waited for, Lieutenant Brown's departure. "Buster" Browns rotation back to the states also known as DEROS, Date Estimated Rotation form Overseas Station, Buster Brown's DEROS day came shortly after I arrived, and he left the 43rd to go home and ETS. Estimated Time of Separation, meaning: Sweet Liberty, the day you got out of the Army. Tagge was left for the rest of us at the 43rd to love and care for. Within hours of Lieutenant Brown's departure from the unit, good old Tagge was winging his own way north on the road to Kon Tum in the back of a deuce and a half truck. Somewhere along the way Tagge ETSed too, only his exit was at 45 miles per hour. This was considered humane, that is it was humane as opposed to being handed over to the local Montagnard village as lunch, which some of the other troops wanted to do. I did not hear that the truck was stopped and then backed up over good old Tagge, but I do think that might have been just the right treatment for this mutt. Of course I wasn't there to witness any part of the revenge that might have been dished out as I had not been with the 43rd as long as some, and had not suffered the bites and nips as often as others. Payback can often be a bitch!

Odd Jobs

In the 43rd Signals repair depot the Signal Corps found in me my real calling in electronics, I was appointed, at my own suggestion, terminal equipment specialist, FUBAR specialist or Equipment Terminator. There was always a percentage of all repaired equipment that was tougher to repair than others, and there was always that one or two pieces that kept coming back regularly with the same complaint again and again. It was not because we were incapable or incompetent; it was just one of those things. We were willing to do our job of repairing gear; there were just those individual pieces that had so much wrong with them that they were always breaking. Damp or wet conditions, humidity, being jolted from place to place, or age all played a part. Without the knowledge of the superiors appointed over us I would quietly slip whatever piece of troublesome gear out of the shop. I was to take these pieces of equipment outside the compound to a nice quiet place, and there put a couple of rounds from an Army .45 caliber automatic pistol or an M-16 through them. On my return I would then write up the equipment for battle damage. The write up I gave the equipment usually contained the acronym FUBAR, Fucked Up Beyond All Recognition or NRTS Not Repairable This Station. After performing this simple task I receiving the undying gratitude of my fellow repairmen who had spent parts of their youth trying to fruitlessly fix the dammed things, and now thanks to me would never be plagued by them again.

With the joy abounding from one end of the shop to the other I was acclaimed the greatest repairman. It was told far and wide, "Let Lennox fix it. If he can't fix it nobody can." What got me puzzled was that none of these bozos had thought of doing this for themselves before I implemented it.

Qui Nhon

Repairing equipment was fine, but the Army had a lot of people around the 43rd who could do that. The First Sergeant needed people to make supply runs to the coast on a regular basis. People he could trust to get there and back with the goods and not get lost along the way. He also needed people who could scrounge for him, pick up this or that, and do a deal or two for the necessities of a First Sergeant. So when a convoy was being organized the names of Big Jon, Orosz and Scotty came up every time. To date I had only gone by convoy between Pleiku and An Khe, and now we were going all the way to Qui Nhon on the coast. Qui Nhon was over 100 miles away, and instead of one deadly and devastated mountain pass to drive through now there were now two. Mang Yang pass between Pleiku and An Khe, and now Do Mang or An Khe pass between An Khe and the coast. With the thought of having to traverse both passes my attacks of the malaria pill blues, (the G.I.s aka the shits), hit an all-time high. I was nervous; everyone was nervous having to traverse these passes.

The road was not a straight shot from An Khe to Qui Nhon; it twisted and turned through many villages along the way. Nor was it a safe road no matter how many gun trucks you had protecting a convoy you were still one big juicy target. The road was swept for mines every morning before anyone was allowed to drive on it. They swept the road and the shoulders with tanks pushing huge rollers. What the tanks could not sweep the engineers swept with mine detectors. So the road was not safe, the shoulder was not safe at all, the villages were not safe and neither were the villagers. Nice, real nice!

Driving down from the mountain highlands to the coastal lowlands I was impressed with how paper flat the land became. Rice paddies and farms stretched into the distance from the base of the foothills, and the road became as straight as a string at times. Driving through, watching farmers plodding behind their water buffalos as they plowed their fields, the white stucco houses with gaily painted stripes and designs, set against the greenness of the surrounding hills made the war seem very far away.

On my first trip, one of the strangest things I saw was a set of unused railroad tracks that ran north and south through a village with a five way intersection. It was not only memorable because of the rails or the five way, but for the Vietnamese national policeman who stood on a pedestal in the middle of the intersection and directed traffic with a flair.

Outside of this village and closer to Qui Nhon was a U.S. Army truck stop. A barbed wire surrounded oasis in a desert of rice paddies, roadside whore houses and the occasional temple. This was a great place to get out of your truck, and stretch for a while and have a pee without getting shot at. Here a weary traveler could choke down a cold coke, if they had any, and get a free can of "C" Rations. The "C" Ration meals offered were the ones least liked by the troops. There would be open cases of "C" Rations available, all with the favorite meals already gone leaving things like Ham and Lima Beans, (aka Ham and Motherfuckers to those who had dined on them before), or the ever popular Ham and Scrambled Eggs. I passed on the C-Rats.

Driving into Qui Nhon we had to navigate through the narrow streets crowded with civilians, civilian vehicle traffic, and their street markets. The smells of Nouc Mam and charcoal smoke were everywhere. The Vietnamese put Nouc Mam on everything, it is a strange pungent sauce, and the Vietnamese thought it was one of Gods greatest inventions. I and a lot of other G.I.s thought it was the closest thing tasting and smelling to shit that we had ever found. I once asked a Vietnamese national how it was made, and this was his description:

Take an empty 55 gallon drum, a barrel or wooden box and cut out both ends.

Put a basin in the bottom

Over the basin, in bamboo racks put a layer of fish, and then a layer of straw, all the way to the top of the barrel.

Cover and let stand.

Check the basin from time to time (over several days) and when the basin is full of liquid take the basin and pour the contents back into the top of the barrel.

Replace empty basin in the bottom.

Continue this sequence till smell is just right. The process is then done, (tastes, yum yum, just right).

Qui Nhon was one of the major port cities in Vietnam for American supplies to be brought in. It was also a scroungers paradise, because it was a major supply port for Vietnam. There were U.S. Army supply depots there that covered acres of ground, and there were also scrap dumps there that also covered acres of ground. The scrap yards were mountains of pieces of tanks, helicopters, and other used up implements of war strewn across the ground. Walking through either dump was a true thrill, as there you could find anything and everything you wanted lying about on the ground. I once found a brand new airplane wing crated and waiting for someone to take it home. Finding things was one thing, getting out the gate with them was another? If you didn't have the proper paper work you were S.O.L. (Shit Out of Luck), and if the sleepy guards on the gate didn't believe the requisition form you had or the other one you had so carefully forged, the alternative was a trip to L.B.J., Long Bin Jail named I'm sure out of affection for the President. To avoid that possibility I resorted to the only things left, a midnight requisition, steal it when no one was looking, or to trade for it with the supply people.

In one corner of a supply dump I could walk from stack of material to stack of material without touching the ground, in the scrap yard the ground was so densely covered with dinner forks and knives you could not see the ground. There were no spoons however. I had discovered shortly after my arrival in Vietnam that the three things required to sustain G.I. life in Vietnam were a spoon, a church key can opener, and a P38 C-Ration can opener. The Vietnamese civilians also believed that spoons and Army "C" Rations were a boon to their civilization, and so spoons were in short supply everywhere. If the Army had used metal detectors when checking out civilian K.P.'s at the base camps they would have been surprised at how much silverware and "C" Rations the Army was supplying to the local economy.

After my first trip to Qui Nhon I knew just how far in the rear Qui Nhon was, as far as enemy action was concerned. It was so far in the rear that the Army had to pipe in the sounds of the war through tape recordings. There were no defensive bunkers visible anywhere we stayed, and the only sounds at night were the insects buzzing. It was so quiet that the Army ran its own beach resort there, and combat troops were sent there for a rest. The resort was no two bit strip of sand with a Popsicle stand. It had a lot to offer in the way of recreation. The resort had sports, palm trees, sun bathing, and no civilians to bother you, and a fence to keep you in. From what else I saw on my first trip I knew that the place was just right for scrounging whatever we needed. So I decided to try my hand at a little trading with the some of the supply and maintenance troops. The one thing I had available for trading right away was my own communist SKS rifle, which was worth its weight in something, because you could bring an SKS rifle home with you as a war souvenir. So I dropped some hints to the rear area supply troops, and on my next trip I brought my rifle with me.

Guns for Butter

On our second trip to Qui Nhon and showing off a War souvenir rifle, I was deluged with requests for more. There were a lot of anxious faces wanting to know if I could get more? "How did I get it?" "Can you do this regularly," and "when do I get mine?" Also, "I want an AK47?" We had struck gold. On this first pass I turned down all offers of money and traded the rifle to a Supply Sergeant straight across for 2 baby refrigerators, a case of steaks, and a beat up old Casablanca ceiling fan. The first refrigerator and fan went back to Pleiku with me, and I traded the second refrigerator to an American advisor team in a village near our camp. The first refrigerator got us two more fans, a dozen sheets of corrugated tin and 10 4 X 8 foot sheets of plywood and some other junk, but I kept the Casablanca fan.

The American Advisor team came through for the refrigerator and we got two AK-47 assault rifles and two old bolt action rifles for the second fridge and a hand-made VC flag, hand made by Vietnamese villagers under the control of the American Advisor team. The AKs were not as valuable as an SKS because they could fire fully automatic, and for that reason you could not take them home in a working condition. No matter, they were in high demand amongst the supply pukes.

So Big Jon, Oroz and Scotty opened their new trading empire with very little out of pocket expense. The AK-47s, the bolt action rifles and the flag went back to Qui Nhon with us, and they got a 35mm camera, eight 4' X 8' sheets of 1/2 inch plywood, and a reel to reel tape recorder and much more. We also got more requests for guns, guns and more guns.

As Big Jon's and my part of this loot I installed the Casablanca ceiling fan in our room, I suspended it by a single nail, in the center of our room back at the barracks, and here it was to provide the next best thing to air conditioning. There were a few draw backs that went with this fan however. I had to practically rewire the motor to get some life out of it, but once it was cleaned up it worked for many months. The fan lasted till the end of my tour in country, and also till the end of Big Jon's tour. When Big Jon left the fan went to a new owner, and is probably the cooling system for someone in Vietnam till this day. They don't build them like that anymore. The fan had all metal blades instead of wood, so you had to be careful what you waved around in the room, the fan could eat fingers or socks with equal relish. The real problem was not with the fan, but with electricity which ran it. The electrical supply was the same as in Camp Enari the quantity of the AC voltage that was supplied to the barracks would vary wildly. It varied by 70 volts some time, so you could count on voltage anywhere from 75 volts to 145 volts. How did I know this, well like any good technician I had found myself a "spare" voltage meter and I hooked it up to the electricity outlet in our room. All I had to do was look at the reading on the meter whenever the fans' speed changed, to know what the heck was going on. At 75 volts the fan blades oscillated harmlessly barely moving the air in the room, but when the voltage rose to its other extreme life could become hazardous. The fans blades would become a smooth silver blur, like an undersized airplane propeller, and the whole fan would begin to swing violently back and forth on its single nail. The sound made by the high speed fan blades slicing through the air became a roar, and I mentioned to Big Jon more than once that I thought we would both be safer outside or under our beds. I was sure the whole thing was going to jump off of its perch and come flying around the room like a giant buzz saw and slice us both into baloney.

The trading expanded from that point on, and people from the coast would telephone Orosz at the repair shop. And Orosz made sure that these people knew to talk to no one else but he. Top blew a gasket after the first message was left at his orderly room by some idiot who wanted an AK47. Once Top knew he could get plywood out of what we were doing he became reasonable, and told us how he wanted things handled. Requests poured in, as did the First Sergeants requests for material. The orderly room would bring us messages they were passed on to us by the First Sergeant. This was sort of a forerunner to the "Home Shopping Network." We expanded my exotic weapons trading, through more village contacts, and we got into Montagnard crossbows, homemade Ho-Chi-Min sandals and home-made knives. All of the luxury items we received in trade were hauled back up the mountains to the 43rd, and we traded those to people from remote locations who brought signal equipment in for repair. Sort of a "Bring and Buy" sale.

Of all the items we traded for, the one item that always cost us the most or we got the most for was sheets of plywood. People would wait in line for it, steel it, kill to get it, and because we had a source for it, our First Sergeant made sure we were well taken care of. As far as duty assignments, we now got only occasional guard duty, or K.P., but when a convoy was being put together there was always the summons to the First Sergeants office.

"Here Scotty, see if you can find any of this stuff."

"Sure Sarge, what have you got to trade?"

"Oh, and Scotty, see if you can find some plywood."

"Sure Sarge, what have you got to trade?"

"I got some paint."

"Paint! I get spit on for paint. Got any floor tile?"

"OK, you can take two cases."

"Oh, and don't forget, get my plywood."

"I need batteries, the Advisor Teams need batteries and the ARVN will pay well for them."

"Take 4 boxes of "D" cells and 4 boxes of anything else you think will go."

"Get some steaks the C.O. wants to throw a party."

"Tell him to get his own steaks. We need something to trade steaks for."

This would go on every time.

The Hazards of Going to the Coast

On our next trip to Qui Nhon, I made this run as the driver of a 3/4 ton truck, with Orosz as a shotgun guard, and we leading a convoy of three other two and a half ton trucks all without canvas each hauling boxy signal shelters. I made the traverse of the steep pass roads safely on the way down, but we were caught in a fire fight in Do Mang pass on the way back.

Traveling down-hill in an Army truck was relatively easy, and you could gain quite a bit of speed even with a governor on the engine. Going up-hill in an Army truck was a different story. Getting a good running start was a good idea, but a running start would not get you that far, the passes were a long hard grueling climb. Eventually you were slowed by gravity and reduced to crawling along in either 2nd gear or in steeper stretches 1st gear. If there was mud on the road then it was 1st gear and four wheel drive. In any case we crawled up-hill at maybe 10 to 15 miles per hour, and that made for an easy target.

The security forces in both passes were both Korean and American, and when this fact about the Korean presence was revealed to me I definitely felt sorry for the enemy. As the saying went, "When the Koreans came to town, everyone shit weak." This meant that the Korean's reputation brutality was well known. If you messed with them their reaction would be brutal enough to make anyone mess their pants.

On our up-hill return journey a fire fight broke out a short distance ahead of our convoy while we were creeping up the pass. The 4th division APC that was part of the road security detachment blocked the road in front of us, and we were forced to take cover along the shoulder of the road. Jumping out of our truck Orosz and I took cover on the downhill slope beside the road, and fired our weapons up the mountain side in the general direction of the enemy. Enemy rounds were slapping into the road in front of us and some were whizzing off overhead and down the pass. The other drivers and shotguns from the convoy followed our example and we popped off hoping we might hit something. We were still firing when the gunner on the APC in front of us yelled at us, "Get the fuck out of there." The APC moved to the side of the road so we could get by and the race was on. We all got up and ran like maniacs while the bullets were still flying, we started our trucks and started to pull slowly out. Orosz spent a little too much time returning the enemies fire, crouching by his open door, facing up the mountain, firing away with his M-2 carbine. He was providing covering fire so the rest of us could get to our vehicles and get them rolling. He was still firing back at the enemy as I put the truck in gear and pulled away. The truck starting to move off brought a shout of alarm from Orosz. He gave up being our protector and he got up and sprinted for the tail gate of the truck. He caught up with it within 10 yards, and he tossed his rifle into the back before he jumped on the back bumper. Unfortunately, the rifle landed painfully into the face of a new replacement soldier, (one of three we were bringing back with us), who was watching Orosz, and was too wrapped up in `would he or would he not make it'. On the run Orosz was able to grab onto the tail gate of the truck, and he swung himself on board over the tail board like a Hollywood stunt man. Once on the word was passed to me and away we roared in 1st gear, while the battered newbie was tended to.

These trips to Qui Nhon always took about four hours one way, barring any unforeseen circumstances, and so we always stayed overnight. This offered some marvelous opportunities to get out and see another side of Vietnam, the quiet side, the side with street lights and gaily colored neon signs, the naughty side not the "Off Limits" side, of Vietnam. We had a chance to see the city of Qui Nhons' night life, up close and personal. The town was not "Off Limits" like Pleiku. Big Jon, Orosz and I took advantage of some of the overnight visits to forge ourselves a pass, steal an unattended Jeep and go and see some of the sights. Blank passes were available in every orderly room of every unit, just wait till no one was looking and they were there for the taking. So getting a blank pass was easy.

Filling it out was a matter of name rank and serial number. Vehicle log books were another matter. However, our buddy Orosz having been in charge at the 278ths motor pool had a locker full of blank vehicle log book forms that we forged with the I.D. of the vehicle that we commandeered. Lieutenant Hanley never refused to sign a pass for us to venture out at night, and we took great pains not to get this Officer into trouble by misbehaving. The local Vietnamese were happy to see G.I.s come and spend money, in the local establishments. I dined out many nights on the local foods, from vendor's street stalls or restaurants. Fish, Prawns, rice, milk and other delicacies, but no matter how I tried I could never get closer than three feet toNouc Man sauce and its smell.

The Glee Club the Second Helping

When back at the 43rd we paid close attention to our growing Glee Club, as we didn't want a lot of trouble with the locals. So we had to make things as light and fun as possible. We didn't want to end up like a meeting of the math or chess club. So we agreed to have weekly meetings, and some not so weekly meetings. Not so weekly was when we all wanted to get together for a beer. Whenever we met for a beer everyone was required to follow "Varsity" protocol. We instituted new rules for drinking, which would add more variety to our evenings. Now we had to drink by the numbers, hey we were in the Army and everything was by the numbers. When someone wanted to drink they requested that the command be given by the most senior member present. That command was "Prepare to drink," everyone would grab their can of off-brand beer and sit expectantly for the next command. Once everyone was prepared the second command was then given, "Ready....., Drink," and everyone would then imbibe. Anyone who missed the cue, or didn't have a beer, had to beg the pardon of his peers to get a catch up drink. The common method to do this was to request, "Permission to be An Idiot," indication that "Gee I was stupid and messed up." If the other members present condescended to grant a second chance to this thirsty individual, they would signify by replying, "Permission granted." Only then could a drink be taken.

Not surprisingly other new members brought new musical material with them to add to our dirty song collection. We were so successful at attracting new members that we eventually had to produce a song book laboriously and secretly typed out on a U.S. Army Teletype writer machine. Using U.S. Army equipment and U.S. Army ink ribbon and paper, plus punched paper tape to record a book of dirty songs was a no, no. People got sent to jail for doing that. The guys in the shop who worked on the Teletype machines bitched about us using up all their supplies. So what the hell we did it all in a couple of hours during the middle of the night. The people in charge never knew, the guys in Teletype repair never knew, and nobody went to jail. We did eventually find replacement paper in Qui Nhon for the teletype guys so they would stop bitching about our usage.

The glee club was either so loud or so much fun that the C.O. of the battalion, the colonel, came down to join us one evening. By that time our membership was over a dozen, and we had our secretly printed song book for everyone. The colonel sat and had a beer or two with us, observed our drinking rules, and sang a few songs with us. The colonel was generous enough to buy us all a round of Carling's, at 25 cents a can, that we felt obligated and gave him a song book as a souvenir of his visit. Heck, it was his unit budget that ultimately paid for it.

We experimented with other ways to entertain ourselves. One new twist was added for a short time. When a brew was finished the empty can was banged down on the table so that everyone knew it was empty. The owner would them turn the can sideways and smash it into his forehead, and finish it off by slamming the dented empty back on the table. This was quite a manly fete, as these were `tin' cans, not the aluminum ones of today. This was all well and good until the club got a shipment

423

of something called "Antler" beer from some were, whose claim to fame was that it came in the "Patented Stainless Steel Can." Orosz was the first to try one of these, and after burping to show how much he liked the contents he then commenced to bash his brains out with the can. He hit himself in the head with a resounding clang, and his head then bounced off of the wall behind him. He was out cold. "All right you idiots, no more can crushing." was the word from the First Sergeant the next day.

We were never requested to sing at social functions, hell, there we none, but everyone in the battalion knew who we were and what we were. As usual we were told to "Shut the fuck up," from Qui Nhon, Ahn Khe and many other places and on many occasions. Eventually, the Varsity became so popular that we decided to show outwardly our involvement with our club. We developed our own shoulder patch, with our own original character. We wanted to design a pie shaped shoulder patch, for mom and apple pie, that would fit our image, and what we came up with we were very proud to wear around our compound. Of course these patches were unauthorized by the Army and we were not allowed to sew them onto the shoulders of our uniforms. We had to be content with having them encased in plastic and wearing them buttoned on the breast pocket of our fatigues. We started with a pair of good looking female legs, naked female legs, spread into a "V" shape, "V" for victory, (what we were fighting for), of course, and then we placed a foamy mug of beer strategically between the knees of those shapely legs. Lightning bolts shot into the foamy head on the mug of beer, (we were in the Signal Corps), and the inscription, "VICTORY IN VIETNAM" was placed above the beer across the top of the patch. It was beautiful! All of this was mounted on a blue background, and bordered in yellow. It was breathtakingly sublime as far as unit insignias go. We had them hand sewn in Qui Nhon, at Joe's cut-rate shoulder patch shop, for all our members, and along with the shoulder patches we had a guidon flag made with a larger version of the patch in the middle. The guidon we flew on the lead vehicle of any convoy that Big Jon, Orosz and I participated in. We definitely rivaled the rebel flags, skull and cross bones, stars and stripes, and unit flags that were flown by various other trucks while on convoy. I won't say that the patches were coveted by all who saw them, but the colonel never got one, neither did the First Sergeant or the C.O. I carried on correspondence with several people who thought that they deserved membership in the Varsity, and therefore they deserved a patch. This correspondence went on long after I left Vietnam.

35 Friggin' Miles an Hour

For all of our motoring back and forth on highway QL-19 I was never not scared on a convoy, it never became routine. What scared me most of all was possibility of getting stopped for speeding in one of the two passes we went through. Yes I was NOT amazed by the infrequent ambushes that occurred in the passes, those scared the hell out of me, but at least you expected that was the place where you would get ambushed. I was absolutely flabbergasted that Vietnam had a nationally enforced speed limit of 35 miles per hour. Nationally enforced by Americans on Americans, it wasn't going to be a Vietnamese White Mouse or whatever QC stood for on an ARVN M.P.'s helmet, and it sure as hell wasn't going to be a Korean who pulled you over. This speed limit was mandatory for all U.S. Army personnel and only U.S. Army personnel, and to back it up the American M.P.s had radar, other speed traps, and traffic tickets available for enforcement. We abided by this speed limit; we abided by it when we had an officer or NCO were present in our vehicle, and we abided by it involuntarily going up-hill in one of the passes. But our attitude on this speed limit was catch us if you can. Driving anywhere in Vietnam at 35 mph was not what any of us lower enlisted men considered safe, sane or healthy, and so with each trip along QL 19 we bumped the limit up a few miles per hour till we were going just as fast as we could get an Army vehicle to go. No matter what the enemy or the M.P.s threw at us, all of us considered ourselves bullet proof or invisible to enemy observation only after our vehicles reached a velocity of light speed, 55 mph or better.

What idiot dreamt up a 35 mph national speed limit in a war zone none of us ever knew, but the idea must have come from some "Big Brain" somewhere. No matter, the M.P.s sure knew when and where we would be exceeding it the most, there they set up their speed traps. Their Jeeps had sirens and red lights, and they would pull you over just like getting a ticket in the states. The fine for speeding was nothing compared to the thrill of having to sit by the side of the road in open country and wait while an M.P., with his foot on your bumper, filled out a ticket. I didn't care how many Korean or U.S. troops I saw securing the roads, anytime I was outside of a base camp I thought of myself as a target. Any fast moving target was a lot harder to hit than one going no more than 35 miles per hour.

Orosz and I got several speeding tickets between us, and mostly for cruising through the speed traps that the M.P.s had set up in and around Qui Nhon. No M.P. I ever encountered was stupid enough to stop a speeder in one of the mountain passes, and no Army driver I ever knew was stupid enough to let an M.P. stop him in one of the passes. I don't know if there was an M.P. stupid enough to pull a vehicle over in either Man Yang or Do Mang pass. There might have been! Convoys were usually sheparded through those passes with heavily armed gun trucks in front, middle and rear of the convoy. (Gun trucks carried machineguns up to 50 caliber on their corners, as well as M-79 grenade launchers, and several gunners all surrounded by heavy armored plate. They also had menacing names painted on their sides. "Grim Reapers," "Exterminators," or "Death Squad" were some of them). Heavily armed G.I.s were not willing to be pulled over for speeding by M.P.s armed only with one or two M-16 rifles.

When Orosz or I were stopped for speeding we always presented our 278th Signal Company drivers license instead of our license from the 43rd. Since the 278th no longer existed the tickets were usually thrown out when the ticket finally found their way to the battalion C.O.'s desk. The C.O. had no time to chase down delinquents, and handing out Article-15 punishments to non-existent drivers from a non-existing company. That much investigation took too much effort.

None of the M.P.s caught on to our deceptions or the fact that the 278th no longer existed. Both Orosz and I presented them with drivers licenses with phony names on them. Some of the names we dreamed up for our phony licenses' were right out of high school and pretty hilarious. Names like "Will I. Graduate," "Rodger A. Dodger," and "Phermineas Bundersnatch" to mention but a few. As I have mentioned, Orosz had been the person in charge of issuing drivers licenses, but when his job ended at the 278th he had somehow came away with a stack of drivers license blanks. All we needed was a typewriter in some unguarded office and he or I could create a new persona for the M.P.s to chase.

Local Traffic Problems

Besides our struggle to avoid their entrapping ways, we figured that our own M.P.s and our government being against us. We had one more problem on the roads that just would not go away, and could it was a problem that could not be ignored. It was the Vietnamese drivers themselves; with discussions with different drivers from different units we figured that the South Vietnamese drivers posed a greater threat to our safety than anything else.

A big part of the problem was perceptions. The South Vietnamese, who owned the country we drove through, also liked to perceive that they also owned the roads. We had a different perception, and at times liked to prove that they didn't "Own the roads." Vietnamese drivers in the towns and cities

427

were one thing, a crazy mishmash, but you expected that in town. We normally didn't get shot at in the towns. Out on the open road the locals were a hazard to us and themselves. A lot of Vietnamese had gotten away from the bicycle and adopted the 50 cc motorcycles as a form of family conveyance, a big step up for a nation still using Water Buffalo as a mode of transportation. Under powered motor scooters were also a popular means of transportation in the suburbs. The problem with bikes, motor scooters and small engine motorcycles was they were slow, and when you put a load on them they were even slower. Out on the open road motor cycles could be seen with a husband driving and wife plus one or more children on board, plus there might be chickens and other animals as passengers too. Motor scooters they made into taxi cabs in the towns and would hang a cage with seats on the back end. Add lumber, several passengers, and livestock and you had big trouble. The trouble generally was that any one or more of these conveyances could be in front of you doing 5 miles per hour if they could. Which side of the road they used did not matter to the locals both sides were fair game.

Because of the Vietnamese local driving customs people on Army convoys devised their own devilish schemes to get the local Vietnamese and their local vehicles out of the right of way and off to the shoulders of the roads.

The taxi cabs made out of motor scooters did not block the roads in our area, as much as the motorcycle drivers did. As I have explained, the drivers for the 4th division had a habit of pulling up beside these motor scooter taxis, and the shotgun guard would open his door and reach out a boot and kick the taxi over on its side. So these taxi cab drivers were very wary of any Army truck, and stayed to the shoulder of the road.

Out on the open road, roaring along, and not stopping for anything that wasn't bigger than us was our way of convoying. Driving down the road we would have our windshield flipped up out of the way or completely removed and replaced with some armor plate. Sticking out of the windshield would be one of a variety of weapons we carried with us. M-16 rifles, an M-60 machine-gun, or my all-time favorite traffic control weapon the M-79 40mm grenade launcher.

The M-79 when fired made a very distinct "Pooooohhh" sound when it coughed out a round, and I think I can say without contradiction that everyone in Vietnam, including the enemy, knew that sound by heart. Oroz and I spent one morning before going on a convoy breaking apart 40mm Buckshot, (canister), rounds and putting them back together the way we wanted them. I took four canister rounds which contained several pellets of buck shot each, and I removed the shot and the one inch plastic wad that held the shot in place, and that left the shell casing. We dumped out all but a spoonful of the powder, and we then packed a wad of paper tightly into the end of the shell to keep the powder in place, and the paper replaced the plastic wad and shot. Big Jon, Orosz and I had done some experimenting outside of base camp with this paper wad and the different amounts of powder until we got the right amount required to tap someone on the shoulder from100 feet away. We wanted to scare them not tear their stupid heads off. Riding down the road as a shotgun guard this day I kept my M-79 out of sight until we came up behind a Vietnamese on a motorcycle doing ten miles an hour down the middle of the road, and in the middle of nowhere. I stuck the barrel of the grenade launcher out through the windshield opening, and while we were still far behind him I loaded one of our doctored rounds. "Scotty what the hell you going to do with that?" asked an incredulous The Mummy the driver for today. "I'm gonna do a little traffic control," I replied. I took careful aim, and when my target got to 50 yards I fired. The Vietnamese heard the distinct "POOOOOHHH" sound of the M-79 first, and my targets head popped up as he sat bolt upright. The target then pulled his head down as far as he could get it between his shoulders. The wad of paper bounced harmlessly off of the road nowhere near him a second after the sound, and the rider made hastily but shakily for the far shoulder of the road.

"Beats the hell out of begging them to get out of the way," I said.

"Hey if we was Koreans," said The Mummy, "we would just run the fuckers over."

Nose Art

During the Vietnam War people in the U.S. services were prone to name anything, everything from latrines "Sergeant Potts Pisser", helicopters "Death from Above", to tents "Tinmon's Teepee". It was sort of self expression much has our fathers had done during World War II in adding nose art to the front of their airplanes. We, it turns out were no different than our Dads.

With all this motoring around Vietnam I began to see the same vehicles again and again on different trips. There were convoy gun trucks of all designs and paint schemes, armored Jeeps, Tanks, Armored Cars, Armored Personnel Carriers, and other exotic vehicles cruising the roads everywhere we went. Trucks Jeeps and other vehicles were personalized by the owner/driver with a name painted on the vehicles side or under its windshield. A truck displaying the name "Miss Virginia" denoted the affection felt for some home state, town, or a sweetheart and this was the most common type name displayed. Some people got very creative in naming their vehicles. An armor plated Jeep with twin M-60 machineguns on top was named "GONADS," a chaplains Jeep, (it could only be a chaplain), and with the word "REPENT" painted in white reverse letters under the windshield. That way the word "REPENT" showed in your rear view mirror when the Jeep came up behind you.

I was finally and permanently assigned as driver to the same deuce and a half truck. This truck had an all metal box mounted on the back instead of an open bed with a canvas cover; this trucks' original purpose was to be used as a mobile repair shop. Because this metal box had a metal door on the back and could

430

be locked it was ideal to haul valuable stuff back and forth to Qui Nhon. Having my own assigned truck was a boon to our getting from place to place, but this particular truck had a problem or two when I first acquired it. The first problem was that the truck had a stand up exhaust stack in front of the passenger side of the cab, but half of the exhaust pipe was missing. The exhaust system ended level with the top of the passenger door, and both the driver and the shotgun were asphyxiated by the diesel fumes being blown into the cab as they drove down the road. I had fixe that problem first after suffering severe nausea on my first ride in this beast.

I made a modification to the exhaust system after the Motor Pool Sergeant told me to go and fuck myself when I asked him to requisition the correct part I needed. So being not one to take a no for an answer I liberated an exhaust stack from a scrap pile over at the engineers when no one was looking. Teach that Motor Pool Sergeant to talk nasty to me. I found this unused five ton exhaust stack and modifying it with a hacksaw, a sledge hammer and a scrounged "U" bolt until it fit my truck.

The second problem the truck had was the lack of a spare tire. Some scrounger before me had liberated the wheel and tire that had been bolted to my new truck. So knowing the reception I would be given by the Motor Pool Sergeant I knew what to do. I waited till it got dark then performed a midnight requisition of a spare tire from someone else's truck. Problem now transferred to someone else. Screw em!

Once I was told that this truck was now "MY" truck I decided that I too needed to do some personalizing of my own vehicle. I wracked my brain for several days. What to do? What name? I was no artist, how am I gonna do this? Why put a name on it, and end up looking just like every other G.I.'s truck in Vietnam. Why not, it was one of the only ways we got to show our individuality. Somehow "Grim Reaper" just didn't fit, "Bunch of Buggers," "Scroungers" or "Thieves Delight" did fit. But not "Flying Finger," which were my first choices. So after much thought and consideration I settled on a bastardized

431

saying by a famous cartoon pig that I always enjoyed greatly. It was a saying that I was very fond of quoting my entire time in the Army; I painted the following across both doors of the cab, "Abaddi....Abaddi....Abaddi.....AW FUCK IT!"

Pictures 4

Figure 19. 43rd Signal area showing transmission screens that made it an excellent target area. Author's collection.

Figure 20. 43rd Signal from QL14. Author's collection.

Figure 21. Big Jon trying to dig his way back to Texas. Author's collection.

Figure 22. Three young amigos showing off a rare treat, cans of a brand name beer. L to R Orosz, Big Jon and Scotty. Author's collection.

Chapter 17

The Monsoon Coffee Company

My arrival at the 43rd was followed shortly by the South East Asian Monsoon. This weather phenomenon arrived with a loud clap of thunder and a torrential down pour. I had heard of the Monsoon from many veterans, but their descriptions did not do it justice. The Monsoon is not a thing or a weather event; it is a weather season that lasts for several months. It doesn't rain all day but when it did rain it rained in buckets and more buckets. It rained daily on what seemed to be a regular schedule, and you could practically set your watch by when the rain would start and stop.

With the Monsoon came thankfully cooler weather and the sky was covered for most of the day by a low hanging sheet of grey. The clouds cut off the tops of the surrounding hills and mountains from view, and everything was dull and gloomy. When it wasn't raining then puffy grey clouds raced across the heavens at a tremendous speed. For the first few days it was a novelty to stand or walk outside in the cool rain, and let it soak your fatigues. Back inside your uniform would dry in 20 minutes, and you could go outside and start all over again. I saw more than one G.I. running outside naked with a bar of soap in his hand going to catch a warm afternoon shower. The rain turned the distant brown hills back into a lush green inviting countryside, and with all the new growth bits of the local villages became hidden from view. What had been white stucco and red tile was now nothing but green, and what had been a glimpse of a thatched roof was now nothing but banana leaves.

During the Monsoon everything was soaked, you walked in red mud, you ate in red mud, you worked in red mud, and you carried red mud everywhere you went on the soles of your Army jungle boots. The mud was on all of your equipment, inside and out, inside and outside of every vehicle, in all your possessions, it was even caked on the walls in places. I had seen dried read mud smears on trucks, tanks, APCs and other vehicles before, but I chalked it up to camouflage. It wasn't camouflage it was just red mud on vehicles that had not been washed for years.

The barracks area at the 43rd had raised wooden walkways between each barracks and the latrine, and until the rains came I didn't realize what they were for. They helped you avoid plodding to the latrine in six inches of mud, for if you stepped off of the walkways deep red mud is what you ended up in. Stepping into this red slop could suck the boots off of your feet if your laces were not tied securely.

The Monsoon did not stop the rocket attacks, but all the mud just allowed the missiles to bury themselves deeper in the ground. The rain and low clouds never caused the enemy's aim to waver once. The wet red soil did absorb most of the blast and shrapnel, but not much of the BANG! The explosions just slung the red mud far and wide from the impact zone but it was laced with shrapnel.

Early one rainy morning the enemy sent us a series of 122mm rockets that crashed in giant strides through the length of our compound, and through half of our buildings. There were some large holes punched in the ground, but even larger holes were produced when one round hit the officer's latrine dead center and the next one hit the mess hall also dead center. Good-bye to those flush toilets the officers had, they would now

436

have to crap like the rest of us. During this attack Big Jon and I ended up jammed into the same bunker shortly after the first round had hit the ground, and we both watched from the doorway of the bunker, (We both liked to watch what was going on from the doorway. That way we could defend ourselves if there was a ground attack. We were both more than fatalistic, we figured that if a rocket hit your bunker you were dead whether you sat inside or in the doorway), we watched as the shrapnel and pieces of water pipe rained down all around us from the one round which hit the mess hall. From my perch in the doorway I reached out and picked up a piece of sizzling, hissing metal about one inch square in my bare hands and burned my fingers and I dropped it immediately back into the red mud. To show Big Jon how hot it was I leaned my body out of the bunker door, and placed my unlit cigarette against another piece of hissing shrapnel, the metal lit the cigarette in just a second.

Sitting in a bunker during a rocket attack I started to have strange thoughts. I was passed the stage where you worried where the next round would land, and I started having random abstract thoughts about rocket attacks in general. I wondered why the Army didn't build blast walls around its outhouses. Why they didn't do the same for mess halls? Or why the Army didn't put a blast wall around the places guys worked the shop buildings in the compound? Was it because you were not supposed to go to the latrine when under attack, as that is what you had your pants for? Anyway, these strange thoughts kept popping up in my head.

It was during this attack a strange thought came to me and I shared this one with the other G.I.s toughing it out waiting for the "All Clear" to sound. I thought that the 43rd First Sergeant should take special action to safe guard the majority of the troops. Every outfit had a few men that were considered duds, (the bozos, the idiots, the guys who were constantly screwing up), and I thought of a novel way of employing these individuals. The C.O. should assemble all the duds into one special squad, and when a rocket or mortar attack occurred the squad would move about the compound trying to catch the incoming rounds. The idea of the "Rocket Squad" was born, and all close by in the bunker thought it a great idea. Those present in our bunker started to volunteer names for admission into the "Rocket Squad." They could all visualize one of our company duds running around the motor pool, a baseball catcher's mitt held out in front by outstretched arms, head thrown back searching the sky and yelling, "I got it, I got it," at the top of their voice.

Mud Sports

Because of all the red mud carried in by boots the floors of the barracks and work shop areas had to be cleaned constantly from the comings and goings of all those muddy feet. Mopping was the usual method, scrapping with flat nosed shovels would have been easier, but the Army had plenty of mops and men to use them. The main danger about the mud on the floor was that this red goop was as slick as a sheet ice, and when walking on it your feet could sail out from under you at any time. Buildings were not the only place that mud would accumulate; the roads would get covered with an inch or two of this red slime from mud slides, thrown up by tank or APC tracks, and other vehicles carrying it onto the roads. Many times I spent a few anxious seconds looking out the drivers or passengers side window to see ahead as my truck slid down several hundred yards of roadway spinning its wheels on the sheet of mud. Other times I sweated blood, and willed my bladder not to let go, while feeling the trucks rear end slip from side to side. Even in four wheel drive you slid, and many times I wondered if we were ever going to make it straighten out or end up in the ditch. The only thing you could do when sliding around on the road was to gingerly compensate for the swing, and hope for the best. At times I would have given a months' pay to see the expression on my shotgun's face as we slid, but I was too busy, I had my own troubles at the same moment.

One day I being, as usual, in the wrong place at the wrong time, I was given the job of organizing the floor clean up at the repair depot. This involved mopping the entire area at least twice a day, and having been in the Army over two years I definitely knew a lot about mopping. I was not content just to swab down the floors which just moved the mud from place to place. I had other organizational talents. So twice a day I would organize a team of moppers to do the entire floor in one pass. I called it "The Mop Squad," and it consisted of six men with mops mopping their brains out in a line moving from one end of the shop to the other. From the first day that I put the squad into operation it attracted a lot of attention from those sitting on top of the benches as the squad sped by with mops flying. It got to be a lot of fun to mix elbows in this way, instead of the clean up being a dreary drudge of a chore. Often those not on the squad would liberate mops from other buildings just so they could participate in 10 minutes of "Mop Mayhem." The squad would mop and shove each other from one end of the depot to the other while those not on the squad would shout encouragement from the bench tops. To a bunch of bored G.I.s it really broke up the day.

The Steam & Cream

After I had been living in the 43rd area for a week or two I got into a conversation, one night, with a couple of my new work mates from the repair shop. The subject of our discussion was "what do you guys do for fun or entertainment around here?" I was hoping that there was more to do than what we had for entertainment at the 278th. The explanation started with a list of the standard Army amenities, AFVN radio, taped music, records, and writing letters. I was hoping one of them would say U.S.O. show, but neither one of them mentioned the U.S.O. .

439

"Yes, yes, but what do you guys get in the way of entertainment?" I asked again.

"We get movies in the EM club," came the reply. We were getting warmer.

I let them ramble on for a little while.

"No," I said, "I said fun and entertainment,"

"Oh!" they both said in unison and gave each other a knowing look.

"Well there's always Thunder Alley," said the first one.

"What's that?" I asked.

"Well," began the second one, "Thunder Alley is where all of the whorehouses are, and even though they're off limits you can still drive through it."

"Driving through is not exactly what I want to do," was my response to this bit of information.

"There's always the steam bath," said the first one, and this brought a conspiring look and a nod from the second guy.

"Yeah, the Steam and Cream," said the second.

The Steam and Cream was the local bath house that resided, surprisingly enough, inside the MACV, (Military Assistance Command Vietnam), compounds barbed wire. It was about a half mile walk from our compound, there was a road that led through the MACV living area which was compound next door to us. This was a steam bath run by the Army P.X. service, and was manned entirely by Vietnamese women. This sounded better all the time. My two companions also told me that the specialty of the house was a steam bath, followed by a massage, followed by a hand job. I decided that I would visit this palace of delights when the feeling was right.

It was two weeks before I deciding that I had that certain feeling, and it was time for me to make the pilgrimage down the hill to the steam baths. As it turned out, I had waited a week too long for the feeling to arrive.

In the intervening period of my feeling finally erupting the 43rd Signal had received a new Chaplain. He had arrived right after I had transferred into the unit. This Chaplin was a Baptist and a nice family man fresh from the states. After he got acquainted with the members of his congregation, and each of their far flung locations he settled down to life in the base camp. Somehow he learned that there was a steam bath located nearby, and he decided to visit it for a bath and massage. After getting his bath and massage the young girl servicing him asked him in her best broken English "you wan spe-c-ial o' house?" and the padre said sure. When I finally made the trip down the hill all I found in place of the steam baths was an empty boarded up building, and that's the way we both remained for the rest of my tour.

Jeep for Dinner

One of the staples served at dinner in the 43rds' mess hall was roast beef, and this was a delightful change from the 278ths' S.O.S. that Sergeant Grayson was so fond of. The beef was carved right on the serving line and made your mouth water just to watch the carving being done.

On my first helping of 43rd roast beef I set my steel divided tray down on an empty table, and without waiting for Big Jon or Orosz to join me I dove right in. The first mouthful convinced me about the origin of the meat served. I chewed my first mouthful till my jaws ached. When Orosz and Big Jon sat down to join me I was only partially able to warn them about the meet on our trays. I had a giant, bulging wad of beef in my mouth, and tried to talk around it.

"Waawaa Buflooo," is what I got out without spraying the table with spittle.

"What?" They both asked in unison.

"Waawaa Buffaloo," was my strained reply.

"Water Buffalo, where?" asked Orosz.

"Thitth ith Waawaa Buffalo," I said pointing to my mouth.

"Bull Shit!" said Orosz.

"No Boo Shiii, Waawaa Buf," I tried once more to explain.

They both took a mouthful of meat and immediately the little light bulbs went on over their heads. To say the least the meat was tough, and digestion was only aided by sawing through portions and devouring it in little bites. We ate it, we would eat anything they put in front of us, but that beef had to have been Water Buffalo.

The rumor going around the mess hall was that "A supply truck had hit a Water Buffalo on the way to the 43rd, and they were serving the Water Buffalo and we were destroying the evidence."

At one evening meal the cooks were having a particular hard time slicing the beef with their extremely sharp knives. On seeing their efforts I quipped, "What happen' a Jeep hit a Water Buffalo and you guys are serving the Jeep?" Those around me immediately concurred with my estimate of the situation.

Gordo's Big Trip

It was at this same time that my feeling wilted that Gordo showed up. Gordo was a former member of the 278th, and he and I had shared many a pleasant evening admiring the world, while peering through the gun slit of a bunker. I had spent my first guard tour in Vietnam with Gordo. He had shown me the world as it appears at night through a Star Light Scope. If you have never peered at the world through a Star Light Scope the world is Green bright Green. Gordo Explained how the only person the VC could possibly hide from the view of this scope would have to be the Incredible Hulk or Herman Munster. Gordo and I had shared a lot like this in the short time I had known him. We were both from LA, and we had compared a lot of stories about our growing up, while we whiled away the hours. On this occasion I was sad to see him, Gordo had come to the 43rd to be court-martialed.

What had brought Gordo to this was an even while we were both still in the 278. I had attended one of the outdoor movies, and was half awake while engrossed in this black and white epic, displayed on white painted plywood, when a shot rang out from close by. I like all the troops present went flat while others ran for the cover of the nearest barracks or bunker. The shot was immediately followed by loud shouts and a scuffle in the back of the movie crowd. I was more dismayed by having nowhere to hide, than wondered what the hell was going on in the back.

It was Gordo he had been bullied out of his seat before the movie started by another troop, and instead of taking his lumps gracefully he had gone back to his barracks and he had come back with his M-16 rifle. Luckily his approach had been seen by someone and Gordo was jumped as he was taking aim on the bully. The shot went wild, and the ensuing scuffle was caused by three or more G.I.s pummeled Gordo into a bloody unconsciousness.

Two months had passed since the shooting incident at the 278th movie. I had really thought no more about it, until Gordo showed up at the 43rd. The Gordo I knew in the 278 was a short, dark, soft spoken, family man, (a wife and two kids in Los Angeles), who smoked a pipe as his only vise. We were buddies, and it was sad to see him under these circumstances. Big Jon, Orosz and I made an effort to sit with him at meals, tell him stories and jokes, and try and keep up his spirits.

The inevitable finally happened, Gordo was convicted of armed assault, and because of the severity of his crime he had been sentenced to several months in prison. The Army had but one prison in Vietnam, a place infamous for its reputation of racial unrest as well as cruelty. L.B.J., Long Binh Jail. Those three letters meant but one thing to any US Army soldier, and it wasn't the president of the United States. I had first heard of it in Fort Riley Kansas, and from the tails told I wanted no part of it. Good news always got around far and wide in the Army.

The day after the conclusion of Gordo trial our very bald First Sergeant sent for Big Jon, Orosz and myself. He needed a prisoner escort to take Gordo to L.B.J. prison in Long Bin outside of Saigon. Remembering my own time spent as a prison guard, and also having no desire to deliver my buddy to jail, I begged off leaving Big Jon and Orosz with this distasteful job.

It was not without reason that Big Jon and Orosz had been chosen for this assignment as both of them had escorted prisoners to prison before. Big Jon, being the biggest guy in the company if not the battalion was a good choice for escorting the more belligerent prisoners. This he had done at least once before when we were back in the 278.

On this particular assignment, Big Jon was to take a very angry and vocal G.I. to jail for the crime of almost beating an NCO to death. This G.I. was not particularly happy with the idea of spending time in jail and said so in not so many words. To Big Jon he said in a private moment, "You ain't takin me to no jail! I'm gonna take that 45 away from you and shove it up your ass." Big Jon did not take well to being talked to this way, but he made no reply. To get the prisoner to jail required getting him out of Camp Enari to the air base, and then to Saigon and jail. It was a long way to go, with lots of places where anything could happen.

Big Jon got a ride to the air base in the back of a ¾ ton truck. He and his handcuffed prisoner rode in the back of the truck, and he only got out of the truck at the main gate of Camp Enari where Big Jon, prisoner and paperwork were all inspected by the M.P.s. Inspection over, it was back into the back of the truck and off to the air base. Maybe a hundred yards past the main gate Big Jon called for the driver to stop. The truck halted on the road next to the camp's perimeter wire, and all aboard dismounted the truck. Big Jon muscled his prisoner by the arms over to the ditch by the side of the road. There Big Jon sat the prisoner in the dirt and then he drew his .45 Army from its holster, and all eyes were suddenly on Big Jon. Big Jon had the trucks shotgun guard hold onto the prisoner and Big Jon blasted a .45 slug into the ground of the shoulder of the road. Big Jon then picked up the spent brass casing from the bullet he had just fired. Then in front of the prisoner Big Jon put the brass casing into his top shirt pocket, and said "OK let's get going." The prisoner resisted getting back on the truck and said, "What did you do that for?" Meaning why did Big Jon shoot into the ground. Big Jon smiles at the prisoners, and drawled, "That was your warning shot." He had no more trouble with Mr. Big Shot all the way to jail. This made Big Jon the right man for the right job.

Big Jon and Orosz set off for a trip that would normally be one day there and one day back, Big Jon and Orosz were gone the amazing time of five days, amazing in that Saigon was 300 miles distant, three hours away by plane. So upon their return we passed the word for a "mandatory" Varsity meeting. We wanted to hear all the gristly details of their trip first hand. The story when told was a true saga from beginning to end. As they told their story at the club the night of their return we all got more and more intrigued. Their story went: The prisoner and escort party had proceeded as ordered; they headed for the Pleiku Air-Force base on their first leg of the trip to L.B.J. Once out of the 43rd friendship took over from duty, and the prisoner's handcuffs were removed with a promise of not trying to escape. Side arms were stuffed into an overnight bag, and Gordo was treated to a few beers in the Air-Force bar.

With Gordo and his escort properly lubricated they managed to make their flight and headed off on their way. First stop being Tan Son Nhut Air base, outside of Saigon. As Orosz put it, "Once in the air Big Jon and I decided to give Gordo one last taste of freedom, and we went along to make sure he did it right." So once on the ground at their destination and their papers checked. Away they went, and outside the air base they took a cab to Saigon instead of Long Binh.

There was one anxious moment during their trip. There had been no thought that Gordo might escape, especially after giving his word, after all where could he go? Once Gordo, big Jon and Orosz had arrived at Tan Son Nhut they dressed properly as prisoner and escort, donning their side arms and hand cuffs. Orosz had Gordo hold his pistol while Orosz arranged for billeting and transportation. The Air Force Sergeant behind the information counter became very nervous after reading the orders presented to him. He kept glancing around and clearing his throat nervously and loudly while nodding his head toward Gordo. He got no reaction from Orosz so he finally beckoned Orosz to come close, and leaning over the counter, whispered at Orosz, "I don't want to alarm you or anything, but your prisoner has your pistol." Orosz's eye-brows shot up in surprise, and he turned and faced Gordo. In mock indignation he said out loud, "God Dammit Gordo, will you stop trying to make a break for it every five minutes. If this continues I'm going to be forced to ask you to give me back the bullets for my .45." He followed this with, "Prisoner is your weapon properly on safety?" "Yeah, Uh sure Jerr," came the reply. "Very good prisoner. At ease!" The Air Force Sergeant looked at the three of them and mopping his perspiring brow rolled his eyes and muttered how uncivilized the Army was. They got their billet in seconds.

Once in the Army hotel, a shower with plenty of hot water was in order. Big Jon went out to find some beer, while Orosz went down the hall for a shower, leaving Gordo to his own devices in the room. When he came back from his shower Orosz found Gordo sitting on the bed with pistol parts all around cleaning and oiling his guards .45s.

Pooling what money they had they found a civilian restaurant with reasonable rates and once well fed set out from there to find that exciting animal, the Saigon nightlife. Gordo was treated to a trip down one of life's little gutters, a night of gaudy glittering night clubs, scantily clad bar girls. All of the sex, drugs and rock-and-roll he could cram in, sweetened by lots and lots of ICE COLD Vietnamese beer.

But what the three of them found out was that they had more money than sense, and one night on the town would not be enough to get rid of it. So they stayed on, and a telephone call back to the First Sergeant was all that was needed for the extension, that along with the brightest flimsy excuse their beer fogged brains could come up with. So with careful husbanding of their resources and the all creative excuses they could muster. The three of them stretched an overnight, two day at best, trip into a five day debauch.

The sad part of this road trip was the final delivery of Gordo to his new life at L.B.J. Orosz and Big Jon marched Gordo from where the Vietnamese taxi let them off on the asphalt road, down the short dirt road they trudged, to the guarded entrance to the prison. The cab ride had been solemn, but an occasional smile or wink reminded all three that the world was not ending. The now handcuffed prisoner was marched to the guard shack at the entrance, where the orders transferring the prisoner were handed to the guard. After close inspection of the papers, hand cuffs were removed and the M.P. guard said to Gordo, "Take your clothes off." Gordo stood where he was confused and dumbfounded, and made no move to comply with the guard's instructions. The M.P.'s night stick came around in a wide round house and caught Gordo on the side of the head just above the ear. It landed with a loud crack, and the impact of the blow sent Gordo sprawling in the dirt. "I said, TAKE YOUR FUCKING CLOTHES OFF," the command more distinct now. Orosz and Big Jon just stood there agonizing over their friends' predicament; they stood by and watched as their buddy stripped. Gordo then walked on unsteady legs into LBJ, naked, and rubbing the side of his head.

"So that is how it is done in L.B.J." concluded Orosz at the meeting.

The Monsoon Coffee Company

I had held many jobs since being in the Army, and had certainly had my share of diversity since coming to the 43rd. Along with mud clean up, infliction of battle damage, convoys to the coast, and repair work I was now sent out by the warrant officer in charge of the repair depot to find a coffee pot. This warrant officer wanted to set up regular hot coffee for the troops, and also because he wouldn't have to walk so far when he wanted a cup. So with only his instructions to build it, I went out and got him all that was need so he could have that hot cup of Joe any time he wanted. He did get a place to get himself a cup of coffee.

We opened the Monsoon Coffee Company on scrounged, borrowed or stolen material, and we did it in a place without running water. First Big Jon and I found a 100 cup coffee percolator in one of the supply dumps in Qui Nhon, but it was missing its basket and cord. Orosz scrounged the basket up during a midnight trip to the 43rds mess hall, when no one was looking, and the electrical cord I hand wired. Big Jon then had to talk the cooks into letting him have some ground coffee, and when they refused to let us have any, we resorted to what I knew best. We filled out a midnight requisition; we liberated the coffee in the middle of the night from the mess hall supply shelves, when they weren't there to say no. We were ready to go into the hot coffee business once we found a source for water. The source turned out to be right in front of our eyes. During the day water was trucked into the 43rd and so it was only available in the mess hall or in the showers. We had a ready source for water right outside the shop; it fell from the heavens daily. So I requisitioned a 20 gallon pot from the same supply dump I found the coffee pot in. I got Louis G. to stand outside in the rain with me and with him holding one handle of the pot the two of us would catch the rain water as it poured off of an inside corner of the shops tin roof. So the Monsoon Coffee Company was born, and each day we had loads of fresh hot coffee for all.

Because of the 4th Division's edict about all men below the rank of E-6 were not eligible to buy booze, I had written home about this inequity. My brother would send me Scotch through the mail inside a package of cookies or popcorn. To make sure that some government snoop or some other rear echelon twerp didn't steal it, my resourceful brother would send it disguised as bottles of Listerine mouth wash. The color of the bottles contents were the same, Listerine was not a product to be found on the local PX shelves, and Listerine came in its own corrugated cardboard wrapper. It was very nice of him, but I forgot to tell him that with the 4th Division's edict about booze I had given up drinking the hard stuff and I drank only beer. So on a whim, one day I had just brewed a fresh pot of Monsoon Coffee, I opened the lid of the pot and poured in a generous slug of "Listerine," and I told those present that it was part of the water purification process. From that day on the line for coffee got longer and more demanding. No one knew that there was anything but Listerine in the bottles, and I didn't tell them otherwise. To advertise the fact that you had Scotch was to invite every barracks thief for miles to come and go through your possessions.

One day Big Jon took a bottle of my "Listerine" to breakfast with him, and he did this to brighten up his otherwise dull meal. He added a shot of Scotch to his cornflakes and reconstituted milk in an attempt to improve the taste. He swore that the Scotch made the meal taste like he had added a banana to it. I didn't argue with him, I went and tried it myself, and I'll be damned if it didn't taste like bananas, sort of.

Odd Jobs

It rained so much during the Monsoon that sandbagged bunkers would begin to disintegrate and collapse, and a constant battle was waged to rebuild or replace disintegrating defensive positions. Needless to say that the lifers in charge of us went into panic mode at the sight of the disintegrating bags, and Big Jon, Orosz and I plus several others spent several pleasant days pouring the contents of one sandbag into another while being ankle deep in mud.

The normal way to do any sandbag work was, you went to the local sandbag emporium and bought the sandbags you needed, already filled. Outside base camps some enterprising Vietnamese had set up a shop on a piece of cleared land, and sold bits of their motherland by the bag full. You would pull up to his establishment in a truck and give the entrepreneur an empty sandbag and one penny, and he would give us a sandbag full of Vietnam in return. Of course this was not done one sandbag at a time; the number was in the hundreds. To fill the sandbags the shop keeper had wife, kids, and other relatives hard at work, and he certainly had enough of Vietnam to go around. Whether this enterprising business person owned the land put into the sandbags was never in question, and it really made no difference. During the Monsoon season however, this little roadside stand closed down, and the owners and employees went into other business ventures.

It didn't take me long to become acquainted with my new work mates at the repair depot, and as I became more familiar with the troops they became more familiar with me, Big Jon and Orosz and our comings and goings. Becoming acquainted was one thing, fitting in was another? Like in the 278 most of the troops in the 43rd had acquired nick names, usually displayed boldly hand lettered on helmets or flak vests, and these were a lot easier to remember than their last names stenciled over their breast pockets. I was still called Scotty, and now I met a guy named Jimmy Olsen who was known as, naturally enough, Superman's pal. I was introduced to a 6' 6" giant named Perkins who was called the Jolly Green Giant by one and all. This Perkins guy was a rather secretive and mysterious fellow. For one he worked a night shift all by himself, and also he was sort of a mad professor of electronics, who was kept in the back room and brought out only occasionally. He was so gifted electronically that all the exotic radio gear that was causing a problem were given to him, and 99.9% of the time Perkins "The Jolly Green" found a solution. Once we got to know Perkins there was a lot to like about this lanky tall person, and he was quickly voted into membership of the Glee Club.

Almost everyone below the rank of Sergeant had a nick name applied, but the troops had their own names for individual

Sergeants and others above, names that were not necessarily kind or affectionate.

Because of the rain the warrant officer in charge of the repair depot wanted to send all repaired electronic equipment back to its unit wrapped or bagged in plastic. To me and others this sounded like a reasonable thing to do as most of the equipment was transported in or out in the backs of open trucks. The problem with this idea was where to get the plastic, and so I was sent out to scrounge. I found a good supply of large plastic bags at the A.P.O. (Army post office), and made a deal to take the bags off of their hands on a regular basis if the depot fixed their broken stereos and other electronic gear. This transaction for the plastic bags pleased our warrant officer, and he was like a kid with a new toy watching equipment leave his shop wrapped in plastic. The man had fulfilled his mission.

One day the post office refused to give out anymore plastic bags and as the A.P.O. now had its own use for its own formerly surplus plastic bags. I was sent back out to find another source. I looked all over everywhere but plastic bags were in short supply. I finally returned to the depot with a stack of heavy plastic bags I had gotten free. The warrant officer was in seventh heaven again with my find, these were heavy gauge plastic, in his favorite color O.D. Green, and each one was four feet wide by eight feet long, and the best part was they were free.

I brought back an arm load of these new bags to the shop, and was greeted by Oohs, and Aahs, from my warrant officer and his NCOs. The questions came rapid fire.

"What you give away to get these Scotty? The farm?"

I smiled smugly, "Nev-a happen Sir," was my reply, "I got them free."

"Free" was his second favorite word, Army was his first.

"Free, were did you get these, they are great?"

"You really got these Free Scotty, that's amazing."

"Can you get anymore?"

"Sure sir, the guy said I can have all I want."

"where did you get these?"

"I got them at Graves Registration, Sir."

"Oh!"

We didn't use these plastic bags, for some reason.

Our officer should have spent some time researching what happened to all the nice plastic wrapped equipment he sent back to be used by the out-lying signal sights. The sides' of the roads leading out of our base camp, for maybe a mile, were littered with discarded plastic bags. These bags that had been blown off of the equipment being sent back to units, usually traveling in the backs of open trucks, from the 43rd Signals repair shop.

Soldiers in Vietnam had a rather fatalistic attitude toward rain. "If it rains, you get wet." So no one bothered with ponchos or other rain gear, they were too much trouble to put on or take off. When caught outside in a down pour you didn't run to avoid getting wet, you trudged along and got soaked like you always did. It rained and it rained, and there was no way of avoiding it.

Smokeless Lou

Louis G, or Lou, the hairiest Italian American alive, didn't have any money. That is a fact! He got paid the same as everyone else, but Lou never had any money. We didn't know if it was gambling, women, drink, drugs or stupidity, but Lou was broke, always broke. Because he was broke he was always bumming cigarettes off of someone, and Lou was known by one phrase for his time in the 43rd. "Have ya got a smoke?" Lou was Orosz's roommate, and he was fun to be around. He was one of the first guys we inducted into the Glee Club, but even so Lou was a Bum. Lou had no shame about being a bum; he bummed smokes from everyone and anyone. After several times of Lou bumming cigarettes off of me I got tired of it. I asked Lou, "Why don't you have any cigarettes of your own?" Lou replied, "I'm broke."

I didn't get mad, I didn't yell at him for not having any money. I did the soldierly thing, the brotherly thing, I gave Lou two dollars in M.P.C., (the price of a carton of cigarettes at the P.X.), and told him to go buy himself a carton and to stop being a bum.

Lou left, and hitch hiked to the P.X., and he was gone quite a while. Lou returned, but without a $2 carton of his favorite cigarettes. Lou had in his possession five candy bars and three comic books.

Lou was a bum for the rest of the time we were together, but he knew better than to ask. Lou would sneak an occasional cigarette out of my pack that I usually left in plain sight, but he sneaked a smoke from me when I wasn't around.

Sports

It was a dark and stormy night, and a group of us, Perkins, Louis G., Superman's Pal and my two regular buddies Big Jon, Orosz were walking through the compound one night. Yes we had been drinking, and yes we had been singing our songs. We sang so much that we were feeling no pain. On our way back to the barracks we had to cross the battalions' main motor pool entrance drive. As luck, which was usually terrible, would have it the roadway was gated. It was late, and as usual there were no lights to guide our way, and no one in the group was sissy enough to carry a flashlight. It was raining hard, and the rain pounding on us as we strolled along chatting amongst ourselves. We all long ago had accepted getting wet as a part of life during the monsoon season. The gate for the motor pool was in the form of a steel cable drawn across the road about 18 inches above the ground. The cable was suspended between two buildings so there was no way to skirt around it. To add insult to injury there was the usual giant puddle of rain water that stretched from shoulder to shoulder and for six feet in front of the cable and two feet behind. Normally we would just wade through the three or more inches of water in the puddle and then

453

climb over this cable obstacle when we came to it. There were reflectors dangling from one or three places on the cable, but because of the clouds above there was nothing to reflect off them.

The cable was there every night and it was used to keep people from gaining unauthorized use of the U.S. Army vehicles parked there. I don't think that the Army trusted any of us.

We were young and daring, and also a little stupid from all the Carling's Black Label Beer we had consumed. So some idiot said "Lets jump the chain," said stupid me, and the other stupid idiots with me agreed, it was a slow evening and this was something to do. We all ran like excited children toward the cable splashing through the ankle deep puddles, and just before the cable we all leaped in the air to clear the obstacle. Stupid me was first, but I had leapt too early and when I came down from my leap I was surprised. I had not cleared the cable but had landed on it with my leading foot, catching on the angle between the heel and the sole. The cable stretched taught under my weight and held my body stiff and erect for what seemed seconds at an angle while I watched the rest of the group whizz by me and over the cable. They all cleared the cable that I now held in place for them. Their heads turned back as they passed me to look at me in amazement, and after they had each landed safely, on the other side of the puddle, they watched as I slowly fell backwards off of the cable waving my arms like a frantic pelican. I landed on my back in the middle of the puddle with a world class splash. The water was so deep that the water nearly covered my whole body completely. I lay there almost submerged in the red muck looking up at the black sky with the rain pouring on me, and I tried to ignore the tremendous pain I now felt from the several sharp rocks that I had located with various parts of my body. Big Jon, Perkins and Orosz splashed over to me and looked down at my prostrate being. Perkins was the first to speak, and said to no one in particular, "Damn! I think he's dead." I felt dead. But I managed a small groan. "Damn Scotty that was numba one, how'd ya do that?" "Hey, I missed it can you do that again Scotty?" called out Jimmy Olsen. I lay there looking and feeling painfully stupid, "you guys wouldn't mind pulling me out would ya?" I asked hopefully, "I don't think I can move." "Fucking A, Scotty, that was great man," and Big Jon and Orosz both felt around in the muck for my arms. As their efforts broke the suction and they pulled me erect Orosz added a comment about the mud for emphasis, "Man this shit's so thick it can suck your boots off just like a Saigon whore." We all giggled over that one all the way to the showers.

Guard Duty

Many evenings and week-ends that I spent in the 43rd I spent in performing guard duty. It was a lot more lonely vigil here at the 43rd than it had been at Camp Enari; here I pulled my two hour guard shift, all alone on top of a 100 foot guard tower. Just me a field telephone, my M-16 and a search light for company. The weather helped to keep you awake when a chilling rain blew into your face propelled by a stiff breeze. Many was the time that I pitied the poor slob who had not brought his field jacket to 'Nam, or who had been talked out of it by some supply puke. It was damn wet and cold.

On guard at the top of the tower was particularly hazardous when a rocket or mortar attack occurred. Being one of the few people awake you got to see these events first before anyone else in the 43rd. During a rocket or mortar attack your job in the guard tower was to crank up the field phone and tell those in charge where the enemy rounds were falling and how many, and then to get the hell out of that guard tower. It was a long way down in the pitch dark with only the flash of nearby explosions to show the way, and more than one guard damaged himself trying to speed his descent by jumping or falling.

If those in charge did not know that we were under attack by the explosion of the first round then there was something definitely wrong at headquarters. Why they wanted to have an on the spot report of how many rounds and where was beyond me. I could count the explosions as well as they could.

If I was at the top of a tower when a rocket or mortar attack began it was usually a welcome distraction to a very boring evening. To liven things up at the HQ bunker during an attack of this kind I would ring into the command bunker and report the event to the officer of the guard in the following manner:

"Sir, this is Lennox in tower number one."

"Yes Lennox, what is going on?"

"Sir I have a cannon report."

"Yes Lennox, what is it?"

"Baker Oscar Oscar Mike Sir," (Baker is military phonetic for "B" Oscar "O" and Mike "M" so B O O M), and with that I would hang up. I guess fun is what you made of it.

Vacation

After weeks of rain, rain, rain I began to wonder if this was not the time to think of dryer places. I had been working hard for six months, so I thought it was time to take my R&R. R&R in the Army stood for Rest & Recuperation or Rack & Ruin, but those of us down in the mud looked forward to it as I&I Intercourse & Intoxication. Every soldier in Vietnam was allowed five wonderful days of vacation from the war. Transportation to and from was provided at government expense. When I first expressed my desire to Big Jon he thought the idea wonderful, and we made plans to go on R&R together.

We began to kick around ideas of when and where to go, and on a Sunday we had a discussion about it over a steak dinner at the Air Force steak house. Big Jon and I had been walking around the Pleiku Air Force Base on our way from our $2 steak dinner, and we were walking back to our vehicle past a row of neat Air Force air-conditioned barracks. You could definitely tell that the Air Force took good care of their people, they had real windows on their barracks; even the blast wall around the building was neat and painted an Air Force blue. As we walked along a window next to us opened, and surprised us both. Neither of us had seen an honest to goodness window since we had left the states. The window slid quietly up and wonderful feminine voice attached to a pretty face and a curly head of brunette hair, said "Hiya big guy." That was all that was said. I had just turned my head in the direction of the brunette when in one swift motion Big Jon leapt through the window and was gone. As if to put an end to all conversation the brunette disappeared and the window slid shut behind her and real curtains closed on the inside.

I had been deserted before, but never for a woman, I felt cheated, I felt alone, and I felt like getting the hell out of there. If there were women around there was bound to be the Air Forces version of the M.P.s hanging around. Waiting for Big Jon around an Air Force barracks where women were kept was asking for a skull bashing from the M.P.s. So I went and found our ¾ ton truck and took a seat behind the wheel and waited to see what was going to happen next.

A few hours later a whistling Big Jon appeared acting like nothing had happened. He got into the passenger's seat, and motioned for me to get going.

"Wait a minute," I said.

"No Hi Scotty. No how's it going. Just get moving Scotty!" I said with anger in my voice.

"Just a minute lil' buddy, three was a crowd back there," replied Big Jon.

"Did you tell her you had a buddy waiting outside?"

"Did you ask her if she had a friend?"

"Did you ask her if she wanted a threesome?"

"Well no, but I did get invited back," said Big Jon with a large smile on his face.

"Well, who was she?" I asked.

"She is a Red Cross Donut Dolly," he said proudly.

"And that is the barracks where they keep all them Donut Dollies."

"And she gave it to you one for free?" I asked incredulously.

"Yep, and she asked me to come back too."

"You can come back. For free!" I said even more incredulously.

"I ain't buyin' this it's too good to be true," I said.

The rumor was that Donut Dollies went for officers, and they went for the price of $50.

With that the final insult to being left out in the cold, we drove off and back to the 43rd and the $50 dollar smile of satisfaction on Big Jon's face was there for days.

When we next discussed where to go on our R&R was the first dilemma we had to solve, and there were several delectable and tantalizing names on the R&R list to choose from. For a couple of single guys with lust on our minds and money in their pockets there were some tough choices to be made. We could have gone to Bangkok, (to us that name said it all), Kuala-lumpur, Hong Kong, Japan, or Taiwan to name just a few. Soldiers stories about each and every place on the R&R list were graphic to say the least, and highly improbable in their content. It seemed from the G.I. stories that there was nothing, NOTHING, the Asian women would not do to please an American soldier on leave. I had learned a long time ago that nothing NOTHING is never ever that good, especially when it is being described by a teenage, under paid, over sexed, and generally over imaginative soldier who has been away from home for too long.

So Big Jon and I decided to go to Australia, not to see what an Australian woman would or would not do for an American soldier on leave. Incredulous as it may sound; my object of going on to Australia was to visit with my relatives. My mother's brother lived outside of Melbourne, and I had communicated with him once I had gotten to Vietnam with the idea of visiting during an R&R in Australia. I was invited to visit if I could. By accepted G.I. standards there had to have been something seriously wrong with the both of us.

So once we settled on Australia we put in our papers with Australia as a first choice, and we both settled back and thought no more about it. Our plan called for us to depart within two weeks of our paper work being submitted, and there was no reason that the Army should turn us down. However, there was one thing we didn't count on. Before you could go on R&R to Australia you had to have a blood test, a recent blood test, and the results had to precede us to the R&R center. "Blood test!" We're not going to get married down there I complained when I first heard of the requirement, but marriage was not one of the reasons I suspected that they required it. Big Jon and I both neglected to get a blood test in the time we waited for our R&R approval, and when the approval finally arrived we had the facts of Army life explained to us by our bald headed First Sergeant. No blood test, no R&R. We were both slightly uneasy by Top's revelations, but Big Jon and I discussed it and we decided that we could get a test after we got to the R&R center. After that we dismissed it from our minds.

Big Jon and I arrived at the R&R center in Da Nang via the U.S. Air Force and another terrifying flight over mountains while in the midst of a cloud bank. This time the trip was complete with terrifying special effects, thunder and lightning. We arrived two days early, OK so we had a tough time with numbers, but our Sergeant had the same problem as he let us go two days early. We were in sunny and dry Da Nang and enjoying the weather so we checked in at the R&R center we were told by the clerk that we hadn't had a blood test. Well, B.F.D., (Big Fucking Deal), we knew that. The R&R clerk then informed us that it was a B.F.D., and he also informed us that a blood test took five days to process. SHOCK is a good word to describe our reaction to this revelation.

"Well what do we do now Big Jon?" I asked, after what we had been told finally sunk in and had been accepted by my screaming brain. "Don't worry lil' buddy," said Big Jon, "we'll get it together." Somehow his slow southern words reached a resonate spot in my brain, and I believed he was right and I calmed down.

Da Nang was beautiful, a barbed wire paradise stretching along a beach at the foot of steep mountains. The Monsoon was doing its thing in the highlands, so the lowlands were sunny and dry. In Da Nang there was one enormous air base for jets and another for helicopters, and Da Nang was an enormous base for the U.S. Marines. The Da Nang base complex was so big that it had its own mountain captured behind chain link fences and barbed wire. No bunkers or blast walls encased the barracks, I didn't see any weapons in sight, and it was definitely peaceful It was so peaceful at the R&R center that there was a U.S.O. Canteen pumping out free soda pop and Snow Cones all day long, and when you got bored with that you could wander down to the base bowling Alley and P.X. We spent some time marveling at these unheard of luxuries that the Marines had in Da Nang.

The two of us had spent our first afternoon lounging around the bowling alley snack bar; it was well lit and spotlessly clean. This made us feel that we were back home hanging out. After a line or two of sport we went and lingered over an ice cold Coke in the Marine snack bar. This was great, but a table of likewise lounging Marines next to us decided to have some fun. There has always been some rivalry between the Marines and the Army, and this table full wanted to see if we were game to carry on the conflict. We were.

Leaning back in a chair with his legs stretched out in front of him a Marine called over to us.
"Hey you two, are you doggies?" I first looked around to see which two he was referring to, and then I looked at Jon and said, "We're it."

"Y'all talking to us?" drawled Big Jon.

"Yeah I'm talking to you.... Doggie," was the reply.

"That's Mr. Doggie to you Jar head," I shot back.

"This a slow day for you birds from the Bird, Ball and Hook, or is this how you normally pass your time off?" I asked.

This brought all of the Marines to a sitting position at their table, and now more of them wanted in on the verbal exchange. The verbal abuse now flew hot and heavy from one table to the other.

"Say Marine, have you been to any dances lately? Isn't that what the Navy's got you guys for." I asked.

"You're so ugly you ought to shave your ass and walk backwards." Shot back the Marines.

"Swabby Fucker, Swabby Fucker!" Shouted the Army.

"If I had a head like yours I'd put it on a pole and wash windows with it." Said the Marines.

"All you got to do to become a Marine is have someone take your brain out, stomp USMC on it, pound it back in, and you guys believe you are one." Said Big Jon.

"You was whipped with the ugly stick." Marines.

"Oh, the Marine Corps' flag is a dirty old rag, and the commandant is a queer." Army.

"You're so ugly you gotta sneak up on a glass of water to get a drink." Marines.

"Yeah! Yeah! Yeah! You can brag all you like about invading tropical islands, but the biggest invasion ever didn't have one Marine hit the beach - D-Day June 6th, 1944." Army.

"You came to a battle of wits - unarmed." Marines.

"Laugh it off, smart ass, your mother had too." Army.

"If I had a nickel for every time I've heard that said, I'd be a nickel-air." Marines.

"You might but I Fucking doubt it." Army.

"Fuck a bunch of doggies." Marines.

"If I washed my dick would you suck it? You dirty Cock sucker." Army.

"Fuck ya doggies!" Marines.

"Your dentist called, it's time for your hair appointment." Army.

We gave as good as we got, some of the Marines had jumped out of their chairs and were leaning on their table trying to get an opening to heave an insult at us. When everyone ran out of their favorite high school gym insults the verbal exchange slowed down and we were left with the dilemma of either fight, fuck or go for your hardware. We ended up by grinning stupidly at each other, and then laughing out loud. We spent the rest of the afternoon swapping stories, and finding out where everyone was from. It was just like we did when hanging out at our own EM club. We drank the Marines version of beer; it was the same off-brand stuff that we got.

Back at the center we discovered with delight that there was an unlimited supply of hot water spewing from the shower heads in the latrines, and there were flush toilets for all. For a lot of guys like myself who had spent the last several months living in squalor this was a vacation in heaven, but what other delights the city of Da Nang held I never had time or a chance to discover.

Da Nang was a huge U.S. Marine Corps base, and surprisingly enough those guys looked remarkably like us, O.D. green and everything except for their funny hats. Aside from their strange Marine Corps terminology we were able to get our message across, WE NEEDED BLOOD TESTS, NOW! We would do almost anything to get on that R&R plane. After asking instructions of one or two local Marines Big Jon and I hitch hiked out of the R&R center, across Da Nang and into the foot hills. We had to get rides with three separate Marines. We jolted along on the steel beds of a series of Marine 6 x 6s, same same Army deuce and a half, passing sand dunes, valleys, and row upon row of grey buildings. Da Nang was huge, but we finally got close to our destination, thanked our last driver, and headed out on foot. After a mile or two winding down a dirt road, through the scrub covered hills we found it. There in a deep valley were a number of large tents that held a U.S. Navy medical unit. Once there Big Jon and I presented our case for a blood test to a Navy corpsman. Whether it was our washed out and dirty fatigues or the eloquence of our plea I'll never know what convinced this Navy Corpsman to give us what we wanted. Inside a medical tent our blood was drawn, and within

462

of an hour we had our blood test results in our hands and were hitch hiking back to the R&R center.

What they were looking for in the blood test was evidence of gonorrhea or other venereal disease. Big Jon felt none too good about his blood test, and all the way up to the Navy medics he was crying the blues about not feeling well. This was very uncharacteristic of Big Jon, and after the test I asked him what was the reason for him dragging his feet. Big Jon thought that he might have a dose of the Clap coming on, and that is why he was reluctant to get a blood test. The incubation period for gonorrhea was between 36 hours and seven days, depending on your state of physical health, and I questioned him about why he thought he had a case of the Clap.

"Not the Donut Dolly?" I asked.

"No not her," Big Jon replied.

"Hey roomie, I don't know how or when you were close enough to anything else that was female get to anything social. Big Jon just didn't seem the type to go looking for guys. If you have found yourself another lady friend, you dirty dog, you sure kept it a secret," I told him.

Thinking over who else he possibly could have had a tryst with. Our aging laundress was no prize, and outside of a few of the younger K.P.s at the mess hall there had been nothing around the 278th or the 43rd to attract anyone's attention.

Big Jon finally confessed to me of a recent liaison with the same American Red Cross girl the same Donut Dolly he had deserted me for when we had been at the Air Force base having a steak dinner. She had indeed invited him back and he had gone. He even admitted to spending the night with her the day before we left for R&R. I was shocked, I said, "I didn't think you had $50 to part with on anything that frivolous." Big Jon replied, "I don't, I got it free again."

I had known Big Jon now for several months, and to me it was not that surprising that he made out like that. The one thing that I knew about Big Jon was that he knew everyone, and everyone knew Big Jon. He was the man to see when you needed anything or wanted something accomplished. Big Jon even came up with a birthday cake, a professional looking iced birthday cake for Billy "Bad Ass" Barnes birthday, (a feat unparalleled in the military history of Vietnam), and how or where it came from no one knew. There were no bakery shops in our part of Vietnam, and the mess hall cooks didn't produce a cake in anything under 2 X 4 feet sheet size. Who was Billy Barnes, or more accurately Billy "Bad Ass" Barnes, he was a guy in our supply room who got us the parts we needed to fix the communication equipment that broke down all over the place. Billy was a fellow Texan to Big Jon, and Texans that stick together. Billy was the only supply guy who had a personality, a big mouth, but personality. Billy was half the size of Big Jon, but his Texas size personality made up the rest. Hence the "Bad Ass" add on to his name and he was just one of the guys in the repair shop.

How did Big Jon come up with a birthday cake for Billy? As it turned out, Big Jon was in tight with a Vietnamese Colonel at MACV, and the Colonel had a wife who lived in Pleiku. Big Jon had merely asked the Colonel where to get a birthday cake and the Colonel's wife gladly produced one the next day. The cake was beautiful. Pink icing, candles on top and it looked like it came from the corner bakery. We were afraid to cut into it. Not because of the source, but it was so beautiful we didn't want it to be destroyed. Big Jon truly was a master at resourcing anything, and I think that I could safely say that Big Jon knew everyone, and everyone knew him, he was truly amazing.

When we arrived back at the R&R center I tried to talk him into talking his chances and coming along anyway, but it was no use the itch he felt in his pants had his Texans mind made up. For me, this was a trip that I could not possibly give up, and I agonized over going without Big Jon. Big Jon insisted that I go. It was his dose of the clap not mine. He said, "I didn't share my Donut Dolly why should I share her clap." I was left to go to Australia by myself. Big Jon reluctantly went back to the medics and the 43rd on the next available flight. The only thing left for me to do was to buck up my own resolve, and march right down to the Marine Corps P.X. and buy some civilian clothes to wear to Australia.

The funny thing about the civilian clothes for sale in a military P.X. was that there was darn little to choose from and most of what there was were funny looking and the wrong size. I had to settle for a pair of almost orange, skin tight pants that were four inches short of my shoe tops, and two shirts both plaid and looking like they belonged to my big brother. Getting on the plane to Australia I felt right at home, as everyone had shopped at the same place as I, and looked about as hideous as I did. The short hair be damned we were advertising to the world, and anywhere I went in that odd civilian get up everyone knew that they were looking at an American soldier on R&R.

I will never forget the breath taking view I saw as the commercial jet lifted off from the Da Nang air base on the first leg of my trip. Mist covered mountains; stacked one in front of the other marched down to the sea in different shades of grey. The sea was a flat calm and shimmering with silver sun light. "Right out of a Japanese calendar," said the guy sitting next to me. I never realized that Vietnam could be so beautiful.

I liked what I saw, even though I knew in my heart that every foot of the beautiful scene below me was crawling with the enemy.

I went to Australia and had a WONDERFUL time. I took pictures so Big Jon could see what he had missed of the standard R&R flesh pots of Sydney. After getting off of the plane in Sydney and being released from the R&R center, I went to the first clothing store I found and bought some clothes that fit, and threw my P.X. garb in the trash. I then traveled to Melbourne, and eventually ended up in a little town called Warnahbool visiting my uncle and other relatives. I did spend most of my time in saintly virtue, sight-seeing and visiting with my relatives who I hadn't seen in years, but I did find some time to try to drink all of the beer on the continent. My relatives already had a head start on me, in the let's drink Australia dry department, and they drug me from pub to pub showing me off to friends and neighbors. I found out about the famous hospitality of the Australian people, I could not buy a drink. I drank for free in every pub we visited. I was shown off to one and all as a "Yank" here from the fighting in Vietnam. Besides all the family visits and the beer I also spent a good deal of time standing underneath a shower head trying to remove the odor of Vietnam from my body, and it took some hard scrubbing to begin to remove the smell of Vietnams' red mud. Waking up in the mornings it took some pinching to remember where I was, and to realize just how far I was from the 43rd Signal Battalion and Pleiku.

I hopped a plane back to Sydney for my last night of vacation and I put myself up in a nice high rise hotel. I didn't mind the expense I wanted one last night of luxury before I headed back to Vietnam. I ate and drank and slept to my heart's content. I had an R&R that I would long remember, and I couldn't wait to write and tell Mom about my experience.

When my vacation ended I did not come back to my buddies at the 43rd, as a lot of my peers had done, they came back with sordid tails of wild debauchery, and damn little else. I came back with a little money still in my pockets, a souvenir boomerang, and a clean body, but a smile on my face none the less.

Chapter 18

The Stuttering Pig and Superman's Pal

Getting back to the 43rd after R&R was like falling from paradise into purgatory. I descended back into those pungent aromas I had so recently rid myself of under hot soapy water in Australia. I had spent as much time as I could in the R&R center at Da Nang, enjoying the amenities, but I had to finally face reality or jail by not returning to my unit. Reality won. "I'm not crazy about reality it stinks but it is still the only place to get a decent meal," to quote the great Groucho Marx.

I no sooner stepped in the door of the 43rd's orderly room than the First Sergeant announced, "Lennox, good your back. Get your shit. You're going to Than Chan," almost in the same breath. "What? No hi Scotty? No did you have a good time Scotty? No kiss hello? By the way where's Than Chan?" I asked. Top had done his homework, and he showed me Than Chan, it was a speck on a map that looked more like fly shit than a town. Than Chan is a dot 70 miles north of Pleiku, on twisty turney highway QL14. There was nothing that came to mind that associated any importance to Than Chan. But my attitude toward Than Chan changed instantly when I noticed that the next door dot on the map was Dak To, a name that struck a chord with me and anyone who had read or heard the news in recent months. They were sending me into the bad part of town, and I was to go by truck. Worst of all I was to go north in a one truck convoy. I looked a long time at the First Sergeant; I wanted to see if he was kidding. He wasn't I was to make the run solo. Shit!

I had enough time to put down my bag, securely locking up my new civilian clothes and my souvenir boomerang, and head off to the motor pool to prepare my Stuttering Pig truck. I was being sent north to help out a remote signal detachment from the 43rds signal company in Kon Tum, the 146th Signal Company. The detachment was on a signal relay sight in Than Chan, which was an ARVN base, and the 146th guys were having trouble staying on the air because of equipment failure. This time it was not going to be the Scotty and his two buddies, Big Jon and Orosz, putting on the show. Big Jon and Orosz were not equipment repairmen, well Orosz had been one a long time ago, but he was out of shape for this one. I would have liked to have either one of them on this trip as a shotgun guard. It was to be the Scotty and another technician putting on the show. I was taking Superman's Pal (Jimmy Olsen) with me, and he was definitely excited to be given the opportunity and privilege of getting to spend a few nights away from home. The two of us backed up by a truck load of electronic equipment. Olsen little realized that getting out on the open road, was dangerous. But so was sleeping in strange places, and eating "C" Rations three times a day. That may have screamed excitement to some people, but I wasn't one of them.

Jimmy was a tall dark haired kid from Nebraska, who wore extremely dark rimmed glasses. He was young and slim like the rest of us; he had a dark crop of hair that fell into his eyes covering his bright brown eyes. He was usually one of the most vocal guys in the barracks or repair shop. He was constantly voicing his desire to go home and be with his young wife once more. We all wanted to go home and be with Jimmy's young wife too, but we kept quiet about it after he got extremely mad on hearing of out desires. I liked Jimmy, aside from his distinctive comic book name he did a good job at whatever he was sent to do, and he had a great sense of humor.

By the next morning I mustered my war gear and my resolve to be ready to go. We loaded the truck with the gear we would need, and I checked out "Piggy" making sure that he was ready to make a long trip. I didn't care much for the idea of having to drive all the way to Than Chan in a lone truck convoy, even in broad day light. I was driver, and Superman's Pal was shotgun guard, I gave him my by now standard lecture on what I expected a shotgun guard to do if we got in trouble. Before I started my engine a clerk from the orderly room came running up and gave me instructions to meet with a north bound convoy that would accompany me all the way to Kon Tum. That brought a smile to my face and a sigh of relief as well.

The trip started off OK. Luck was with us. Top had done right, he had found out news of the north bound convoy through the "Old Sergeants" network, and Olsen and I smiled to each other as we cranked a round into our M-16s as we set off out the 43rds back gate. Kon Tum was the half way point to Than Chan, and half way was better than nothing. It was bright and early when we arrived at the designated truck stop to pick up the convoy. Actually the truck stop was just a wide spot in the road, just enough room for several trucks to pull over safely. Here we parked and waited nervously, I kept the engine ticking over, my M-16 ready, and nervously hummed "we're at the rendezvous, where's the convoy," over and over in my head. There was always a certain feeling I got if I thought I was in the wrong place at the wrong time. On convoys Orosz and I had both felt it a time or two, and when I got it I just knew the best thing to do was get out of there fast. As I sat in the truck that morning I had that creepy feeling. No sooner had our truck rolled to a stop than six Vietnamese children climbed on the running boards, and several adult women were gathered around the cab. All of them were hawking their wears, shoe shine, shoe laces, drugs, a little Boom Boom in the bushes, it was all for sale. After looking over the displayed wares I decided just

469

to stay in the truck. Through broken English a young boy and I made a deal. I made a deal with this kid on the running board to have the crystal of my watch cleaned. He started at one dollar, but he finally settled for 25 cents in M.P.C., and I had my trusty old seventeen dollar Timex watch crystal cleaned. My watch face was so dinged up you could barely tell the time through the scratched and nicked crystal, so polishing for 25 cents didn't seem like a bad deal. The kid dripped a drop or two of Brasso brass polish onto the crystal and rubbed like hell with some emery paper for ten seconds, and to my amazement the watch glass was like brand new. I had him perform this feat with the watch still firmly strapped to my wrist, after all my seventeen dollar Timex meant a lot to me. It meant seventeen dollars.

The convoy of five deuce and a halfs arrived and without allowing any time for shopping the Sergeant in charge told me what was what. They were not going to Kon Tum, Shit! They were going to a road junction 15 miles up highway QL14 and then turning off. I was to follow them and then make my own way after they turned off. Double Shit! With those instructions we immediately left the roadside department store and all its entanglements. Superman's Pal and I were now heading north at a sedate 35 miles per, observing the speed limit. The convoy took us the first 15 miles of our journey, and then turned off to one of the camps along the way. Once on our own I opened the throttle as hard as I dared on that twisting turning mountain road, and we roared on our way to Kon Tum. Road security was in evidence by the sandbagged emplacements, APCs and troops around bridges and at different points on the road, and we slowed slightly passing each of these. Even with this display of security there was not a lot of protection on many stretches of this mountain road, and I felt very vulnerable in one lone truck. No matter how fast I got Piggy going our luck finally ran out.

On a stretch of highway without any evidence of security we got hit. As we negotiated one long sweeping turn to the right someone opened fire on us. The stretch of the road we were on was not flat and wide open, there was a shear drop off cliff on the right side and a brush and tree stump covered hill side on the left. The shots were fired from high up from our left front, by one or more people using small arms and luckily nothing heavier. Whoever fired on us probably couldn't resist a target as big as a house, which is what that shop van on the back of Piggy resembled. I first realized our peril when I heard the bullets slamming into Piggy's metal body with loud snapping and pinging sounds over the roar of the engine. We were driving with the windshield flipped up, so that we could fire out if necessary and I jumped two inches straight up with the explosion in my right ear when Superman's Pal returned fire without being told. Hot brass casings were dancing around the cab, bouncing off the canvas roof, and some going out the windows. I fumbled with my own M-16, but driving with one hand at what I thought to be around 200 miles per hour, screaming, and keeping from peeing my pants was just enough for me to handle at one time. I let my rifle lay leaning up across my lap and concentrated on driving. Olsen was firing blindly out the front window, holding on to his rifle pistol grip with his right hand and clinging to the center post of the windshield for balance with his left. He let go of the center post only long enough to grab my unused M-16 and then continued to return fire. His body shook with each burst he put out with his rifle. We were both hunched over our respective tasks, trying to offer as little a target as possible. But Piggy was just too good a target, and as we made it around the curve bullets still pinged and slammed into the truck. Both Jimmy and I were still screaming and firing we had made it through the right hand curve and started to make the turn to the left around the next bend when the enemy managed to put a few more rounds into the truck. One round hit the engine compartment and blew the upper radiator hose off of the engine. The scalding contents of the radiator immediately evacuated their steaming hot container through the new opening and the force of the water hit the fold down side wall of the engine compartment, which immediately

471

folded down, sending scalding water out into Piggy's slip stream. The wind blew the water into the cab of the truck through the open windshield, and into our faces. Jimmy Olsen was lucky he was wearing his glasses, but I was not wearing any. So now we were driving at 300 miles per hour, screaming, firing blindly out of the front window, and driving near sightless down a twisting mountain road. Superman's pal stopped firing and dropped the M-16 and grabbed the wheel until I managed to wipe my eyes, and by that time we were cleanly out of the ambush, our rifles were out of ammunition, and the truck had reached invisibility speed (301 plus mph). We were to say the least relieved, but we did not slow down until we saw the next road security post.

Empty shell casings were sliding and jingling around on the floor of the cab as we drove on, slower this time, I was having a lot of trouble seeing clearly. We pulled over at the next bridge security post, and reported our encounter to the Sergeant in charge. We then tried to do what we could to repair the damage to our truck. Jimmy and I spent a few moments grinning and laughing at each other and the state we were both in. We both felt really glad to be alive, and it took a few moments to get my knees to stop shaking. Jimmy didn't seem displeased with our safety either, though he said that did require a change of pants. Me. Hell, to get out of the truck on the jelly like legs was a miracle. It also took a crowbar to break the suction my butt had on the seat cushion.

We both smelled of diesel oil, rusty old water and both of us had red mottled and blistered faces. Piggy was still drivable, and we both decided that rather than hang around waiting for a tow in the mountains we would proceed. We patched up the hose as best we could. Being in electronics we had a large supply of electricians tape, and we bound up Piggy's wounded radiator hose with that and then drove on, steaming down the highway.

The rest of the run to Kon Tum was thankfully uneventful, and we got to the 146th Signal Company without Piggy's water pump or engine freezing up. All those we passed along the road could hear and see us coming from a long way off, the fan belts were squealing like banshees, and clouds of white steam were boiling out the sides of the engine compartment and from one or two bullet holes in the engine hood.

It was noon when we arrived at the 146th Signal, and after taking our truck to the motor pool for repairs Superman's Pal and I went to the medics to get something for our burns. My eyes were watering and stinging, and I wanted to get them taken care of. The local medics didn't want to treat eyes so they sent us to a doctor at the Kon Tum air base. There the doctor coated my eyes liberally with an ointment which cooled the stinging and burning. Rust, diesel oil, and hot water were not the best things for washing eyes I was told, as tiny particles of rust had been imbedded in both eyes. After the ointment had been applied I noticed something really odd, I could now see double, double out of each eye. I spent some time staggering around and walking into things while Olsen tried to keep me from hurting myself.

After much wiping and other attempts at washing out of my eyes failed, and waiting for quite a while the double vision did not clear up. The doctor knew only one thing that he could do, and that was to have me med-evaced me back to Pleiku and the 71st Evac. Hospital. A med-evac helicopter or "Dust-off" was a normal means for evacuating wounded soldiers from the battlefield; however I was not a wounded soldier.

Instead of calling a "Dust-off" helicopter for me the doctor had me put on the regular courier helicopter which was leaving shortly from the Kon Tum chopper pad. I was apprehensive about my eyes, but this was over shadowed by the excitement I felt of going on my first helicopter ride. Up until this time I had always been envious when helicopters flew over, envious of their ability to fly above it all. For months I had witnessed the different types of helicopters whizzing overhead. Small Loaches (LOH Light Observation Helicopters), daring Dragon Flies, darting and hovering like wasps, sleek cobras (gunships) lethal mosquitoes, Huey's (gunships and transport) dragon fly shaped work horses, and Chinooks (shit hooks - cargo and transport) twin rotered behemoths that roared overhead like freight trains.

I was transported to the chopper pad by medics, and led by the arm to the UH-1 (Huey) helicopter sitting on the pad with its rotter blade turning overhead, and by counting the number of heads visible on board, then dividing by two I could see that the courier helicopter was already full. Majors, Colonels, and Staff Sergeants stared back at me with blurred faces while the medics talked with the crew chief and the pilot. The solution was an easy one. The door gunner was kicked off of the Huey, and I was kicked on. This was going to be my first helicopter ride, and I was going to get to do it in style. I was given the door gunners helmet and his M-60 machinegun, and after strapping in the pilot talked to me over the intercom. "Be sure and shoot now if you see anything," he said. "Yes sir, just tell me which one to shoot at........!"

My first helicopter flight was beautiful though dizzying with double vision. We flew just under the solid grey cloud bank all the way back. The clouds cut the mountains and hills off in a straight line, making all of them the same height. We flew over the vivid green country side cut up by brown snakes of rivers, and brown and red patches in the green turned out to be base camps and villages. Vietnam came alive as it all flowed beneath us. To me it was wondrous to behold even if I saw it in stereo. The flight ended all too soon and the couriers were all dropped at the Pleiku Air Force base. The pilots next delivered me at the 71st, but first they performed three very low 360 rotations at a better than 45 degree angle. This maneuver was made while the pilots waited to clear the flight path of the Air Force Base. This maneuver left me hanging onto my machine gun as if I was in mid-air, and hanging on for dear life, lest I fall straight down. I was left at the chopper pad of the 71st Evac. Hospital. I stepped off of the helicopter onto the Red Cross on the metal plates of the pad and was greeted by three medics with a trolley, but as I was mobile they allowed me to walk into the hospital. Inside I lay on the trolley and waited for my turn to be treated. Within a few minutes of my arrival there were two wounded cases brought in after me, bleeding and moaning, they laid them on other trolleys beside mine. I lay there quietly; my troubles seemed small compared to theirs. The doctors and nurses worked on these two frantically. Removing blood soaked clothing, inserting I.V.s, talking gently to the wounded. Then the two of them were wheeled away, leaving me alone with my thoughts and my silent view of the double ceiling.

By coincidence my Platoon Sergeant Staff Sergeant Fullcup was at the hospital when I arrived, and he was rather shook up when I told him how and why I had gotten back to Pleiku so quickly. Sergeant Fullcup was a strange guy, but on reflection he was from a strange place, West Virginia. As he told it he wasn't from JUST West Virginia, he was from "West by God, Stand up, Take your hat off, Virginia," and to say the least he was proud of it. After our conversation the medics took care of me, and within minutes of landing my eyes were being treated by a doctor who place my head tightly into a vice, and then told me, "Don't move!" The doctor then painfully scrapped the imbedded rust and crud out of one eye and then the other. I did not move as directed, while the scrapping was going on I wanted to kick the doctor in the balls, but I did not move. I spent the next 12 hours with my eyes bandaged, and when they took them off my eyes were both fine. The red scalded and blistered skin on my face remained for a few more days, but I was over all I was much relieved.

After the bandages were removed I was sent back to my unit. When I arrived at the company orderly room I was warmly welcomed home. Everyone I met back at the 43rd had heard some wild rumors going around about what happened to Scotty, and when I showed back up at the orderly room the next day people were a little disappointed. I was only a little worse for the wear and tear. Here I was without bandages, a few burns on my face, and nothing else to show for the battle I and

Superman's Pal had fought. I was a combat story let down. I was supposed to be full of bullet holes like my truck, but I was very glad to be a disappointment to them.

Within an hour I of my return I was back on board a helicopter, this time a small Kiowa (a regular courier four man helicopter), and I was the door gunner once again as I was whisked back up to Kon Tum. We flew again over the same green and brown territory with its triangular forts and other brown islands in a sea of bright green. I had viewed all this the day before, but this time it was in much better focus. On this helicopter ride I had a chance to think about my circumstances. Here I was heading back to finish a job that any self-respecting repairman could accomplish, and a question came to my mind. Was I the only guy in the repair shop on salary?

I landed back in Kon Tum to resume our trek north by truck. Piggy was ready to go again, with Superman's Pal, and we had a passenger, a kid named Davis from the 146th. Both of them were all ready and waiting when I arrived at the chopper pad. My cheeks clenched on every corner in the road and I held my breath a great deal, but we made the rest of the road trip to Than Chan in wonderfully uneventful peace and calm.

Davis I had known before. I had worked with him on details when he was first assigned to the company and in the replacement pool; this was before he was sent up to Kon Tum. Davis was a nice pleasant guy, who smiled all the time, and went around with a sort of "Hey how ya doing buddy" attitude. He was husky and blond, and looked like he could take care of himself. We got well acquainted over the next several days, and had a lot of laughs in the process.

At Than Chan I found a different world, one stranger and more remote than life had been at the 278th. The signal detachment we were to help was in place in the middle of an ARVN base camp outside the town of Than Chan, and beside a team of American Advisors these 12 signalmen were the only other U.S. personnel around. The base camp was surrounded by the usual barbed wire and sand bagged bunkers, but there

476

were several tanks on the line also. These were old World War II vintage M-24 Chaffee light tanks, and their gun barrels pointed out of the perimeter at all angles. I noticed that there never was any maintenance done on these tanks and that each ones position never varied from day to day, so one afternoon I got curious enough and went and took a close look at some of them. I crawled up on one of them after banging on the side and got no response. On closer examination, looking down the open turret hatch, I discovered that the tanks were derelict, and were full of trash. The ARVN immediately lost my vote for a sense of security, and a sense of our own well-being.

Jimmy Olsen, Davis and I set about curing the equipment problems that the detachment was having, and getting acquainted with our hosts at the same time. At night we could go to bed at mid-night, and we would sleep in the still warm bunk of one of the men on night shift. After two days and the equipment was back on the air 100 per cent, and things had shaped up so well we decided to see what there was to see in Than Chan. Than Chan was a whistle stop of a dozen one story dingy white moldy stucco buildings, plus several dozen wood, tin and cardboard shacks. The town was set out in the typical Vietnamese jumbled fashion. One road led through town and there was one intersection. In the middle of the intersection or always nearby stood the grey uniformed Vietnamese National Policeman, (the White Mouse). The one good thing about Than Chan was that it was so far from any major American military installation that there were no M.P.s stationed there, and being soldiers we didn't have to be told what that meant. To me it meant screw the 35 mph speed limit.

On our third day there I escorted Davis down to the local whorehouse to get him what he wanted most. He wanted his teenage itch scratched. He had been chomping at the bit ever since we had got there and found out about the absence of M.P.s and three days was all I could stand of his begging to fulfill his most fervent wish. (My most fervent wish was for a Fried Chicken dinner, or a 1931 Model A Ford. I wasn't about to achieve either one of those any time soon so I agreed to help him achieve his wish). He wanted to get laid, and he wanted it in the worst way, and I wanted him to shut up about it in the worst way. It was here that Davis discovered first-hand the biggest deterrent to sexual intercourse in Vietnam. Davis pole vaulted out of our truck and in to the local whorehouse and got himself situated, while I parked the truck and then sat outside the whorehouse with my M-16 waiting for him. Before the start of his wish completion there came the startling sound of VUBB,UBB,UBB,UBB .....VUBB,-UBB,UBB,UBB,UBB,UBB. It was the sound of an M-60 machine-gun being fired somewhere nearby. I jumped out of the truck and inside the front door of the whorehouse and I lay on the ground, poking my M-16 out at the ready. Davis came scrambling out of the cubicle he had been occupying, naked, and with a drawn .45 automatic in his hand. There was no enemy action going on outside, and no more firing was heard. However, the wishing was over for today. Davis's manhood had deflated and he was too nervous after the gun fire to muster what it took to get his money's worth.

On our fourth day at Than Chan Sergeant Fullcup and his new replacement Sergeant Stubaby arrived by helicopter to see what their brave lads at Than Chan were doing. I recognized Sergeant Stubaby right off. I had known him when I was stationed at Fort Riley, Kansas, and I always thought he was decent to the troops. I called his name as I saw him step off of the chopper, and gave him the finger in welcome. This brought me a smile back and a mild ass crewing from Sergeant Stubaby, I was reminded of the niceties of military courtesy and the penalty for insubordination. Two subjects I was obviously not real strong on. I stood their grinning at him while he delivered his speech. It was nice to see old, friendly faces once again.

Both Sergeants made a tour of inspection of the signal facilities, and my team's efforts to support them. Satisfied with our help and suggestions to improve this or that were made. There was nothing to do. After a few recommendations were made about what to do due to the lack of M.P. supervision and the Sergeants decline to do any of them. Sergeants Fullcup and Stubaby found themselves with some hours to kill before their helicopter was to come back to pick them up. What to do in hostile territory, when there is no place to go and nothing to do, and no bar close by. I suggested that we spend the time profitably by showing Sergeant Stubaby how to fire an M-79 grenade launcher. Sergeant Stubaby had never fired one, and all of the territory outside of the camp was considered a firing range because we were in a free fire zone. Superman's Pal, the two Sergeants and I made up a foursome, and we marched out of camp and found a suitable spot for having a little target practice. We enjoyed ourselves, sending H.E. (High Explosive) rounds out their full 300 yards. We spent a good hour blowing up pieces of Vietnam, and using up all but five of the 40mm rounds we had brought with us. So with target practice over we strolled back into camp, passed the dozing Vietnamese gate guards and the decomposing tanks. We strolled along the dirt road passing the time of day in idle chit-chat, when the loud yell of "Hey! You men! Stop where you are," brought us back to the real military world. The shout had come from a Full Bird Colonel who came storming out of the first building we had passed. He was a surprise to all of us, and Sergeant Stubaby was even more surprised when the colonel demanded, "Who's in charge of that formation?" All of us looked around, and after a quick tally of who had the most stripes all eyes settled on Sergeant Stubaby. Your "IT." Sergeant Stubaby was marched into the building by the colonel and given a half hour lecture about shaking up the local population with our gun fire and explosions.

When Sergeant Stubaby caught up with us he was very red faced, and not very happy. We had been re-acquainted less than three hours and already he had been given the finger and an ass chewing, he was not pleased. To calm him down and to offer some form of compensation he was offered a tasty cup of homemade booze, "Jungle Juice," the specialty of the guys in the signal detachment. There was no allowance for beer on supply runs as space on the helicopter was for "C" Rations and water only. The 146th guys had no beer or booze so they made their own out of fruit, in their underground bunker. This mollified Sgt. Stubaby somewhat, for which I was glad, being I was going to be working for this man soon.

The one thing I did accomplish before I left the guys of the signal detachment was to put them on to my trading network as a possible supply of weapons to trade. They gave me an old PRC-10 radio to trade before I left. The forerunner of the PRC-25, but trading material was trading material. Later they provided a valuable source for Montagnard crossbows, which were a hot item in Pleiku as well as on the coast. Eventually the PRC-10 got traded for a case of steaks, and we thanked the guys at Than Chan when we B-B-Qed them in their honor. After all business was still business. Not to be a "Prick" about it I made sure that 12 steaks headed north on the next supply run. They were cleverly disguised as a case of signal parts. I didn't trust those supply people either.

Superman's Pal and I drove Davis back to his home in Kon Tum, and spent the night in his barracks at the 146th. With nothing to do in the evening we found ourselves hanging around the bunker line watching the lights of the other compounds nearby when a few mortar rounds came in landing in and around the 146th's compound. We found cover with some of the 146th people in their defensive bunkers. The bunker we ended up in faced two other compounds, one left and the other right, 200 to 300 yards away. These two compounds belonged to different factions of the Vietnamese Army. The one on the left belonged to the ARVN and the one on the right to the Chi-Hoi, VC and NVA who had been converted to the South Vietnamese government cause. There was a flat open space of three or four hundred yards between both compounds, and on slow nights the men of the 146th would entertain themselves by starting fire fights between the ARVN and the Chi-Hoi. "Hey man, watch this," said one of our hosts in the pitch blackness of the bunker. Olsen and I peered out the bunkers fire slit as one of the men fired two rounds at the ARVN with his M-16. Two rounds were then fired at the Chi-Hoi compound, and two more at the ARVN. Within seconds the ARVN and the Chi-Hoi opened fire on each other and a tremendous fire fight ensued which lasted for a good half hour. The men of the 146th were delighted, and some of them came out and sat on top of their bunkers to watch the show. Olsen and I watched the red tracers flying back and forth, the flares drifting through the heavens, and the explosions from grenades and claymore mines. Our hosts informed us, "Shit man, that ain't nothin'. Those assholes hate each other, and you should see the fire fight they have anytime a dog wanders between their compounds." In the morning Superman's Pal and I said good-bye to Davis and made the rest of the trip back to Pleiku and our home at the 43rd without further incident.

Monopoly Money Shuffle

Superman's Pal and I got back to the 43rd just in time. The day after we arrived we participated in an M.P.C., (Military Pay Certificates), currency exchange. All of the money of all of the troops in Vietnam was to be changed periodically, and on exactly the same day. And this amazing feat was to be done on an unannounced basis. The idea, I was told, behind this was to put the Black Market's own currency exchange program out of business. The exchange involved replacing all our current multicolored bills for a new set of different multicolored bills. The powers over us then made the old set of Monopoly bills worthless.

On M.P.C. change day all of the Vietnamese employed on base were kept outside. All of the compounds had their gates closed and guarded, and all of us G.I.s were assembled first thing in the morning, and we were held there in that formation until our money was exchanged. This formation thing was in itself a ticklish business. Morning formations were prone to attract the undue attention of the enemy in the form of rocket and mortar attacks. We older wiser troops stood the formation just as close to the local drainage ditch as we could get. We were ready to pounce at the slightest hint of incoming rounds. The newbie troops, the F.N.G.s stood the formation just like in the states, with neat orderly ranks, and occasionally turning around and wondered why we were hovering near the drainage ditch. We stood around nervous and grumbling for hours, waiting our turn. During this assembly we were individually marched in front of a pay officer who swapped our money for us. No secret handshake, no secret words this time. No ceremony what so ever. We just plunked our money down and new money was counted out, then the "Next!" Out you went. Lord help you if you were a big winner at poker and had more than your normal pay amount. Then you had to "Tap Dance an explanation in front of the C.I.D. and hope they believed you. When we were finished we were allowed to go to work. After my money had been swapped I strolled down by the perimeter barbed wire to see what was going on. Outside the wire groups of Vietnamese civilians were milling about on their side of the wire trying to attract the attention of us on our side. The whores from Thunder Alley were tossing rolls of bills big enough to choke a water buffalo over the fence, and trying to attract the attention of a former or future customer to exchange it for them. There were ARVN soldiers, merchants from downtown, even laundresses and K.P.s from our own compound trying to get in on the money swap. To our amusement, the whores parading noisily up and down on the outside of the wire some in their black French underwear, all trying to get someone on the inside to make a deal with them. Offers flew back and forth through the wire; the usual starting point was 50 cents on the dollar then the addition of "Numba One" Boom Boom as an incentive. The second installment of negotiations went to 25 cents on the dollar, with a "Two Dolla Short Time" added on. If there were no takers the next negotiating point was 10 cents on the dollar, which is what all merchants, laundresses, or other P.X. cowboys tried to get if they could.

Several G.I.s picked up rolls of bills, and shouted back encouragement to the owners. Most of these bills found their way into the battalion chaplains, (The same guy who had closed the "Steam & Cream"), fund, for support of the orphanage run by Catholic Nuns, that both the chaplain and the battalion helped to maintain in one of the nearby villages.

Downtown After the Money Change

A week after the currency exchange I was sent to town to buy ice to be used to cool beer for a company party. I drove a regular Deuce and a half truck as Piggy, (complete with bullet holes), was being patched up at the motor pool. I was given a total stranger for shotgun guard for this trip to downtown Pleiku, to the Ice House. It was interesting to see the effect that the M.P.C. change had had on the local economy. Shopkeepers were now standing out in front of their stores yelling at G.I.s as they drove by, trying to get them to stop and buy something. Before the exchange the shopkeepers had been content to sit in the cool shade of the stores and let mama-san and baby-san take care of business.

I went about my business at the Ice House, while the shotgun guard went and checked out a tailor shop and clothing store next door. While I paid for and had the ice loaded my companion got cornered by a very anxious tailor trying to make a sale. As I watched from a few steps away the price for a hand-made suit of clothes kept coming down as the guard tried to wriggle out of the grasp of the shopkeeper. Finally the tailor asked, "OK G.I., how much yo' pay fo' suit?" My guard replied, "10 bucks." "OK yo' got," said the tailor, and he dashed into his store and came out with a suit on a coat hanger. From where I was standing it definitely looked like a 10 dollar suit, and the shopkeeper tried to give this to the guard who was now back in the truck and looking at me desperately trying to tell me to get him the hell out of there.

We did and on the way back I decided to take a little side trip down Thunder Alley, to see how the local economy was doing in the red light district. Thunder Alley was two rows of the ever present one story flat roofed stucco houses that were set back from the road by their 30 foot deep fenced front yards. This alley was outside of the "Downtown" Pleiku shopping district, north of the main town area. The road through was dirt and turning onto this dirt road we became one of two strings of trucks and jeeps passing each other slowly in opposite directions. The American and Vietnamese M.P.s, (the Vietnamese M.P.s had the letters "QC" printed on the front of their helmets, and I do not know what it stood for), were there watching to see that no one stopped or got out of their vehicle, or that no one got a chance to scratch a certain itch. The whores were there in quantity if not quality, hanging around the fronts of their houses, yelling at the passing G.I.s in the best English they could manage. The whores were trying to do the same thing as the downtown shopkeepers, and drum up some new cash flow. There was a parade of black, red or white lacy underwear, a grand display of limbs and other strategic flesh, and much yelling and vulgar gestures. This pantomime of sexual stimulation was done all to the delight of the honking, hooting and hollering G.I.s passing by. Whenever an M.P.'s back was turned or their gaze was diverted an O.D. Green fatigue body would leap from one of the moving vehicles or out of one of the houses. The figure would disappear diving through a door or window of one of the houses or into a passing vehicle. So while driving back to the 43rd we had drug our feet as much as we could to watch the titillating show in Thunder Alley.

We got the ice back to the 43rd safely, in spite of the danger of its melting from the heat put by the torrid display the hookers put on in Thunder Alley. The ice had been brought in for a good reason; a company party was being thrown. It was announced to one and all, that it was now time for a little relaxation around the 43rd. A company party had been proclaimed by the C.O., part of which Orosz, Big Jon and I had contributed to with the steaks from the PRC-10 deal.

These parties were rather formal affairs. The NCOs had their party away from the rest of us, the officers undoubtedly had theirs, and we lowly enlisted men had ours. A sign would be posted somewhere in the compound. The bulletin board was usually a good spot, right next to the guard and K.P. rosters. And the statement usually went rather like this:

A DAY OF FUN IN THE SUN
EM PARTY FRIDAY
BAR-B-Q AND BEER BUST

VOLLEYBALL
HORSE-SHOES
STEAKS

THERE WILL BE ICE

BRING YOUR WEAPON

Stubaby's First Trip to Qui Nhon

With the special trip to Than Chan now over I was now back in the old routine, repair work, guard duty, and convoy duty to Qui Nhon. We were due to make another run to the coast, and this time we were going to have to break in Sergeant Stubaby on how and what to do and who to see. Our convoy for this trip consisted of two Jeeps and two trucks I drove the lead Jeep with Sergeant Stubaby and the 6' 6" Jolly Green Giant Perkins crammed awkwardly into the back seat. On the rutted and well-worn roads in Vietnam a Jeep was much easier to handle than a deuce and a half truck and so we whizzed through Mang Yang pass to An Khe, and made our first stop at the new

4th Divisions' base camp, Camp Radcliffe. We were paying a visit to the company of the 43rd stationed with the 4th, but we found the road inside Camp Radcliffe blocked by a solid row of trucks, in both directions, while a grass fire burned in a field ahead of us by the side of the road. Sergeant Stubaby sent me on ahead on foot to find out what was holding us up. I was glad to be out of the Jeep for a while. The groans, moans and creaking joints of the 6' 6" giant wriggling in the back seat were disturbing. I walked up the road past the first five trucks in line and then climbed up on the running board of the next. I greeted the driver and then asked, "Say man, what's the hold up?" "Man, the M.P.s is burning a pot field and all the heads have stopped to take in the breeze." I strolled back to my Jeep and explained things to my passengers, and so we had to sit and wait for the air to clear as well as the heads of the drivers in the traffic in front of us.

Continuing on past An Khe and down Do Mang pass we got separated from the rest of the convoy when it became intermingled with a Korean truck convoy. The only person I had ever known with the balls to try and pass a Korean truck convoy was a crazy man from the 278th named The Mummy. The Mummy could get a deuce and a half going faster than I believed possible. You could say that he drove hard and he lived hard, and he maintained that that way if anything happened he would leave a good-looking body.

I had been the shotgun guard for The Mummy the day that he passed a Korean convoy, and I mean to say that this was no simple little thing to do. The Mummy and I were making a solo run to Qui Nhon and as we were coming to the area before Do Mang pass we came up on the rear of a Korean convoy. Not one to wait for anyone The Mummy pulled out into the clear on-coming lane and raced our truck down the side of the Korean Convoy. The Koreans usually kept a tight interval between vehicles to prevent having their convoy broken up. We were doing OK until I noticed that there was a vehicle coming towards us very rapidly. What was coming down the

486

lane we were in was an ARVN convoy, (You could tell by the Orange strip along the front of their vehicles hood). There was no need or use in shouting a warning to The Mummy he just kept moving forward, just as fast as he could go. With inches to spare The Mummy cut our truck in front of the first Korean truck as the ARVNs roared by in the opposite direction. I could not tell who was ready to pee their pants first, me or the ARVN driver of their first truck, but The Mummy acted like this was an everyday thing. To The Mummy it was an everyday thing. On conferring to Orosz upon my return I found out that yes, The Mummy was a maniac behind the wheel, and yes he would pass anything that got in his way. I did ask if The Mummy had a death wish, but Orosz wasn't sure, after all the longer you were in Vietnam the more fatalistic you became.

Sergeant Stubaby had me pull off of the road so we could wait for the others in our split up convoy to catch up, so I pulled off at the entrance of a Korean fire base. It was a lot safer than just pulling off to the side of the road and waiting to see what came along first, your companions or some of the enemies flying lead. As I brought the Jeep to a stop at the front gate of the Korean base my eyes were greeted by an amazing sight. There before us were 40 or more Korean soldiers in the front leaning rest position, (the old prone supported, militarily known as the push-up position). There was what I assumed to be a Korean officer walking up and down the ranks of the prostrate troops screaming at them and smacking some of them on the back of the head with a swagger stick as he strode up and down the rows. "Boy is he pissed," I said as I looked over at Sergeant Stubaby, and he stared back at me open mouthed. "Sure, glad I'm not in their Army," I commented as I put the Jeep in reverse, and backed out the way I had come in.

I drove down all the way off of the pass and we waited for the rest of our vehicles at the bottom amongst the farms and rice paddies. Against my advice Sergeant Stubaby had me pull over on the shoulder of the road to wait. Even after I informed him that the shoulder was where the enemy put most of their mines.

All of us got out to relieve ourselves, and I was the only one who took my rifle out of the Jeep and carried it under my arm as I watered the roadside ditch. "What you bring that for?" asked Sergeant Stubaby. Remembering my own first days in Vietnam and the first time I was shot at I smiled and replied, "If we get shot at, what are you gonna shoot back with? What's in your hand?" The other two sheepishly went and pulled out their M-16s and held onto them while we waited.

Qui Nhon was, now that we knew our way around, always an adventure to Big Jon, Orosz and myself, plus anyone we cared to drag along. We would forge our own travel pass using the names of Sergeant Saunders or Lieutenant Hanley', (names from characters in the TV show combat), as authorization for us to be out driving around after dark. Once we got completely lost and ended up at a Korean base camp. We were lucky when we got out of there two minutes later all five of the tires were still on our Jeep. The lug nuts had been loosened on the spare tire, but we got out before we lost anything to that bunch of opportunistic scroungers.

Being out on the town, enjoying all the bright lights and "B" girls was not all there was to do in Qui Nhon. The Army had clubs for all ranks to enjoy cheap beer, and at times cheap booze. We, being Big Jon, Orosz and I decided to go drinking, but we wanted to go drinking with Sergeant Stubaby. There were Army rules against this, Stubaby was an Army E-7 in rank, and we were not. Sergeants E-6 and above had their own club to do their drinking, and we lower ranks had our own club. Sergeant Stubaby couldn't come and have a drink with us at our club, and we couldn't go to his club for the same. It just wasn't done to fraternize! There was only one solution to this Big Jon, Orosz and I went to the closest P.X. and bought Sergeant E-6 pin on stripes, and then we took off our own current rank pin on ranks and instantly became Sergeants E-6. Problem solved, or so we thought.

The three of us along with Sergeant Stubaby marched right into the E-6 and above club, sat down and ordered a drink. We were so smug, so sure that we had pulled a fast one over on the Army that we became quite talkative. Our drinks arrived, and at that same moment in walked the scrawny Sergeant Major from our own battalion HQ in Pleiku, the very same spit shined and starched Sergeant Major I had run into on my first day in the 43rd. This was trouble, big trouble, if he recognized any of us we would be in the stockade for a very long time. We would be in for some serious jail time if we were caught impersonating a "Lifer." No more talkative, we just sat there trying not to look at him. The Sergeant Major sat down with his own cronies two tables away. I would say that we were petrified, petrified into silence. We did our best to duck our heads or try not to let him have a good view of us. "Big Jon said, "I'll bet he is saying, I wonder when those guys got promoted?" Orosz responded with, "20 minutes ago, is the answer." We drank up and left, and vowed never to impersonate an E-6 again, well maybe never. All of us avoided the Sergeant Major back at the 43rd from that moment till we all left for good.

On the occasion of bring Sergeant Stubaby on his first trip to Qui Nhon we took the time to visit the Army's private beach resort, known lovingly to us lower ranks as "Shit Beach." Shit Beach was known formally as Qui Nhon's Red Beach, and was known as a recreation center for G.I.s, run exclusively for and by the U.S. Army. This place was called Shit Beach by the G.I.s because the beach was situated several hundred yards south of the beach the Vietnamese used as a toilet. The oceans tide was not in Red Beach's favor, and the deposits made by the Vietnamese would frequently wash down to Red Beach. On my first visit to this beach I verified its colorful G.I. name in a rather graphic way; I met a certain floating object while swimming.

On this particular trip back from the coast we passed the usual sight of a wrecker in the pass, pulling an upside down deuce and a half truck back on its wheels. None of us thought anything about it until we got back to the 43rd, and upon entering the orderly room we were greeted by the company clerk with, "Did you guys hear about those guys from the 146th? They got killed in a truck wreck on the way to Qui Nhon." I immediately put two and two together, "Who was it I asked?" "Some guy named Davis." Orosz said that I turned white as a sheet, but the next thing I knew I was outside puking my guts into the drainage ditch. I was upset for days.

Private Discussions

With Sergeant Stubaby and the rest of us phony NCOs safely back in the barracks of the 43rd Signal life went on as it had. To break the monotony of life in the barracks Big Jon, Orosz and I would congregate some evenings in Orosz's room even though it was cramped it was bigger than the room that Big Jon and I shared. Orosz's room was laughingly called Santa's Workshop, and this was probably because of all the mischief that was created there. We would always invite Orosz's roommate Louis G., Lou the Hairy Italian, he had to join in, he had no option. Lou would be there anyway, performing his favorite pastime, Sleeping. When you had no money sleeping didn't cost anything. This pastime of sleeping was otherwise known in Army circles as checking his eyelids for holes. But when Big Jon and I showed up in an evening Louis G. never got to practice his pastime. If our loudness didn't keep him awake, our sitting on his bed or on him, plus our constant poking at him with words and deeds made him eventually come out from under the blankets and participate

If on the other hand we were having a regularly scheduled Varsity Glee Club meeting we would meet at the club where our dozen or more members could all attend without feeling too confined. We would crowd together using all the tables and chairs we could commandeer. Once so assembled Orosz was charged with calling the roll and we promptly "Booed" anyone not present. Then we would sing and drank to our hearts content no matter who yelled "Shut the fuck up will ya" at us.

490

These get-togethers in Orosz's room were not only a source for fun, horse play and kidding around, but also a source to show off our somewhat perverted culinary ability. Collectively we had thought up a way to avoid eating in the mess hall; as we had all become jaded as to institutional food. As our impromptu affairs in Orosz's room became more frequent we often missed meals because we were joking around and it slipped by. One evening Orosz pulled out his steel helmet and an electrical hot plate, and into the pot were tossed whatever he had stashed under his bunk. It was a mixture of "C" Rations and Vienna Sausages. It was a really gross concoction, but it fed us all and we were glad to have it. From that evening on we called this type of cookout a "Spaghetti Roast", and at these we cooked up dinner in the same steel helmet over the same old electric hot plate. The menu at these "Spaghetti Roasts" was diverse. We would cook beans, Vienna sausages, hash, "C" Rations, left over LRRPs Rations, spaghetti, whatever we had scrounged, bought at the P.X. or had been sent from home. Not to mention, what we had managed to requisitioned on a midnight raid on the mess hall. What we had we mashed all of it together and liberally applied Tabasco sauce, ketchup, and other condiments that we found. The food was wolfed down by the spoonful, as we all whipped out our white plastic "C" Rations spoons from our pockets and dug in. Without plates, napkins or other silverware the food was devoured in uproarious laughter. Too bad for you if you forgot you spoon you had to run out and get one or wait till someone lent you theirs.

The conversation at these get-togethers ranged from dirty jokes, to dirty songs, to the banalities of military life. If the talk wasn't lively it was always loud. All of us yelled back and forth with voices raised more often than not in an attempt to be heard above the sound of the monsoon rain pounding on the barracks tin roof, than in raucous good spirits.

We would sit talking and listening to the local AFVN (Armed Forces Vietnam or Americans for Vulgar Nonsense as

491

we called it) radio station, or listen to a record or tape player grinding out something more raunchy like "Cream" or "The Rolling Stones." The general topics of discussion were: food, fast cars, faster fast cars, women, what I'm going to do when I get home, sports cars, hot cars, race cars, women, motorcycles, women, getting out of the Army, food, gossip about different events and people in the company and women. Whenever the conversation did occasionally turn somewhat philosophical in nature we would all sit in reverent silence and listen. The one philosophical topic we all liked the most was WOMEN.

"I'm a leg man," was one offered opinion.

"Yeah man! Me too," said someone else in agreement.

"Not me man, I'm a Tit man first and foremost," was the opinion of another.

"There is only two kinds 'Big ole' Good uns, or Good ole' Big uns!" Said another connoisseur of the female form.

On this night Orosz chimed in, "I used to be a leg man, but now I'm an upper thigh and bush man." end of discussion on women.

The above statements were generally in reference to one of the "Girly" magazine fold out pictures that proliferated as wall paper in the barracks. For myself I was in two minds about the girls in the "Girly" magazines. First I thought, "Well if they are going to show it, well then I was going to look." My second mind said, "I read "Girly" magazines for the same reason other guys read the magazine about travel and exploration in foreign countries. I read them to see places I wanted to go but was never going to get there."

When I say women, I do not mean "SEX" I mean girls/women babes, pin ups, center folds, our mental image of what was at home. Sex was a sacred, reverent subject not discussed in any group unless you wanted to be labeled a pervert. If you mentioned sex at all it was mentioned quietly and solemnly and a general reminder of just how lonely we felt. After all none of us had any real experience about SEX, we all knew about it, but we were somewhat afraid to talk about it. (I

492

only knew one expert on SEX and he was my younger brother. According to his letters he knew all about SEX, and he had women tripping over each other to get in bed with him. What he had I didn't know, but as he once told me, "He got more ass than a toilet seat.") Most of us were afraid of saying something about SEX that was completely stupid, and that way give away the information that you were an idiot about sex. Or worse yet a VIRGIN! Which is what we really were, but none of us want to admit it. Some of us may have HAD SEX, but none of those that had had SEX were in any way an Expert. None of us were knowledgeable enough to educate anyone else about SEX. My own statement about this subject was, "I'm so lonely, I gotta get a broad!" I think that for me it summed up the subject nicely.

The general consensus of opinion was that the perfect woman for a G.I. returning from Vietnam was a Nymphomaniac who owned a liquor store. However, Orosz staunchly held out to the bitter end for a wealthy widow or heiress of 80 years who had one foot in the grave. The one subject that was our most fervent desire, the one thing we all wanted most and could not have was the company of Women. You couldn't get women unless you were Big Jon and got invited into lady's bedrooms right in front of your roommate.

Whatever the desires of the group present one of the best topics of conversation was not women it was food. What your Mom cooked, how your Mom cooked it, prepared it, what ingredients went in to it. We were fascinated with what anyone's Mom cooked. We spent hours listening with rapped attention while Louis G. described in great detail how his Mom made a spaghetti dinner. It was a night of mouthwatering delight. Orosz devoted a night to Meat Loaf, and Big Jon to BBQed ribs. We craved and wanted good home cooking. Food never failed to lift our spirits from the deep lonely depression they could occasionally slip into. No mention of that precious commodity a girlfriend, or when you were going home could do so much for your spirits as the mention of home cooked food could do.

On some of these occasions the conversation did get around to something else, the question, "What will be the first thing you are going to do when you get home?" came up. By now I had been in Vietnam for over eight months and I was only now beginning to allow myself the luxury of thinking of home. There was the usual "I'm going to screw the wife and then I'm going to put the bags down," bit of bravado contributed by Jimmy Olsen, Superman's Pal. Sergeant Fullcup had often told us his first act upon arriving home would be to kiss the wife and then grab a salt shaker and head out to the tomato patch. Big Jon was going to "put on his cowboy boots and then put on a horse." I too stated my own fantasy about my own home coming, "I'm going home in my jungle fatigues, with all my war gear and my rucksack on my back. I'm going to slowly back up the side walk to my front door firing off bursts from the hip with my M-16. I'm then going to bang on the front door with the stock of my M-16 and when it opens I'm going to say, `Well here I am, they're right behind me!'"

Some of the discussions about going home were quit spirited, and the theme of getting out of the Army was always a big topic for discussion. The general consensus of opinion was "I'm gonna get the hell out of the Army, and stay out." But one evening I think I summed up my plus a whole bunch of other opinions on this one subject. I stated that, "The next time I pick up a rifle and put on a uniform, my mother will be doing the same thing. Then we are both going to head for the beach to help repel the invasion." This brought a chorus of "A-Mens." As an afterthought I added, "When I get out of the Army I'm going to keep my uniform in my closet. Each year on the anniversary of my E.T.S., (Date you get out of the Army), I am going to take it out, tie it to a tree, and torture it." Light applause.

Another big topic of discussion was cars, and what car are you going to buy once you get out of the "Green Machine." To us money was of no object as we really had nothing to spend our money on, but what we had in the way of money was damn little anyway. Cars, cars, cars and cars occupied a lot of awake and asleep hours for a guy a long way from home. Cars were safe, as most G.I.s knew a lot about cars, and each G.I. had his own preference. Thinking or dreaming about women was not safe, it could be very dangerous at times, as women would cause guys to do stupid things. To a young men, we figured that cars and women cost about the same, and that was in U.S. dollars not the funny money we had. In a neighborhood where the majority of the residents were bachelors, we had no real idea of the expence of a woman. It seemed to me that all of us young guys wanted was a "Kick Ass" home stereo, and a hot rod set of wheels. They were both in high demand, and women were a luxury item that would be there after the car.

Once we got talking about cars and which ones were the best or better than the best, and what features were the most desirable. There was no stopping the discussion as we all wanted to chime in. Next came the topic of how much to spend on a car, and where was the money coming from. Getting a real job did not seem to be a problem to us single young men, we could get a job, getting a woman when you didn't have one seemed harder. Of the four or five of us that hung out in Oroszs and Lou's room I was the only one that had a girl friend. Nothing permenant or promised, we went out together, it was a sort of detached kind of relationship for the three years I was in the Army. So I was looked on as some kind of woman expert, but mostly I played dumb when questions about relationships came up. Women were complicated, relationships were complicated, but money was not complicated. Most of us had money stashed away some where. In an envelope in the company safe, savings bonds sent home, or in some bank somewhere.

Here is where I formulated another of my Lennoxisms. I told my group one day to be careful with their money and their banking. "Why" they asked? "Never put your money in a bank that can't get the time and temperature correct," I told them. We all agreed.

Two U.S.O. Shows in Two Weeks

A U.S.O. show showed up one day at the front gate of the 43rd, and it was like a traveling circus had come to town. There were several duce and a half trucks loaded with things and a Jeep with a Sergeant driver and civilians in colorful dress. All of us made much of this rare occasion, and we all made plans to attend the show that night to be put on in the EM club. This was not Bob Hope and his troupe, but had he come up to Pleiku he would not have been greeted with more excitement. The show turned out to be a little disappointing, it was a tap dancer, a guy who played the singing saw, (this is no joke), and two or three overweight women who helped act out skits. What the hell, it was all the entertainment we could get, and we all applauded loudly and laughed politely at their antics before yelling, "The HOOK, get the HOOK!" after each act. We were not ungrateful; we just had a little too much Carling's on a very festive evening.

Surprise upon surprises within a week of the first one another U.S.O. troupe appeared at our front door. Amazing, two shows within two weeks. The news of our entertainment starvation must have gotten to the right ear of some bigwig in the U.S.O. This glut of U.S.O. shows broke a long standing record of time between such events. This second show was an Australian Rock-N-Roll band complete with scantily clad, shapely, Go Go dancers. This show was received with the same enthusiasm as the Tap Dance of the first show, and all that were not on duty went and had a great time. The place was packed with soldiers it was Broadways' S.R.O., (Standing Room Only), G.I.s were standing along the walls, and seated on the floor in front of the stage. The crowd was really with the band on every song. Names of favorite songs were yelled from the G.I.s in the audience, and groups of guys sang along with every song rendered. "Those were the days," had everyone in the place singing. So did "The Letter" and "We gotta get out of this place." Things were great until the band played "The Green,

Green Grass of Home," this, I was to discover, was the trigger for the main event.

In the repair shop there was a big strong farm kid of 19 years named Giagantus, who worked with us. He was a great help in the carrying of huge heavy pieces of heavy electronic equipment in and out of Electronic Repair Shop. A nice kid, easy going, the kind who took everything in stride and never caused trouble, but we found out the hard way that he had one idiosyncrasy. Whenever he heard the song "The Green, Green Grass of Home" he came unglued, mentally unstable, and became fighting mad, especially it turned out he had had a few beers. I never found out what he was so upset about, I guess there is something about a song about a hanging that makes you think of Mom and apple pie. To look at this kid you would never think that that round soft face hid the temperament of a music critic.

His going to pieces on hearing this song wasn't the bad part, but what was the bad part was that the kid usually tried to take the place to pieces with him. I was sitting sedately at a table listening to the band, when the problem with Giagantus and the song was pointed out to me by Louis G., I saw a chair went sailing through the air. (Lou knew this kid had a problem with this song and had kept it to himself. Why? We never knew), who I was sitting with. As soon as that certain song begin Louis G. began to look around to find Giagantus, and Louis G. nudged Orosz to make him aware that something close by was happening. The band was doing its level best to give a credible performance of this lovely song when a great sob went up from a table to our right, and a chair sailed through the air towards the stage. Giagantus had made his presence known, and had announced to one and all that he was displeased with the performance of the band. The EM club where the show was taking place was crowded with three or four hundred G.I.s. The chair sailed part way across the room and exploded into a group of unsuspecting G.I.s, knocking them and their table over. Those knocked over immediately jumped up, those that could, to see why it was ruining chairs. At the same time this kid Giagantus stood up bawling his eyes out and tried to send a table after the chair. The table was kept on the floor by other G.I.s and thank goodness it did not follow the chair. Like dropping a pebble in a still pond the ripples spread rapidly throughout the room and the fight was on.

Big Jon, Louis G. and I were all up on our feet and trying to make our way through a mass of swirling O.D. Green bodies to subdue this sobbing, flailing, gigantic monster that was loose. Chairs, tables, G.I.s and drinks went crashing to the floor all around. The band wavered slightly, but continued on like the true troopers they were. People descended on Giagantus from all sides. I wondered if he would be alive by the time we got to him. Orosz, Louis G. and I went pushing our way through the milling crowd trying to reach the kid. I got to where the mass of G.I.s was the thickest, and over some heads I could see some arms waving and figured that this was it. I climbed on a still standing chair to see better, but someone crashed in to me and my chair sending me flying into the group around Giagantus. My extra weight tipped the scale. Giagantus and several bodies, mine on top, crashed to the floor. While more and more bodies mixed it up in small fist fights all around the heap on the floor. The kid was beside himself, he was also beside a lot of other bodies, and as more bodies were pushed or fell on top of us he was beside a great many more people than he realized. Finally the weight of numbers won out and the kid ceased to struggle, and the fight slowly subsided all around. Chairs and tables were righted; bodies picked themselves off of the floor and sat down like nothing happened. The band played courageously on. While they were still untangling the mass of flesh on top of Giagantus someone yelled, "Hey Big Jon's down there," and many hands dug in to pull Big Jon erect and with him came the crying kid. Big Jon and Louis G. hauled the kid away to the medics for his overdue bout at mental hygiene, but the next morning the kid was back with us like nothing had happened. From then on, whenever the kid came around, entered any of our rooms, joined us at the club, or was in our presence we made sure all music was turned off.

Chapter 19

"You Lost Your Jeep in a Mud Muddle!"

The monsoon quit, just like that, the rain stopped as abruptly as it had started, and it left me wondering where all that moisture went, now that it wasn't being dumped where I lived. The dark dank low flying clouds that used to hand around the mountains were gone, but were replaced by nice bright, sunny white fluffy ones that drifted slowly by. With the absence of the rain the Monsoon Coffee Company sort of went out of business temporarily. To keep the coffee flowing it now required that two large strapping guys from the shop be assigned each day to haul a pot of water from the mess hall. So Lou and I now sat back and watch the new guys fetch and carry the water so that our own morning pot of coffee got made on time.

With the start of the new dry season there was now more and more outside activity, and a flurry of dirty details were caught up with. One of the most unrewarding details Big Jon, I and several other "Seasoned Troops" or former F.N.G.s were assigned to by the First Sergeant was training the "Newbies."

New F.N.G.s were to say the least frustrating. Some of them came in with the attitude that they knew it all, and some of them were as dumb as post. Those in between, we found out, were reachable. There was an unwritten agreement between the

First Sergeant and we dumb butts that he sent to train them. The rule was "whatever it took, just don't be seen by no Officer." So for the very hard cases there was the bunker line. Get one of the hard of hearing in there and one or more of us would shove him around or in extreme cases beat the crap out of them until they did it our way. The beatings were never severe, just a little shoving and slapping to put some fear in them, and it worked. Then we would threaten them with immediate death or being hunted for the rest of their lives if they squealed. It worked out pretty well. If they fought back we really did them up right. Top got what he wanted and we had a little recreation on the side. Any of the Newbies that went whining to Top got a sympathetic ear and little else, and if the whining persisted the whiner was usually invited back to the bunker line for a second helping by Top himself. I guess I was lucky that I had not spent some time in a bunker with a couple of "Seasoned Troops" myself, when I had first joined the 43rd.

The Rifle Range

One of the most unrewarding chores Big Jon and I was assigned was the day we had to take the newly arrived troops in the unit out to the rifle range. Getting familiar with your individual weapon, and the care and feeding thereof, was part of being a soldier. We all had gone through Basic Training, and hopefully all the Newbies had gone through stateside Vietnam prep. Training. So at first this seemed like no big deal, take the Newbies out somewhere and get them familiar with their weapons. Standing on the back of the deuce and a half, and looking down on the body of troops milling around beneath me made me cringe. What stood out was how un-alert they all were. We would look over the mob of bright new F.N.G. faces in their dark green F.N.G. fatigues, and say to myself, "These guys haven't got a clue!" They were totally unaware of what was going on around them, they were more interested in getting acquainted with each other or talking about what they had for chow. It was depressing to watch these young eager F.N.G. people, who didn't know where they were or what was going on.

Our first and biggest challenge was to try and educate these F.N.G.s about security, and the importance of it. God was I this stupid when I showed up in country? Probably! Before we got on board the trucks we first had to assemble them, and then get their attention. Then we would show them how to ride a truck while traveling outside a base camp. In Vietnam you rode facing outboard, looking for trouble instead of facing in while talking with your neighbor. We showed them that in Vietnam they had to carry their weapon and ammunition for easy use. We had to make them aware that not paying attention is how you accidentally shoot your neighbor, while you were talking with him, when you should be alert and looking out for trouble by riding facing outboard. And the need to keep both eyes open and watch any and all of the Vietnamese people and their activities around you, so you could stop talking, and point your rifle before you became a casualty. We did all of this and more, as we were going outside of all this nice safe barbed wire, and I believe we went through all of this preparation more for my own preservation than theirs. Goddamn they were fucking stupid!

"Yes Jones, you keep your flak vest done all the way up, if its open nasty stuff can get in."

"Kooner put your helmet on; it will only get dirty there on the floor."

"No you idiots put the selector switch to `SAFE' and leave it there until we get shot at. Yes Jones I will tell you when that happens."

"No Bunker I don't know if there will be chow where we are going."

"If you haven't loaded an empty magazine with bullets from a stripper clip don't you think you ought to before we get on the road?"

Big Jon drove on this trip and I stayed in back with one of the old timers from supply, we had an M-60 machinegun resting on its bi-pod on the roof of the trucks' cab and so I rode standing up so I could turn around and badger these F.N.G. troops. As we drove through the outskirts of Pleiku on the way out to the range I and the supply guy spotted some heavy ARVN activity around some houses to our right. ARVN running around with rifles was unnerving, as there was no way of knowing what they were doing. We saw it, so did Big Jon, and so did the First Sergeant Buddha riding shotgun up front. All of us had our weapons out and were ready. I turned around to check my charges, and was dismayed at their total unawareness of what was going on around them. I woke them up to the facts as I cranked a round into the M-60 and began yelling and pointing out the danger to them. The usual ten per cent started asking "Where? Where?"

"Stop talking and pay attention," the F.N.G.s were told,' said the supply guy.

"Listen for any directions that Scotty and I give you," he added.

"Don't shoot you fucking idiots, just be ready," I yelled over the noise of the trucks engine.

"Jones put that weapon back on 'Safe' or you'll be wearing it like a bow tie if I come over there."

"That's right Jones, this would be a good time to put your helmet back on."

This day we were lucky, and there was no shooting. No enemy action was for the ARVN to take care of, and no ARVN M.P.s trying to stop us from going where we were going. The action was far enough away from us that Big Jon was able to drive on by, and I gave a great sigh of relief.

We arrived, without further incident at Camp Holloway, on the south side of Pleiku. This was the place where we would find the rifle range, I was thankful that we were all in one piece. We jumping down from the back of the truck, and sorted out the Newbies. At least they knew how to line up, and we set up for individual instruction in the M 60 Machinegun, the M-79 Grenade Launcher, and the M-16 rifle. The range at Camp Holloway was anything but a rifle range. It was a wide clear spot of ground that backed up onto the side of a hill. No safety stuff of any kind like they used in the states, we just had to wing it. Big Jon and I now became rifle instructors. We had to listen to the "Aw gee whizz, I had this in basic," crap by smiling and sawing, "well let's just run through it again to see what you remember." I was tempted to add, "You little prick," a few times, "If you don't go through this till we are satisfied then you don't get to fire the nice Machinegun or the M-79." Every newbie fired and zeroed his weapon, every one of those little shits fired a few rounds through an M-60 Machinegun, and every one of them fired one round through an M-79 Grenade launcher. We got through that without any one getting shot, and Big Jon and I sat down on some empty ammo boxes at wait for the next thing that Top wanted done.

"Ya know Big Jon," I began, "I sure as shit am glad that we ain't thrown' grenades with this bunch."

"I don' think this bunch of F.N.G.s could handle them," replied my big friend.

There were other "seasoned" guys helping with this rifle range exercises Big Jon went and found something to entertain ourselves with. We were both no strangers on killing time during the Army's hurry up and wait game. With what seemed like a great deal of time left before we reloaded the trucks Big Jon and I talked about our recon days at the 278th, and how now those days were gone.

With a broad smile on his face Big Jon picked up an empty M-60 ammo box Big Jon said for me to grab an M-79 and follow him. He and I went as far from the now milling band of F.N.G.s as we could get to a quiet clear area at the base of the hill we had been shooting against. Once we were out of site of the mob Big Jon produced three M-79 buckshot canister rounds from his pocket and declared, "Let's have us some fun Scotty

McNasty, we can shoot Skeet with this here ammo box." We practiced "Skeet Shooting" with and M-79.

Since he brought the ammunition Big Jon got two tries to hit the ammo box after I had hurled it into the air by its handle. But Big Jon being the excellent shot that he was just couldn't connect. Three things need to come together to hit a target; front sight, rear sight and target. Well Big Jon had his try now it was mine. So Big Jon heaved the ammo box up into the air by its handle, and I tried to blast it with a 40mm canister round of double-aught Buck-Shot from the M-79. I shoot with both eyes open and always have so front sight and rear sights didn't matter. On my one and only try I hit the ammo can dead center, and the double-aught buck pellets tore the metal box to shreds. "Great shot!" Exclaimed Big Jon, but in the time it took to make that statement the inch and half round, inch and three quarter long plastic wad that held the pellets came bouncing back on me from 25 feet away. The plastic wad bounced off of the front of my helmet with a loud resounding CLANG. Surprise, is a good word to use for my expression at that time, I was completely surprised. That sound was greeted by "Rang your bell that time," didn' it lil' buddy," as Big Jon handed me the badly bent plastic wad he had just picked up from the ground. The ensuing head ache and lack of ammunition ended our skeet shooting club permanently. As always with Big Jon and I, fun in Vietnam was where you made it up yourselves.

A Seasoned Vet

We were not done with the Newbies, and we were now to cross paths with these new green troops more and more often as the First Shirt would have us working as Acting Sergeants of the Guard or Acting Charge of Quarters more frequently. Because of these two new entanglements I spent many happy evenings way into the wee hours shepherding new troops on guard duty and other tasks. I spent many an hour explaining the intricacies of our defensive system to many a new and shining face, usually while at the top of a 100 foot guard tower. This was the very same tower I had spent many an evening on my own, and the view in the middle of the night was exactly the same. I explained the meaning of all this barbed wire and sandbags, and the need for them to stay alert and above all awake during their tour of duty. The intricacies of the Off and On switch on the searchlight, and how to sweep it around to see if anyone was creeping up on you.

The ever popular topic of "What to do if there is a Rocket or Mortar attack," and that was usually followed by "What to do if there is an enemy ground attack." How to crank the field telephones' handle so you didn't break a nail, and how to "Report" in if there was trouble, "Don't just yell or scream for help and run away," was often practiced as the correct form of communications by F.N.G.s, but we tried to show them a better way. We talked to them about, when to open fire, when to get the hell out of the tower, and most importantly how to get the hell out of a 100 foot tower without killing yourself. I found that I now knew this stuff by heart, and needed no notes or other reminders to help me explain things to the F.N.G. I had in front of me.

At times this education seemed boring and repetitive, but most of all I felt disgusted with these new troops. Not one of them knew or could recite any of their 11 General Orders, which were the guide for every soldier ever placed on guard duty. I wasn't no starched and polished soldier, but I did know the rules I had to follow.

Together we would lean over the parapet, pointing out to them what a lookout should know. We looked out past the barbed wire at the hump backed landscape I now knew so well. To the left I would point out the perimeter lights of Artillery hill, to the center Engineer hill, and way off to the right was the Air Force base and the 71st Evac. Flares would occasionally arc up and over some position on a bunker line in the distance and the bright blobs of light would float slowly back to earth like lazy comets with crooked tails. I never got tired of seeing the navigational lights of helicopters. They could be seen floating above the distant base camps at all hours of the night. At times the red rain of a gunship's mini-guns would be working out on something unseen around a camps perimeter. A mini-gun was an electric Gatling gun that could fire up to 2000 rifle bullets per minute, every fifth bullet was a red tracer that would glow red against the night sky as it fell to earth. So what looked like red rain was a stream of red tracer bullets accompanied by many hundreds of unseen bullets. It looked like somewhere in the heavens a hose was turned on, and red drops of water would cascade to earth snaking from place to place until the tap was turned off. All this I had seen many times before, but now I was using my past experiences to break in the new guys. "Holy crap," I once told myself, "I'm becoming an old man."

"Hey man, what do I do if I see someone out there?" This was the most asked question I was given. The answer was right out of the First Sergeants hand book for new troops, had there been a hand book. The answer had probably been recited to troops, by some First Sergeants, every time that a trooper screwed up on guard duty. I now recited the exact script as it had been handed down to me.

"Up here in your 100 foot penthouse you have the world at your fingertips," I said.

"If you have not already done so, turn on this fucking great searchlight."

"Here is the switch see!"

"Next pick up the field phone and crank the handle, if someone speaking Vietnamese answers hang up!" That one always drew a puzzled look.

"Tell the people on the end of the phone what you have seen, and look over your parapet to see if they are still there," I continued.

"Have your rifle ready, and only shoot if you have a clear shot," I instructed.

"Do not shoot the person climbing your ladder That will be me coming to rescue you." End of lecture.

The routine for stopping an intruder, as it had been explained to me many months ago by another First Sergeant at the 278th, consisted of the following:

1. You yell halt, three times in English.
"HALT!"
"HALT!"
"HALT!"
2. If the individual doesn't stop, you yell halt three times in Vietnamese.
"DUNG LAI!"
"DUNG LAI!"
"DUNG LAI!"
3. If the suspect still doesn't stop, you fired a warning shot over their head.
4. If the individual hasn't stopped after the warning shot, shoot to wound.
"Shoot to wound.... How the hell do you do that Sarge?"
"How the fuck should I know Lennox, just shoot to wound... OK."
5. If the individual hasn't stopped by then, shoot to kill.

By the time I got around to explain this procedure to the new men things had changed. At this time in my Army life, I had somewhat abridged the 11 General Orders. I had lost the little card with them printed on it, and I was not too prone to trust anyone, especially someone sneaking through the barbed wire in front of my bunker. Somehow that intricate litany and procedure I had learned from the First Sergeants, for challenging someone in Vietnam, had become somewhat abbreviated, and what I now performed for a Newbie was what could be considered as the Readers Digests version of the First Sergeant's instructions.

508

I took a deep breath and then instructed, "Under your breath you mutter in the same breath, 'HaltthreetimesinVietnamescandEnglish." This statement was followed very rapidly by three rifle shots, the "Kill" shot, the "Wound" shot and then the "Warning" shot. We were jaded about Vietnam and the Vietnamese, to say the least.

Paranoia or Premonition

Rocket attacks still occurred, and as I had less and less time to go on my tour I had been keeping track of their frequency of the attacks when I began to noticed something strange. On days that I didn't eat breakfast we had a rocket or mortar attack within 24 hours. "Was I that far gone?" I asked myself. "Am I just gun shy from living on this bullseye?" I first explained my suspicions to Big Jon, but only after the fourth time in a row that the MINUS breakfast PLUS rockets happened. His reaction to this revelation was he started checking with me each day to see if I had breakfast. I guess we were both "That far gone, or H.E. Happy." After the next "Hey Scotty, you eat breakfast today?" Got a "No" reply and a rocket attack appeared shortly thereafter many more people started checking with me each day about my digestion. By the time I left Vietnam my record was eleven out of eighteen missed breakfasts resulted in high explosives arriving in the company area. That was a 61% success rate, if success can be called the right word of getting rocketed. There were a lot more than 18 attacks during this period of time. However, I couldn't explain the results; I was just not hungry on certain days so I didn't eat. The results made me skinnier, and a believer in these predictions, and hell, so were Big Jon and many others.

So much high explosives had been thrown our way we with any time at the 43rd though that we were a screwy lot.

Pappy's Article 15

Despite being rockets frequently so far there had been few or only minor casualties from all this enemy attention. During one of the rocket attacks a former member of the 278 we called Pappy, rescued another former member Hippy, who had been wounded by shrapnel. Pappy was late getting to his bunker, and on the ground outside his bunker he found Hippy an unconscious Hippy with a huge hole in him. The hole was as big as your fist, and it was punched through his chest, from back to front. Hippy could not be revived, and stayed unconscious and bleeding badly. Pappy picked him up and threw him into the back of a nearby Jeep intending in driving Hippy to the nearby hospital. The Jeep was locked with a chain and padlock around its steering wheel, as was Army regulations. Pappy was not perturbed; he took aim with his M-16 and shot the lock off. Once the Jeep was running he drove through the compound, through the incoming rockets to get to the road to the 71st Evac. Hospital. With rockets still coming in, the gate guard was hiding in his sand bagged guard post, and wouldn't come out and open the gate. Pappy had to threaten the 43rd's gate guard with his M-16 before the guard would open the gate. Pappy got Hippy to the 71st and undoubtedly saved his life.

This action by Pappy undoubtedly saved Hippy's life, and earned Pappy a Bronze star with a "V" for Valor. This action also earned him punishment and a fine of $15.00 under Article-15 for destruction of Army property, and unauthorized use of a military vehicle. Go figure.

In the Signal Corps not many people earned medals, that is, not many but fat Mess Sergeants. Pappy was toasted and cheered from one end of the 43rd to the other he couldn't buy himself a beer for at least a week, and we all celebrated having a hero in our midst.

I visited Hippy at the 71st Evac. One day about a month later. Hippy was alive and well, and waiting to go home. The poor guy had a four inch square scar in the middle of his chest, but a smile on his face.

Further Losses

A day or two after Pappy's brave deed two more 43rd people were ambushed on the road leading to Plei Ping Montagnard village. They had been driving back to their signal site in the village at dusk, just like they were told not to do. The driver was killed outright, shot in the head from behind, and his shotgun guard just managed to save his own life. The shotgun drove the truck from the passenger's side of the cab, and managed to get out of the ambush. The shotgun guard had returned fire by pointing his M-16 out the back window of the cab and keeping the enemy away. The guard drove out of the ambush on a shot out front tire and an M-16 that was out of ammunition. The truck was brought in to our motor pool the next day by a wrecker, what a mess. Not just the shredded left front tire, but the distinctive bullet hole in the back metal plate behind the driver made us think just how vulnerable we all were. These Army vehicles were not as bullet proof as we thought after all. It gave me the shakes just looking at the wreck, and I relived my own ambush.

Within a week further losses for the old 278 gang were incurred. One of the water truck drivers from the 278th was badly wounded by another G.I. This driver, Paco, was stationed in the 43rds detachment at Kon Tum, and we had not seen him since the deactivation of the 278th. The deactivation had happened some months ago, but we were always keeping tabs on who was from the 278th and not the 43rd. Word always filtered in about who from the 278th had ended up where. Paco was a nice guy, and we had eaten together, talked together, and showered together with the water he had delivered.

This poor guy was sitting in his room in Kon Tum when a bullet came through the wall and hit him in the chest. The bullet had been fired by a G.I. in the next room who was despondent, depressed, or just plain stupid, and wanted to end it all. The G.I. with the sadness problem had merely given himself a flesh wound and a dishonorable discharge from the Army. Mr. Sadness had given Paco several weeks in hospital.

Back to the Medics

Since my arrival in Vietnam I had battled with toilet problems that were never ending. I called these problems my personal case of the malaria pill blues. Also known as, the G.I. shits, the runs, or the G.I.s. My G.I.s suddenly changed into full-fledged dysentery, and quite frankly a huge pain in the ass, the head and the gut. I had never had it so bad, I couldn't sleep, I couldn't eat, there was only one thing I could do, and I had been doing that every hour, and sometimes more often on the hour and the half hour. It was misery, and I was spending more time on the way to or from and in the latrine than in doing anything else. So after two days of pain and misery I finally gave up and went and to see the medics at the 71st Evac. Hospital.

I walked down that now familiar road to the 71st Evac. I went on sick call and sat back under the sign that read, "Is Moby Dick a social disease?" and for my trouble I got to spend some time with a beautiful woman. I got to tell my problem to a Captain of nurses, a very feminine, blond, American, female, Captain of nurses. At first, standing on one side of a small table, I could not make the words come out of my mouth that described my ailment. I was embarrassed; I was dumb struck by her closeness and her beauty. I lingered over her delicious aroma, having first seen her from the entrance of a room crowded with other G.I.s. From there I had to elbow my way through the sea of other G.I.s who wanted the same thing that I did. They wanted to have this vision of loveliness all to themselves. Finally I mustered the courage and the words, but forgetting my military courtesy. "Lady," I said, "I got a bad case of the G.I.s that won't quit." The G.I.s was the soldier's

512

common name for what is otherwise known as the runs, the trots, the sniveling drizzles, blow hole, and the shits. "What's the G.I.s?" She asked in response to my announcement. Her blue eyes shone and were amazing as they gazed only on me. I felt shy having to explain things to her right in front of a crowd of leering troops who delighted in my callousness and her seeming naiveté. Red in the face I went on to describe in detail my ailment. She listened without batting an eye, and I knew that the romance was gone. She became very business-like and gave me a bottle of little white pills, "take these," she said, like my problem was just like every other guys problem. Yes but even though my problem was just exactly like every other guys' there I wanted more. She ended our relationship with one word, "Next!" And it was over. That ended my problem and my visit with the blond Captain. After taking her pills I couldn't go for a week. I thought I might explode before the medication released the lock on my rear end. I was happy to have been that close to a beautiful woman, and happier still not to be visiting the latrine every five minutes.

Vietnamese Language 101

I now that I was getting "SHORT" I now spent more time in the repair depot than I did on the road to Qui Nhon. The trading for weapons still went on, but I was not needed for that anymore. The First Sergeant had taken over the role of weapons overseer, and had a new Buck Sergeant running the Qui Nhon shuttle service. I was finally getting to use my two favorite words in the Army "Short Timer." I had less than 100 days to go before going home, and getting OUT of the Army.

Now that I was one of the men working in the repair shop regularly, I had the task assigned to them of training Vietnamese soldiers in the repair of sophisticated electronic communication equipment. This was all part of some great plan, somewhere that some "Big Brain" had dreamed up. In the Grand Scheme of things there must have been a paragraph in that plan that said, "The men of the 43rd Signal Repair Shop will train Vietnamese soldiers in the repair of electronic equipment. The Vietnamese will not speak English nor the Americans Vietnamese, and furthermore the Vietnamese will have no back ground what so ever in electronics." Well, what the hell, neither did I have any grasp of electronics when I started.

This was the score that myself and my colleagues had to deal with, first the language barrier, and then the technical barrier. Pigeon English had become a major part of life in Vietnam for all of us. It was how you communicated with the Vietnamese laundresses in the barracks if you had a laundry problem you used pigeon. (My O.D. Green G.I. socks kept diminishing in number was the usual thing). If you wanted a hair cut by the civilian Vietnamese barber, you needed pigeon to get your thoughts across. (Many were the times that I sat in the barber's chair with a loaded and cocked .45 automatic on my lap under the barber's sheet. I was edgy about any Vietnamese working on me with a razor blade. I was especially skittish the shorter time I had left, also since I didn't know the barber's political affiliations). If you wanted a refill of beer or any form of drink service at the EM club you needed to know pigeon to get the civilian bar girl to bring you the right thing.

Now I and the rest of the guys in the shop tasked with implementing this task all scratched our collective heads. We had to transfer these Pigeon English language skills over to the technical training of ARVN soldiers in the repair depot. Not all of us in the shop had been in country as long as I and not everyone spoke good English or English good. Somehow "Hey mama-san where be for socks, yo' bring tee tee sock, yo' numba ten mama-san," didn't translate into anything electronic or technical. (Rumor had it that the mama-sans used G.I. socks as Tampax, and it was for this reason that they kept disappearing).

To a G.I. there was a whole series of key words and or phrases that communication with anyone Vietnamese was centered around. All of us picked them up, in the gutter, as we

514

went along, but the words we all learned got across the meaning of what we were trying to convey. I now present a partial list of Vietnamese G.I. speak to illustrate my point.

For you Vietnam or Vietnamese language purists don't expect them to be spelled correctly.

Baca Noyk (Ba-ca Nook)	- Lets screw
Beau Coup (Boo Coo)	- many
Beau Fucking Coup (Boo Fucking Coo)	- a whole bunch
Boo Shit (Boo Shit)	- Bull Shit
Choi Oy (Ch-o-ee Oy)	- The very idea!
Choi Duc Oy (Ch-o-ee Duck Oy)	- How about that!
Di Di (D D) (short for Dee Dee Mow)	- go away, beat it
Dinky Dau (Dinky Dow)	- Crazy
Numba One (Number 1)	- The Best
Numba Ten (Number 10)	- The Worst
Numba Huckking 10 (Number Huk-king 10)	- Worse than Number 10
Du Miami (Doo Miami)	- Worse than numba Huckking 10
Hubba Hubba (Hubba Hubba)	- Hey Baby
Dung Lai (Dun-G La-ee)	- Stop
La Dai (La Da-I)	- Come here
Nev-a Happen (Never Happen)	- No way

No Bic (No BIC)	- Don't understand (Nothing to do with ball point pens)
No Lie (No Lie)	- you tell truth
Same Same (Same Same)	- Just like
Sin Loi (Sin Loy)	- sorry about that
Souvenir mo (Souvenir M.)	give me free
Sup Sup (Sup Suo)	- Eat
Tee Tee (T T)	- a little
Xin Loi (Sin Loy)	- Sorry
Xin Loi Min Nhoi (Sin Loy Min Noy)	- sorry about that sweet heart
You be for (You Be 4)	- Are you

There were many more, but any conversation held with a Vietnamese person would include at least two or more of the above words or sayings.

So with a lot of gesticulating and pointing from both nationalities, a lot of "You do, you do" or "You no do, you no do," and more pointing, head nodding, head shaking, and some great pantomime from both sides we went to work. I was surprised, one day, when one of the ARVN soldiers slapped the flat of his hand against his forehead with a loud slap. I thought that was an American expression, but our fathers had been to this country long before we arrived. It was nice to see that we had got at least one point across.

When I became involved in this training process it was explained to me that if you told a Vietnamese, "If you pulled this certain switch while the equipment was operating it would result in a particular electron tube blowing up and that would be followed by a certain transformer melting, the fuse blowing and the world ending." The Vietnamese would pull the switch during operation of the equipment to see if it would indeed do what you said it would do. And the answer was, "Yes it did do what we said it would do. So training was a long involved daily process. I had a great respect for these ARVN we were training. They all tried hard to learn and do a good job, and to have some fun now and again. There idea of fun was to pull the right switch at the wrong time; sometimes faking you into thinking they were pulling the right switch at the right time. My kind of fun was removing Orosz's dog Whore from their ankle.

Horse Play

Working regularly in the shop I became more acquainted with my fellow repair people and the daily workings of the shop. I was still the "Secret" combat damage specialist for equipment, or "Equipment Terminator." I was still in charge of the Monsoon Coffee Company, and still leader of the mop squad.

Now back in the shop on a regular basis I added a couple of new fun things to the repair guy's day; just little things to help get your mind off of your electronic troubles. At any point during the work period, day, hour or week I would yell out, "Attitude Check?" This question was an open invitation for those in earshot to vent their feelings. "Fuck it!" "Who gives a shit," were some of the normal status shouted replies, but it did let guys let go of some of their frustrations. Another fun game I thought rather fun till it was played on me as a payback, was to walk up to a guy and ask, "How high do your boots go up?" A split second later I would kick the individual in the shins. The result was the victim hopping around on one leg for a few seconds. The guy's in the shop liked that one so much they would play it on each other.

517

I wasn't the only one cutting up on the job. There were others who needed diversion as well as I, and they contributed to keeping it lively in the shop. Once in a while from across the main room of the shop, the teletype repair section, some one from over there would yell out, "Anyone who can't tap dance is queer." That would set off a frenzy of up wards of 12 or more prancing, jumping men their feet flailing around in rubber soled jungle boots trying to look like they were tap dancing. I don't remember that I saw anyone not try to tap dance when this challenge was hurled from across the room. I certainly did my best impersonation of Fred or Gene, as I was not wanting to be counted amongst those people on the other team. It was a great two minutes when it happened.

Even with my heady responsibilities of coffee making, mopping and damage infliction I found time to fit in one of the more enjoyable Army activities that made a slow day in the rear become quite fun and that was rumor mongering.

Wherever I was in the Army, Vietnam, the states, there was a never ending string of rumors coming out of the latrine, anyone who went to the latrine came back with a juicy bit of gossip that everyone else was just waiting to hear. No matter how ridiculous or improbable the story, there were always people ready to believe what was reported in the latrine. It seemed that soldiers lived for rumors. If you were not following a rumor you just weren't happy.

"Hey Scotty did you hear, there is an NVA division on its way here from Cambodia. They have just over run the Oasis, (a fire support base half way between Pleiku and Cambodia), and the NVA are heading here to overrun Pleiku." This was a staple of the rumor mill. "Yeah, and the Air Force is setting up a B-52 Arc Light mission to wipe them out." This is one of the more radical rumors. In camp Enari I had heard this same rumor with a slight variation. "The VC are coming to take back Dragon Mountain, cause it's the birth place of Ho Chi Min." The more normal but just as untrue rumors had to do with arrivals of luxury items in the P.X., "Hey, I heard that the P.X. just got a truck load of (inset product here), Pioneer speakers, reel to reel tape recorders, 35mm cameras, etc." Stories like this were greeted as gospel every day. "Yeah! No shit Scotty I heard it from this puke, the Colonels driver, he was on the next hole to me at the crapper. He said that the Colonel has a case of the clap so bad that his balls swole up like melons and they turned blue too." That was indeed a juicy tidbit of information, but knowing the source of the information I doubted it. I wished it was true of certain NCOs but not the Colonel.

Whether they were true or false there was enough of them, and they certainly were colorful. The more frequent juicier rumors were:

"One of the cooks got hepatitis and we are all gonna have to get shots in the ass to clear it up."

"Oh shit! Find me a place to hide." This one turned out to be true.

"They got burgers and fries in the mess hall for chow."

"My Ass! That will be the day!"

"There's a round eye U.S.O. show at the air base and they got a stateside stripper."

"I would not put this one past the Air Force. They really saw to their troops comforts."

"They got steaks for dinner tonight."

"Who do you think you're kidding, there never are no steaks."

So to fit in a little more with the daily workings of the repair shop I figured it was only right that I start my own rumor. So one day I took time off from the job and I went to the same notorious, rumor spreading, latrine as everyone else. Sitting down with my neighbors I casually opened the conversation with, "Hey you guys read in the Stars & Stripes about that Sergeant Major jungle telegraph uncovered in Vietnam?" This was greeted by nods and "Yeah Man" from the more gullible, or "No shit Scotty what happened?" From the gullible. Then came the question from the group of green clad conspirators sitting on the holes close by. When I had finished my story, and my explanation of the crimes nods and concurrence came from the guys. "Well I heard that the C.I.D. (Criminal Investigation Detachment) just arrested the commanding general of the 4th division on charges of corruption in association with this Sergeant Major thing. He was taking kickbacks from all the Sergeant Majors in his area, cause the Sergeant Majors were operating brothels for officers only, on the side." This opened up a steady discussion on the crimes of the C.O. of the 4th Division and all officers in general. I smiled to myself, I next brought up, "How our own 43rds' Sergeant Major looked like a crook, yeah, to me he did look like a crook, those shifty eyes, how all Sergeant Majors were a shifty lot and not to be trusted." My job in the latrine done I sat back and spent my time reading a week old version of The Stars & Stripes which had no mention of any such arrest or scandal.

By the time I got back to the repair shop I was greeted with my own rumor, and I must add it had grown somewhat in the severity of the charges. In addition to my story the general was now charged with operating and illegal diamond smuggling operation operated through the use of the diplomatic pouches going back to the U.S. from the division. Now this was a new twist. The ARVN troop trainees were even in a huddle and chattering loudly in Vietnamese, and it could only be about these recent disclosures from the latrine. Someone in the rumor mill must have been bi-lingual.

Within a half hour of my visit to the latrine the rumor had made the rounds of the company area and was in Jeeps heading for the 4th division headquarters, II corps headquarters, and the MACV compound. I smiled inwardly on a job well done and went back to work.

Perkins Crime

I was doctoring the morning tub of coffee for the guys, and I had just gurgled my last drop of Listerine in to the pot when Sergeant Stubaby grabbed me by the arm. This was just after my rumor spreading exercise, and when he grabbed my arm I thought that I had been caught. I was prepared with my Listerine story, but Sergeant Stubaby had something he wanted to share with me. What he shared was a new fact about my buddy Perkins. Perkins, "The Jolly Green Giant," it turned out was a Ham radio nut, and had brought his addiction with him to Vietnam. Sergeant Stubaby had caught Perkins trying to requisition a piece of radio equipment through Army channels that could only be used on a ham radio rig. Sergeant Stubaby had him cold, now what should we do about it. Showing me the papers that Perkins submitted, the F.S.N. Federal Stock Number and the signature on the requisition were enough to put Perkins into an Army slammer for a long time.

I liked Perkins, he was a unique kind of guy, he lived and breathed electronics, but he could still communicate with the rest of us in understandable English language terms. Besides being our electronics mad genius in the back room he had helped me and others in the past solve tough problems, and Orosz, Big Jon and I had inducted him into the Varsity to show that anyone who could carry a tune was alright with us.

But Perkins had been caught red handed trying to requisition a directional coupler (whatever that is) through the Army supply system. After Sergeant Stubaby explained the whole thing to me, and that he intended to do "nothing" about it. I had a suggestion to the contrary that might be fun to pull on the old "Jolly Green." I would join Sergeant Stubaby in harassing Perkins. Stubaby would make threats like, "You're not going home, you're going to Leavenworth Prison," and I would chime in with "Sergeant Stubaby's got your requisition Perkins, the C.I.D. will be banging on your door tomorrow, so be prepared for the flashlight up your butt trick."

Men from M.A.R.S.

Even though he had a larcenous side Perkins was a good egg, and he performed one very important duty for us in the electronic repair depot. He provided some of us with occasional telephone calls back home to the world. Perkins had the talent needed to repair the M.A.R.S. equipment for the local M.A.R.S. radio station. This was a big feather in the warrant office in charge's cap, and our warrant officer went out of our way to get us all the M.A.R.S. business he could drum up. This talent of Perkins was not an everyday occurrence; in fact it was quite rare. The one thing Perkins knew was radios and how to make them tick. Long range radios, not the short range ones we normally worked on. So Perkin's talent was in high demand by our warrant office and the M.A.R.S. people. Perkins only had their short wave equipment to work on one or two days a month, but he managed to make the very most of it.

I had been a big fan of the telephone company ever since I had been drafted and left home for my time in the Army. The phone company was a soldiers' vital link with home wherever you ended up in the Army. That is, any place but overseas in the Army. I don't think it would be possible to make a payphone call from Vietnam at that period in history. I was even fonder of the telephone company after I was shown that you could make telephone calls home or to your girl or anyone else for free. This was a revelation that just astounded me. I learned it from a college student while I was on my way to my new duty station Fort Riley in the great state of Kansas. I was standing in the Kansas City Airport counting my massive amount of pocket change to see if I had enough to call home. I was standing in front of a bank of pay telephones when a young man in civilian clothes walks up to the phone next to mine, and he dropped a dime in. He next asked the telephone operator how much to make a call to a number in New York City. Once he had the amount needed this young man started dropping coins into the pay phone next to the one he was on, and holding

522

his own phone's hand piece up close to the phone he was dropping the coins in. All the while he was doing this he gave me a big conspirator smile and a wink. His call went through, I was amazed, he finished his call and walked away, leaving me to contemplate a life of telephone crime, as well as my handful of pocket change.

M.A.R.S. stood for Military Affiliated Radio Station. But what M.A.R.S. did was to provide a radio link between Vietnam and the U.S. through the Ham radio operators in America. The M.A.R.S. people would set up a radio link to a Ham station somewhere near your home and a Ham radio operator would patch in a telephone, reversed charges of course, and link to your home phone for you to talk for a few minutes. That is technically how it was supposed to work, but it was not the way that it usually worked.

This M.A.R.S. stuff was wonderful stuff in theory, but I never could, never, NEVER , EVER get a M.A.R.S. radio station to patch me through to my home, in any of the dozens of attempts I made. They were too busy, the atmosphere was lousy, the air was too crowded, and I heard every excuse from the M.A.R.S. station people. Perkins on the other hand provided us with the same service as the M.A.R.S. station through his personal known network of ham radio operators, and his knowledge of how to operate the M.A.R.S. gear had on his work bench for test. Perkins never had trouble with the atmosphere, the crowding of the air or other funny business. The reason he could get us through to the U.S. when nobody else could was Perkins would tweak and tweak the equipment until it gave him what he wanted. The M.A.R.S. people were not tweekers, they were knob turners. The M.A.R.S. people would bring him all of their short wave radios to repair, and while they were in his hands he had to test them to see if they worked properly. You can see now why Perkins became a member in good standing of the Varsity.

My first exposure to the people from M.A.R.S. was when one of them entered the repair shop one day and announcement,

"I'm from the M.A.R.S. station." This announcement normally brought the response of, "So what!" from the troops within earshot. The M.A.R.S. guys were just as popular with the rest of the repair shop troops as they were with me, and this was because the rest of the troops couldn't get a call through to home through the M.A.R.S. guys either. Here standing in the entrance to the shop was a guy who spent his entire tour in Vietnam in air-conditioned comfort, somewhere deep on a base camp, his feet up on a desk, in front of a Ham radio. He looked like John Wayne, Audie Murphy and Roy Rogers all rolled into one. He was wearing camouflage jungle fatigues, (made exclusively for Ranger contingents), an Australian bush hat, three or four brass Montagnard bracelets, and a pilot's .38 caliber revolver in a shoulder holster. I had a hard time holding a straight face when I saw this guy, and a harder time not saying, "Why don't you go and fuck yourself." But he was from the M.A.R.S. station.

Perkins took care of these guys personally, and all paperwork was immediately approved by our warrant office. All needed parts were ordered on a Priority One basis and were given special express handling. We ruffians on the repair bench figured that someone was getting telephone calls through to the states. Perkins took care of all their needs with a smile and a professional air, he was their man. In no time had their equipment out of their hands and into his own for him to do with what he wanted and that was to talk to his Ham radio friends. After the M.A.R.S. guy had departed Perkins would erect his own antenna and was on the air in no time. The A.S.A. (Army Security Agency in charge of finding people like the enemy not using radios correctly or talking to people in the states without permission) came looking for Perkins' antenna regularly, and they stayed in the area for weeks but never did find it. Perkins became our own personal M.A.R.S. station, equipment permitting, and gave us great service.

There was one more strange thing about Perkins. It turned out that Perkins and I had another unusual link in our relationship besides our connection through the Varsity Glee Club. We had known each other for almost three months when we finally got around to talking about our homes. Perkins and I were from the same home town, and one more thing revealed through our talk. Our mothers worked at the same place and if that wasn't enough; our mothers knew each other and had for years.

Mandatory Morning Formations

Things were constantly changing at the 43rd, people came and went every day, and we had new faces and new names of F.N.G.s to familiarize ourselves with. Old faces and old names just faded away as old timers went home. One of the new faces and names we HAD to learn was that of the new C.O. for Headquarters and A companies. A new C.O. was a big thing to us troops with the most time in country. We were concerned to know what stupid rookie mistakes the new C.O. would make that might endanger us. By this time in my Army life, (Getting closer to three years), I had seen my share of 1st and 2nd Lieutenants over the years, and I had seen a lot of bonehead orders issued. Like anything else in life there were good ones and there were bad ones, and you had to be able to catch on to which was which fast. Unfortunately this new C.O. took the cake for idiocy. His first act as Commanding Officer was to announce that there would be mandatory formations every morning. Loud "Groans" could be heard from those reading the announcement on the company's bulletin board. This was insanity. "More loud groans" from the same group at the bulletin board. Formations had been rare when I was in the 278th, the First Shirt there had been able to persuade the 278th's C.O. that formations were dangerous, and were a health hazard to the well-being and good morale of the troops. The same had been true for the C.O. who had just left the 43rd. That C.O. had had his education delivered too him on the tip of a communist 122 mm high explosive rocket.

525

That C.O. had tried to initiate morning formations when he was a new guy, and I had arrived about the same time as the morning formations started. Formations had only been a daily occurrence in the 43rd for a few days and that was enough for Charlie to make book on the 43rd. All he needed was what time of day would all those lovely targets be standing there in all those straight lines. Charlie knew where and when we held these get-togethers. The local barber, one of the mama-sans, garbage haulers or any other member of the smiling Vietnamese civilians employed by the Army gave them the info. So it was easy for him to lob in a few rounds, and on one morning that is exactly what he did. Right between this nice flashing red lights on top of the giant antennas. It was only a day or two after I had arrived from the 278th; about 5 rounds fell on the 43rd's formation area with me plus 100 plus people standing in neat ranks. Within seconds of the screeching sound of the incoming rounds 100 plus people were trying to crowd into the nearest cover, the drainage ditch was 3 deep. A knot of bodies blocked the entrance to the nearest bunker. Charlie's marksmanship was off this day as he missed the entire formation by 100 feet. His rockets screeched in hitting the NCO club and the mess hall. The NCOs were shocked and dismayed, as for the time being they would have to do their drinking in the EM club along with us hoi polloi. Either that or get used to the new air conditioning that the VC had just installed in their club. As for the mess hall, most of us were delighted in our enemy's accuracy. To those not familiar with the contents, the advent of "C" Rations instead of cooked food provided some delight with a great change in menu. Those of us more familiar with "C"s wanted to go A.W.O.L. or transfer to a unit with a functioning mess hall.

This ended formations for the duration of that C.O.s tenure with us, that was until this new C.O. came into the company. He decided all on his own that morning formations would be a great way of giving the troops the word. I guess that nobody took this guy outside of his office and pointed out the giant antennas with the flashing red lights on top, or showed him the red circle with the white circle that we lived on. Nor had anyone explained to him that this had been tried and had failed before. By this time I was getting too short for this nonsense. For that first morning formation I did reluctantly show up and attend, but I made sure I placed myself in the rear most rank. I was standing by myself, right next to the drainage ditch until Sergeant Stubaby saw me and made me get back into ranks. The next morning formation I tried to form an entirely new rear most rear rank, and on the third day of formations I got a few troops to stand with me IN the drainage. This was pointed out to me, by a rather red faced First Sergeant, that this was detrimental to the other troop morale. I told him that I did it for MY morale, but as usual he failed to see my side of it. So I ended up once again going back to setting a good example for the new troops, by settling for standing in the normal rear rank of the formation.

The C.O. persisted with these formations, and it wasn't long before Charlie sent him his thank you card, in the shape of a few 122mm rockets. The morning of the attack we were standing there in the ranks waiting for the "word" to be disseminated to one and all. When First Sergeant Buddha showed up Big Jon yelled from the rear rank, "Hey Top! Y'all didn't see no mam-sans this morning did ya." "The bus is probably late," came the reply from Buddha. No mama-sans was a sure sign that we were going to get hit by something, and Big Jon knew what he was talking about. Too bad his warning was not heeded. "My ass!" Shouted back Big Jon. Within seconds we heard the whistle of the first incoming round. The first landed in the perimeter wire, and the rest marched further up the hill crashing closer and closer to our formation area. The last landed between a barracks but closer to our latrine, wounding an unfortunate trooper in the butt who was still blissfully sleeping in bed instead of standing in line like the rest of us. That taught him not to miss a formation.

When I along with most of others heard the rockets coming, I reacted like a coiled spring, but the whistle of the incoming caught the First Sergeant in mid-sentence. I dived immediately into the drainage ditch I had been standing next to. I landed on top of a screaming fat Irving Slomo, my weight landing on his back knocking the wind out of him and thankfully stopping his screaming. But I had made it into the ditch in the split second before the VC rockets hit us I wondered how this fat guy who had been standing in front of me in formation could beat me into a ditch behind us. My thoughts were cut short by the defining explosion of the first round, and the whine of shrapnel whizzing overhead. The last round slammed into the latrine 60 feet behind our formation area scattering debris everywhere (Orosz and I had told them that the VC had a shit seeking rocket, months ago). Miraculously no one was seriously hurt, the latrine building was a smoldering mess, but aside from some minor wounds from rocks and debris everyone had survived. The best part of all this was watching a chagrined C.O. dusting off his nice new O.D. Green fatigues.

After I was sure that the INCOMING had ceased I climbed out of the ditch pulling a wheezing Irving with me. "How'd you get here so fast," I asked him. I noticed he had the impression of a jungle boot on his back in red dust. "I was pushed," was all he said. The jungle boot had belonged to big Jon.

Needless to say those in command got the message, and this ended mandatory formations again. I resolved after this event that the next formation I stood in, I would again be standing next to the drainage ditch, if not in it, or it would be back in the U.S.A. and I would be collecting my discharge certificate.

The Sinking of the Good Ship M151A1

I was down to a three weeks from the end of my tour in Vietnam, and I was sent on an errand to another base camp on the other side of Pleiku. I was riding as shotgun guard, with my M-16, in an open topped Jeep driven by a big guy from the repair shop named Sheisskoff, and it was explained to us by Sergeant Stubaby that we were on a mission of mercy. We were being sent out to retrieve a very important piece of equipment by our Warrant Officer; he had sent the item to be repaired at another maintenance depot. The equipment's return to the 43rd was vital. It was the movie projector for the officer's recreation room. Being close to going home I was a little apprehensive of making this trip, and this close to going home nervous was now my middle name. To show my anxiety I constantly fidgeted in my seat, craning my neck this way and that, and I smoked half a pack of cigarettes within the first five miles of the trip.

Our route took us along some dirt roads that lead around some of the more outlying Vietnamese villages, and this made me very jumpy. The rainy season was over, but there were still lots of mud and puddles around left from a tropical storm that had blown through the highlands over the past few days. The storms were left over from a Typhoon that had hit the coast of Vietnam. I liked to avoid puddles as much as possible as they were a good spot for the enemy to hide mines in their soft mud. My backside told me I was nervous as I sensed my pucker factor climb to a new high. I got that old "We shouldn't be here feeling on the back of my neck." I also felt like I was sucking the seat cushions up through the seat of my pants. We cruised along on our mission at the recommended 35 mph. Sheisskoff wasn't one to get into trouble by speeding, and I think that is the reason he was assigned as driver on this trip. We were traveling a quiet, straight and isolated stretch of road, and I could clearly see something ahead I didn't like. We had come upon a large puddle of water that covered the road from shoulder to shoulder. Sheisskoff slowed the Jeep to a crawl as he approached the water, and I stopped my head twisting from side to side long enough to utter instructions. "Sheisskoff, skirt it and skirt it wide."

Sheisskoff complied and took the Jeep onto the grass on the left shoulder of the road, but his two right tires were still in the water. Why he went to the wrong side of the road I did not ask, he was driving and it was his decision. As we made our way slowly into the water the Jeep veered sharply right, the nose of the Jeep pointing straight into the middle of the puddle, and started to submerge. What we had run into was not a puddle in the road but an artillery or bomb crater that was full to the brim with rain water.

Within a tenth of a second of the Jeep making its swerve into the puddle, rifle in hand I climbed out of the Jeep's passenger seat and was out of the Jeep by stepping onto the rear seat and jumping over the back. My feet touched the soggy ground behind the Jeep as the nose of the Jeep dipped further into the brown water. Sheisskoff slammed the gear shift lever into reverse and his right foot crammed the accelerator to the floor. The Rooster tail of mud and brown water covered me from head to foot. Without skipping a beat Sheisskoff reached out his right hand and put the Jeep into four-wheel drive, still the slide forward continued. Still the Rooster tail continued, but I managed to move out of its way spitting out a mouthful of brown water as I moved. Sheisskoff sat with the steering wheel straight armed, leaning back in his seat trying to pull the Jeep out of the puddle by will power alone. It did no good. The engine's high rpm scream ceased as Sheisskoff realized the tires did nothing but spin on the mud, and threw it all over me standing behind the Jeep. He realized that he was losing the battle, so he sat with his right foot poised over the accelerator pedal, and the Jeep's engine ticking over as the front end of the Jeep slid deeper and deeper into the puddle, and he tried to decide what to do next. I stood muddy but dry shod in the grass and watched the front of the Jeep's hood disappear under water. Sheisskoff sat bolt upright stared straight ahead, (like a demented Captain slowly going down with his ship), full of determination, and the Jeep's engine reached a higher level of rpm as Sheisskoff tried one more time. His foot must have found an extra sixteenth of an inch of play in the accelerator pedal as his foot raced his mind in reaction time. The Jeep sank lower. All that was needed now was a naval captains' hat for him to wear, and for him to salute as he sank out of sight. I awoke from my own transfixion on the Jeep and took a 360 degree look around the area. We were definitely alone. All of a sudden the Jeeps motor ceased it's protesting, and silence prevailed. I turned back from my inspection of our surroundings to see that the Jeep had sunk past the middle of the hood. Deep enough for the water to flood the carburetor and kill the engine. Water was now coming in over the Jeep's sides, so Sheisskoff abandoned his efforts to save our sinking ship, and grabbing his own rifle he exited the same way I had. The Jeep finally stopped its down ward slide; it had sunk all the way up to the front of the drivers' seat at an angle of 45 degrees. We were all alone with our puddle and our submerged Jeep. The birds chirped, the grass grew, but other than that there was complete silence.

In a few seconds we had been put on foot in a hostile environment, the two of us now stood naked to the Vietnamese country except for the M-16s we carried. I looking from our vehicle, laying half submerged in the puddle, to Sheisskoff in search of a solution to our predicament. "Jess H. Christ that's deep," I offered. "Yeah! And it's cold too," replied Sheisskoff showing me his drenched fatigue pants. He pointed and laughed at my mud splattered face and uniform front.

I once again went back to my examination of our surroundings, and as no enemies were visible I gave a sigh of relief. So we stood there looking at our vehicle and each other until another sound caught our attention. The hum of a small engine that grew louder from our left, the direction we were headed before our sinking. We both looked down the road and saw two male Vietnamese civilians coming our way riding a small motor scooter. As they came closer I noticed a couple peculiar things about this duo. They both were wearing bright colored flowered shirts instead of the usual white shirts usually worn by Vietnamese males, they were both smiling happily and the one in the rear seat had a guitar strapped diagonally to his back. They were also traveling toward us down the middle of the road, the very same road our Jeep was parked at 45 degrees in. These two on the motor scooter were not slowing down. I looked at Sheisskoff and he was staring fixedly at the motor scooter and its passengers, so I looked once more at our Jeep. I had to make sure I was seeing what I was seeing. Yep, the Jeep was still there. The motor scooter was heading our way down the center of the road, and the Jeep was half sticking out of the puddle in the middle of the road.

The Vietnamese grew closer and still did not slow down. My jaw worked up and down like I was trying to shout a warning, but nothing came out. It started to rain, but I didn't notice at first. The sound of the motor scooter's engine grew in my ears as I watched its steady progress toward us. The motor scooter drove straight on without swerving or slowing, straight into the far side of the puddle. The water of the puddle parted and with a plop swallowed the motor scooter, two Vietnamese, the flowered shirts, the guitar, and the sound of their engine. All that remained was a small ripple on the top of the water.

I looked at Sheisskoff and he was looking back at me, and we both looked back at the puddle as the ripples on the surface reached the far side and returned. After what seemed to be a minute an object erupted abruptly on the water's surface and settled back onto it. It was the guitar. Seconds later two dark objects emerged on the surface of the puddle, but the heads were several feet closer to us from when we had seen them submerge. These were the two Vietnamese heads, and they were attached to two Vietnamese bodies which were dragging a submerged and silent motor scooter. Sheisskoff and I still stood and stared by the side of the pool as these two drenched figures came crawling out and pulled and drug their steed from the murky depths.

While the scooter was being retrieved I finally gave in and nearly wet my pants I was laughing so hysterically. I laughed so hard my sides ached and I found it hard to catch my breath. Sheisskoff caved in and fell on his wet butt in the wet grass by the side of the road, laughing as hard as I. It continued to rain harder still, but it didn't dampen our spirits we roared with laughter.

Once out of the water the two Vietnamese and the motor scooter lay in the middle of the road exhausted from their efforts. After a few minutes one of the men waded back into the puddle and re-submerged once more trying to retrieve the guitar. Once the guitar was retrieved and all four parts were reunited on the dry road way, the motor scooter was set upright and the two muddy and bedraggled Vietnamese remounted it and tried to start it. This brought fresh laughter from myself and Sheisskoff who joined me again, laughing so hard he had tears in his eyes. All this time the two Vietnamese paid no attention to Sheisskoff or I, and never looked in our direction. The motor scooter failed to kick over so the Vietnamese began pushing it down the road until it did start about 400 yards further on.

This left Sheisskoff and I in our original predicament, parked in the middle of the road, miles from any base camp, in "Indian Country," and now it was raining very hard. The Vietnamese and their scooter disappeared behind the curtain of rain, down the way we had come. Now Sheisskoff and I were completely alone. "Well Ollie, here's another fine mess you've gotten me into," was all I could manage.

We stood there soaked to the skin for half an hour snickering and giggling before another vehicle came along. This one was a U.S. Army Engineer five ton dump truck, and it came down the road from the direction we had come. In seconds the driver recognized a couple of motorists in distress, and threw a chain around our back bumper. In no time our Jeep was popped out of the puddle and back on the road. A little priming of the Jeep's carburetor with gasoline and we had the Jeep fired up and all the water blown out of the engine. Sheisskoff and I thanked out rescuer, and retracing our steps, found a dryer way to pick up what we had been sent to pick up. We smiled and grinned all the way back to the 43rd, and gave no mind to the fact that we and the Jeep were soaked to the skin and coated in a brown film. We spent an hour or two cleaning up the Jeep and ourselves, and then we each enjoyed reliving the afternoon's events by relating them to the others in the shop.

Chapter 20

Going Home

In my last month of my tour I had joined the ranks of a very exclusive club, the "Short, Short Timers". This was the club I had been trying to join since Basic Training. All through my tour in Vietnam and most of my time in the Army I had been passed by people yelling "SHORT" to anyone who would listen. In Vietnam this was a signal to all that this person did not have much time left to spend in country, and was on his way back to the world. There were other funny sayings used by short timers, "I'm so short I can sit on the edge of a dime and dangle my legs." "I'm so short I can't even pay attention." "I'm a two digit midget," or "I'm so short I gotta climb a ladder to take a pee." So to celebrate being short I got myself a short timers calendar, (A chart that counted down to one, and each day was Xed off in turn), and I too would yell "SHORT" to the people I met. No matter how short I got there was always others who were shorter, so there was a constant comparison of the amount of time each of us had left with other short timers. It was the Short contest and it went like this:

"How many days you got Scotty?"
"Thirty two and a wake up."

"Man that ain't short, I got twenty and I'm outta here," or the reply could be "FIGMO man, FIGMO." (Pronounced FIG MO, an acronym standing for Fuck It, I Got My Orders).

"How many days you got Smithy?" I asked a guy I met in the mess hall, and the answer was, "Hours!" The true winner of the contest and the best answer I ever got.

The days crawled by one at a time. It was a long hard climb, that last month till going home, and you just had to pray that we wouldn't get rocketed until I was out of here. That was a fact that didn't happen

Perkins Crime Revisited

Perkins was shorter in time left than I was, but Sergeant Stubaby kept telling him that he was going to be extending because of a certain piece of paper that Stubaby had in his possession. Namely one requisition form for a directional coupler, which had Perkins signature on it. Alternatively Sergeant Stubaby brought in a reenlistment blank and thrust it under Perkins nose, and then told him to sign it to get the criminal evidence torn up in front of him. Perkins turned pale and slowly shook his head back and forth, but refused to sign.

But the day did come for Perkins to go home and he showed up at the regular time for work in the morning, but this time he had his bags in his hands and smile on his face. He certainly had been sneaky about getting close to going home. He had made no announcement about how close he was to DEROS or saying goodbye. He never went around yelling "Short!" To anyone and seeing him standing in the shop with his bags in his hands was certainly a surprise.

With his showing up, bags in hand, I realized that we hadn't planned anything as a sendoff for him; people came and went all the time in Vietnam. Good pals were always made a fuss over by their friends, and doing so was always a break from work. However, when I saw that grinning tower of O.D. Green

536

I couldn't let him just walk away like that. I called Orosz, Big Jon and six other guys from the repair shop together, and I told them what I wanted done. We all sprang into action at one time. Six of us grabbed and picked up the 185 pound giant Perkins bodily and two more tackled his 175 pounds of bags. We then marched with Perkins on our shoulders through the camp to the back gate. There we demanded that the gate guard unlock and open his portal of wood and barbed wire, which he did. We then marched outside the gate and threw Perkins to the ground, effectively throwing him out of camp, and his bags were hurled after him. We marched back into the compound leaving a prostrate and bewildered Perkins outside. The gate guard was then commanded to lock the gate, while we stood and watched a confused Perkins dusting himself off. We then marched off and left him outside for two hours. Occasionally someone would report that they saw him, bags in hand, wandering around outside the barbed wire and looking in expectantly. We finally relented and several of us went and picked him up in an open deuce and a half and hauled his big tall butt to the Air Force Base to begin his trip home.

At the air base Sergeant Stubaby made a big thing of tearing up his incriminating evidence against Perkins. Perkins exhibited a huge smile and a big sigh of relief on seeing this done. Amidst good wishes and pats on the back, I presented Perkins with a small cardboard box, sealed with tape and marked with the FSN (Federal Stock Number) of a directional coupler, the very same device that Perkins had coveted. Perkins was touched, he gave me a sheepish grin, and he deftly opened his duffel bag and shoved the box in without opening it. "A little going away present" I remarked, and Sergeant Stubaby shook his hand and assured him that there were no hard feelings. The warrant officer showed up with a tear in his eye; he was loosing his M.A.R.S. brownie points with Perkins sudden departure. With all official destruction of the evidence Perkins was a free man, and we all said our good-byes and he was off.

Perkins got all the way down to Cam Ranh Bay before he opened the box. Inside he found two of the best rocks I could find in the company area packed securely in Styrofoam peanuts.

Orosz Departs

Shortly after Perkins my best friend and closest buddy left Orosz departed for Cleveland and freedom from the Green Machine. His leaving us was an event that many from far and eide came to honor. Some of our trading partners came to see him off, guys from the MACV compound. Cooks, guys from outlying signal sites made the trip to the Pleiku Air Force Base to see him off. On his day of departure the supply guys proudly carried Orosz to a waiting deuce and a half while others carried his bags. Sergeant Stubaby made it sort of a shop holiday and many if not most of the guys just dropped their tools so they could go to the Air Force Base and say their goodbyes. The enticement of a $2 steak dinner had nothing to do with it.

It appears that the two years Orosz had been in country did not go unnoticed for his reputation or repute was known far and wide. A gifted Bull Shit artist, Orosz had talked his way in and out of situations, made and kept deals and got things done for people everywhere. At his departure were artillery men, engineers, as well as Infantry who all came to say farewell to a guy who over two years had made friends and influenced people. The size of the crowd at the Air Force Base was huge.

At the air base Big Jon and I presented our pal with the guidon of the Varsity Glee Club as a remembrance of our time together. The very same flag we had flown from our trucks on our many trips going back and forth to Qui Nhon. Orosz's dog Whore had come to the air base with us to say goodbye. Though he wanted to, the Army made it too difficult for a G.I. to take pets back to the U.S. with them. Big Jon and I would look after her for him. Time was definitely getting "Short," that old gang that had been a big part of my life in Vietnam was definitely breaking up.

Big Jon, Jimmy Olsen, Louis G. and I posed for farewell pictures with Orosz, along with many others. Even our Warrant Officer, who was not a fan of Orosz, showed up, and took pictures to add to the festivities. We were all happy that Orosz was going home to Cleveland, but we were sad at the same time that he would no longer be part of our lives. This union the three of us had forged, of brains and brawn, had been going on so long and had been such a big part of our lives that Big Jon and I did not want to see it end. We had been getting in and out of trouble together for so long that the excitement we generated by doing that was almost intoxicating. This was a bitter thing to say goodbye to a buddy who meant so much to us. It was bitter in the parting, but sweet that this guy was finally getting to go home safe and sound. Safe, but maybe a little worse for the wear we had put on him. In the future I would miss his sly pointed comments, the drinking, his attitude, and his know how on how to get people to work with you not against you.

The goodbyes finally all said, Big Jon and I gave him a final salute and a hand shake all around, each of us gave him our home addresses for good measure. We were sure that we would all meet again.

Re-Up and Buy a Brand New Car

It was required that before you left Vietnam to go home and exit the U.S. Army that the Army be given one last shot of getting you to stay on in the old job. My departure from the 43rd Signal was just around the corner when the summons arrived. I was to be given the obligatory Army reenlistment talk by the obligatory Army Reenlistment Sergeant. I was summoned to the reenlistment office, and upon entry into the palace of reenlistment I was completely astounded. There was no red mud visible anywhere. The whole place was spic and span just like it was in the states. The place was spotless! Sure it had the usual government or Army furniture, but the whole place was completely clean from top to bottom. After an appropriate waiting period in the reenlistment waiting room I was ushered into the Reenlistment Sergeants office. Once I became used to the immaculate surroundings I was cordially greeted by my host Sergeant Reenlistment. There I was given a reenlistment enticing cup of coffee and a reenlistment donut, (Where this guy got donuts in Vietnam I have no idea. Maybe he knew Big Jon's MACV Colonels wife too. I had not seen a donut since before I left the U.S.A.). Once properly entertained and the idle chitchat was over, I was then given the reenlistment pep talk. I had the test scores, I had the physical requirements, (I breathed), and I had the technical skills to have a great Army career. I listened politely, it all sounded remotely familiar. I then thanked the Sergeant for his hospitality, but I was not interested in his offer of 10,000 tax free dollars for six more years of my life. I had had enough of having Neanderthals with stripes push me around and telling me what to do. If I didn't do what they told me to do I was told then I would get to go to jail. It just was not enticing enough. I had had all the K.P., guard duty, bad food, and Neanderthals that I could stand. Thanks but no thanks. I had had my share of Sergeants Bigbelly, Kookwell, Grayson, Fullcup and other feeble minds. To me Sergeants were like diapers, they were full of shit and all over your ass."

The Glee Club had a song about reenlistment, and we used to sing it loudly especially in front of Lifers. It went:

> Re-Up and buy a brand new car,
> Re-Up and stay the rank you are,
> Re-Up and get the bonus,
> And you can phone us from Vietnam.

I had no desire to remain in my present position of duty slave. No matter how much money the Army offered. My mind was made up all the way back in Basic Training. An Army life was not my cup of tea.

Paranoia Sets In

As my time for going home drew nearer I became increasingly anxious about going safely getting home, and I was like a kid waiting for Christmas. I became more paranoid about getting home without any further scratches on me. I began getting up earlier each day, and I would make my bed, clean up and head for the mess hall for breakfast. I wanted to make sure that I had breakfast, to me that was the only true way to prevent a rocket attack. That is one reason why I got my butt out of the barracks early because we all knew by now that the barracks was a very prime target for enemy gunners. Knowing how anxious about breakfast I had become one or two people would get up early and have breakfast with me. I appreciated their efforts in trying and get me to calm down. It was Sheisskoff's turn on the morning when I had ten days to go, and he asked me the night before to come and get him on my way to breakfast. When I got up and got going it was pitch dark and I glanced at my watch, yep it was "Zero Dark Early." When I was ready I went and woke Sheisskoff and he got up and dressed immediately, and we trudged off across the compound to the mess hall. When we got there the place was dark and deserted, not even the cooks were there. Sheisskoff looked around and then at me, while I just stood there and shrugged my shoulders. Sheisskoff looked at his own watch, and exclaimed loudly, "You got me up at four A.M., its four A.M. Scotty you need to go home." At least there was coffee! Sheisskoff said, "Scotty, you are jittery enough and you do not need any coffee."

A Speed Bump on the way Home

Going home was not an easy process, especially when other people started putting up roadblocks in my path. A weekend before I was to leave I heard strange voices in the barracks throughout the weekend. The voices were female voices, and they were giggling and carrying on in someone's room down the hall from mine. No need to explain what was going on, someone was having some friends over and they were playing house. Women, Thunder Alley Whores, had been smuggled in to the 43rd in an empty water truck by a couple of enterprising G.I.s. No one said anything; no one went snooping to see what was going on. We all knew, someone had smuggled some Vietnamese whores onto the base and were having a wild weekend. However, if we lower life forms knew it was going on so did the powers appointed over us. These women were not what you would say, quiet.

Bright and early Monday morning the whore smugglers were discovered and drug before the C.O., and the smugglers turned out to be a couple of Lifer wanna-bes. Two low rank NCOs who and more than one hitch in the Army and wanted to make a carrier out of it. Getting caught bringing whores onto the base was definitely a carrier limiting maneuver.

First Sergeant Buddha explained it to us later that one of the whore smugglers got a smart idea on how to save his shattered Army Carrier and get it back in the good graces of the C.O. The smart smuggler told the C.O. that he and his buddy knew who was selling drugs in the barracks, and were willing to point them out if the C.O. would forget the whole whore thing.

Because of this bright idea, all of the residents of the barracks were immediately summoned back from work and we were told to assemble in front of the barracks. I was there along with Big Jon and the others, and the First Sergeant came out and formed us into three ranks. What next? I and everyone else wondered what this was all about. There had been no warning that they were looking for drug dealers and this assembly was a so called police lineup. This was a first for me, and I thought it might be one of those shakedown inspections that I had participated in at Fort Riley. No this was entirely new. Out of the C.O.'s office comes the C.O., the smugglers, a civilian, (I knew he was a civilian because he wasn't wearing what we were wearing. This guy had on a white shirt and jeans. This was the C.I.D., the criminal Investigation Division. The

542

Army's Gestapo to us. Our collective blood ran cold), and all three of the C.O.s company were accompanied by two very large M.P.s. Curiosity seemed to be all around me, and I came to attention with the rest of the ranks when the command was given. The C.O.'s party marched slowly down one ran and then down the next.

What was going on was these two smugglers were going to point out to the police who was selling drugs in the barracks, and the M.P.s were there to put the cuffs on whomever was pointed out. Standing there I began to sweat, I was in the middle of my biggest might mare. I was in a "Police Line Up" and my night mare was I knew they were going to pick me. "Lady you said the guy who molested you had two heads and three arms?" "No, it's him!" As the woman in my night mare pointed me out. I began to sweat harder, I had a week to go and I was sure that these two Assholes were going to pick me. Just to make my dream come true, shit! Down my rank they came looking at each man. One more man then they were going to see me. Where can I hide? I will never see my home again! They walked passed me. I breathed out, and the sun shone again, birds chirped, and the grass grew. I would go home. They walked right by me and didn't put the finger on me. I was more than relieved I was on cloud nine. They didn't pick anyone out of the "Line Up" they just marched back into the C.O.'s office. We were dismissed with great relief. I continued my one week to go.

Farewell to Army

With all the papers filled out, the formalities over there was only one thing left for me to do, and that was to leave. So I did, in my own style, the style I had become known for around the 43rd. After signing out of the company I walked back to the barracks threw my shaving kit, what civilian clothes I had, and a few personal items into my duffel bag and then tipped the rest of my lockers contents onto the floor. Big Jon added to the festivities by kicking my old gear into the hall way. None of it would fit him. I was done, and so I walked away. First Sergeant Buddha and Sergeant Stubaby arranged a ride for me to the air base in the back of a deuce and a half. A few members of the repair shop came along, Big Jon brought along Whore, all to say goodbye. It was my sad but happy day. At the air base they presented me with a phony set of orders for leaving Vietnam, which had some humorous passages in them. (See Appendix A). I was also presented with an engraved Zippo cigarette lighter. Instead of the usual unit insignia on one side and a map of Vietnam on the other, the unit had had engraved some of the sayings I was more renowned for using around the 43rd repair shop. (See Appendix B). I was touched, but not touched enough to remain. I did leave them all with one Scotty McNastyism before they left me to make my own way home; I told them that I had missed breakfast that morning.

As I said my last goodbye to my roomie, my savior at times, my playmate, and my best pal ever. I had one thing that puzzled me, as I stood there on the concrete of the Pleiku Air Force Base. This one thing remained a puzzle for many years to come. I was leaving, and my good buddy Big Jon, was staying. I was having a hard time leaving him behind. I understood the Army's tour of duty thing, however, Big Jon had been here in Vietnam long before I arrived at the 278th, and here he was remaining after I departed. How can this be, what crime had Big Jon committed for the Army to keep him when I got to go home? It was a conundrum, a puzzle, and a sad state of affairs. We said a tearful goodbye, but I knew our spirits would never part.

So I departed the 43rd, and made my way back to where I had entered Vietnam, Cam Ranh Bay. My exit was as uneventful as my entrance. The place was so crowded with troops waiting to leave that I could not find a bed to sleep in on my first night in the replacement depot. So I slept out under the stars on top of one of the bunkers. I slept, that is, until some idiot woke me up and told me to go and find a bed. So I went

544

and found another vacant bunker roof, but they found me there. I finally had to go and prowl around in the overcrowded barracks till I found a patch of bare floor, and there I spent a peaceful night.

The next day was the usual Army routine. Hundreds of us sat around on the sand and waited to be told what to do. While sitting in the sand of Cam Ranh Bay waiting to process out of Vietnam I had time to sweat, sweat and think in the 100 plus heat and humidity that I would not miss. I reflect on the time I had spent "In Country." I had been here a year and I definitely had some good times and some sad times. I had met a lot of good people, and we all had one hell of a good job keeping the Armys' communications systems up and running. And we had had one hell of a good time together doing our job. I realized sitting there in the shade that I would miss all of what I had gone through, but especially I would miss all the friends I had made. We had looked out for each other, and that meant a lot. I had grown up in Vietnam; it definitely wasn't the same guy going home who had left there for the Army almost three years before.

Quite by coincidence I ran into one of the guys I had arrived in Vietnam with, I was reacquainted with one of those who I had shared my bottle of Canadian Club with on the flight over. He was the "Fucking Grunt," from Fort Lewis Washington. He had spent his time as an infantryman in the 4th Division, and so we swapped stories for a while. We had both experienced Camp Enari and the territory around the Ia Drang valley. When he first saw me he asked, "Hey Lennox that you?" "Yeah it's me," I replied. "Christ man I could hardly recognize you, you look like a skeleton." I had lost over 30 pounds in Vietnam and hadn't noticed it. I was a six-foot stick, as skinny as a rail. I hadn't noticed it, but apparently it showed. Wow! Would my Mom recognize me when she saw me?

My old travel buddy and I would not be on the same return flight together, but we past the time waiting for a flight together which made the long three day wait for a plane pleasant enough.

He had been in the infantry, and I was a little bit jealous. I had done a little bit of his job on the recon patrols, but I had to admire a guy who had spent his entire tour out in the bush. We swapped stories, and we were both glad to be going home in one piece.

The flight home was full of anticipation. So we all anticipated together because there was not a lot to see out the windows. The flight home was identical to the flight I had getting me to Vietnam, it was long and boring. There was nothing to do on the flight to help pass the time, and I found sleep impossible from the noise and from being so excited to be going home. There were no stops on this flight, no Japan, no Alaska, just straight back to the U.S. It was on the same airline, and had an identical set of disinterested stewardesses as the one I had arrived on. By the time the plane touched down in the U.S. I didn't even know the time of day, or what day of the week it was. My 17 dollar Timex watch had stopped somewhere over the Pacific. Not that it mattered. I arrived back to Fort Lewis Washington, in a down pour of rain, the exact same conditions I had left in, and at same time of day, the middle of the night. The rain was probably a continuation of the down pour I had left Washington in a year ago. Weather wise it was 70 degrees cooler at Fort Lewis, than where I had come from, but because of the rain there was just as much humidity in the air. I processed in and in doing so I was separated from the mass of G.I.s, and I was told to go and get my steak dinner. About a dozen of us who were exiting from the Army found ourselves standing in front of an Army mess hall, the infamous Steakhouse, for that steak dinner promised to each returning vet. The mess hall was closed. This is what we were told, as we stood outside in the rain and getting soaked, by a cook in a white T-shirt and paper hat. The cook had just popped his head out the door to inform us "they wereclosed", and twelve wet angry and hungry arms grabbed portions of his T-shirt and hat and pulled him outside with us. "Now you are open," Mr. Cook was told. Soon we were inside waiting in the warmth while steaks were prepared to order.

Uncouth Youths

The processing out of the Army was long and involved, and to be sure not as easy as when I processed in. Funny thing about processing out of the Army, there were no Sergeants screaming or yelling, but just as many forms to fill out and no standing at attention. I only remember a few things that happened because I had been awake for 48 hours straight, and I was rather numb. What really stands out in my memory is the fact that it took about another 24 non-stop and sleepless hours to complete the process, and the fact that none of us going through the procedure complained about it or bitched to one another is remarkable. We had as much paperwork to fill out as we had had at any time in the Army, but I didn't mind. While we were being instructed on the intricacies of separation from the Army, the officer conducting our separation session informed us, "When you fill your Army form such-and-such and you come to the box that asks for your military occupation, do not put down KILLER."

We were all paid off in nice crisp brand-new bills by a G.I. in a wire cage. We got paid for unused leave, and they made sure that we had no missing Army gear that we had to pay for. We got the usual travel pay to our homes, and then we were shown the door and told to take the bus outside to the airport.

With the forms all filled out it was finally over, finished, my military life was at an end. The Army just dropped us back into civilian life without any period of readjustment or anything. I think they could have spent some of the tax payer's money to prepare us for our re-entry into polite society. As it was it would take years for certain speech habits acquired in the Army to disappear, they could have done something about my swearing before I went home to Mom. By the time we had two or three years in the Army we were what could be referred to as a bunch of foul mouthed youths. Or what we considered ourselves to be, under paid, under fed, over sexed, teenage professional killers. The Army should have had a form of couth school that they could have run us through. Something that would have helped remove some of our fucking language problems.

I can see a group of us sitting in a class room, some fresh from combat and the field, mingling with us R.E.M.F.s, (REMF was a derogatory term for those not fighting on the front lines. It stood for Rear Eschelon Mother Fuckers), all of us nodding off to sleep while some officer or NCO lead us through a couth exercise. The instructor holds up an everyday object, and has us name it. "All right men, this is a fork, everyone say FORK." A disorganized mumble comes from his charges, "That'safucking fork, Yeah fuckingfork." "No, no, no men, this is a fork, SAY FORK, say it." Again the disjointed mumble, "ThassaFork." This would continue until we had some language skills that didn't use four letter words. So that we could speak in sentences that were without a four letter word as every third fucking word.

This way we would have been able to go home and perform some everyday civilian task, like dinner with the family, without embarrassing ourselves. Like I did on the first family sit down in a long time, I sat there and asked my mother to, "pass the fucking salt."

One More Battle to Fight

The papers signed, the uniform fitted, and the shoes shined. The Army let us go. We got a free bus ride from Fort Lewis to the Seattle Tacoma airport in an O.D. Green Army bus as a parting gift, and I and the rest of my small party sat silently but happily on the midnight ride to the airport. The process of exiting the Army had taken a long time to get to this point. Not the three years I had just spent in the "Green Machine," but the

24 plus hours plus we had spent since the plane from Vietnam had touched the ground. I was happily exhausted.

The airport was quiet and deserted when we entered, but some of the ticket counters were still open for us to buy that one-way ticket home. It was the happiest money I had ever spent, and with the ticket clutched in my hot little hand I went and found a place to sit down.

For a soldier, and I was still a soldier till I took off the uniform, there was only one place to go, and that was the U.S.O. . There is one in every major airport. I found the U.S.O. tucked away in a corner of the terminal building, and found it to be a quiet, crowded barracks like room complete with double Army bunk beds and sleeping G.I.s, but run by kindly old ladies. These were the exact same kindly old ladies I had met at the draft board in my home town so many many years ago. I found an empty bed, stashed my crumpled duffle bag, crawled in, uniform and all, and went right to blissful sleep. I slept the sleep of kings for at least two hours until the call of nature reminded me of my duty to myself. I got up straightened my uniform and checked with the kindly old lady at the desk. I found the closest men's room and went in. The men's room was crowded when I went in, there were two long haired civilians in there and they were pounding their fists into the body of a guy dressed just as I was. At this time in my life I did not have to be asked to join a fight, I did not need to be told to fight, and I certainly was not afraid to fight. No little tickle feeling in the pit of my stomach this time, just pure anger and rage filled me. (I had an affidavit in my pocket from everyone I had ever hit in the mouth, they were always satisfied). As skinny as I now was, as tired as I was I just erupted. I just smacked the closest long hair too me. I hit him on the right side of his jaw with my right, and sent him bouncing into the wall, which he banged into hard and then slowly dribbled down the wall on his back till he sat upright on his ass. This second long hair looked up from the G.I. he had been pounding on, and I caught him right under the chin with a left hand. I could hear his teeth crunch together, and his eyes opened in giant circles of surprise. I hit him in the right eye with my right and he went down on his face on the tile floor with a loud clunk. The anger and rage I had just felt, faded away in the next second, as I helped the beat-up G.I. to his feet. I did not know this guy, I had never seen him before, but because of the O.D. Green uniform we shared he was my brother. From between split lips his bloody teeth whispered "Thanks man!"

We got the hell out of that bathroom, it was too noisy in there, and we went and found another and cleaned ourselves up.

Back in the Land of the Big P.X.

Going home was pure elation, and I enjoyed it even more when I boarded my plane in Seattle and discovered that the flight attendants were wearing the latest fashion, Mini-skirts. To the delight of the G.I. sitting across the aisle from me I asked a lovely, blond, and long-legged attendant if she would get me a pillow. She reached above me into the overhead compartment, and when her arms went up so did the hem line of her skirt. I was anticipating anything and everything, but what I got a glimpse of was a pair of shorts, the same color and style as her uniform skirt. The G.I. across the aisle did a double take, and he had to ask the attendant for a pillow for himself so that we could both verify that we had seen what we had seen. With this as my re-indoctrination to civilian life I was sure that I was once more in the land of the big P.X., that I had made it home to "The World" with all its perks and perversions, and I was very glad to be there.

Looking Back

I only brought one souvenir home with me from Vietnam, and I am very fond of it. I sit on it every day.

My butt was certainly skinnier than it had been when I left for Vietnam; I had lost 30 pounds over there and had not noticed. My family hardly recognized the gaunt figure that entered their front door, but they were glad I was home none the less.

I found out that I had finally grown up as a man I had matured a great deal in three short years of Army life. I had learned a lot, about myself and about life in general and I had learned it in a very short span of time. I knew that I could assume responsibility without hiding from it. I had the ability to stick up for myself at any time and in any place. I wasn't going to be pushed around in life, by anyone. Coming home was more than fried chicken or a hot turkey dinner; it was the realization of just how good we in the U.S.A had it compared to the rest of the world. In the U.S.A. the roads were not mined, trash did not seem to lay everywhere, barbed wire was not visible on every town street or corner and Americans knew that their Army would fight for them. I was proud of my service as a soldier and as a new citizen of this great nation, and I will always remain proud. I may not have been in the infantry, but I did participate in patrols outside the base camp wire, and I had certainly had my share of being shot at. I am also proud of the nation that I represented. If nothing else, the U.S. Army did these things for me and I will be eternally grateful.

I had come home with one determining, one want in my head. I wanted normal. I wanted the sanity that normal life would bring. I wanted home cooked meals, a wife, the kids, the home, the mortgage, and most of all I wanted normal. No more guns, no more explosions, no more institutional food. This was the driving force in me when I came home and took off that O.D. Green uniform for the last time. However, it took me years to be able to face a meal containing Pork and Rice together.

I faded into the woodwork and have had a happy life ever since. I married, had the kids and the mortgage, and that was all the excitement I needed. That is my success story; I am a successful husband, father, home owner, a citizen and a bill payer. To me this is wonderful, and I can truly say that I am a happy man.

In my work life I was always given new or unusual challenges to perform, challenges that everyone else sunned. "Give it to Lennox, he can do it!" Seemed to be the reputation I was known by. I was not afraid to try something I had never attempted before and I could usually fix the customer and fix the problem. I made a success out of what ever job was given to me.

Big Jon, Orosz and I have stayed in touch with each other ever since that day when we all finally got home. For years it was just a Christmas card with a note in it, or a phone call to tell each other of a birth or just to say hi. The three of us have been a big part of each other's lives and we shall remain so forever. Friends like Big Jon and Orosz just don't grow on trees; you don't find people you can trust with your life just anywhere. When you do you keep hold of them. We have been, and will be, pals for life.

Others have joined in keeping in touch. Louis G. from Philadelphia has stayed in touch and joined our note passing and phone tree. Perkins, the Jolly Green and I have been pals and part of each other's lives since we both got home. We being from the same home town made that easy. Recently we caught up with Billy "Bad Ass" Barnes, and he is now back in the group that can now have mini reunions together.

We are old and slow, and some of us have had health problems and parts replaced, but we are all Veterans and proud to be so. We salute the fag, take our hats off wehen the national anthem is played and stand at attention the best we can. The Vietnam War is now far behind us but we will never forget the times we had, both rough and smooth. And we will never forget the people we met in the U.S. Army.

We have all been as successfully and normal as I have. We have managed all the normal things that Vietnam made us crave. Of the six of us there are some remarkable American success stories.

Louis G. found a carrier in Electronics and became a very successful salesman.

Scotty did the same.

Billy "Bad Ass" made a good living as a business man.

Big Jon was a Master Electrician for a long time, but craving excitement and became a Dallas Cop.

Perkins went back to college and worked himself through to become a full-fledged Electronics
Engineer and had a great carrier in aerospace. (We all knew that this was the path for him and he certainly didn't let us down).

Orosz was our one true shining star success story. Orosz is the one that we all brag about. Orosz is the envy of us all. He became the maintenance engineer in the biggest, loudest and most raucous topless bar in Cleveland. Orosz truly lived the dream of us all.

THE END

Figure 23. Orosz goes home. Sent off with our Glee Club guidon as a momento. L to R Superman's Pal. Scotty, Sgt. Stubaby, Orosz, Lou, and Big Jon. Author's collection.

Figure 24. 278th Recon Patrol Patch. Author's collection.

Figure 25. Glee Club patch. Big Jon's collection.

Figure 26. Glee Club members reunion in Florida 2014. L to R Orosz, Billy Badass, Perlins, Scotty, and Lou. Big Jon had an excused absence for the meeting. Author's collection.

Figure 27. The Glee Club 2014, Big Jon in chair and L to R Orosz, Billy Badass, Lou, Perkins, Scottys wife Nancy, Scotty, and Big Jon's wife Cindy. Authors collection.

Appendix A

Phony Orders

DEPARTMENT OF THE ARMY
HHD. 43RD. SIGNAL BATTALION
APO SAN FRANCISCO 96318

SPECIAL ORDERS
NUMBER 12
EXTRACT

12. TC 246. FOL INDIV DIR. WP TDN 642358 01-4857-5149-
4858-4193-14985-4951-121-15948-4007- P-1445 SON Q127
CAH-12/365.
LENNOX, ROBERT M. XXX-XX-XXXX SP/4 P31L207
HHD 43RD SIG BN (WDQZAA)
APO 96318
ADMINISTRATIVE ACCOUNTING DATA
AUTH: SCCIV-IA-JEUP-CCN MSG DTG 2405207 SEP XX
ALOC: ACN 13553
OPO C &.L NO: 00XX DEC XX
LV ADRS XXXX XIMENO APT 203 LONG BEACH, CALIF
90815
MO OS (CURR TOUR): 12 (NT12)
PCOD: X OCT XX
ULTIMATE ASG: FORT HOME APO 90815
DEROS: XX DEC XX
DDUS: XX DEC XX

SPECIAL INSTRUCTIONS:
VERY SOON THE ABOVE NAMED INDIVIDUAL, WILL
ONCE AGAIN BE IN YOUR MIDST. BE HE HUSBAND,
SWEETHEART, FRIEND, SON OR BROTHER TO YOU HE
IS STILL YOURS. HE MAY ACT A LITTLE STRANGE
AND LOOK STRANGE BUT THIS IS TO BE EXPECTED
AFTER TWELVE (12), MUD SPATTERED MONTHS IN
VIETNAM. IN MAKING YOUR PREPARATIONS TO
WELCOME HIM INTO RESPECTABLE SOCIETY, YOU
MUST MAKE CERTAIN ALLOWANCES FOR THE CRUDE

ENVIRONMENT IN WHICH HE HAS SUFFERED FROM THE ADVANCED STAGES OF VIET-CONGITIS, OR TOO MUCH BOM-DE-BOM BEER. THIS MAN HAS SURVIVED THE WORST THAT THE FAR EAST HAS TO OFFER: MUD, RAIN, HEAT AND HOMESICKNESS.

FOR THE INDIVIDUALS NEXT OF KIN:
1. GET THE WOMEN OFF THE STREETS, HIDE THE SCOTCH, AND KEEP THE CHILDREN OUT OF EARSHOT.

2. DON'T SAY ANYTHING TO HIM IF HE JUST SITS AND STARES AT SUCH THINGS AS CHAIRS, SOFT MATTRESSES, SMOOTH ROADS, HOT SHOWERS, AIR CONDITIONERS OR BLONDS. OR IF HE STANDS AROUND MUTTERING VIETNAMESE SAYINGS SUCH AS, "XIN LOI," SORRY ABOUT THAT, "DI DI," GET LOST, "XIM LEI," EXCUSE ME, AND DO NOT ARGUE WITH HIM WHEN HE ASKS FOR SULPHUR TO PUT IN HIS BATH WATER, OR IF HE IS CONTINUALLY FLUSHING THE TOILET. JUST GO ALONG WITH HIM AND HE WILL EVENTUALLY GET OVER IT. IF HE MUMBLES SUCH THINGS AS, ":BLACK MARKET," "GOOK," "SLOPE," OR OTHER ODD SAYINGS IN HIS SLEEP IGNORE HIM. MAKE NO FLATTERING REMARKS ABOUT THE EXOTIC SOUTHEAST ASIAN SCENERY, AVOID MENTIONING THE BENEFITS OF OVERSEAS DUTY AND ABOVE ALL DO NOT ASK, "DOES IT RAIN MUCH IN VIETNAM?" THE MERE MENTION OF ANY ONE OF THESE SUBJECTS MAY TRIGGER AN AWESOME DISPLAY OF VIOLENCE.

3. IF HE PREFERS TO SIT CROSS-LEGGED ON THE FLOOR AND INSISTS ON EVERYONE EATING WITH CHOPSTICKS, PLEASE HUMOR HIM. PAY NO ATTENTION WHEN HE STIRS SOY SAUCE INTO HIS

POTATOES OR MIXES SNAILS WITH HIS RICE IN
HOPES OF MAKING BOTH TASTE BETTER. PLEASE DO
NOT SAY ANYTHING ABOUT POWDERED EGGS, "C"
RATIONS, DEHYDRATED POTATOES, FRESH MILK, ICE
CREAM AND ESPECIALLY DO NOT MENTION THE
FOOD DELICACIES OF THE FAR EAST, SUCH AS "NOUC
MAM" (FISH).

4. ACT LIKE NOTHING HAPPENED IF HE TAKES A
NOTION TO PEE IN THE GUTTER WHILE IN TOWN,
WHILE HE IS CROSSING THE STREETS, TAKE SPECIAL
CARE OF HIM FOR HE HAS BECOME COMPLETELY
OBLIVIOUS TO OUR HORNS, WATER BUFFALO AND
OTHER SUCH THINGS FOUND IN THE STREETS OF
PLEIKU. IF HE OFFERS YOU 200 P FOR CHOP-CHOP
HUMOR HIM AND GO ALONG WITH IT.

5. SHOW NO ALARM IF HE WALKS AROUND IN
SHOWER SHOES AND A TOWEL. BE TOLERANT WHEN
HE TRIES TO BUY EVERYTHING AT LESS THAN HALF
THE PRICE AND ACCUSES THE GROCER OF BEING A
THIEF AND REFUSES TO ENTER ANY ESTABLISHMENT
THAT DOES NOT HAVE STEEL-MESH SCREENS OVER
THE DOORS AND WINDOWS.

6. IN A RELATIVELY SHORT TIME HIS PROFANITY
WILL HAVE SLOWED ENOUGH TO ALLOW HIM TO
ASSOCIATE WITH MIXED GROUPS. IT MAY BE QUITE
A WHILE BEFORE HE STOPS COMPLAINING ABOUT
SLEEPING IN A ROOM OR STOPS REFUSING TO GO TO
BED WITHOUT A MOSQUITO NET.

7. ANY OF THE FOLLOWING SHOULD BE AVOIDED
SINCE THEY CAN PRODUCE AN ADVANCED STAGE OF
SHOCK. PEOPLE DANCING, T.V., AND "ROUND-EYED"
WOMEN. FOR THE FIRST FEW WEEKS, (UNTIL HE IS

HOUSE BROKEN), BE ESPECIALLY WATCHFUL WHEN
HE IS IN THE COMPANY OF WOMEN. HIS FIRST
REACTION UPON MEETING AN ATTRACTIVE "ROUND-
EYE" MAY BE TO STARE. WIVES AND SWEETHEARTS
ARE ADVISED TO TAKE ADVANTAGE OF THIS
MOMENTARY STATE OF SHOCK AND MOVE THE
YOUNG LADIES OUT OF REACH.

    8. REMEMBER THAT BENEATH THIS ROUGH AND
WATER-SOAKED EXTERIOR THERE EXISTS A HEART
OF GOLD, SWEET AND PURE THOUGH SLIGHTLY
MILDEWED. TREASURE THIS FOR IT IS THE ONLY
THING OF VALUE HE HAS LEFT. HE MAY NOT LOOK
OR ACT LIKE IT, BUT HE IS YOUR VERY OWN. TREAT
HIM WITH KINDNESS, AND AN OCCASIONAL FIFTH OF
SCOTCH AND YOU WILL BE ABLE TO REHABILITATE
THIS HOLLOW SHELL OF A MAN THAT YOU ONCE
KNEW. JUST ALLOW HIM A FEW WEEKS TO GET USED
TO BEING BACK IN CIVILIZATION.

    9. SEND NO LETTERS TO APO S.F. 96318 AFTER THE
OF   19 . EXCUSE THIS SORRY LOOKING, GOOD
FOR NOTHING, BLEARY EYED, MUD SOAKED
DRUNKARD AND IDIOT SOLDIER OF YOURS. HE'S ON
HIS WAY TO THE LAND OF THE BIG
P.X.....HOME....................

Appendix B

Commerative Lighter Inscription Given to me by the Men of 43rd Signal ELM Shop

Inscription on cigarette lighter presented to me on leaving Vietnam.

Front:

FROM THE MEN OF
THE 43rd SIG BN
ELM SHOP

DRUNK LAST NIGHT
ROW ROW YOUR BOAT
I WANNA GO TO THAN CHAN
IM SO LONELY
I GOTTA GET A BROAD

Back:

PRESIDENT
ROBERT McNASTY
LENNOX

GET MARRIED
UP YOURS
COMMIE PINKO BASTARD
PREPARE TO DRINK
I HATE EVERY ONE
EQUALLY BUT SEPARATELY

74078829R00340

Made in the USA
Middletown, DE
24 May 2018